Scots-English
English-Scots
DICTIONARY

LOMOND BOOKS

Abbreviations used in this book

adj	adjective
adv	adverb
art	article
conj	conjunction
imper	imperative
interj	interjection
n	noun
npl	plural noun
phr	phrase
prep	preposition
pron	pronoun
pp	present or past participle
v	verb
v aux	auxiliary verb

Published by Geddes & Grosset an imprint of
Children's Leisure Products Limited

Compiled by David Ross and Gavin D. Smith
for RLS Limited

Cover photograph courtesy of Chris Close Photography

© Text 1998 Children's Leisure Products Limited,
David Dale House, New Lanark, ML11 9DJ, Scotland

First published 1998, reprinted 1999

ISBN 0 947782 26 5

Printed and bound in India

Introduction

The Scots language has had an independent existence for more than eight hundred years. It shares its beginnings with Northumbrian English, the language spoken by the Anglian invaders who settled in the area between the Humber and the Forth. In the time before the Scottish kingdom was formed, its home was Lothian, sometimes a kingdom in its own right, sometimes a protectorate of either Angles or Scots. The principal language of Scotland was Gaelic, but in the southwest an early form of Welsh was spoken, and in the far north, from the ninth century, the dominant language was the Norse of different Scandinavian groups. From its base in the southeast corner, Scots gradually spread, forcing the older Gaelic language back into the glens and uplands of the Highlands. As control of the north and the Hebrides was wrested from the Norsemen, their language was forced out (although it was Gaelic that largely filled the gap). During this lengthy process, many Gaelic and Norse words were borrowed into Scots – this legacy is one of the elements that make it a distinctive language. Later, other languages made important contributions, especially French and Dutch, languages of the countries with which Scotland had the most important commercial and political ties.

Students of Scots recognise that the language, developing in a country with poor communications and where until the Reformation most people were illiterate, varied within itself from region to region. Lothian, Clydesdale and Aberdeen all spoke Scots but with a rich supply of local idiom and pronunciation in each case.

What makes a language? It must be sufficiently distinct from any other not to be merely a dialect. It must be the prime means of communication for a distinct group of people. Some would say that it should also display a literature or at least a store of legend and fable. On these grounds, Scots was indeed a language up to the nineteenth century, but ever since the union with England in 1707 it had been under threat. Just as it had once usurped the place of Gaelic, first at court then among the traders, churchmen and teachers, so now a 'standard' English crept across the land. The Scots diction and vocabulary were felt to be provincial and quaint. As mass communications and mass printing improved, this trend intensified until Scots as a written language fell into disuse. Because of this, there was no process of standardisation of the spelling of Scots, with the result that there is no recognised orthography and many words have variant forms.

Scots was rescued as a literary language in the first part of the twentieth century by the determined efforts of a group of writers and poets, among whom the most distinguished was Hugh MacDiarmid. This 'Scottish Renaissance' brought with it the use of the word 'Lallans' (Lowlands) since it was the language of Lowland Scotland as distinct from the tenuously surviving Gaelic of the Highlands and Islands. The later decades of the twentieth century brought a new appreciation of Scotland's cultural past and a new school of writers prepared to combine an uncompromisingly demotic Scots with a tactical deployment of standard English. This period also brought the admirable efforts of the Scottish National Dictionary Association in documenting and describing the Scots language. Not least, the realisation is still growing that language is one of the factors that serves most effectively to define and unite a nation.

Scots-English Dictionary

A

a *adj* all.
aafie *adj* awful.
aar *n* alder tree.
aback *adj* aloof. • *adv* away; behind.
abad, abade *n* delay.
abaid *n* abode.
abaisit *adj* abashed.
abaitment *n* diversion; sport.
abandon *v* let loose.
abandoun *adj* at random.
abay *v* astonish.
abbacy *n* abbey.
abbeit *n* dress; clothing.
abee *v* let alone.
abeelitie *adj* ability.
abeese *v* abuse.
abeigh *adj* aloof. • *adv* at a distance.
abeis *prep* compared with.
abin *prep* above.
ablach *n* carrion; dwarf.
ableeze *adj* ablaze.
ablow *adv* below. • *prep* below.
abodie, a'body *n* everybody, everyone.
abone, aboon *see* abuin.
aboot *adv* about; in addition. • *prep* about.
abraid, abreid, abreed *adv* abroad; widely.
abrede *v* spread abroad.
abreed *adv* abroad; asunder.
abreid *see* abraid.
abreist *adv* abreast.
abstrack *adj* abstract.
abstractness *n* aloofness.
abstraklous *adj* outrageous.
abuin, abone, aboon, abune *adv* above. • *prep* above; about.
abuinheld *adj* overhead.
abuise *v* abuse; revile; violate.
abune *see* abuin.
abuse *v* stop using.
abusion *n* deceit.
aby *v* suffer for.
abye *adv* ago.
accep *v* accept.

accres, accresce *v* accrue; increase.
ace *n* smallest part.
acherspyre *v* sprout.
achil *adj* noble.
ack *n* act; deed. • *v* act.
acker, ackre *n* acre.
ackwallie *adv* actually.
ackwart *adj* awkward; gawky.
aclite *adv* awry.
acquant *v* acquaint.
acquantance *n* acquaintance.
acquent *adj* acquainted. • *v* acquaint.
acquentance *n* acquaintance.
acre-braid *n* width of an acre.
acteeve *adj* active.
actioun *n* affairs, business.
adae *n* ado.
adap *v* adapt.
addeetion *n* addition.
addikit *adj* addicted.
addle *adj* foul.
addle dub *n* filthy pool; cesspit.
adeas *npl* difficulties.
adew *adj* gone; fled.
adhantare *n* phantom.
adist *prep* on this side.
adrad *adj* afraid.
adred *adv* downright.
adreich *adv* behind.
adreigh *n* distant.
adresly *adv* skilfully.
adverteese *v* advertise.
adverteesement *n* advertisement.
advisement *n* advice.
advocate *n* barrister.
advoutrie *n* adultery.
adwang *adj* tiresome.
ae *adj* only; sole. • *art* a. • *n* one.
ae-haunt *adj* single-handed.
aefauld *adj* faithful; sincere; single-minded. • *n* honesty.
aefauldlie *adv* honestly.
aeger *n* auger.
aer *n* oar.
aesome *adj* single; solitary.

aet *v* eat.

aeter *n* eater.

afauld *adj* honest.

afaynd *v* attempt.

afeard, afeared *adj* afraid.

afen *adv* frequently, often.

aff *adv* off. • *prep* off; **aff an on** *adv* intermittently; **aff the knot** *adj* crazed.

affa *adv* away from.

affcome *n* result.

affeck *v* affect.

affer *n* condition, state.

aff-hand *adj* plain-dealing.

afflickit *adj* afflicted.

afflufe, affluif *adv* off the cuff. • *adj* impromptu; offhand.

affoord *v* afford.

affordell *adj* alive.

affpit, affput *n* delay, procrastination; procrastinator.

affpittin *adj* dilatory.

affray *n* fear.

affrichted *adj* afraid.

affset *n* disadvantage; ornament; outset.

affside *n* far side.

afftak *n* deduction (of something); jeer; mimic; mocking remark.

afftakin *n* sarcasm; mockery. • *adj* mocking.

afit *adv* afoot.

aflaught *adj* lying flat.

aflocht *adj* distraught.

afore *adv* previously; prior to. • *conj* before. • *prep* before, prior to; **afore the pint** *adj* premature.

aforgane *adj* opposite to.

aft, aften *adv* often.

agait *adj* astir.

agane *adv* again.

agate *adv* afoot.

agee *adv* one side.

agent *v* manage.

agin *adv* against. • *prep* against.

aglee, agley *adv* astray; awry; askew; obliquely.

agrufe *adj* grovelling.

ah *pron* I.

aheid *prep* ahead.

ahin, ahind, ahint *adv* behind. • *prep* after; behind. • *adj* late; **ahin the haun** overdue.

ahomel *adv* upside-down.

aiblins *adv* perhaps.

aidder *n* udder.

aidle *n* liquid manure.

aifternune *n* afternoon.

aigars *npl* pot-dried grain.

aiger *adj* eager, fervent.

aigh, aight *v* owe.

aigle *n* eagle.

aiglet *n* tagged point; jewel.

aigre *adj* sour.

aik *n* oak.

aiken *adj* oaken.

aikit *adj* owed.

aile *n* transept.

ailickie *n* best man; groomsman.

ailin *n* sickness.

ain *adj* own.

aince *adv* once.

aince-eeran *adv* specially.

aincin *adv* quite, fairly.

aind *v* breathe.

aindless *adj* breathless.

ainlie *adj* familiar; only.

ainsel, ainsome *n* one's own self.

aip *n* ape.

aipple *n* apple.

air¹ *adv* before, ere; early.

air² *n* oar.

airch¹ *adv* scarcely.

airch² *n* aim; arch. • *v* take aim.

aircock *n* weathercock.

aird *n* ridge.

airgh *adj* hollow.

airgument *n* argument; contention.

airish *adv* chilly.

airlie *adj* early.

airm *n* arm.

airn *n* iron.

airnin *n* ironing.

airschip *n* inheritance.

airt for *v* make for.

airt¹ *n* art.

airt² *n* direction; locality; quarter; point of the compass; tack; way. • *v* direct; point; urge on; guide; incite; manoeuvre; pilot; steer; **airt oot** detect.

airtie *adj* artful.

airtily *adv* artfully.

airtiness *n* artfulness.

airy *adj* showy; pretentious; conceited.

aishan *n* generation.
aislar, ashiler *n* ashlar.
aisle-tuith, asil-tooth *n* molar.
aisment *n* accommodation.
aist *n* east.
ait *n* habit, custom (bad).
aitcake *n* oatcake.
aiten[1] *adj* oaten.
aiten[2] *n* partridge.
ait-farle *n* oatcake.
aith *n* oath.
aither *conj* either.
aithland *n* infield.
aits *npl* oats.
aiver *n* carthorse; neutered he-goat.
aix *n* axe, hatchet.
aixman *n* axeman.
aixtree *n* axle.
aizle *n* hot ember.
ajee *adj* ajar; disturbed; awry.
alaft *adv* aloft.
alagust, allagust *n* suspicion.
alaigh *adv* under.
alairm *n* alarm. • *v* alarm.
alane *adj* alone.
alang *adv* along.
alaw *adv* beneath.
albuist *conj* although.
aleen *adj* alone.
alenth *adv* at full distance; at maturity.
algait *adv* anyways.
alhale *adv* entirely.
alicht *v* enlighten.
alist *adj* alive.
allagrugous *adj* grisly.
allagust *see* **alagust**.
allan *n* skua.
alleadgance *n* allegation.
allege *v* advise; confirm.
allenarly *adj* solely.
aller[1] *n* alder.
aller[2] *adv* wholly.
allerish *adj* chilly.
allevolie *adj* volatile.
allister *adj* sane.
alloo *v* allow.
allover *prep* over and above.
allow *v* approve; commend.
allowance *n* approval.
allryn *adj* weird.
allryns *adv* all together.

allstryne *adj* ancient.
allthocht *adv* although.
almain *adj* German.
almous, almows *npl* alms.
alood *adj* aloud.
alous *v* release.
alow[1] *adv* below. • *prep* below; under.
alow[2], **a-lowe** *adj* alight, blazing.
alpe *n* elephant.
alpuist *conj* although.
alquhare *adv* everywhere.
alsame *adv* all together.
alse *conj* as.
alswyth *adv* immediately.
alunt *adj* ablaze.
alycht *v* enlighten.
alytre *adv* little.
amaist *adv* almost.
amang *adv* among. • *prep* among.
ambry, amry *n* (food) cupboard.
ameise *v* mitigate.
amene *adj* pleasant.
amerand *adj* green; emerald.
amerciat *v* fine.
amichtie *adv* almighty.
amirale *n* admiral.
amissin *adj* missing.
amitan *n* fool lunatic.
amoont *n* amount, quantity.
amove, amow, amowe *v* anger, vex; disturb.
amry *see* **ambry**.
amshach *n* accident; misfortune; calamity.
amshack *n* noose.
an *conj* and; if; then. • *adv* then; **an a** also, besides; **an siclike** et cetera.
anarmit *adj* armed.
anciety *n* antiquity.
ancleth, ankleth *n* ankle.
ane[1] *art* a. • *adj/n* one; **after ane** *adj* alike.
ane[2] *v* agree.
aneath *adv* beneath; underneath.
anefauld *adj* honest.
aneist *adv* adjacent, adjoining.
anely, ainlie *adj* only.
anent *adv* concerning. • *prep* about; alongside; opposite.
anerly *adj* lone. • *adv* only.
anew *adj* adequate. • *adv* beneath.

angersome, angersum *adj* annoying, provoking.
angir *n* grief; vexation.
anie *n* little one.
anither *adj* another.
ankerly *adv* unwillingly.
ankleth *see* **ancleth**.
annere, annerd *v* adhere; consent.
anse *conj* else; otherwise.
anter *v* chance; happen.
antercast *n* misfortune.
antrin *adj* chance; haphazard; occasional; rare; exceptional.
anxeeitie *n* anxiety.
anygates *adv* everywhere.
apairt *adv* apart.
apayn *adj* furnished; supplied. • *adv* unwillingly.
apen, appin *adj* open. • *v* open.
apersmart *adj* bad-tempered.
apert *adj* bold; brisk; open.
apiest *adv* although.
aplace *adv* here present.
aplight *adv* completely.
apon *adv* upon.
appair *v* injure.
appearinlie *adv* apparently.
appell *v* challenge.
appeteet *n* appetite.
appin *see* **apen**.
appleis *v* satisfy.
apprise *v* appreciate; approve; prefer.
appruve *v* approve.
Aprile *n* April.
aqual *adj* equal. • *adv* equally. • *n* equal.
aquavitae *npl* spirits.
ar *v* plough.
arbiter *n* arbitrator.
arch *see* **argh**.
archilagh *n* turn to stand.
archin *adj* smooth-flowing.
aready, areddies *adv* already.
arend *v* rear up.
argh, arch *adj* reluctant. • *v* hesitate.
argie *v* argue.
argie-bargie, argle-bargle *n* dispute, argument. • *v* dispute; haggle.
argufy *v* argue.
aricht *adv* aright.
arit *adj* ploughed.
ark *n* chest.

arle, erle *v* give a pledge; betroth.
arles *n* earnest; token.
arlich *adj* sore; chafed.
armless *adj* without weapons.
arn *n* alder tree.
arnit *n* pignut.
aroads *adv* everywhere.
aroon *prep* around.
arr *n* scar.
arra, arrae *n* arrow.
arrachin *adj* tumultuous.
arras *n* darts.
arreik *v* reach.
arreird *adj* confused; slow.
arrondell *n* swallow.
arsecockle *n* pimple.
arselins *adv* backwards.
arval supper *n* funeral meal.
as *adv*/*conj* than.
asclent *adv* aslant.
ascrive *v* ascribe.
ase, ass *n* ash; ashes.
ase-backet *n* ash bucket.
ase-midden *n* ashpit.
ashet, aschet *n* large plate, platter; pie dish.
ashiler *see* **aislar**.
aside *adv* near. • *prep* beside.
asil-tooth *see* **aisle-tuith**.
ask *n* eft; newt.
ask for *v* ask after.
asklent, asklint *adv* askance; askew, aslant; obliquely.
aspert *adj* cruel.
aspre *adj* keen.
ass *see* **ase**.
assailye *v* attack.
asseer *v* assure.
asseerance *n* assurance.
assession *n* complicity.
asshole *n* ashpit.
assilag *n* storm petrel.
assize *n* jury.
assoilye, assoilzie *v* acquit.
assyth *v* compensate.
astarn *adv* astern. • *adj* insolvent.
asteer *adv* astir; confusedly.
astit *adv* rather; as soon as.
astren *see* **austern**.
aswim *adv* afloat.
at *conj*/*pron* that.

athegither *adv* altogether.

athings *npl* everything.

athir, ayther *pron* either.

athoot *adv* without.

athort *prep* across; through.

attercap, attercop *n* spider.

atterie *adj* festering; infected; septic.

atterlie *adj* angry.

attrie *adj* festering, purulent; grim; fierce.

atweel *adv* assuredly, truly.

atween *adv/prep* between.

atwix *prep* between.

auchmutie *adj* mean.

aucht¹ *adj* eight; eighth. • eight.

aucht² *n* ownership. • *v* possess, own; owe.

aucht³ *adj* possessed.

auchteen *adj/n* eighteen.

auchteenth *adj* eighteenth.

auchten *adj* eighth.

auchtie *adj/n* eighty.

auchtlins *n* anything.

audie *n* fool.

aul *adj* old; oldest.

auld *adj* old.

auldfarran, aulfarran *adj* droll, witty; wise; old-fashioned; quaint; precocious.

auld-father *n* grandfather.

auld lang syne *n* long ago.

auld-warld *n* antique.

auld-young, aulyoung *adj* middle-aged.

aumrie *n* cabinet, cupboard; larder, pantry.

auncient *adj* ancient.

aunter *v* hazard.

aunterous *adj* adventurous.

aunty *n* aunt.

Aunty Beeny *n* old-fashioned woman.

austern, austerne, astren *adj* austere; severe.

austrous *adj* frightful.

author *n* ancestor; informant.

ava *adv* of all; at all.

avail *n* worth.

avenand *adj* elegant.

aventure *n* chance; accident.

aver *n* carthorse.

averie *n* livestock.

Averil *n* April.

averins *npl* cloudberries.

avillous *adj* contemptible.

avise *v* deliberate.

avisement *n* advice.

aw *adj* all. • *adv* all. • *pron* I.

awa *adv* at all; away; distant; asleep.

awall *v* let fall.

awald *adj/adv* prostrate, supine.

a-wastle *prep* to the west.

awaur *adj* aware.

awband *n* check; restraint.

awe *v* owe.

awee *adv* slightly.

awesome *adj* appalling.

awey *adv* everywhere.

awfie, awfu *adj* awful, atrocious, frightful, dire; lamentable; shocking. • *adv* very. • *n* lot.

a'where *adv* everywhere.

awld *adj* longing.

awkart *adv* athwart.

awkwart *adj* hostile.

awmon *n* helmet.

awmous *n* alms.

awn *v* acknowledge, admit; claim, confess; contact; own.

awner *n* owner, proprietor.

awnie *adj* bearded.

awns, yauvins *npl* beards of corn.

awpron *n* apron.

awrangous *adj* criminal.

aws *npl* windmill sails.

awsome *adj* horrendous.

ax *v* ask.

ay *adv* still; yes. • *prep* of.

aye *adv* always; constantly; ever; forever; still. • *n* yes.

ayeways *adv* always.

ayont *prep* beyond.

ayther *see* **athir**.

B

ba¹, baw n ball.
ba² n/v hush; lull.
baa, bae v bleat.
baach, bauch adj bad-tasting.
bab n nosegay. • v dance.
babbis v sneer.
babbity-bouster n last dance at a feast.
babby, babbie n baby.
babbie-clouts npl baby clothes.
bacheleer n bachelor; third-year university student.
bachie n bachelor.
bachle see **bauchle**.
back adv behindhand. • n address; backstairs; brewing vessel. • v address.
backart adj backward.
back-birn n load on the back.
backchap n retort.
backcome n recrimination.
back coort n backyard.
back-door trot n diarrhoea.
back-drawer n apostate.
backend, back-en n autumn; later part.
backga'en adj receding; declining.
backgain n decline; sickness.
backgang n/v relapse.
backie n bat.
backin n/v address.
backings npl remnants.
backland n tenement.
backlins adv backwards.
back o prep after.
backowre adv some way behind.
backrans adv backwards.
backset n setback.
backsey n loin.
backside foremaist adj inside out.
backsprent n spine.
backyett n back gate.
bad adj unwell.
badgeran n beating.
badly adj poorly.
bad-money n gentian.
bae see **baa**.
baff n blow; hit.
baffie n slipper.
baffle n trifling thing.
bagenin n snogging.

baggie n belly.
bagrel n child; dwarfish person.
bagrie n trash.
bahookie n buttocks.
baid, bud n bribe.
baigle v walk with short steps.
baik, beek v warm; bask.
baikie¹ n ash bucket, coal bucket.
baikie² n tethering post or stake.
bail, bale n fire; signal fire.
bailie, baillie n civic dignitary; magistrate.
bainie adj large-boned.
bainish v banish.
bair n boar.
baird¹ n bard, poet.
baird² n awn; beard.
bairdie¹ adj bearded.
bairdie² n loach.
bairge n barge. • v collide; strut.
bairman n bankrupt.
bairn n child; infant; offspring. • v impregnate.
bairnheid n childhood.
bairnie adj childish. • n baby; child.
bairnlie adj puerile.
bairnlik adj childlike; immature.
bairnly adj childish.
baisdlie adv confusedly.
baise n hurry.
baiss¹ v baste, sew loosely.
baiss², baist v beat, drub.
baiss³ adj sorrowful.
baist¹ n beast, creature; cow.
baist² adj afraid.
baist³ see **baiss²**.
baists npl cattle; vermin.
bait¹ n boat, ship, ferry.
bait², bayt v feed.
baith adj/pron both.
baither n trouble; annoyance. • v trouble; annoy.
baivenjar n ragamuffin.
bajan see **bejant**.
bake n biscuit.
balapat n family pot.
balderie n orchid.
bale see **bail**.

ballant *n* ballad.
ballfire *n* bonfire.
ballion *n* knapsack.
ballish *n* ballast.
ballycog *n* milk pail.
bamling *adj* clumsy.
bammer *n* mad person, lunatic.
bampot *n* idiot.
ban¹ *n* choir.
ban² *n/v* curse.
ban³ *see* **band**.
bananie *n* banana.
band, ban *n* bond; marriage bond; hinge;
   leather strap.
bandstane *n* anchor-stone.
bane¹ *adj* ready.
bane² *n* bone.
bang *adj* fell, cruel; violent; ferocious,
   fierce. • *v* excel, outdo, surpass; move
   suddenly; trounce.
bangie *adj* irritable.
bangrel *n* shrewish woman.
bangster *n* bully.
bangstrie *adj* bullying.
bankrape *v* bankrupt.
bankrout *n* bankrupt.
bankset *adj* hillocky.
bannet *n* bonnet.
bannock *n* barley-meal cake, oatcake.
bansel *see* **hansel**.
banstickle *n* stickleback.
bap *n* bread roll.
bapper *n* baker.
bapteese *v* baptise.
bar *n* barley.
barbour *see* **baurber**.
bard *n* minstrel; poet.
bardach, bardy *adj* bold; pugnacious.
bardin, bards *n* harness trappings.
bardish *adj* insolent.
bards *see* **bardin**.
bardy *see* **bardach**.
bare *adj* unsheathed.
barefit *adj* barefoot.
barelies *adv* barely.
bargane *v* fight.
baries *npl* bare feet.
bark *v* strip bark.
barken *v* clot; harden; encrust; tan.
barkenit *adj* encrusted.
barker *n* tanner.

barley *n* truce.
barley bree *n* whisky.
barm *n* yeast. • *v* ferment.
barmie *adj* frothy; hasty.
barnat *adj* native; ancestral.
barnman *n* thresher.
barra *n* barrow, trolley.
barrace, barras *n* barrier.
barrie *adj* good.
barsk *adj* hoarse.
bask *adj* arid.
bass *n* doormat.
bass mat *n* table mat.
bate *adj* defeated.
bate *n* bet. • *v* bash, beat; bet.
bather *v* bother.
batie, bawty *n* big dog.
bating *n* drubbing.
batter *n* glue, paste. • *v* paste.
bauch¹ *adj* (*implement*) blunt; seedy;
   sheepish; sorry.
bauch² *see* **baach**.
bauchelt *adj* distorted, misshapen.
bauchle, bachle *n* old shoe; trifling
   thing; clumsy person. • *v* distort; shamble.
bauchled *adj* bent.
baud *adj* bad. • *adv* badly.
baudrans *n* pet cat.
bauk *n* balk; beam, rafter; narrow
   unploughed strip.
baukie *n* bat.
bauld *adj* audacious, bold.
bauldaur *adj* dashing.
baumy *adj* balmy.
baun *n/v* band.
baunk *n* bank.
baur *n* bar; comic story, gag, joke.
baurber, barbour *n* barber.
baushfae *adj* bashful.
bausie *adj* big.
bavard *adj* worn-out.
bavarie *n* greatcoat.
baver *v* shake.
baw *see* **ba¹**.
bawbee *n* halfpenny.
bawbies *npl* money.
bawd *n* hare.
bawty *see* **batie**.
baxter *n* baker.
bayt *see* **bait²**.

be *prep* by.
beadle, betheral *n* gravedigger, sexton, verger.
beal *v* suppurate.
bealach *n* mountain pass.
bealin *n* abscess, ulcer.
beamer *n* blush.
bean *adj* cosy.
bear[1] *v* denote, mean.
bear[2] *see* **bere**.
bearward *n* bearkeeper.
beast *n* animal.
beastie *n* insect.
beb *v* swill.
bebble *v* sip rapidly.
bechle *v* cough.
becht *adj* tied.
beck[1] *n/v* bow, curtsy.
beck[2] *see* **baik**.
beddie *n* cot, cradle, crib.
bedene *adv* quickly.
bedfast *adj* bedridden.
bedink *v* bedeck, decorate.
bedlare *adj* bedridden.
beds *n* hopscotch.
beek *see* **baik**.
beenge *v* cringe; fawn.
beeny *adj* bony.
beerial *n* funeral.
beerle *v* bury, inter.
beescap *n* beehive.
beet *v* refuel a fire; praise publicly.
beetraw *n* beet, beetroot.
beezer *n* outstanding person.
befa *v* befall, betide.
beflum *v* befool.
befyle *v* foul.
begane *adj* covered.
begarie *v* decorate in different colours.
begeck, begeek *v* disappoint; deceive, trick.
begot *n* bigot.
begotted *adj* bigoted.
begottit *adj* besotted.
begouk *v* jilt.
begouth *v* began.
begowk *v* beguile; betray; cheat.
begoyt *adj* foolish.
begrutten *adj* marked with tears.
beguess *adj* random.
begunk *v* jilt.

behaud *v* behold; hold on.
behauden *adj* beholden, indebted.
behecht *v* promise.
behin *adv/prep* behind.
beho, boho *n* laughing stock.
beik *n* beak.
beild, bield *n* shelter, protection, refuge.
  • *v* shelter protect.
beinlike *see* **bienlike**.
beir[1] *v* bear.
beir[2] *v* signify.
beir[3] *see* **birr**.
beit, bete *v* help mend.
beizless *adj* extreme.
bejant, bajan *n* first-year undergraduate.
belang *v* belong, belong to.
belch *n* monster.
beld, bell *adj* bald.
belike *adv* probably.
bell[1] *v* bubble up.
bell[2] *see* **beld**.
belleis, bellies *npl* bellows.
bellie *v* bellow.
bellies *see* **belleis**.
belling *n* rutting call of deer.
bellisand *adj* elegant; imposing.
belloch *v* (*cattle*) low.
bellralve *v* rove about; be unsteady.
belltowe *n* bell rope.
bellum *n* noise.
bellwaver *v* straggle; stroll.
bellythraw, bellythra *n* colic; stomach ache.
belshach *n* brat.
belshie *adj* short and fat.
belt *n* thump.
Beltane *n* May festival.
belth *n* whirlpool.
beltin *n* clump of trees.
bely *v* besiege.
belyve *adj* immediately.
bemang *v* hurt, harm.
bemangt *adj* injured.
beme *v* resound; boom.
bemean *v* degrade, humiliate; demoralise.
ben[1] *n* mountain.
ben[2] *adv* inside.
bend *v* drink heavily; **bend the bicker** carouse.
benew *adv* below.

benichtit *adj* benighted.
benjel *n* heap.
benmaist, benmost *adj/adv* innermost.
benorth *adv* north of.
bensel, bensell *n* force; violence; exposedness.
benshie *n* fairy woman.
bensome *adj* quarrelsome.
bent *n* coarse grass.
bequeyst *n* bequest.
bere *n* barley.
beremeal *n* barley meal.
berge *v* scold without effect.
bern *n* man.
berries *npl* raspberry picking.
berry *v* thrash.
berry-pickin *n* raspberry picking.
beseik *v* beg, beseech.
beshacht *adj* torn; twisted.
besle, bezle *v* chatter.
besom *n* broom; hussy, slut.
besouth *adv* south of.
besplatter *v* besprinkle.
bestial *n* farm animals.
best maid *n* bridesmaid.
besturted *adj* startled.
beswackit *adj* soaked.
besweik *v* allure, beguile.
bete *see* **beit.**
betech *v* put in trust.
bethankit *n* grace.
betheral *see* **beadle.**
betimes *adv* by and by.
better *adv* more. • *n* advantage.
better-faured *adj* better-looking.
better-mais *adj* better-class.
betterness *n* improvement; recovery.
beuch *n* branch, bough.
beugle-backed *adj* crook-backed.
beukit *adj* baked.
bevie *n* fire.
bevvy *n* liquor.
bew¹ *adj* good.
bew² *n* blue.
bewaur *v* beware.
bewave *v* make to waver; shield.
bewith *n* poor substitute.
beyont *adv/prep* beyond.
bezle *see* **besle.**
bibble *n/v* bubble.
bick *n* bitch.

bicker¹ *n* beaker, drinking bowl, cup.
bicker² *v* move rapidly as in fighting.
biddin *n* command.
bide a wee *v* wait a while.
bide in *v* inhabit.
bide *n* agony; pain; stay. • *v* abide; await; bear, put up with; remain; reside, stay.
bidie-in *n* cohabitee; resident girlfriend; concubine.
bield *see* **beild.**
bien *adj* complacent; cosy; prosperous, rich.
bienlike *adj* well-to-do.
big¹ *adj* conceited; stuck-up.
big² *v* build.
big coat *n* greatcoat.
big hoose *n* mansion.
bigg¹ *n* kind of barley.
bigg² *v* build.
biggar *n* builder.
biggin, bigging *n* building.
biggit *adj* cultivated; built.
biglie *adj* habitable; large, commodious.
bike, byke *n* building; wasps' nest.
biking, byking *n* hive swarm.
bilbie *n* shelter.
bilch *v* limp.
bile *n/v* boil.
biler, boiler *n* boiler; kettle.
bilin *n* boiled sweet.
bill *n* bull.
billie *n* man, fellow.
Billy *n* Protestant.
bilsh, bilshie *adj* short and plump.
bin¹ *v* bind.
bin², binner *v* run fast.
binch *see* **bink.**
bind *n* size.
bine *n* tub.
bing *n* heap; pile; slag-heap. • *v* dump; pile.
bink¹, binch *n* bench; dresser; hob; plate-rack; shelf; bank; hive.
bink² *v* press down.
binkie *adj* gaudy.
binna, binnae *prep* except.
binner *see* **bin.**
binwood *n* convolvulus.
binwuid *n* ivy.
bir *see* **birr.**
bird, burd *n* woman, lady.

birdalane *n* only child.
birdie's een *n* tapioca.
birk¹ *n* birch tree.
birk² *v* answer tartly.
birken *adj* of birch.
birkenshaw *n* birch wood.
birkie *adj* perky. • *n* young fellow.
birl *n* turn. • *v* dance; turn round; spin, rotate; pour out; whirl around; revolve.
birlinn *n* oared boat, galley.
birn¹ *n* burden. • *v* burden, encumber.
birn² *n* burn; burn mark. • *v* burn.
birn³ *n* hill part of a farm.
birnie, byrnie *n* armoured vest.
birr, bir, beir *n* energy; enthusiasm; force; vigour; pace; whirring noise.
birse¹ *n* anger, ire; irritation.
birse² *n* bristle; bruise. • *v* bruise.
birsie *adj* hairy; hot-tempered, passionate.
birsle *v* parch; roast; scorch; toast, warm at the fire.
birslet *adj* burnt.
birst¹ *n* brunt.
birst² *v* weep profusely.
birstle *n/v* bristle.
birth *n* current.
birthgrun *n* birthplace.
birze *n* press; pressure. • *v* press.
bismare *n* whore.
bisming *adj* horrible.
bisset *n* gold ornamentation.
bit¹ *adj* small. • *n* place.
bit² *conj* but.
bittle *n* bit, small piece.
bittle *n* mallet; masher.
bittock *adv* little. • *n* morsel, small piece; dagger.
bizz *v* buzz; fizz; hiss.
bla¹ *n* blow. • *v* blow; vaunt.
bla² *see* **blae**.
blab *n* blob.
black *adj* absolute. • *adv* completely, entirely.
black-avised *adj* dark-complexioned, swarthy.
blackberry *n* blackcurrant.
black coat *n* clergyman.
blackie *n* blackbird.
blacklie *adj* ill-coloured; unwashed-looking.

blackmail *n* protection money.
blackman *n* goblin.
blacks *npl* mourning clothes.
blad¹ *n* portion; piece.
blad², blade *n* leaf; tea leaf; page; blotting pad; portfolio.
blad³ *v* drive; strike; defame.
bladdry, bladrie, blaidrie, blathrie *n* nonsense; ostentation.
bladoch *n* buttermilk.
blae¹, bla *adj* blue; bluish; livid; bleak.
blae² *v* bleat.
blaeberry *n* bilberry.
blaff *n* bang.
blaflum *v* bluff.
blaid *n* pimple.
blaidrie *see* **bladdry**.
blain *n* bare patch; blank space; cicatrice.
blait *see* **blate**.
bland *v* blend.
blander *v* scatter.
blandish *n* flattery; unharvested grain.
blare *v* bleat.
blash *n* heavy fall of rain. • *v* soak drench.
blashy *adj* thin; watery.
blason *v* announce.
blast *v* breathe hard; smoke; boast.
blastit *adj* paralysed.
blate, blait *adj* bashful, shy; diffident, modest; simple; slow; naive; timid.
blather *n* bladder.
blathrie *see* **bladdry**.
blatter *n* hailstorm; tempest; rattle. • *v* rattle.
blaucht *adj* pale; livid.
blaw¹ *n* gust; blow; boast. • *v* blow; boast, brag; exaggerate; **blaw up** compliment.
blaw² *n* oatmeal.
blawdoon *n* back-draught.
blawort *n* bluebell; cornflower.
blawp *v* belch; retch.
blear *v* blind.
blearie *n* gruel.
blearit *adj* debauched.
bleb *v* sip.
blebbit *adj* blurred.
bleck¹ *adj* black • *n* blacking; negro. • *v* black; defame.

bleck² *n* challenge; puzzle. • *v* puzzle, baffle; exceed.

blecken *v* blacken.

bleckguaird *n* blackguard.

bleeze *n* blaze. • *v* blaze; flare; turn sour blaze; brag.

bleffert *n* snowfall; squall.

bleib *n* blister.

bleir *v* calumniate, lie.

bleirie *n* lie.

blellum *n* wastrel.

bleme *n* blossom.

blenk *see* **blink**.

blent *v* shine; flash; blink.

blether *n* chat; chatterbox; nonsense. • *v* babble; chat; gossip; talk nonsense, jabber.

bletherie *adj* talkative.

bletherin *adj* chatty, garrulous.

blethers *n* babble, chatter; gibberish, nonsense.

blethers! *interj* rubbish.

blethersay *n/v* talk.

bletherskite *n* babbler; braggart.

blibberin *adj* slobbering.

blichan *n* poor specimen.

blicht *n/v* blight.

blide *adj* blithe.

blin *adj/v* blind.

blin bargain *n* pig in a poke.

blindlins *adv* with eyes shut.

blinee *n* dogfish.

blinman's buff *n* puffball.

blinsmoor *n* snowdrift.

blink, blenk *n* beam; moment. • *v* look upon; ogle; bewitch; enchant; turn sour.

blinker *n* star.

blinlins *adv* heedlessly.

blinners *npl* blinkers.

blinter *v* glimmer, shine weakly.

blinterin *adj* gleaming.

blirt *n* squally gust. • *v* weep noisily.

blissin *n* benediction.

blithe *adj* festive; glad, happy, joyful. • *adv* gladly, happily.

blitheness *n* gladness.

blithesome *adj* merry.

blizzen *v* parch.

blob *n* drop.

blocher *v* cough.

block¹ *n* bargain. • *v* plan; bargain.

block² *n* pulley. • *v* hinder.

block³ *n* codfish.

blonk, blouk *n* horse, steed.

blooter *v* blurt; bungle.

blootered *adj* drunk.

bloss *n* buxom girl.

blot *v* puzzle.

blotch *v* blot; **blotch out** blot out.

blot sheet *n* blotting paper.

blouk *see* **blonk**.

bloust *v* boast.

blouster *n* bluster; boaster, braggart.

blout *adj* naked.

blowstrie *adj* breezy.

bluebell *n* harebell.

blue bunnet *n* bluetit.

bluefly *n* bluebottle.

bluff *adj* credulous.

bluid *n* blood. • *v* bleed.

bluidie *adj* bloody.

bluidie puddin *n* black pudding.

bluidshed *adj* bloodshot.

blume *n* bloom. • *v* bloom, flower; flourish.

blunk *v* mismanage.

blush *n/v* blister.

bluthrie *n* thin porridge; phlegm.

blyter *v* besmear.

boab *n* bob.

boak, bock, bok, bowk *n/v* belch; retch; vomit.

boakie *n* sprite, brownie.

boal *n* niche, wall opening.

bob¹ *n* bouquet, posy.

bob² *n* dance.

bobbinquaw *n* quagmire.

bocht *v* bought.

bock *see* **boak**.

bockie *n* hobgoblin.

bod *see* **bode**.

bodach *n* old man.

boddom *n* bottom.

bode, bod *n* bid, offer. • *v* offer; portend; press on.

bodement *n* foreboding.

boden *adj* prepared. • *conj* provided.

bodie, body *n* human being, person.

bodle *n* two Scots pence.

bodword *n* prediction.

body *see* **bodie**.

bog *n* bug.
bogan, bolgan *n* boil.
bog-bluiter *n* bittern.
bog-cotton *n* cotton-grass.
boggard *n* bugbear.
boggle *v* protrude.
bogle *n* ghost, bogy, hobgoblin; phantom; scarecrow.
boglie *adj* haunted.
boho *see* **beho**.
boich *v* cough constrictedly.
boiler *see* **biler**.
bok *see* **boak**.
boldin *v* swell up.
bole *n* alcove.
bolgan *see* **bogan**.
bon *adj* borrowed.
bonailie *n* farewell drink.
bone *n* petition; boon.
bonk *n* bank.
bonnet fir *n* pine.
bonnet flook *n* brill.
bonnet laird *n* small landowner.
bonnie, bonie, bonny *adj* attractive, pretty, beautiful; considerable.
bonspiel *n* competition in archery or curling.
bonxie *n* skua.
boo¹, bow *n* bend, curve; bow; curving street; archway. • *v* bow; bend, curve.
boo² *n* bull.
booder *n* boulder.
bool¹ *n* glass ball, marble; cannonball.
bool² *n* dotard.
bools *npl* marbles; taws.
boon¹ *prep* above.
boon² *adj* prepared. • *n* extent; width. • *v* bound.
boondinner *n* harvest dinner.
boonmost *adv* uppermost.
boontie *n* bounty.
boorach *n* group. • *v* cluster.
boord *n/v* board.
boose *n* cattle stall.
boost *v* dispel.
bootch *v* botch.
borch *n* surety, bail.
bord *n* hem; ruffle.
bordel hoose *n* brothel.
bore *n* crevice.
bosie *n* bosom; embrace.

boss¹ *n* tussock.
boss² *n* void; hollow. • *v* undercut.
bot *conj* but.
bote *n* help.
bothan *n* shebeen.
bothie, bothy *n* wooden hut or booth; cottage.
bothne *n* cattle park.
bothy *see* **bothie**.
bottick *n* boat hook.
bouch *n/v* bark.
boucht *n* curve; knot; twig.
bouet *n* lantern.
bouff, bowf *v* bark; bay.
bougar¹ *n* crossbeam.
bougar² *n* puffin.
bougars *npl* cross-spars.
boughtie *n* twig.
bouk¹ *n* size, bulk; carcass; corpse. • *v* bulk.
bouk² *see* **buik**.
bouke *n* solitude.
boukit *adj* large; pregnant.
bouksum *adj* honourable.
bouky *adj* bulky.
boun *v* make ready.
bound, bund *adj* pregnant.
bounder *v* limit.
bount *v* spring.
bountith *n* bonus; reward.
bountree, bourtree *n* elder.
bour, boure *n* bower; chamber.
bourach *n* enclosure; confused heap.
bourd *v* jest, joke; mock.
boure *see* **bour**.
bourie *n* burrow; den; lair.
bourtree *see* **bountree**.
bouss *n* pout.
bouster *n* bolster.
bout *v* sift.
bouzie, bowsy *adj* bushy, wooded.
bow *see* **boo¹**.
bowand *adj* pliant.
bowat, bowet *n* hand lantern.
bowbard *n* coward.
bowbert *adj* lazy.
bowder *n* tempest.
bowe *n* buoy.
bower *n* bowmaker.
bowet *see* **bowat**.
bowf *see* **bouff**.

bowie *n* barrel; bucket, pail; butt; cask; small tub.

bowk *see* **boak**.

bowl *n* basin.

bowlie¹ *adj* bent, crooked.

bowlie² *n* basin, bowl, dish.

bowlieleggit *adj* bandy-legged.

bowpot *n* bouquet.

bowsieman *n* bogyman.

bowsome *adj* compliant; obedient; flexible.

bowsplit *n* bowsprit.

bowsy *see* **bouzie**.

bowt *n/v* bolt.

boxbed *n* wall-bed.

boxin *n* panelling, wainscoting.

boy *n* bachelor.

boyickie, buygie *n* small boy.

boyn, boyne *n* washtub.

boytach *n/v* bundle.

bra' *see* **braw**.

braal *n* fragment.

brace *n* chimney piece.

brachell *n* game dog.

brachen *n* bracken.

brack *n* salty liquid; flood.

bracken *adj* broken.

brade *v* move fast; spring out; take after, resemble.

brae *n* brow; hill; slope; upland.

braehead *n* hill-top.

braeshot *n* landslip.

brag *n* challenge. • *v* reproach; defy.

braggie *adj* bombastic.

braid *adj* broad; wide. • *adv* indiscreetly.

braid claith *n* broadcloth.

brain¹ *n* spirit; voice.

brain² *v* wound.

brainge, breenge *v* run rashly forwards, barge.

brainyell *v* break out.

braisant *adj* shameless.

braith¹ *adj* violent; severe.

braith² *n* breath.

brak *n* break; bankruptcy. • *v* break; stave.

brakfast *n* breakfast.

brakker *n* lawbreaker.

bramble, brammie *n* blackberry.

brammel *n* fish bait.

brander *n* gridiron. • *v* grill.

brang *v* brought.

brangle *v* shake; wave.

branit *adj* brindled.

brank *v* cavort, prance; bridle; hold back.

brankie *adj* gaudy.

branks¹ *n* bridle.

branks² *n* mumps.

brash *n* short sickness.

brast *v* burst.

brat *n* apron; bib; clothing; rag; cloth.

brathly *adj* noisy.

brattle *n* clatter; gunshot; peal; thunder. • *v* make a clattering noise.

bratts *n* scum.

braverie *n* bravado.

braw, bra', brave *adj* fine; handsome; splendid; admirable; handsome; well-dressed; worthy.

brawlins *npl* cowberries.

brawly *adv* finely.

brawn *n* boar; calf of the leg.

brawness *n* beauty; splendour.

braws *npl* beautiful things; finery; best clothes.

bray *v* push; squeeze.

braze *n* bream; roach.

breach *n* breaking waves.

brechle *see* **breechle**.

breckan *n* bracken.

bred *n* board; lid.

bree¹ *n* soup, broth; gravy; stock; liquid.

bree² *n* eyebrow.

breechle, brechle *v* waddle.

breed *n* pancreas.

breedie *adj* prolific.

breeks *npl* trousers; breeches.

breekums *n* small boy.

breel *v* move rapidly.

breels *npl* spectacles.

breem *adj* keen.

breenge *see* **brainge**.

breengin *adj* bustling.

breer¹ *n* briar; rose.

breer² *see* **brere**.

breerie *adj* sharp clever.

breeth *n* breadth.

breeze *n/v* bruise.

brehon *n* local judge.

breid¹ *n* bread; loaf.

breid² *n* breadth.

breids *npl* oatcakes; sweetbreads.

breife, breve n writing; spell. • v write down.

breist n breast. • v spring forward or up.

brek n breach; break, breaking; tumult.

breme see **brym**.

brenn n/v burn.

brent adj precipitous, steep; straight; smooth, unwrinkled.

brenth n breadth.

brent-new adj brand-new.

brere, breer v germinate.

bress n brass.

breve see **breife**.

brewster, browser n brewer; publican.

bribour n beggarly type.

bricht adj bright.

brickle adj brittle.

brid n bird.

bridecake n wedding cake.

bridie n small meat and vegetable pie.

brief n certificate.

briestane n sandstone.

brig n bridge.

briganer n brigand, thief.

bril n wishbone.

brile v broil.

brime n brine.

brisket n breast.

brither n brother.

brither-dochter n neice.

brizz v squash.

broach v cut stones roughly.

broch n burgh; fort; halo.

brochan n thin porridge.

brochle n lazy person.

brocht v brought.

brod[1] n goad; spur.

brod[2] n board, plank; table; book-board; collection plate.

brod[3] n brood; litter.

brog n awl, bradawl.

brogle v persist ineffectually; bungle.

brogue n light deerskin shoe.

broig, broich v be in a sweat.

broken, brokken adj outlawed; bankrupt.

broo[1] n bureau; job centre; dole.

broo[2] n eyebrow; forehead.

broo[3] n liquid.

broo money n unemployment benefit, dole money.

broofle see **broostle**.

brook n soot.

brookie adj begrimed; grimy; smutty.

brookit adj neglected; soiled; streaked.

broon n brown.

broostle, broofle n bustling.

brooze v browse.

brose[1] n keep, livelihood, living.

brose[2] n oatmeal pudding.

brosy, brosie adj glutinous; bloated; inert.

brother v initiate, accustom.

broudster n embroiderer.

broukit adj part clean, part dirty; tear-stained.

browden, browdin adj devoted; enamoured; fond. • v pet.

browl n firewood.

brownie n domestic sprite.

browst n brewing; brew of malt liquor.

browster see **brewster**.

brub v check; restrain.

bruckle adj brittle, fragile; crumbly; unsettled.

bruik, bruke v enjoy; possess.

bruilyie v broil.

bruilyie, bruilzie n fight, brawl.

bruit[1] n brute.

bruit[2] see **brute**.

bruke see **bruik**.

brumble v rumble hollowly.

brume n broom.

brunds npl glowing embers.

brunstane n brimstone.

brunt adj keen; burnt.

bruntie n blacksmith.

brushie adj spruce.

brussel v push forward.

brust n/v burst.

brute, bruit n report; rumour.

brym, breme adj stormy; raging.

bubbies npl breasts.

bubble n snot, mucus. • v blubber.

bubblie adj blubbering, tearful.

bubblyjock n turkey cock.

buck[1] n beech tree.

buck[2] n body. • v butt.

bucker n smuggling boat.

bucket n bin, dustbin, wastepaper basket.

buckie n whelk or other spiral shell;.

bucksturdie *adj* stubborn.
bud *n* gift; bribe.
budden *adj* invited.
buddie *n* body.
buff¹ *n* lung.
buff² *v* buffet.
bugaboo *n* hobgoblin.
buggle *n* bog, marsh.
bught *n* ewe-milking pen.
bughtin-time *n* milking time.
Buik *n* Bible.
buik, bouk *n* trunk of the body; book.
buikbuird *n* bookshelf.
buiklair, buiklare *n* learning, erudition.
buird¹ *adj* well-built.
buird² *n* board; table; bier; fishing net. • *v*
   board.
buirdlie, buirdly, burdly *adj* burly, stalwart; imposing.
buist¹ *n/v* brand.
buist² *n* box, chest; coffin.
buit *n* boot.
buith *n* shop; booth.
bullace *n* axe.
buller *n* bellow; loud gurgling.
bullie *n* bullfinch.
bulty *adj* large.
bulwand *n* bulrush.
bum¹ *v* buzz; hum; drone; boaster.
bum² *n* slattern.
bumbaze *v* astonish; bamboozle.
bumbazed *adj* bewildered, perplexed.
bumbazit *adj* dazed.
bumbee *n* bee, bumblebee.
bumfelt *adj* puffed out; rumpled.
bumfle *n/v* bulge; pucker; rumple.
bumflie, bumfly *adj* bulging; rumpled.
bumlack *n* stumbling block.
bummle¹ *v* blunder; bumble.
bummle² *v* boil up; bustle.
bun *n* rabbit's tail.
bunce *v* bounce.
bund *see* **bound**.
bung¹ *n* nag, old horse.
bung² *adj* drunk.
bunker *n* bench seat; sandpit.
bunkle *n* stranger.
bunnel *n* bundle.
bunnet *n* bonnet, cap.
bunnle *n* pack.
bunsucken *adj* beholden.

buntin *n* bantam.
bural *n* burial.
burd *see* **bird**.
burdalane *n* only child.
burden *n* drone.
burdenable *adj* burdensome.
burdenous *adj* burdened.
burdly *see* **buirdly**.
burgh *n* borough.
burial letter *n* intimation.
burian *n* mound.
burn, beck *n* brook, stream.
burnet *adj* brown.
burran *n* badger.
burrow duck *n* sheldrake.
burry man *n* scapegoat.
bursary *n* scholarship.
bush *v* sheathe; enclose.
busk *v* adorn, deck, decorate; dress;
   equip.
busker *n* dresser.
buskit *adj* well-dressed.
buss¹ *n* bush, shrub; clump, thicket.
buss² *n* herring fishing boat.
bussie *adj* bushy.
busteous *adj* huge.
buster *n* fish, chips and peas.
bustine *n* fustian cloth.
but¹ *adv* though. • *prep* without; outwards.
but² *n* outer room.
but and ben *n* two-roomed house.
butch *v* butcher.
butchach *n* curse.
butch-hoose *n* abattoir.
butt *n* isolated piece of land; archery
   ground.
butterie *n* butterfly.
buttery rowie *n* breakfast roll.
buttery-lippit *adj* flattering.
butts *npl* fire engine.
buy *v* bribe.
buygie *see* **boyickie**.
by *adv* beyond. • *prep* past; **by himsel/**
   hersel *adj* of unsound mind; **by wi** *adj*
   over and done.
byaak *v* bake.
bycommon *adj* unusual.
bydand *adj* waiting.
bygaen, bygane *adj* passing by; bygone.
   • *adv* past.

bygate n byway.
bygoing n passing.
byke[1] n beehive; hive; wasp's nest.
byke[2] see bike.
byking see biking.
byoors n overtime.
by-ordinar, by-ornar adj unusual, exceptional, extraordinary, outstanding, special. • adv exceptionally.

byous adj remarkable.
by-pit n makeshift; substitute.
byre n cattle shed, cowshed.
by-rins npl arrears.
bysenless adj utterly worthless.
byset n substitute.
byspel n uncommon individual.
bystart n bastard.
by-time n leisure time, spare time.

C

ca[1] n greeting. • v call; drive; order; urge on; **ca awa** proceed with care; **ca canny** slow down; **ca doon** knock down; **ca the feet frae** astonish.
ca[2] n hill pass.
caak v cackle.
caar see cair[2].
cab v pilfer, steal.
cabbitch n cabbage.
cabbrach adj greedy.
caber n beam, rafter; long pole; tree trunk.
cabroch adj skinny.
cackie v excrete.
cacks, cackies npl excreta, turds.
caddie, cadie n errand-runner; cadet.
caddle n nail.
cadge[1] v hawk, peddle wares; beg.
cadge[2] v drive; toss; jolt; shake up.
cadger n driver; carrier, carter; pedlar.
cadgie adj exuberant; hospitable.
caff n chaff.
cag n keg.
cahute n ship's cabin.
caibe n cabinet-maker.
caibin n cabin.
caif adj tame.
caigie, caidgie adj wanton; sportive.
caik n stitch, side pain.
cailleach n old woman; corn dolly.
caip, cape n top part; coping.
caiper n/v caper.
caipstane n coping stone.
cair[1] v rake up.
cair[2], **caar** adj left.
caird[1] n card (comb used to comb cotton).
caird[2] n map, chart; card.

caird[3] n tramp; travelling tinker.
cairds npl cards.
cair-haundit adj left-handed.
cairn n marker of heaped stones.
cairney n hillock.
cairngorm n precious stone.
cairpet n carpet.
cairry v carry, convey.
cairry-oot n takeaway, drink or hot food bought to consume elsewhere.
cairt[1] n card.
cairt[2] n cart.
cairt-draucht n cart-load.
cairter n carter.
cairtin n card-playing.
cairts npl playing cards.
caiver v waver in the mind.
cald n cold.
callant n lad.
caller adj bracing, refreshing; fresh; vigorous. • v freshen; refresh.
callet n cap.
calsay n causeway.
calshie adj crabbed.
cammock adj crooked. • n hooked stick; game of shinty.
camp adj brisk; active.
campie, campy adj bold, intrepid; brave.
camshachelt adj disarranged; misshapen.
camshachle v distort.
camshack adj crooked; unlucky.
camstairie, camstarrie, camsteerie, camstrary adj insubordinate; perverse; unrestrained; tumultuous; disorderly; unmanageable.
camstane n pipeclay.
camy adj crooked.

canallie n mob.

canass n canvas.

canaul n canal.

candent adj red-hot.

candibrod n sugar-candy.

cangle v cavil; quarrel.

canker n ill-humour. • v fret.

cankert adj lowering.

cankry adj cantankerous.

canna, cannach n cotton grass.

cannas n coarse cloth; canvas.

cannel n cinnammon.

cannel n cinnamon.

cannel-bane n collarbone.

cannel coal n bright-burning coal.

cannie, canny adj cautious; prudent; shrewd; thrifty; tactful; unassuming.

canny-wife n midwife.

Canongate breeks n venereal disease.

canse v speak saucily.

canshie adj cross.

cansie adj conceited.

cant¹ adj playful.

cant² n custom.

cant³ v recite, chant; set a stone on its edge; fall over; ride rapidly.

cantel n fragment.

cantie adj comfortable; contented.

cantily adv cheerfully.

cantle¹ n ledge.

cantle² v erect.

cantlin n corner.

cantrip n charm, spell, magic; frolic, trick; mischief.

cantrips npl antics.

canty adj lively, cheerful, pleasant.

canyel v jolt, shake.

cap¹ n wooden eating dish.

cap² v seize; excel.

cape see caip.

caper n pirate.

capercailzie n mountain cock.

caperonish adj good, excellent.

cappilow v get ahead.

cappit adj peevish.

capul n horse, mare.

car¹, caur n sledge; hurdle.

car², ker adj left; left-handed.

carb v carp.

carcat, carcant n necklace; garland.

carcidge n carcass.

carebed n sickbed.

carfuffle, curfuffle n agitation; disorder; fuss.

carie adj soft.

cark n load.

carlage adj churlish.

carle n man, fellow; commoner; candle-stick.

carlie n little man.

carline, carlin n old woman; witch.

carlish adj coarse.

carmovine n camomile.

carnail adj rotten.

carnaptious adj cantankerous, quarrel-some.

carnell n heap.

carp v speak, relate.

carping n narration.

carsackie n blouse; overall, smock.

carse n low-lying land by a river.

carte n chariot.

carvel n sailing ship.

carvie n caraway.

case n chance.

cashie adj luxuriant, blooming.

cashle v squabble.

cassie, cazzie n straw basket for carry-ing peat.

cast n appearance, aspect, bearing, de-meanour, deportment; assistance, help; twist. • v throw off, shed; use; coat with lime or plaster; swarm; **cast oot** disa-gree; fall out; spurn.

cast-bye adj useless.

casten adj faded.

castings npl old clothes.

casual adj accidental.

catalogue n register.

catechis n catechism.

cateran n bandit, brigand.

cat-kindness n cupboard love.

ca-through n disturbance.

cat's een n speedwell.

catsherd n cataract.

cat-tails n cotton-grass.

catterbatch n quarrel.

cattle npl lice.

cat-wittit adj foolish, silly; unbalanced.

caudron n cauldron.

cauf n calf.

caufkintra n birthplace; native district.

cauk *v* pay dearly.

caul *n* dam; weir.

caulcreeps *npl* gooseflesh.

cauld *adj* cold.

cauld-bark *n* coffin.

cauldrid *adj* chilling.

cauldrife *adj* causing coldness; apathetic.

cauld-watter *adj* apathetic; unconcerned.

caulk *n/v* chalk.

caulker *n* bumper.

caum *adj* quiet.

caunle *n* candle.

caunle-dowp *n* candle-end.

caur[1] *n* car.

caur[2] *see* **car**[1].

cause *conj* because.

causey *n* pavement; roadway; street. • *v* pave.

causey stane *n* cobblestone.

caution *n* security; pledge; bail.

cave *v* push; toss.

cavel *see* **kavel**.

cavie *n* hen coop.

cay *n* jackdaw.

cazzie *see* **cassie**.

ceepher *n* cipher.

cele *v* hide.

cerse, cerss *v* search.

certaint *adj* certain.

certie *adv* certainly.

cess *n* tax.

chaave *n/v* struggle; toil.

chack[1] *n/v* check.

chack[2] *v* clack; clink; nip. • *n* ouzel; stonechat.

chack[3] *n* wheel rut.

chackert, chackit *adj* chequered; tartan.

chackie *adj* uneven.

chackie mill *n* death-watch beetle.

chackit *see* **chackert**.

chad *n* compacted gravel; small stones forming a river bed.

chaddy *adj* gravelly.

chaff *v* chafe.

chaft *n* jaw.

chaft-blade *n* cheekbone; jawbone.

chafts *npl* chops; jaw.

chaipe *v* escape.

chaipel *n* chapel.

chairge *n* cost; expense. • *v* charge.

chaistifie *v* chastise.

chaker *n* chessboard.

chalmer *see* **chaumber**.

cham *n/v* chew.

chammer *v* settle; quash.

champ *n* morass. • *v* chop; mash; pound.

champer *n* pestle.

champit tatties *npl* mashed potatoes.

chance n perk, perquisite.

chancy *adj* lucky.

chandler *n* candlestick.

change-house *n* tavern.

channel *n* gutter.

channel-stane *n* curling stone.

channer *v* fret; chide.

chanter *n* bagpipe drone.

chantie-beak *n* chatterbox.

chanty *n* chamberpot; lavatory pan.

chap *n* blow, knock, tap; choppiness. • *v* knock; strike; mash; ratify, sanction; pick out; **chap hauns** shake hands.

chape *adj* cheap.

chapman *n* pedlar.

chapper *n* knocker.

chappit *adj* cracked.

char *v* stop; turn aside.

chark *v* grind; gnash.

charker *n* cricket.

chase *n* hunt, case; hurry.

chasie *v* chase.

chate *v* cheat.

chaterie *adj* cheating.

chatter *v* shatter.

chattert *adj* frayed.

chattle *v* nibble.

chaum *v* gobble.

chaumber, chaumer, chalmer *n* chamber, room; bedroom; parlour.

chaunt *v* chant.

chauve *adj* black and white.

chaw *n* hawthorn.

chaw *n* snub; chagrin. • *v* chew; fret; provoke.

chawed *adj* vexed.

chawsome *adj* galling.

cheat *n* cat.

cheatrie, cheatry *adj* fraudulent. • *n* fraud.

check *n* key.

cheek *n* jamb; side.

cheen n/v chain.

cheenge n change; patronage. • v alter; convert; transform; vary.

cheeny n china.

cheer n chair.

cheerisome adj cheerful.

cheetle v chirp.

cheggie n chestnut.

cheim v divide equally.

cheip, chepe v chirp.

chese v choose.

chess n sash; window-frame; segment of fruit.

chessart n cheese-press.

chessie n chestnut.

chessoun v accuse.

chib n knife. • v knife; slash.

chibbie adj chubby.

chice n choice.

chickenwort n chickweed.

chief adj intimate.

chieftain n chief.

chiel n fellow, lad; servant.

childe n servant; man.

childer npl children.

chilpie adj chilly.

chim v make up to.

chimes n main dwelling.

chimley n fireplace; grate; chimney.

chine n/v chain.

chingle n shingle.

chinglie adj gravelly.

chinkie n chin.

chippie n marble.

chippit adj damaged.

chirk, jirk v gnash; grate noisily.

chirl v chirp; warble.

chirle n chin.

chirm n warble.

chirr, churr v chirp.

chirrie, chirry n cherry.

chirt n/v hug; squeeze.

chitter v chatter; shiver.

chitterin adj trembling.

chizel v cheat.

chizors npl scissors.

chock n croup.

choice v choose.

choller n jowl; double chin.

chookie see **chuckie**.

chop, chope n shop.

chore v steal.

chork v squelch.

chow n chew; mouthful. • v chew.

chowk v choke.

chowks npl cheeks, chops.

chowl v twist.

chree adj/n three.

Christendie n Christendom.

Christenmas n Christmas.

chucken n chicken.

chuckie[1], **chookie** n chick, hen.

chuckie[2], **chucky** n pebble, stone.

chuckie-stane n throwing pebble.

chuddue n chewing gum.

chuffie adj chubby.

chuffie-cheekit adj chubby-cheeked.

chug n/v tug.

chuggie n chewing gum.

chye n chaffinch.

chynge n change. • v change; decompose; go off.

cinner n cinder.

circumjack v agree; correspond to.

cissie adj girlish.

cistren n cistern.

clabbydhu n mussel.

clachan n village, hamlet.

clacher v move with difficulty.

clack n gossip; insolence. • v gossip.

clackan n racquet.

cladach, cleitach n talk.

claen adj clean.

claes npl clothes, attire.

claffie adj disordered.

clag n encumbrance; clot; dried-on excreta or dung. • v clog; stop up.

claggie, claggy adj glutinous; adhesive, sticky.

clag-tailed adj dirty-bottomed.

claik[1] n barnacle.

claik[2] n clucking; idle talk. • v cluck.

clair[1] adj clear.

clair[2] v scold; beat.

claith n cloth; clothing.

claiver v talk idly.

clam[1] adj clammy; mean; low.

clam[2] n scallop.

clamant adj urgent.

clamjamfry, clamjamfrie, clamjamphry n company; crowd, rabble; jumped-up people; junk, rubbish.

clammer v clamber.

clammersome adj clamorous.

clamp n clump.

clampers npl clogs.

clams, clamps npl pincers.

clap[1] n moment; stroke, pat. • v adhere, cling; flop; pat; press down.

clap[2] n rabbit's burrow.

clapman n public crier.

clappit adj flabby; gaunt; sunken.

clark n clerk. • v compose; write.

clart n dirt, grime; mud; muck. • bedaub; make dirty.

clarty adj dirty; muddy; adhesive.

clash n idle talk, rumour; heap. • v gossip; throw; strike; slam.

clasher adj/n telltale.

clashmeclaver see **clishmaclaiver**.

clat see **claut**.

clatch n slut. • v daub; patch up roughly.

clathes npl clothes.

clatter n prattle; rumour. • v gossip.

clatterer n scandalmonger.

clattie adj disagreeable; nasty; dirty.

claucher v snatch up.

claut, clat n clod; clot; lump. • coagulate; clutch.

claver n clover.

clavers npl gossip, tittle-tattle.

claw v scratch.

claymore n two-handed sword.

clean-fung adv cleverly.

cleanin n placenta.

clear adj certain, sure.

clearance n revelation.

clearin n beating.

cleas npl clothes.

cleck v give birth; breed; conceive; hatch; invent.

cleckin n brood of chicks.

cleed, cleith v clothe.

cleedin n attire, clothing; garment; suit of clothes.

cleek, click n hook; crochet hook; girlfriend, boyfriend. • v hook; clutch; ensnare.

cleekie n staff; hooked stick; golf club.

cleekit adj linked.

cleeks npl cramp.

cleepie n heavy blow.

cleester v anoint; plaster.

cleg n horsefly; gadfly.

cleik adj lively.

cleisher n monster.

cleitach see **cladach**.

cleith see **cleed**.

clem adj mean; low.

clem adj queer.

clench v limp.

clep n gaff.

clep, clepe see **clype**.

clesp n/v clasp.

cless n class.

clett n sea rock.

cleuch, cleugh n hollow between rocks; gorge; chasm.

cleuk n/v claw.

cleuks npl clutches.

clever v climb.

clew n ball of thread.

cley n clay.

cley davy n navvy.

clibber n pack-saddle.

click see **cleek**.

clift[1] n cavern; cleft, fissure; plank; crotch.

clift[2] n cliff.

clim v climb.

climp v catch quickly.

clink[1] n money, cash; telltale. • v beat, strike; join metal; **clink up** v snatch up.

clink[2] v compose.

clint n flinty rock.

clip n colt; tearaway; yob.

clip v embrace; grapple.

clipe see **clype**.

clippin n sheep-shearing.

clippin time n nick of time.

clish v spread gossip.

clishmaclaiver, clashmeclaver n busybody; tittle-tattle; lengthy debate.

cliver adj clever; nice; quick, swift.

cliveralitie adv cleverness.

cloak n clock.

clocher v cough thickly.

clock[1] n beetle.

clock[2] n cape, cloak.

clock[3] n cluck. • v cluck; brood.

clocker[1] n broody hen.

clocker[2] n cockroach.

clockin adj broody.

clockin hen n broody hen.

clod n sod. • v pelt, throw.
cloff n split; fissure.
clog n log.
cloit n afternoon nap.
cloitery adj damp; slimy.
cloor v cuff; thump.
cloorer n chisel.
cloot¹, clout n cloth; rag; bandage; nappy; patch. • v patch.
cloot², clout n blow.
cloot³, clute n hoof, cloven hoof.
cloots npl clothes; rags.
close¹ adj constant, continual.
close² n alley; staircase of a tenement building; passageway; courtyard.
closin n congestion.
closs adj close.
closter n cloister.
clottert adj caked.
clour v beat; thump.
clout see cloot¹, cloot².
clow n clove.
clowe n talon.
clowen adj cloven.
clud n cloud.
cluddy adj cloudy.
cludgie n lavatory; toilet.
cluf, cluif n hoof; claw.
cluff n blow; thump.
clung adj empty.
clute see cloot³.
clyack sheaf n last sheaf of harvest.
clype, clep, clepe, clipe n telltale. • v tell tales; report.
clyre n tumour.
clytach n balderdash.
coaf v cough.
coal bing n pit heap.
coalie-back adv/n piggyback.
coal neuk n coal cellar.
coal-ree n coalyard.
coat n petticoat; skirt.
coat-weasel n ermine.
coble n fishing boat; ferry-boat.
coch v cough.
cock v indulge; pick up; set up.
cockapentie n snob.
cocker v totter.
cockernonny n snood.
cockieleerie n cockerel.
cockle v cuckold.

cockle-headed adj whimsical.
cocky adj vain.
cod¹ n cushion; pillow.
cod² n pea pod.
codgie adj relaxed, contented.
codroch adj rustic.
cods npl testicles.
coff n/v purchase, buy.
coft adj bought.
cog¹ n bucket, pail; wooden dish.
cog² n chock.
cog³ n small sailing ship.
cog-wame n potbelly.
coggie n small wooden bowl.
coggle v rock; unbalance.
cogglie, coggly adj unsteady.
coin, coyn n corner.
coinyelled adj pitted.
coist n flank.
coit v jostle.
cole n haycock.
colfin n wadding.
coll¹ n coal.
coll² v cut; clip; shape.
college n university.
collegener, collegianer n university student.
collet n collar.
collie¹ n sheepdog.
collie² v abash; domineer.
collieshangie n controversy; disturbance; dogfight.
collogue n conference; interview; symposium. • v conspire, plot.
collop n steak.
come n growth; bend. • v expand; happen; come by come in; come in collapse; come ower befall; come tae comply; come to calm down.
come awa! interj come on!
come-doon n degradation.
commandin adj disabling.
communin n discussion.
compaingen n companion, comrade.
compare n comparison.
compeir v appear in court.
complain n moan.
complainer n prosecutor.
compliment n donation, gift.
complouter, compluther v coincide; comply; collaborate; cooperate.

compone *v* compound; settle.
comprise *v* evaluate.
con *n* squirrel.
conand *adj* knowing.
conceitie *adj* conceited.
concioun *n* assembly; speech.
condescend on *v* particularise, specify.
condinglie, condingly *adv* agreeably; lovingly.
conduck *n* conduct; safe-conduct.
confabble *v* converse.
confeerin *adj* corresponding. • *prep* considering.
confeese *v* bemuse; confuse.
conflummix *n/v* shock.
confoon *v* confound.
conformity *n* concession.
connach *v* waste.
conneck *v* connect.
consait *n* conceit.
considerin *n* considerate.
consither *v* consider.
consolement *n* consolation.
constant *adj* plain.
consumpt *n* consumption, ingestion.
conter *adj* adverse; contrary. • *contrary; opposite; reverse. • prep* against. • *v* contradict; counteract; oppose; thwart.
contermit *adj* determined.
continuation *n* postponement.
continue *v* postpone.
contrack *n* contract.
contrair *adj* contrary; opposed. • *contrary; opposite. • v* contradict.
contramashous *adj* wilful.
contrufe *v* contrive.
convener *n* president.
convenient *adj* satisfied.
convick *v* convict.
convoy *n* escort. • *v* accompany; carry; conduct; convey; escort; transport.
cony *n* cognac.
conyng *n* knowledge.
coo *n* cow.
cooard *n* coward.
cooardiness *n* cowardice.
coo-cracker *n* campion.
cood *n* cud.
coof *n* simpleton.
cook, couk *v* appear and disappear.
cookie *n* sweet roll, bun, teabread; trol-

lop.
cool *n* cowl.
coolriff *adj* cold.
coom *n* coffin lid; coal dust, peat dust, dross.
coomed *adj* vaulted.
coonger *v* cow, intimidate.
coont *n* count. • *v* calculate, count.
coonter *n* counter.
coonter-lowper *n* shop assistant.
coontie, coonty *n* county.
coonts *npl* arithmetic; sums.
coop *n* small heap.
coopat *n* cowpat.
coor *v* cower.
coorag *n* forefinger.
coordie *adj* cowardly, craven.
coorie *v* cringe; crouch, stoop; cuddle; snuggle; **coorie doon** crouch; **coorie hunker** squat; **coorie in** nestle, snuggle up.
coorse¹ *adj* barbarous; boorish, coarse, crude; disreputable; hard, inclement; naughty; rascally; disobedient.
coorse² *n* course.
coort *n* court.
cooser *n* stallion.
coost *n* physique.
cooter *n* coulter.
coper *see* **couper**.
corbie *n* crow; raven.
corbie stanes *n* crowsteps.
corbie-steps *n* stepped gable.
cord *n* accord. • *v* harmonise.
cordiner *n* shoemaker.
corf *n* basket, creel.
cork *n* contractor; employer.
corky *adj* airy.
corn *n* oats.
cornet *n* standard-bearer.
cornt *adj* tiddly, tipsy.
cornyaird *n* stackyard.
coronach *n* dirge, lament.
corp *n* cadaver, corpse.
corp-lifter *n* body-snatcher.
corrie *n* mountain hollow.
corrie-fister *n* left-handed person.
corrieneuchin *adj* murmuring.
corruption *n* anger.
corrydander *n* coriander.
corse, cors *n/v* cross.

cosh *adj* cosy, snug.

cosie *n* scarf.

coss *v* exchange.

cot¹ *n* coat.

cot² *n* cottage.

cottar *n* cottager.

coudle *v* float.

couk *see* **cook**.

coulie, cowlie *n* boy.

coulter-neb *n* long nose.

countra *n* country.

coup, cowp¹ *n* fall, tumble; rubbish dump, midden. • *v* fall over; overbalance; capsize; topple; upset; tilt.

coup, cowp² *n*/*v* exchange.

coupen *n* fragment.

couper, coper, cowper *n* dealer; broker.

cour *v* crouch.

courage-bag *n* scrotum.

cout *n* yearling horse, colt.

couter *v* cosset.

couth, couthie, couthy *adj* familiar, known; pleasant; affable, agreeable; sociable; kind, humane; sympathetic.

couthless *adj* unfriendly.

cove *n* cave, cavern.

covine *n* fraud.

cow¹ *n* twig; scarecrow.

cow² *v* exceed; clip.

cowclink *n* whore.

cowd *n* short sailing trip.

cowdach *n* heifer.

cowdrum *n* beating.

cowe¹ *n* haircut. • clip.

cowe² *v* outdo, surpass; **cowe the cuddie** surpass everything.

cower *v* recover.

cowlick *n* tuft of hair on the forehead.

cowlie *see* **coulie**.

cowmon *adj* common.

cowp *see* **coup, cowp¹**, **coup, cowp²**.

cowper *see* **couper**.

cowshus *adj* cautious.

cowstick *n* caustic.

cowt *n* cudgel; colt; boor.

cowzie *adj* boisterous.

coxy *adj* coaxing.

coy *adj* quiet.

coyn *see* **coin**.

crabbit *adj* crabbed, crusty, ill-tempered, irascible, irritable, testy, tetchy.

crabbitness *n* bad-temper.

crack *n* anecdote, story; chat, free talk; boasting. • *v* chat, converse, talk freely.

cracker nut *n* hazelnut.

crackers *npl* castanets.

crackie, cracky *adj* affable; talkative.

crackie-stool *n* three-legged stool.

craft *n* croft.

crag, craig *n* neck.

craichling, creichling *n* itching cough.

craig¹ *n* cliff, crag; rock.

craig² *see* **crag**.

craik *n* corncrake; croak. • *v* creak; croak.

craitur *n* creature.

craize *v* creak.

cramasie, cramasye *adj* crimson. • *n* crimson; crimson cloth.

crambo-clink *n* doggerel.

crame *see* **cream**.

cramp *v* contract.

cramsh *v* grit.

cran¹ *n* crane (bird and machine); trivet.

cran² *n* swift.

cran³ *n* barrelful of herring.

cran⁴ *n* tap.

cranachan *n* dessert of honey cream and cheese.

crance *n* chink.

cranch *v* crush.

crank *adj* weak; sickly.

crankie, cranky *adj* insecure; testy.

crannie *n* recess.

crannog *n* lake dwelling.

cranreuch *n* hoar frost, rime.

cranshach *n* cripple.

crap *n* top part; craw of a fowl, crop. • *v* fill; stuff.

crape *n* crepe.

crappit *adj* stuffed.

crat *adj* weak.

crave *v* dun.

craw *n* crow, rook.

crawberry *n* cranberry, crowberry.

crawdoun *n* coward.

craw's aipple *n* crab apple.

craw-taes *n* crow's feet.

craw widdie *n* rookery.

creagh, creach *n* raid, cattle raid; plunder.

cream, crame *n* booth, stall.

creck *n/v* crack.

creeks an corners *npl* nooks and crannies.

creel *n* wicker basket; peat basket; lobster pot.

creenge *v* cringe.

creepie *n* footstool.

creepie stool *n* stool of penance.

creesh *n* fat, grease. • *v* grease, lubricate; creesh a luif bribe.

creeshie *adj* fat; greasy.

creichling *see* craichling.

creil *n* creel.

cress *n/v* crease.

crib[1] *n* beaker.

crib[2] *n* coop.

crib[3] *n* kerb.

cricklet *n* runt.

cries *npl* banns.

crimp *adj* scarce.

crimpet *n* crumpet.

crinch *v* crunch.

crinchie *adj* crunchy.

crine *v* shrink; shrivel; reduce.

crinkie-winkie *n* contention.

cripple *adj* lame.

crock *v* crouch.

croft *n* small upland farm.

crofter *n* upland farmer.

cromag *n* staff; crook.

crone *v* wheedle.

cronnie *n* crony.

croo *n* hovel.

crood *n* crowd, multitude.

croodle *v* hum; coo; croon.

crook *n* fireplace chain and hook.

crook-tree *n* beam of the crook.

croon[1] *n* crown.

croon[2] *n* lament. • *v* mourn; murmur.

crooner *n* gurnard.

croop, croot *v* croak.

croose, crous, crouse *adj* cocky; confident; courageous, valiant; exuberant, jaunty, merry; self-satisfied, smug; assured. • *adv* boldly.

cross-and-pile *n* coin.

cross-speir *v* cross-examine.

crotal *n* lichen for dyeing.

crote *n* grain, tiny particle.

crottle *n* crumb.

crouchie *adj* hunchbacked.

crouds *npl* curds.

croup *v* caw, croak; speak hoarsely.

crouple-craw *n* raven.

croupit *adj* croaking.

crous, crouse *see* croose.

crove *n* chisel.

crowdie *n* kind of cream cheese.

crowdle *v* crawl; draw together.

crowl *v* crawl.

croy[1] *n* crustacean.

croy[2] *n* fish trap; groyne; breakwater.

cru *n* enclosure.

crub *n/v* curb.

cruck *v* make lame.

crud *n* curd.

cruddie *adj* curdled.

cruddle, crudle *v* curdle.

cruds *npl* curds.

cruels *npl* scrofula.

cruet *n* carafe, decanter.

crufe *see* cruive[1].

cruik *v* bend; cruik yer hochs kneel.

cruisie, crusie *n* oil lamp.

cruive[1], crufe *n* pen, pigsty; hovel.

cruive[2] *n* wicker fish trap.

crummet, crummie *adj* crooked-horned.

crummle *v* crumble.

crummock *n* shepherd's crook, staff; walking stick.

crump *adj* crisp. • *v* crunch.

crumpie *adj* crackly; crisp.

crumshie *adj* crackly; crisp.

crunkle *n/v* crease; crinkle.

crusie *see* cruisie.

cry *n* summons. • *v* call; summon; proclaim, publish; shout; name; cry in call in; cry on call on.

cuchil, cuthil *n* forest.

cuddle, cuddy *n* donkey; horse; ass.

cuddieheels, trenkets *npl* iron heels on shoes.

cudding *n* char.

cuddom *v* tame.

cuddum *v* train.

cuddy *see* cuddie.

cufe *n* simpleton.

cuff *n* nape; scruff.

cufie *v* excel.

cuik *n/v* cook.

cuil *adj/v* cool.

cuir *n/v* cure.

cuit, cuitt, cuite, cute *n* ankle; fetlock.
cuiter *v* coddle, pamper; indulge; nurse.
cull *n* testicle.
cullage *n* sexual organs.
culpable homicide *n* manslaughter.
culroun *n* rascal.
culyie *v* coax, cajole; fondle.
cumber *adj* numbed.
cummer[1] *n* godmother; midwife.
cummer[2] *n* vexation; gossip.
cundie, cundy *n* culvert, drain, tunnel; conduit; apartment; hidden space.
cuningar *n* warren.
cunner *v* scold.
cunyie *n* coin; corner.
cupple *v* couple.
curator *n* guardian.
curch *n* kerchief for the head.
curfuffle *see* **carfuffle**.
curie *n* search.
curjute *v* overthrow.
curl-doddie *n* plantain; scabious.
curl-doddies *n* curled cabbage.
curling *n* game of bowling on ice.
curling stane *n* stone used in curling.
curly kail *n* colewort.
curmud *adj* cordial; intimate.

curmur *v* purr.
curmurrin *n* murmur; stomach rumble.
curn *n* grain of seed.
curny *adj* grainy.
curpin *n* rump.
curple *n* crupper.
curpon *n* rump of a fowl.
curr *v* lean; cower; purr.
currach *n* coracle, small boat.
curran *n* currant.
currie *n* small stool.
curtill *n* slattern.
cushat, cushie-doo *n* wood-pigeon; ring-dove.
cushin *n* cushion.
cut *n* appetite; temper.
cutchin *adj* cowardly.
cute *see* **cuitt**.
cuthil *see* **cuchil**.
cutikins *npl* gaiters.
cutle *v* wheedle; guide.
cutter *n* reaper.
cuttit *adj* peremptory; succinct.
cutty, cuttie *adj* short. • *n* short pipe.
cutty-stool *n* low stool; stool of penance.
cuz *adj* closely.

D

daak *n* lull.
daaken, daakenin *v* dawn.
dab, daub *v* peck.
dab-at-the-stuil *n* pepper and salt.
dabber, dever *v* jabber.
dablet *n* imp.
dacent *adj* decent.
dachle *v* hold back, impede.
dacker, daiker *v* search about; be lightly employed.
dackle *n* suspense; hesitancy.
dacklie *adj* pale, livid.
dad, dawd *n* lump; piece. • *v* dash; gust.
daddle *see* **daidle**[2].
dadie *n* dad, daddy.
dae[1] *v* do; **dae guid** thrive.
dae[2] *n* doe.
daeless *adj* improvident; lazy; useless.
dae-na-guid *n* good-for-nothing, ne'er-do-well.

daff *v* frolic, lark; make sport, sport.
dafferie *n* flirtation; frivolity, fun.
daffery, daffing *n* romping.
daffin *n* fun; merry-making.
daffins *n* daffodil.
daft *adj* stupid, silly, foolish; delirious; mad, insane; crazy; doting, infatuated.
daftie *n* fool, halfwit, idiot, simpleton.
daftlike *adj* stupid-seeming.
daftness *n* foolishness.
dag *v* shoot; rain gently.
daggie *adj* drizzling.
daggle *v* lag.
daible *v* wash imperfectly.
daich, daigh *n* dough.
daichie *adj* doughy.
daidle[1] *n* bib; table napkin.
daidle[2], **daddle** *v* dawdle; waste time.
daidle[3] *v* dandle.
daigh *see* **daich**.

daik v smooth down.
daiken n decade.
daiker[1] v decorate.
daiker[2] see **dacker**.
dailer n dealer.
dailigaun n twilight.
daimen adj rare.
daine adj modest.
dainschoch adj squeamish.
daintie-lion n dandelion.
daintith n dainty.
dainty adj large; thriving; plump.
dairt n/v dart.
daise v rot; wither.
daised adj rotten; spoilt.
daith n death.
daith-cannle n will-o'-the-wisp.
daiver, dever see **daver**.
daizzle v dazzle.
dale n deal; portion, share. • v deal; trade.
dale n diving board.
dale n goal.
dall n doll.
dam n urine. • v urinate.
damasee n damson.
dambrod n draughts board.
dame n maiden.
damishell n damsel.
dams npl draughts.
dancer n outstanding person.
dancle n dancing master.
dancin mad adj frantic.
dander n stroll. •.
dander see **daunder**.
danders npl clinkers, slag.
dandle adj fine; grand.
dandrum n freak.
dang n/v damn.
dannle v dangle.
dant v daunt.
danton, daunton v subdue; discourage.
dare n awe.
darg n day's work.
darklins adv in the dark.
darn see **dern**.
darth n dearth.
dashelt adj battered.
dashing n disappointment.
dask n desk; pew.
dass n layer.

datchie adj penetrating; clever.
daub[1] n dash.
daub[2] see **dab**.
dauble v dabble.
dauch n heavy dew.
daud, dad n dab; drop.
daumer v spellbind; stun.
dauner, dander n/v amble, stroll.
daunton see **danton**.
daupit adj imbecile.
daur n daring. • v dare.
daurk adj dark.
daut v caress, fondle; cosset, pamper; dote; make much of.
dautie, dawtie n darling, dear; darling child; kindness.
daver, daiver, dever v stupefy; stun; chill.
davielie adv listlessly.
davoch n division of land.
daw[1] n daybreak. • v dawn.
daw[2] n sluggard; particle.
dawdie n slut.
dawghie, dawkie adj moist.
dawsie adj stupid; dull.
dawtie see **dautie**.
day n today.
day-daw n dawn.
daylicht n daylight.
dayligaun n nightfall.
daze v stun.
dazent adj damned.
dazzle v daze.
dazzly adj dazzling.
de art the.
deacon n expert.
dean, den n steep little valley; hollow place.
dearch n dwarf.
deart v raise in price.
dearth n price.
deasie adj cold; raw.
deave v deafen; plague, torment, weary.
debosh v debauch.
deburse v spend.
deceiverie n deceit.
decern v decree; judge; determine.
dech see **deigh**.
decorement n decoration.
decree n judgement.
decreit v decree.

decrippit *adj* decrepit.
dede *see* **deid**.
dee *v* die; decease; expire.
deed *adv* indeed.
deedle *v* sing low.
deedlie *adj* fatal.
deef *n* deaf.
deek *n* look; glance. • *v* spy out.
deem *n* dame; maiden.
deemer *n* judge.
deemless *adj* countless.
deem's day *n* doomsday.
deepens *n* depth.
deep plate *n* soup plate.
deevil *see* **deil**.
defaik *v* relax.
defait *adj* defeated. • *v* defeat, vanquish.
defeeckwalt *adj* difficult.
defender *n* defendant.
defenn *n* dirt.
defluction *n* catarrh.
deg *v* strike with a sharp point.
deid, dede *n* death. • *adv* very; **deid auld** very old. • *adj* dead; **deid as a mauk** lifeless.
deid-bell *n* passing bell.
deid-hoose *n* mortuary.
deid-ill *n* mortal illness.
deid-kist *n* coffin.
deidlie *adj* deadly.
deidman's bellows *npl* bugle.
deid throws *npl* death throes.
deigh, dech *v* build.
deil, deevil *n* devil; **deil a haet** damn all, nothing at all.
deil's darnin needle *n* dragonfly.
deil's picter buiks *n* playing cards.
deir *adj* bold; wild.
dek *adj/n* ten.
delash *n/v* discharge.
deleerit *adj* delirious.
delf *n* pit; grave; crockery; clod.
delicht *n/v* delight.
delichtsome *adj* delightful.
delt *v* fondle.
deltit *adj* pampered, petted.
delyver *v* deliberate.
dem¹ *pron* them.
dem² *v* dam.
demain *v* demean.
demit *v* dismiss; resign.

dempster *n* judge.
den¹ *n* forecastle.
den² *see* **dean**.
denner *n* dinner. • *v* dine.
denner piece *n* packed lunch.
dentie *adj* fair-sized.
deny *v* refuse.
deochandorrus *n* parting drink; stirrup cup.
depairt *v* depart.
depart, depert *v* part with; divide.
depone *v* declare; testify.
depute *n* deputy.
deray *n* disorder; mirth.
derbel *n* eyesore.
derf *adj* bold, daring; cruel; hardy; sullen, taciturn; obscure.
dern, darn *v* hide, conceal; hearken.
derrin *n* cake of oatbread.
deturn *v* turn aside.
deuch *n/v* drink.
deugind *adj* wilful.
deuk *n* duck. • *v* dip; duck.
deuk-dub, deuk's dub *n* duck pond.
deule weeds *npl* mourning clothes.
devail *v* descend; let fall.
devel *n* heavy blow. • *v* strike, hit.
develler *n* boxer; fighter.
dever¹, deever *v* be stupid.
dever² *see* **dabber**.
dever³ *see* **daiver**.
deviltry *n* devilry.
devise *v* talk.
devol *v* deviate.
devore *n* service; duty.
dew *adj* damp.
dewgs *npl* rags.
dey *n* dairymaid.
diacle *n* compass.
dib *see* **dub**.
dibler *n* large wooden dish.
diceboard *n* chessboard.
dichel *n* thrashing.
dicht *n* light polish; rub; wipe. • *v* dry, wipe; prepare; polish; rub; decorate.
dichtings *npl* refuse.
dick *adj/n* ten.
dict *v* dictate.
diddle *v* fiddle; shake.
diet¹ *n* journey; outing; meeting.
diet² *n* meal.

diet-book n diary.
diet-oor n mealtime.
differ n difference; dissent. • v dissent.
diffide v distrust.
digestlie adj deliberately.
diggot n scamp.
dike¹ n dig; pick.
dike² see **dyke**.
dildermot n obstacle.
dill v placate.
dilly-castle n sandcastle.
dilp n trollop. • v stalk.
dilse n dulse.
dimple n/v dibble.
din adj dingy; dun-coloured; sallow.
din n report, fame; loud talking.
ding v drive; dash; bash, beat, thrash;
  ding doon overthrow, overcome; **ding
  in** drive in; **ding on** attack; **ding up**
  break up.
ding-dang adv helter-skelter.
dingle v tingle.
dink adj neat; trim. • v deck, dress up.
dinklie adv trimly.
dinnle adj tingling. • n vibration; peal. • v
  peal; shake.
dinnous, dinsome adj noisy; riotous.
dint n chance; affection.
dippen n riverside steps; washing-place.
dird n stroke; bump; achievement. • v
  bump; thrust.
dirdum n achievement; uproar; tumult;
  retribution.
direck adj direct. • adv directly. • v direct.
dirk¹ n dagger.
dirk² v grope in the dark.
dirkin v eavesdrop.
dirl n jar; rattle; stroke; vibration; thrill. •
  v jar; pierce; thrill; rattle; reverberate;
  vibrate.
dirlie-bane n funny-bone.
dirlin n vibration.
dirr adj numb.
dirray n/v disorder.
dirrie n tobacco ash.
dirt n excrement.
dirten adj base; soiled.
dirt-flee n dungfly.
dirt-hoose n privy.
disabuse n/v damage; misuse.

disagreeance n disagreement.
disannul v obliterate.
dischairge n/v discharge.
disconvenience n/v inconvenience.
disconvenient adj inconvenient.
discreet adj obliging.
diseise n discomfort.
disgeest, disgest v digest.
dish v butt; destroy.
dish cloot n dishcloth.
disherten v dishearten.
dish-faced adj flat-faced.
dishins n drubbing.
disjaskit adj depressed, downcast, low-
  spirited; decrepit, dilapidated; tired-
  looking, weary-looking.
disjeckit adj dejected, despondent.
disjune n breakfast.
disloaden v unload.
disparit adj desperate.
disparple v scatter.
displenish v unfurnish.
dissle n light rain.
dist n/v dust.
distance n difference.
distrack v distract.
distrackit adj distracted.
distrubil v disturb.
disty adj dusty.
dit, ditt v indulge.
dite see **dyte**.
ditt see **dit**.
divert n amusement; comic; diversion;
  entertainment.
divider n serving spoon, ladle.
divot n clod of turf, sod.
dizzen n dozen.
dobbie, dobie n dunce; foolish person.
docher n durability; wear and tear; weariness.
dochter n daughter.
dock n backside; stern of a ship. • v clip;
  shorten; spank.
docken n dock (plant).
docketie adj short and jolly.
dockit adj clipped.
dockus n something short.
docky adj short; neat.
dod, dods n petulant fit.
dodd v jog.
doddle v wag about.

doddles *npl* genitals (male).

doddy *adj* petulant; hornless.

dodge *v* jog, trudge along; **dodge awa** trudge on.

dodgel, dudgel *v* hobble.

dodgie *adj* irritable.

dodrum *n* whim.

dods *see* dod.

doer *n* steward, factor.

dog¹ *n* blacksmith's lever.

dog² *v* skive.

dog-hip *n* dog-rose hip, rosehip.

doid *n* dolt.

doif *adj* dulled.

doil *n* piece.

doin, done, doon, doyn *adv* very.

doister *n* storm from seawards.

doistert *adj* confused.

doit *n* small copper coin.

doited *adj* crazy.

doiter *v* stagger, totter.

doitert, doittert *adj* witless; senile.

doittrie *n* dotage.

doldies *n* droppings.

dole *n* fraud; malice.

dolent *adj* mournful.

doless *adj* helpless.

doll *n* pigeon dung.

dollie, dowie *adj* dull; wearied.

dolver *n* anything large.

dominie *n* schoolmaster, teacher.

doncie *n* clown, buffoon.

done *see* doin.

donie *n* hare.

donk *adj* damp.

donnar *v* stupefy.

donnar'd *adj* stupefied.

donn'd *adj* fond.

donner *v* daze.

donnert *adj* doltish, slow-witted; stunned, stupefied.

donsie *adj* over-neat; restive; unlucky, hapless; wretched.

doo, dow *n* darling; dove; pigeon.

dooble *n* duplicate. • *v* double.

doocot, dowcate *n* dovecote; pigeon-hole.

doodle *v* dandle.

doof *n* soft blow.

dook, douk *n* plunge into water; bath; dip. • *v* immerse; bathe; dip; dive.

dookin *n* immersion; soaking.

dool, dule *n* grief, sadness; suffering. • *v* grieve.

doolie¹ *n* hobgoblin; spectre.

doolie², dulie *adj* doleful.

doolsome *adj* doleful.

doolzie *n* light-minded woman.

doom *n* sentence. • *v* condemn.

dooms *adv* very.

doon¹ *v* upset overthrow.

doon², doun *adv* down.

doon³ *see* doin.

doon-brae *adv* downwards.

doon-haud *n* handicap.

doon-hauden *adj* repressed.

doon-richteous *adj* downright.

doon-sittin *n* sitting.

doon-tak *n* degradation, humiliation; disparagement.

doonfa *n* declivity.

doonset *n* settlement.

doonthro' *adv* in the low country.

doonwith, doonwi *adj* descending. • *adv* downhill; downwards.

door-cheek *n* doorway.

doorstane *n* doorstep.

doosht *v* throw down.

doot *n* qualm.

dootless *adv* indubitably.

doots *npl* misgivings.

dootsome *adj* uncertain; undecided; vague.

dorb *n* peck.

dorbel *n* unseemly thing.

dorbie *n* mason, stonemason.

dore-crook *n* hinge; hasp.

dorestane *n* threshold.

dorlach *n* short sword.

dorle *n* piece.

dornel *n* horse's anus.

doroty *n* doll.

dort *n* huff; petulance.

dortie, dorty *adj* supercilious; pettish.

dorts *npl* sulks.

dorty *see* dortie.

doss¹ *n* tobacco pouch.

doss² *v* pay down; **doss doon** toss down.

doss³ *adj* dozy, stupid; neat, tidy.

doss⁴ *n* bow of ribbon.

dote *n* dowry.

dottar, dotter *v* dodder, become senile.

dottelt *adj* senile.

dotter *see* dottar.

dotterel *n* dotard.

dottle *n* small piece; cigarette butt; pipe ash; short person; stopper; dotage.

douce *adj* amiable; decorous; gentle; respectable, sedate, staid; sweet; sober; **douce-gaun** prudent.

doucht *n* stroke, blow.

douchtie, douchty *adj* doughty; valiant.

douf *v* grow dull; slumber.

douff *n* heavy blow. • *v* strike; drive.

doufness *n* dullness.

dought *n* strength.

douk[1] *v* duck; bow.

douk[2] *see* dook.

dount, dunt *n* strike; blow.

doup[1] *v* bend forwards; lour.

doup[2] *see* dowp.

dour *adj* austere, bleak; grim, stern, humourless, intractable; determined, dogged; hardy; sullen, taciturn; unyielding; barren.

dourlie *adv* sullenly.

douse *adv* solid.

dout *n/v* doubt.

douth *adj* dull.

doutless *adv* doubtless.

doutsome *adj* doubtful; hesitant.

dove *v* dote; doze.

dove-dock *n* coltsfoot.

dover *n* nap, snooze. • *v* drowse, nod off, snooze; sleep.

dovie *adj* imbecilic. • *n* imbecile.

dow[1] *n* worth.

dow[2] *v* be able; thrive; dwindle.

dowcate *see* doocot.

dowf *adj* inert; useless; insensitive.

dowfart *adj* delicate, disconsolate, dismal, dispirited, doleful, dull, melancholy, mournful, sad, spiritless, unhappy, glum.

dowie, dollie *adj* sad gloomy. • *v* ail.

dowielie *adv* mournfully; sadly.

dowkar, douker *n* diver.

dowl *n* large piece.

dowless *adj* feeble.

downans *npl* green hillocks.

downby *adv* downwards; down the way.

downcast *n* overthrow.

down-ding *n* heavy shower.

downie *n* duvet.

downset *n* beginning setback.

dowp, doup *n* bottom; backside, buttocks, posterior; **dowp doon** *v* sit.

dowp-skelper *n* bottom-smacker.

dowt *n* cigarette butt.

doxie *adj* lazy.

doyce *v* thump dully.

doyn *see* doin.

dozen *v* stupefy.

drabble *v* make dirty.

drabloch *n* refuse, trash.

drachle *n* slow mover.

drachtit *adj* harnessed.

draff *n* remains of malted barley.

draigle[1] *n* small quantity.

draigle[2] *v* bedraggle; trail in mud.

draigon *n* dragon; kite.

draik *v* drench.

dram[1] *n* tot of liquor.

dram[2] *adj* melancholy.

drame *n/v* dream.

drammach[1], **drammock** *n* mix of meal and water.

drammach[2], **dremmach** *adj* whining.

drangle *v* loiter behind.

drant, drunt *n/v* drawl.

drap *n/v* drop.

drappie *n* drop.

drappit eggs *n* fried eggs.

drars *npl* drawers, pants.

draucht *n* facial feature; sheeps' entrails. • *v* gasp for breath.

drauchty *adj* artful.

draunt *n/v* whine.

drauntin *n* tedious talk.

drave *n* haul; herd; herring fishing; shoal.

draw *v* milk; **draw a leg** pull a leg.

drawl *v* act slowly.

drawlie *adj* slow; slack.

dread *v* suspect.

dredge-box *n* flour box.

dree *n* fear. • *v* endure; undergo.

dreeble *n/v* dribble.

dreedle *v* dwindle.

dreel *n* ploughed furrow. • *v* drill; hustle.

dreep, dreip *n* drip. • *v* drip; drain.

dreezle *n/v* drizzle.

dreg *n/v* dredge.

dreich adj bleak; depressing; dismal; drab; dreary, boring, wearisome, dull; godforsaken; monotonous; persistent; tardy; tedious.

dreichlie adv monotonously.

dreid n dread.

dreik n excrement.

dreip see **dreep**.

dremmach see **drammach**.

dress v iron; neuter; treat well; chastise.

dresser n kitchen sideboard.

drib n drop.

dribble n/v trickle; tipple.

driddle v spill.

drien adj driven.

drieshach n ashes of peat fire.

driffle n drizzle.

drift n delay; flying snow. • v delay; put off.

dring[1] n wretch.

dring[2] v delay.

dring[3] v sing slowly; sing (kettle).

dringle v delay.

drite n excrement, faeces. • v defecate, excrete.

drither n fear, dread.

drizzle v walk slowly.

drob n thorn.

droch, droich n dwarf.

drochie n puny person.

drochlin adj dwarfish; puny.

droddum n backside.

drods n petulance.

drog n/v drug.

droggie n apothecary; pharmacist.

droguery n medicines.

droich see **droch**.

drook, drouk v drench, saturate, soak, sop, steep.

drookit, droukit adj soaked, drenched.

drool v trill; quaver.

droon v drown.

droondit adj drowned.

droop adj dripping.

droosie adj drowsy.

droppie n dram.

dross n coal dust.

drotch v dangle.

drotchel n idle woman.

droublie, drublie adj dark; troubled.

drouchit adj parched.

drouerie n illicit love.

drouk see **drook**.

droukit see **drookit**.

drouth n thirst; drinker, drunkard, tippler; drought, dry weather. • v thirst.

drouthie, drouthy adj thirsty; dry; alcoholic.

drouthieness n drunkenness, intoxication.

drove v drive cattle.

drowe, drow n fainting fit; spasm.

drowie adj moist; misty.

drowrie n troth.

drublie see **droublie**.

drucken adj drunken.

drug v pull hard.

drulie adj dryish.

drulie adj muddy; troubled.

drum[1] n hill; knoll; ridge.

drum[2] adj discontented; glum; gloomy.

drumble v make muddy.

drumlie adj cloudy, turbid; troubled; muddy.

drune n drone; murmur.

drunkart n drunkard.

drunt see **drant**.

drush n bits; dross; peat dust.

drutle v excrete.

drutlin adj piddling.

dryachtle adj dryish.

dry-dam, dry-darn n constipation.

dry dyke n drystone wall.

dry siller n hard cash.

dub, dib n small pool of rainwater; puddle; pond.

dub-skelper n one who goes hell-for-leather.

dud n rag; poor clothing.

duddie adj ragged, tattered. • n rag; poor clothing.

duddroun n slut.

dudgel see **dodgel**.

duds npl rags.

duffart n dull person.

duffie adj inferior; soft; spongy.

dug n dog.

dulce adj sweet.

dule see **dool**.

dulie see **doolie**[2].

dullion n large piece.

dulse n edible seaweed.

dult n dolt.

dumb-deid *n* midnight.
dumbie *n* mute.
dumfooner *v* amaze, astonish, astound, dumbfound.
dumfoonert *adj* aghast; bewildered; speechless.
dummie *n* mute.
dump *v* beat; kick.
dumph *adj* dull.
dun *n* low hill; hill fort.
dunch *n* bump. • *v* butt.
dunch *v* push; jog; thump.
dunchy *adj* squat.
dung *adj* exhausted.
duniwassal *n* follower of a chief.
dunk *adj/n* damp.
dunkle *n* dint; dimple.
dunner *n* reverberation; rumble; thunderous noise. • *v* bang; reverberate; rumble; sound like thunder.
dunnie *n* basement.
dunt *n* bump, blow, thud, thump, dent; impact; indentation; insult, jibe; palpitation; wound. • *v* bash, bump, dent, knock; strike, slap; thud; palpitate.
dunter *n* dolphin.
dunty *n* doxy.
durgy *adj* thick.
durk *v* ruin.
durr *v* deaden pain.
dursie *adj* unrelenting.

dush *v* push.
dusty miller *n* primula.
dute, dutt *n/v* doze.
dwable *adj* flexible; weak.
dwadle *v* tarry.
dwaible *adj* flexible; pliable; pliant.
dwaiblie *adj* frail; infirm.
dwall *v* dwell.
dwallion, dwalling *n* dwelling.
dwam *n* daydream, reverie; faint, swoon. • *v* daydream; faint, swoon; nap.
dwamfle *adj* sagging.
dwamie, dwamy *adj* dreamy; faint.
dwang *n* wooden strut; labour; toil. • *v* compel; constrain; force.
dwine, dwyne *n* decline; waning. • *v* decline; wane; pine; fade; waste away.
dwingle *v* loiter.
dwybe *n* very tall, thin person.
dwyne *see* **dwine**.
dyester *n* dyer.
dyke, dike *n* wall; hedge.
dyke-louper *n* trespasser; libertine.
dyker *n* wall-builder.
dyoch *n* drink.
dyow *n* dew.
dyster *n* dyer.
dyte¹, dite *adj* stupid.
dyte² *n* written account.
dyvour *n* debtor; bankrupt; rogue.

E

e *art/pron* the.
ear *adv* early.
earest *adv* especially.
earn¹ *v* coagulate.
earn² *see* **erne**.
easdom *n* comfort.
easel, eassel *adv* eastwards.
easement *n* ease; relief.
easin *n* eaves; horizon.
easter *adj* eastern.
eastlin *adj* easterly, eastward.
eastlins *adv* eastwards.
easy-osie *adj* easy-going.
eat *n* banquet, feast.
eat-mait *n* parasite.
ebb *n* foreshore, seashore.
echt *adj* eight, eighth. • *n* eight.

eckies *npl* ecstasy tablets.
eckle-feckle *adj* cheery.
edgie *v* be quick.
ee *n* eye.
ee-bree *n* eyebrow.
ee-breer *n* eyelash.
eedol *n* idol.
eejit *n* dunderhead.
eekfow *adj* equal.
eeksie-peeksie, eeksy-peeksy *adj* of one kind; much alike.
eel *n* oil.
eelid *n* eyelid.
eelie dolly *n* oil lamp.
eelist, eelast *n* eyesore; grievance.
eelyin *adj* vanishing.
eemir *n* humour.

eemis adj insecure.

eemock n ant; elf, fairy.

een¹ npl eyes.

een² adv simply.

e'en¹ adj even. • adv even, even so; nevertheless.

e'en² n evening.

eenbright adj shining.

e'end adj even; straight; **eend-on** continuous.

eenil v be jealous.

eenin n evening.

eenlins see **eildins**.

e'enow adv at present.

eeriorums n details

eer pron your.

eeran n errand.

eeran-loon n errand-boy.

eerie adj apprehensive; timorous.

eerisome adj causing fear.

eese n/v use.

eesefae adj useful.

eeseless adj useless.

eesicht n eyesight.

eeswal adj usual.

eet n custom.

eetch n adze.

eetim n item.

effeck n effect.

effeckwal adj effectual.

effeir v relate.

eft¹ n aft.

eft², **efter** adv/prep after.

eftercast, **eftercome** n aftermath, consequence, result.

eftergait adj fit; modest. • n outcome.

efterhend adv afterwards.

efterins npl consequences.

efter ither adj consecutive. • adv one after another.

efternuin n afternoon.

efterwards adj afterwards.

egg-bed n ovary.

ei pron he.

eident adj diligent; efficient; intent.

eiffest adv especially.

eik¹ n codicil; extension; increase; supplement; patch. • v add, augment; enlarge; increase; patch; **eik tae** supplement; **eik up** top up.

eik² see **ilk**.

eild, **yeild** n antiquity; old age; stage of life, age. • v grow old.

eildins, **eenlins**, **yeildins** adj of equal age; **eilins wi** contemporary. • npl persons of the same age.

eildit adj aged.

eind n breath.

eir n fear.

eirack see **errak**.

eirne see **ern**.

eiry see **erie**.

eistit adv rather.

eithlie, **eithly** adv easily.

eizel, **izel** n hot ember.

elaskit adj elastic.

eibuck n elbow.

eld v grow old.

elder n lay officer of the church.

eldin, **eildin** n fuel.

eldren adj elderly.

eldritch adj ghostly, supernatural, unearthly.

eleck v elect.

eleevin adj/n eleven.

eleevint adj eleventh.

elenge adj foreign.

Elfin n fairyland.

elf-ring n fairy ring.

elide v abolish; eliminate; annul; cancel.

eller n elder.

ellwan n measuring rod, yardstick.

elne, **ell** n unit of measure.

eirisch, **eirick** adj elvish; frightening.

else adv already.

elsh, **elsyn** n awl.

ely v disappear gradually.

eme n uncle.

emerant n emerald.

emmis adj variable.

emmit n ant.

emmledeug n offal.

emmock n ant.

empash v hinder.

empress n enterprise.

en, **end** n room; end. • v end; kill.

endie adj enough.

endlang adv along.

endurement n endurance.

eneuch adj adequate; enough. • adv/n enough.

engage v pray.

Englify v anglicise.
English pancake n pancake.
enkeerloch adj hot-tempered.
enkerly adv inwardly; ardently.
enlang adv lengthwise; straight on.
enless adj long-winded.
enlicht v enlighten.
enner adj inner.
ennermaist adj nethermost.
ense, ens, enze adv otherwise, else.
entry n alley; doorway; lobby; porch.
enweys adv straight ahead; successfully.
equal-aqual adj equally. • n balance; quits.
erast adv soonest.
erch n arch.
erd, erde n earth.
ereck v erect.
erethestreen n night before last.
erf[1] adj unwilling.
erf[2]**, erfe** adv near.
ergh adj hesitant; shy. • adv insufficiently.
erghness n timidity.
erie, eiry adj afraid.
erle, arle v betroth.
erlis n earnest.
erm n arm.
ermit n earwig.
ern, earn, erne, eirne n eagle; sea eagle.
ernand adj running.
erp v harp on a topic.
errak, eirack n chicken; pullet.
Erse adj/n Gaelic.
erse n hinterland.
ert v urge; prompt.
ertand adj ingenious.
erthlins adv earthward.
eruction n outburst.
esh n ash tree.
esk n newt.
eskin n hiccup.
esp n aspen.
esplin n youth, growing lad.
ess n ace.
essock n dipper.
est n nest.
estate n social group.
ester n oyster.
estlins adv rather.
eterie, etrie, etry adj keen; sharp; hot-headed.

eth adj easy.
ether[1] n adder.
ether[2] n udder.
etin n giant, ogre.
etion n race, stock.
etnach adj of juniper.
etrie, etry see **eterie**.
ett, eet n habit, custom.
etter n pus. • v fester, suppurate.
ettercap n spiteful person.
ettering adj festering.
ettle n aim, ambition; attempt, effort. • v aim, aspire; assess; attempt, try; guess; guide; intend; **ettle at** get at.
even v compare; equal.
evendoon, evendoun adj perpendicular, straight; honest; emphatic; impeccable. • adv thoroughly.
evenlie adj level.
evenliness n equanimity.
even on adv continuously; incessantly.
ever-bane n ivory.
everich adj every.
evident n evidence.
evill adj worn-out.
evin adj equal; indifferent.
evite n dodge. • v avoid, evade, shun.
evleit adj active.
ewder, ewdruch n bad smell.
ewest adj closest.
ewin adv straight.
examin n examination. • v examine.
excep prep except.
exclaim n exclamation.
exem v examine.
exemp n exemption. • v exempt.
exercise v explain Scripture.
exies npl hysterics.
exoner v relieve.
exoust v exhaust.
expeck v expect.
expensive adj extravagant.
explore n exploration.
expoon, expone v explain; expose.
extrae adj extra.
ey n isle.
eydent adj assiduous; attentive; conscientious; diligent; industrious.
eyn n/v end.
eyven adj even.
ezle n spark of fire.

F

fa¹ *adv* who.

fa², faw *n* fall. • *v* fall; slump; fare; deserve; **fa wi bairn** become pregnant.

fa³ *see* **fall**.

faan *adj* fallen.

faceplate *n* face.

facie *adj* bold; cheeky; eloquent.

factor *n* agent, manager; land steward.

faddom *n/v* fathom.

fader *see* **faither**.

fadge *n* faggot.

fae¹ *adv/prep* from.

fae² *pron* who.

fae³ *n* foe, enemy.

faem, faim *n/v* foam.

faeman, faman *n* enemy.

faff *v* fan.

faffer *n* fan.

fag *v* flag.

faggald *n* faggot.

faggie *adj* tiring.

fagsum *adj* wearisome.

faik¹ *n* razorbill.

faik² *v* fold; reduce a price.

fail *see* **feal¹**.

fail-dyke *n* dyke of sods.

failed *n* infirm.

failye *v* be in want.

failzie *n* failure.

faim *see* **faem**.

fain¹ *adj* damp.

fain² *adj* amorous; fond. • *adv* gladly.

fainness *n* affection.

faintice *n* dissembling.

faints, feints *npl* partly distilled spirits.

faiple *n* drooping lip.

fair *adj* absolute.

fair *adj* apt; ready; likely; complete, utter. • *adv* completely, entirely, frankly, openly; utter; **fair ca'in** smooth-tongued; **fair duin** broken-down; **fair duin** dog-tired; **fair fa'** good luck to; **fair fleggit** terrified; **fair oot** candid, down-to-earth; **fair-faced** suave; **fair-farran** plausible, specious; **fair-farrand** fair-faced; **fair-spoken** frank.

faird¹ *n* course; enterprise.

faird², fard *v* paint.

fairdie *adj* passionate; angry.

fairfle *n* skin eruption.

fairin, fairing *n* gift from a fair; deserts; fare.

fairly *adv* surprisingly.

faisible *adj* feasible; presentable.

faither, fader *n/v* father.

faitly *adv* neatly.

faizart *n* effeminate man; androgyne.

faize *v* fray; roughen; flatter.

fake *v* believe.

fald *see* **fauld**.

falderal *n* gewgaw; whimsy.

fale *v* happen.

fall, fa *n* trap.

fall-by *v* be lost.

fallow *v* follow.

falorum *n* virility.

falsehood *n* forgery.

falt, faut *n* want.

faman *see* **faeman**.

famous *adj* well thought of.

fan *adv/conj* when.

fancy breid *n* dainties.

fane¹ *n* elf; fairy.

fane² *v* protect.

fang *n* suction. • *v* capture; grasp; hold; prime.

fank *n* sheep pen. • *v* pen.

fankelt *adj* tangled.

fankle *n* muddle, tangle. • *v* entangle; ravel; tangle; trap.

fantice *n* imagination.

fanton, fantod *n* swoon; emotional fit.

fantoosh *adj* flashy, showy; fancy, ornate; overdressed; pretentious; trendy.

far¹ *adv* where.

far² *n* appearance.

farand *adj* seeming.

farawa *adj* remote.

far-back *adj* ignorant.

far-ben *adj* intimate.

farcost *n* trading ship.

fard *n/v* paint.

farden *n* farthing.

farder *adv* further.

fareweel *n* farewell.

far i the buik *adj* well-read; erudite; learned.

farl *n* segment of a cake or scone.

farran¹ *adj* starboard.

farran² *n* character.

farrant *adj* wise.

farrest *adj* farthest.

farseen *adj* accomplished.

fas *n* knot.

fash *adj* painstaking. • *n* trouble, nuisance; care; anguish, worry; pain. • *v* trouble; anger, annoy, bother, vex; worry; exasperate, irritate, perturb; care; exert.

fasherie, fashery *n* annoyance, vexation, indignation; trouble; care.

fashious *adj* annoying, bothersome, irksome; maddening; peevish, fractious; troublesome.

fassit *adj* knotted.

fasson, fassoun *n* fashion, trend.

fast¹ *adj* hasty; impetuous.

fast² *adv* tight.

fat¹ *n* barrel, keg, vat.

fat² *pron* what.

fa-tae *n* set-to.

fatality *n* fate.

fatter *v* thresh barley.

fattrils *npl* folds.

fauch, faugh *n* fallow ground. • *v* fallow.

fauchie, faughie *adj* colourless; yellowish; sickly-looking.

faucht *n/v* fight.

fauld, fald *n* bend; enclosure; fold, sheepfold. • *v* bend; enclose.

faur *adv* far.

faur-ben *adj* popular.

faurer *adj/adv* further; farther. • *v* further.

faur-seen *adj* far-sighted.

fause *adj* counterfeit, fake; false; spurious.

fausehood *n* falsehood; fraud.

fausont *adj* decent.

faut, faute *n* fault; want, need. • *v* accuse; find fault with.

fauter *n* offender.

favour *v* resemble.

faw¹ *adj* pale red.

faw² *see* **fa²**.

fawely *adv* few.

faynd *v* attempt; endeavour.

fazart *adj* cowardly.

fe, fee, fie *n* cattle; beasts; possessions.

feal¹, fail *n* piece of turf.

feal², feale *adj* faithful.

fear *n* fright.

feart *adj* afraid, frightened.

feartie *n* coward.

feasible *adj* neat; tidy.

featless *adj* feeble.

Februar *n* February.

fecht *n* battle, combat, conflict, fight, fray; pugnacity; struggle. • *v* conflict, fight, struggle.

fechter *n* fighter.

fechtin *adj* pugnacious.

feck *adj* main. • *n* abundance; greater part, majority; **feck o** most of.

feckful *adj* able; capable; dynamic; effective; efficient; rich.

fecklie, feckly *adv* mainly; almost.

fecklish *adj* feeble.

fee¹ *v* engage; hire.

fee² *see* **fe**.

feedle *n* field.

feek *n* methylated spirit.

feel¹, feil *adj* foolish.

feel², feil *adj* soft; velvety, silky; many.

feel³ *v* perceive.

feem *n* passion. • *v* fume.

feenichin *adj* dandyish, foppish.

feerich *n* trepidation.

feerie *adj* clever; active; weak-looking.

feesan *n* pheasant.

feeth *n* net.

feeze *n/v* screw; twist; turn; **feeze aff** unscrew.

feg *n* fig; worthless thing.

fegs! *interj* goodness! really!

feid *n* enmity; quarrel; feud.

feifteen *adj/n* fifteen.

feifteent *adj* fifteenth.

feignyie *v* forge.

feil *see* **feel**.

feim *n* bodily heat; sweat.

feingle *v* fabricate.

fell¹ *n* uncultivated hill; animal hide, sheepskin.

fell² *adj* acute; adept, astute; ferocious; fierce; forceful; loud; severe; virulent; hot; biting; strange. • *adv* very; much of; energetically; sternly. • *v* kill.

fella n fellow.

felled adj prostrate.

felter v entangle.

feltie n fieldfare.

femmil adj firm.

fen v fend.

fend n defence; effort; resistance.

fend v defend; make shift; maintain; provide; succour; support oneself.

fendful adj resourceful.

fendie adj managing; resourceful; thrifty.

fengie v feign.

fent n faint; slit. • v faint.

fere, fier n companion; friend.

ferlie adj superb. • adv wonderfully. n curio; marvel; strange sight; wonder. • v marvel.

ferm n/v farm.

fermer n farmer.

fermtoon n homestead.

fernitickelt adj freckled.

fernitickle, ferntickle n freckle.

fernowl n nightjar.

fernyear n last year.

ferrier n farrier; veterinary surgeon.

ferry v farrow, produce young.

ferry-louper n mainlander.

ferter n fairy.

fesh v fetch.

fess up v bring up, rear; nurture.

fest adj fast; occupied. • adv fast.

festern's een n Shrove Tuesday.

fethock n polecat.

fettle, fettil n energy power. • v mend, repair; put in order.

feu n land held on payment of a rent. • v grant land rights.

feuar n one who holds a feu.

feuch n whiff.

fewter v bind together.

fey adj close to death. • n omen.

fiall n vassal; servant.

fiar n property owner.

fiars npl fixed grain prices.

ficher v dabble at work.

fickle adj tricky. • v perplex; puzzle.

fidder v hover.

fiddle n violin.

fiddlie n fiddler.

fidge n shrug; twitch. • v fidget; twitch.

fidgin n itching.

fidgin-fain adj quivering with fondness.

fie see fe.

fien n fiend.

fient n nothing of; devil.

fier1 adj healthy.

fier2 see fere.

fiercelins adv hurriedly; impetuously; violently.

fierd n ford.

fifie n sailed fishing boat.

fift adj fifth.

figgleligee adj foppish.

fike see fyke.

fikie see fykie.

filabeg n kilt.

filchans npl rags.

file conj while.

filiation n paternity.

filk adj/pron which.

fill adj full.

filler n funnel.

fillets npl thighs.

fill fou v intoxicate.

fillie n rim.

fillock n filly, young mare; boisterous wench.

filsh n lout.

fin, find n feel. • v feel; grope; discover; find; perceive.

findle n something found.

findy adj full.

fine adj likeable; placid.

fine time o day n pretty pass.

fineer v ornament; veneer.

finger neb n fingertip.

finnan haddie n smoked haddock.

fippil v whimper; snivel.

fir prep for.

fire n fuel.

fireburn n phosphorescence.

firefang n fermentation.

fire-flacht, fire-flaucht n lightning; meteor; shooting star.

fireraising n arson.

firework n firearm.

firm n/v form.

firn n fern.

firnie n quarrel.

firple v whimper.

firron adj of the fir.

first-fit *n* first visit on New Year's Day; New Year visitor.
firsten *adj* first.
firth, frith *n* estuary; long narrow bay.
fir yowe *n* pine cone, fir cone.
fish *n* salmon.
fisher *n* fisherman.
fish supper *n* fish and chips.
fissle *v* rustle.
fit¹ *n* foot; foothold.
fit² *pron* what.
fitba *n* football.
fitbrod *n* treadle.
fitch¹ *n* tare; vetch.
fitch² *v* move a short distance.
fit-dint *n* footprint.
fite *adj* white.
fit for fit *adj* side by side.
fit-fowk *npl* pedestrians.
fit-road *n* footpath.
fitstap *n* footstep.
fitsted *n* footprint.
fittie *adj* speedy.
fittiefie, fittifie *n* quibble; quirk.
fittininment *n* concern; interference.
fittit *adj* satisfied.
fittock *n* sock.
fivver *n* fever.
fizz *n* bustle, hurly-burly. • *v* fuss; rage.
flacht *n* lock, tress.
flae *n* flea.
flaff *n* flap; fan; flutter. • *v* flap; fan; flutter; palpitate.
flag *v* flog.
flaich *n* flea.
flain *see* **flane**.
flaip, flipe *n* fall.
flair *n/v* floor.
flaither *v* wheedle.
flake *n* hurdle.
flam *n* flame.
flamfoo *n* gaudily dressed woman.
flamp *adj* inactive.
flane, flain *n* arrow.
flannen *n* flannel.
flansh *v* flatter.
flanter *v* waver; falter.
flat *n* floor; saucer; storey.
flatlins *adv* flat; horizontally.
flauch *v* flay.
flaucht *n* handful.

flauchter-spade *n* turf-cutter.
flaughter *v* flicker; flutter; shine fitfully.
flaunty *adj* whimsical; eccentric.
flaw¹ *n* storm of wind or snow.
flaw² *v* lie, fib.
fleasocks *npl* shavings.
fleat *n* saddle mat.
flech *n* flea.
fleckert *adj* torn; mangled.
flee *n/v* fly.
fleech *v* flatter.
fleeing *adj* flying. • *n* fly-fishing.
fleeing merchan *n* travelling salesman.
fleep *n* flea.
fleer, flyre *v* taunt.
fleerish *n* steel.
fleesh, flesche *n* fleece; horde.
fleesome *adj* frightful.
fleet¹ *adj* manageable.
fleet² *n* nets. • *v* float; flow; flood.
fleetch *v* cajole, coax, entreat.
fleetdyke *n* breakwater.
fleetful *adj* fleeting.
fleg *n* alarm, fright. • scare, frighten; *v* take fright.
fleggar *n* liar; exaggerator.
fleggit *adj* scared.
flesche *see* **fleesh**.
flesh *n* meat.
flesher *n* butcher.
flet¹ *adj* dry-spoken; flat. • *v* flatten.
flet², flett *n* house.
fleuk *see* **flook**.
flichan¹ *n* flake; snowflake.
flichan² *n* sudden heat; surprise.
flicht¹ *n* mote; speck.
flicht² *n* flight, fleeing. • *v* flee.
flichter *n* flutter. • *v* alarm; flutter.
flichtie *adj* capricious.
flichtrif *adj* fitful.
flichty *adj* flighty.
flicker *v* coax.
fliep *n* silly fellow.
flinders *npl* fragments.
flindrikin *adj* flirtatious.
fling *n* disappointment; jilting; dance. • *v* jilt; kick; dance.
flipe *see* **flaip, flype**.
flird¹ *n* insubstantial thing.
flird² *v* flaunt; move about restlessly.
flirdie *adj* giddy.

flirdoch n flirt.

flisk n caper; flick. • v caper, frisk, gambol, skip; flick.

fliskmahoy n giddy girl.

flisky adj skittish.

flist n explosion.

flist n explosion; rage. • v fly off in a rage; explode.

flisty adj stormy.

flit n removal. • v transport; move house.

flitters npl small pieces; shreds, tatters.

flitting n moving house.

floan v court publicly.

flocht n flight; outburst of feeling; stress. • v agitate.

flochtersome adj joyful.

flodden adj flooded.

flodder, flotter v overflow.

flook, fleuk n flatfish.

flosh n swamp.

flot n scum on hot broth.

flotch n large slatternly woman.

flotter see **flodder**.

flottrit adj splashed.

flourish n blossom. • v blossom; embroider.

flourishin n embroidery.

flow n bog, marsh, morass, moss, swamp; jot, speck.

flownie adj light; downy.

floyt n flute.

flude, flude n flood. • v flood; inundate.

fluffed adj disappointed.

fluffer v agitate; excite.

fluffy adj powdery.

fluise v blunt.

flumgummerie n tomfoolery.

flunce v flounce.

flunge v skip; caper.

fluther n rise. • v be in a bustle; flutter.

fly cemetery n fruit slice.

flype, flipe n brim; turn-up. • v turn inside out; flop.

flyre see **fleer**.

flyte n debate. • v debate; rail, scold.

flyter n scolding.

flytin adj quarrelling.

flyting adj abusive.

fob v breathe hard.

fochten adj wearied.

fode n brood.

fodgel n plump person.

fog n moss. • v be moss-covered; prosper; eat well.

foggage n grass left after harvest.

fogged adj moss-covered.

foggie, fogie adj dull; mossy. • n pensioner; veteran; invalid; old person.

foggit adj mossy.

fogie see **foggie**.

foichel n foal.

foison n abundance.

foisonless see **fushionless**.

foldings npl nappies; diapers.

folk n relatives; family.

follower n young.

fond adj besotted, infatuated, doting; gullible.

foo adv how; why.

fool n fowl.

foon n fund. • v found; base.

foond n foundation.

fooner n breakdown. • v fell, strike down; founder; collapse; prostrate.

foord, fuird n/v ford.

fooroch n bustle; haste.

foos n leek.

foost, foust, fuist n fustiness; mildew; mould; mouldy smell. • v smell bad.

foust, fuist see **foost**.

foostie, fousty adj fusty, musty; mouldy; off.

footer see **fouter**.

for conj because.

forat, forad adj/v forward.

for aye adv perpetually; eternally.

forbot v forbid.

forby, forbye prep over and above; beside; past. • adv also; besides; furthermore; extraordinarily; much less.

force and fear n duress.

forcie adj dynamic; forceful; hustling; lively.

for common adj commonly.

fordel adj progressive. • n precedence; progress; reserve; store; stock.

forder adj/adv further. • n advancement; aid. • v advance; further; promote.

fordwibelt adj enfeebled.

fore n profit.

forebear, forebeir n ancestor.

forebreist n forefront.

foreby *see* forby.
forecasten *adj* neglected.
foredone *adj* worn-out.
fore-end *n* front end.
forefoughten *see* forfochen.
foregainst *adv* opposite to.
foregang *n* apparition.
forego *n* augur, premonition.
forehammer *n* sledgehammer.
forehand *adj* first. • *n* start.
forehandit *adj* provident; rash.
foreheid *n* forehead.
foreleit *v* forsake.
foreloppen *adj* fugitive.
foremaist *adj* foremost.
forenent *prep* facing; opposite.
forenoon, forenuin *n* morning.
foresaid *adj* above-mentioned, afore-mentioned.
foresicht *n* foresight.
foreside *n* front.
foresman *n* foreman.
forespoken *adj* bewitched.
foresta1 *n* manger.
foresta2 *v* forestall.
forethink *v* reconsider.
forethinking *n* repentance.
forethocht *n* forethought.
forethochtie *adj* prudent.
forfair *v* waste; perish.
forfairn *adj* forlorn.
forfeitry *n* forfeiture.
forflitten *adj* scolded.
forfochen, forefoughten *adj* exhausted, tired; enervated; worn out.
forgaither *v* assemble; associate; congregate; convene.
forgaitherin *n* assembly, meeting.
forget *n* forgetfulness.
forgettie *adj* absent-minded, forgetful.
forgie *v* forgive.
forhoo *v* abandon.
forjeskit, forjaskit *adj* jaded; weary.
fork *n* hunt, quest, search. • *v* search.
forkin *n* crotch.
forky *adj* strong.
forkytail *n* earwig.
forlay *v* ambush.
fornent *adv* directly opposed to; against.
fornyaw *v* tire.
fornyawed *adj* tired.

for ordinar *adv* normally, usually.
forpit, forpet *n* fourth part.
forray *v* pillage.
forrit *adj* present. • *adv* forward; onward.
forritsome *adj* defiant; forward, pert.
forsamekil *conj* forasmuch.
forsee *v* overlook; neglect.
forspeak *v* overpraise; enchant, bewitch.
forss *n* waterfall.
forsweer *v* forswear.
fortalice *n* fortress.
fortell *n* benefit.
forten *n* fortune.
forthens *adv* at a distance.
forthiness *n* frankness.
forthink *v* repent, rue.
forthwart *n* precaution.
forthy *adj* forward; familiar.
fortnicht *n* fortnight.
forvay *v* go astray.
forwondrit *adj* astounded.
forworthin *adj* execrable.
foryet *v* forget.
foryoudent *adj* exhausted.
fos *n* pit; drowning pool.
fosie *adj* bloated.
fotch *v* flinch.
fother *n/v* fodder.
fothersome *adj* rash; pushy.
fots *npl* leggings.
fou, fow, fu *adj* full; replete; drunk; pompous. • *adv* fully. • *n* fill. • *v* fill.
foudrie *n* lightning.
foug *n* moss.
foumart, fowmart *n* ferret; polecat.
foundy *v* founder.
fourneukit *adj* four-cornered.
fousome *adj* cloying; filling; squalid.
foust *see* foost.
fousty *see* foostie.
fout *n* spoilt child.
fouter, footer, fulter *n* bungler; slacker; dabbler. *v* potter; trifle; fiddle aimlessly with things.
fouterie *adj* bungling; dithering; fiddly; footling; paltry; trivial; inept; time-wasting.
fouth, fowth *n* fullness; plenty.
fouthie, fouthy *adj* full-seeming; copious; ample; opulent; prosperous, rich.
foutie *adj* ignoble; indecent.

foutsome *adj* meddling.

fouty *adj* mean, low.

fow *see* **fou**.

fowe *n* pitchfork.

fower *adj/n* four.

fowert *adj* fourth.

fowerteen *adj/n* fourteen.

fowerty *n* forty.

fowie *adj* well-off.

fowk *n* folk; humanity; mankind; people; servants, employees.

fowmart *see* **foumart**.

fowsum *adj* over-big.

fowsumlie *adj* unpleasantly over-big.

foy *n* celebration.

foze *v* go mouldy.

fozie, fozy *adj* flabby; spongy.

foziness *adv* flabbiness.

fra, frae *see* **from**.

fraca *n* fracas; friendship.

frack, freck *adj* ready.

frae, fra *prep* from.

fraemang *adv* from among.

fraet *n* superstition.

Fraiday *n* Friday.

fraik *v* flatter, cajole; mollycoddle; malinger; shade.

fraikie *adj* coaxing.

frail *n* flail.

frainesie *n* frenzy.

fraith *n/v* froth.

frane, frain *v* insist; interrogate.

franent *prep* opposite to.

frath *adj* reserved; cold.

fraucht *n/v* freight; hire.

frawart *prep* from.

frawful *adj* bold; scornful.

freak *v* fret.

freck *see* **frack**.

freckle *adj* hot-blooded.

free *adj* brittle; single, unmarried. • *v* acquit; exonerate.

freedom *n* leave.

free-living *adj* self-indulgent.

freen, freend *n* friend, intimate.

freenge *n* fringe.

freenless *adj* friendless.

freenlie *adj* friendly.

freenliness *n* friendliness.

freens *adj* akin.

freesk *v* scratch.

freest *n* frost.

freet[1] *n* butter.

freet[2] *v* fret; chafe.

free trade *n* smuggling.

freff *adj* aloof; shy; frigid.

freik, frick *n* strong man.

freir *n* friar.

freit *n* fad; superstition.

freith *v* lather.

freitie *adj* superstitious.

frely *n* beautiful woman.

frem, frame *adj* strange; foreign.

fremd *n* outsiders.

fremmit *adj* alien; strange; unrelated.

frenauch *n* crowd.

frenyie *n* fringe.

frequent *v* associate; hobnob.

fresh *adj* open; sober. • *n/v* thaw.

frest *see* **frist**[1].

fret *v* devour.

fretty *adj* fretful.

freuchan *n* toe-cap.

fricht *v* fright; petrify; terrify.

frichten *v* frighten.

frichtit *adj* frightened.

frichtless *adj* fearless.

frichtsome *adj* fearful; frightening, terrifying.

frick *see* **freik**.

frist[1], **frest** *n/v* delay.

frist[2], **fryst** *adj* first.

frith *see* **firth**.

fro, froe *n/v* froth.

frog *n* cloak.

froon *n/v* frown; glower.

frosch *n* rush of water.

frost *n* ice. • *v* be frostbitten.

frowdie *n* lusty woman.

frozent *adj* frozen.

frull *n* frill.

frumple *v* crease.

frunsit *adj* puckered.

frunty *adj* open-mannered; healthy.

frush *adj* brash; crumbly; friable; tender.

fry *n* distraction.

fryne *v* fret.

fryst *see* **frist**[2].

fryth *v* fry.

fu *see* **fou**.

fud *n* short tail of a rabbit; genitals (female).

fudder¹ n large quantity.
fudder² n scurry.
fuddie adj short-tailed.
fudgie adj gross.
fuff n/v hiss; puff; blow.
fuffie adj impatient; short-tempered.
fufty adj/n fifty.
fugie n deserter; fugitive; runaway.
fuid n food.
fuil n buffoon, fool.
fuil-like adj foolish.
fuird see **foord**.
fuist see **foost**.
fuit n foot.
fuiter see **fouter**.
fule n fool.
fullie adv fully.
fulyie n excrement; manure; filth.
fume n fragrance.
fumler n parasite.
fummle n fumbling. • v fumble.
fumper n/v whimper.
fumple v crumple.
fund adj found.
fundy v stiffen with cold.
fung n cuff, kick; toss; tantrum, huff. • v cuff; sulk; toss.
funk v strike; kick; become afraid; shy.
funker n kicker.
funtain n fountain.
fup n/v whip.
fure adj firm; fresh. • n strong man. • v carry.
fure-days adv late in the afternoon.
fureing n freight.
furfelles npl furry skins.
furhow v forsake.

furich n bustle.
furk n gallows.
furlenth n furrow's length.
furl o birse n ace of spades.
furr n/v drill; furrow.
furrochie adj infirm.
furth prep outside; beyond. • adv beyond; out of doors; forth.
furthie, furthy adj affable; benevolent; generous; impulsive; unabashed.
furthilie adv frankly.
fush n/v fish.
fushion n nourishment; pith; sensation.
fushionless adj lacking taste, insipid; dull; weak, feeble, ineffectual, wishy-washy; faint-hearted; listless; passive; pithless; withered.
fusker n whisker.
fuslin adj trifling.
fussie, fussy adj dressy, foppish.
fussle n/v whistle.
fusslebare adj exposed.
futebrod n footstool.
futret n ferret.
futtle v whittle.
fuzziness n effervescence.
fuzzy, fuzzie adj effervescent; feathery; fluffy; fizzing, fizzy; hissing.
fyke, fike n restlessness. • v fidget; jerk; grieve.
fykerie n fussiness.
fikie, fykie adj pernickety, finicky, fussy, overparticular; fidgety, restless.
fyle v befoul; defile; desecrate; pollute; sully.
fyow adj few; some.

G

ga n bile; gall; grudge. • v gall.
gaad n gaff.
gab n mouth; beak; chatter; tongue. • v mock.
gabbart n sailing lugger.
gabber v gibber.
gabbie, gabby adj chatty; fluent; loquacious.
gabbit n gobbet.
gaberlunzie n beggar; tinker.

gabers npl fragments.
gack n gap.
gad n fishing rod; bar.
gadder see **gaither**.
gadge v talk idly.
gadgie n fellow.
gae v go; **gae back** deteriorate; lose ground; **gae frae** abstain; **gae halfers** share equally; **gae hame** die; **gae on** fuss; **gae ower the score** misbehave;

gae thegither combine, merge; come together; court; **gae will** stray.

gae-doun *n* swallowing.

gaff¹ *n/v* guffaw.

gaff² *n* hand-net.

gaig *n/v* chap.

gail *v* make a piercing noise; break into pieces.

gaillie *n* galley; garret.

gain *adv* later.

gainer *n* gander.

gainstan *v* resist, withstand.

gainter *v* put on airs.

gair¹ *n* pleat.

gair² *adj* covetous; greedy.

gaird *n* guard; watch. • *v* guard.

gairden *n* garden.

gairdner *n* gardener.

gaired, gairy *adj* streaked.

gairten *n/v* garter.

gaislin *n* gosling.

gaist *see* **ghaist**.

gait¹ *n* goat.

gait² *see* **gate**.

gaither, gadder *v* gather; pull oneself together; recover; save.

gaithering, gaddering *n* gathering; company.

gait's hair *n* cirrus.

gaivel *v* stare wildly.

galashes *npl* galoshes.

gale *n* flock (of geese).

gallant *v* flirt; show attention to.

gallepin *n* domestic servant.

galliard *adj* sprightly.

galliardness *n* gaiety.

gallivant *v* run about idly.

gallus, gallous *adj* mischievous, bold; wild; villainous.

galluses, gallowses *npl* trouser braces.

galore *n* glut; plenty.

galshachs *npl* sweets.

galt *n* neutered sow.

galyie *v* roar; brawl.

gam¹ *adj* cheerful.

gam² *n* gum.

gamaleerie *adj* tall; awkward.

gamf, gamph *v* gape; laugh foolishly.

gamie *n* gamekeeper.

gammal *v* gobble.

gammel *v* gamble.

gamph *see* **gamf**.

gams *n* teeth.

gandy *v* boast.

gane *adj* raving.

ganelie *adj* fit; proper.

gang *n* gait; journey; passageway; pasture. • *v* go; **gang agley** go astray; **gang doon** descend.

gange, gaunge *v* prate.

ganger *n* pedestrian.

gangin body *n* tramp.

gangrel *n* stroller; vagrant.

gangs *n* sheep-shears.

gansald, gansel *n* rebuke.

gansey *n* jersey; guernsey; jumper; pullover.

gansh *v* snatch; snarl.

gant¹ *n* gannet.

gant² *n/v* yawn.

ganting *adj* yawning.

gantry, gantree *n* stand for bottles.

gapus *n* fool.

gar *v* cause to happen; coerce; compel; force.

garbel *n* fledgling.

garderobe *n* clothes cupboard.

gardie *n* forearm.

gardin *n* chamberpot.

gardy *n* arm.

gardy-bane *n* arm bone.

gargrugous *adj* austere.

garmunshoch *adj* ill-humoured.

garnel *n* granary.

garnel *see* **girnal**.

garnisoun *n* garrison.

garrit, garret *n* watchtower.

garron *n* small horse.

garten *n* garter.

garth *n* enclosure; garden.

garvie *n* sprat.

gash¹ *adj* ashen-faced.

gash² *adj* free-spoken. • *n* cheek; prattle. • *v* prattle; talk freely.

gashlie *adj* ghastly.

gasoliere *n* chandelier.

gast, ghast *n* fright.

gastrous *adj* monstrous.

gate, gait *n* way; street; tour; trip; conduct.

gates *npl* habits.

gate-slap *n* gateway.

gaud, gawd *n* trick; goad.

gaudsman *n* ploughman.

gauffin *adj* light-headed.

gauger *n* examiner of weights and measures, excise officer.

gauges *npl* wages.

gauk *v* play the fool.

gaukit, gawkit, gawky *adj* foolish; awkward; blundering.

gaun-aboot *adj* itinerant. • *n* vagrant.

gauner *v* bark; scold.

gaunge *see* **gange**.

gaut *n* boar, hog.

gavel *n* gable; gavel.

gavelock *n* crowbar.

gaw *n* weal.

gawd *see* **gaud**.

gawk *n* clumsy person.

gawkit, gawky *see* **gaukit**.

gawpin *adj* gaping.

gawsie, gawsy *adj* buoyant; imposing; plump; jolly.

gean *n* cherry; wild cherry.

gear, gere *n* clothes; accoutrements; commodity; effects; estate; livestock; property; possessions; armour; weapons of war.

gear-gaitherer *n* hoarder.

geat *n* child.

geck *v* fool; twit; **geck at** scoff.

geckin *adj* playful.

geck-neckit, geik-neckit *adj* wrynecked.

ged *n* pike.

gee *n* offence.

geeg *n* gibe.

geenyoch, geenoch *adj* ravenous. • *n* glutton.

geetsher *n* grandfather.

geg[1] *n* deception.

geg[2] *n* poacher's hook.

geig *v* creak.

geik-neckit *see* **geck-neckit**.

geing *n* excrement.

gell[1] *adj* intense.

gell[2] *n* gale.

gell[3] *n* leech.

gelled *adj* split.

gelloch *n* yell.

gemm *n* game.

gend *adj* comical.

gener *n* gender.

genie *n* genius.

genivin *adj* genuine.

gentie, genty *adj* chivalrous; dainty; neat; genteel; graceful; well-bred.

gentrice *n* person of honourable birth; gentility.

genty *see* **gentie**.

geo *n* coastal chasm; creek.

geordie *n* yokel.

gerss *see* **girse**.

gester *v* gesture.

gestning, guestning *n* hospitable reception.

get *n* bastard; brat; child; progeny.

get *v* become; beget; find; **get a len o** borrow; **get a sicht o** glimpse; **get by** get through; **get by wi** dispense; **get fou** befuddle; **getroon** accomplish, achieve; **get up in years** age.

gey *adj* considerable; fairly. • *adv* considerably; pretty.

geylies *adv* pretty well.

ghaist, gaist *n* soul; spirit; ghost; apparition; wraith.

ghast *see* **gast**.

ghillie, gillie *n* boy; servant, attendant; sportsman's assistant.

gib *n* cat.

gibbery *n* gingerbread.

gibble-gabble *n/v* prattle.

gibcat *n* tomcat.

gidlie *adj* godly.

gie *v* give; grant; accelerate; **gie a lift tae** encourage; **gie a name** christen; **gie a riddie** embarrass; **gie ower** abandon, cede; **gie ower** desert; give up, abdicate; **gie the door** eject.

gien *adj* given.

gien-horse *n* gift-horse.

gif[1] *conj* if.

gif[2] **gyf** *v* give.

giff-gaff *n* mutual assistance; repartee. • *v* bandy.

gift *v* present.

gigot, jigot *n* leg joint of mutton.

gigsie *adj* swollen-headed.

gild *adj* strong; great.

gill *n* cavern; gully; ravine.

gillie *see* **ghillie**.

gillock *n* gill.

gillot *n* filly; young mare.

gilp *v* jerk; spurt; spill.

gilpie, gilpy *n* tomboy; roguish boy.

gilravage *n* revelry; riot. • *v* carouse; feast; guzzle; riot.

gilt *v* gild.

giltit *adj* gilded.

gimmer *n* two-year old ewe.

gimp *see* **jimp**.

gin *conj* before; if; until. • *prep* against; before; by; until.

ginge *n* ginger.

gingebreid *n* gingerbread.

ginger *n* lemonade.

gink *v* snigger.

ginkum *n* mannerism.

ginnle *see* **guddle**.

ginnles *npl* gills.

gip *v* gut.

gird¹, girr *n* moment; girth; hoop.

gird² *v* copulate.

girdle, girl *n* flat iron cooking plate, griddle.

girn *n* grimace; grin; grumbling; snare, trap; snarl; whine, whining. •.

girn *v* grimace; grin; grouse, grumble; snare, trap; sneer; whine.

girnal, girnel, garnel *n* granary.

girnie *adj* whining; peevish; querulous.

girr *see* **gird¹**.

girse, gerse, gress *n* cress; grass. • *v* pasture.

girsie *adj* grassy.

girsin *n* grazing; pasturage.

girsle *n* cartilage.

girslie *adj* gristly.

girslouper *n* grasshopper.

girst *n* grist.

girstle *n* gristle.

girt *adj* great; large.

girten *n* garter.

girth, gyrth *n* protection; sanctuary.

git *v* acquire; get; **git abuin** get over.

gite *see* **gyte**.

gitter *n* gutter.

given name *n* Christian name.

gizen *n* gizzard.

gizz *n* countenance; face.

gizzen *adj* leaky. • *v* dry up; split from dryness.

glaamer *v* grope.

glaff *n* glimpse.

glagger *v* long.

glaid¹, glad *adj* smooth; slippery.

glaid² *n* kite.

glaik *n* glance. • *v* flirt; **glaik wi** trifle with.

glaikit *adj* backward; daft; stupid; irresponsible; thoughtless; clinging.

glaim *v* gleam.

glaip *n*/*v* gulp.

glairie-fairie *adj* glaring.

glaise *n* warm.

glaister *n* thin covering.

glaize *n* gloss. • *v* glaze.

glaizie *adj* glittering; glossy.

glammach *v* grab.

glammis, glaums *npl* pincers.

glamour, glammer *n* enchantment; magic; influence of a charm.

glamourie *n* glamour; witchcraft.

glamp *see* **glaum**.

glance on *v* occur to.

glancie *adj* shiny.

glasenit *adj* glazed.

glassin *n* glasswork.

glassin-wricht, glasser *n* glazier.

glaster *v* bark; bawl; boast.

glaum, glamp *n* snatch. • *v* clutch at; **glaum at** snatch at.

glaums *see* **glammis**.

glaun *n* clamp.

glaur *n* mud; ooze; slime; slipperiness. *v* muddy.

glaze *v* smooth over.

glazie *adj* glassy.

glebe *n* plot.

gled *n* hawk; kite; buzzard; hen-harrier; rapacious person.

gledge *v* look squint.

gleed *n* ember.

gleed *see* **gleid**.

gleek *v* gibe.

gleesome *adj* cheerful.

gleet *n* glistening; shine. • *v* shine.

gleg *adj* perceptive; sharply clever; brisk; clear-sighted; crafty; prompt; speedy; subtle; vivid.

gleg-eed *adj* keen-eyed, sharp-eyed.

gleglie *adv* briskly.

gleg-luggit *adj* sharp-eared.

glegness *n* sharpness; keenness.

gleg-tonguit *adj* glib; voluble.

gleid, gleed *n* spark; burning coal. • *v* spark.

gle-man *n* minstrel.

glen *n* dale; valley.

glent, glint *n* glance, peep; glint; glitter, sparkle; flash; shine; twinkle; intuition • *v* glance; glint; glitter; sparkle; twinkle; flash; slip past.

Glesca *n* Glasgow.

gless *n/v* glass.

glesses *npl* glasses.

gley *n* aim; irregularity; squint. • *v* squint.

gley-eed *adj* cross-eyed.

glib *adj* eloquent; voluble; smooth.

glib-gabbit *adj* gossipy.

glid *adj* slippery.

gliff *adj* instant. • *n* flash; glare; hurried glance; sensation; shock. • *v* look at hurriedly; appal; take fright.

glim *n* gleam; glimmer; glimpse.

glime *v* look askance.

glimmer *v* blink; wink.

glimmerin *adj* peering.

glinkit *adj* giddy.

glint¹ *adj* vestige.

glint² *see* **glent**.

glisk *n* flash; glance; glancing ray. • *v* glance.

gliss *v* shine.

glister *n* brilliance. • *v* glisten.

glit *n* mucus; phlegm.

glittie *adj* very smooth; slimy.

gloamin *n* dusk; half-light; twilight.

gloan *n* substance; strength.

glock, glock *v* gulp.

glog *adj* black; dark.

gloggie *adj* dark and hazy.

gloit *v* work messily.

glooms *npl* depression.

gloove *n* glove.

glore *n* glory.

glorgie *adj* mired; besmeared.

glorious *adj* hilarious.

glose, gloze *n* blaze.

gloss *n/v* snooze.

glotten *v* thaw slowly.

gloum *n* frown; gloom.

gloup, glupe *n* cliff hole; cave.

glour, glowr *v* stare.

glousterie *adj* boisterous.

glout *v* pout.

glowe *n/v* glow.

glower *n/v* gaze; glare; stare.

glowsterin *adj* loud-mouthed.

gloze *see* **glose**.

gluff, glump *adj* sullen.

glumsh *adj* sulky. • *n* sour look.

glundie *adj* sullen.

glunsh *n/v* scowl; pout.

glunt *v* look sour.

glupe *see* **gloup**.

glush *n* slush.

glut *n* draught.

gluther *v* swallow noisily.

glybe *n* glebe, glebe land.

glyde *n* nag; old horse.

gnaff *n* small stunted thing or person.

gnap *n/v* bite.

gnidge *v* press.

gnyauve *n/v* gnaw.

go *n* excitement.

goad *n* god.

goam, gome *v* care for; greet.

goat *n* sea cave; trench.

gob *n* beak; mouth; stomach.

God-left *adj* God-forsaken.

godrate *adj* cool; collected.

goff *n* fool.

goggie *adj* elegant.

goif *see* **gove**.

goit *n* fledgling.

golach *n* beetle.

goldie *n* goldfinch.

goller, gollar *n/v* shout, bawl.

gome *see* **goam**.

gomerel, gomeril *n* silly person, fool.

goo¹ *n* gull (bird).

goo² *n* liking.

goodman *see* **guidman**.

goods an gear *npl* belongings.

goodwife *see* **guidwife**.

goom *n* gum.

goon *n* gown.

goonie *n* nightgown.

goor *n* mucus; slime.

goose-seam *n* goose grease.

gorb *n* glutton.

gorby *n* raven.

gordy *adj* frosty.

gorlin *n* fledgling; urchin.

gormaw n cormorant.

gornal n button.

gos n goshawk.

goshens! interj gosh!

goss n simpleton.

gote, got n creek; ditch; drain.

goud, gowd n gold.

gouden adj golden.

goudspink n goldfinch.

goudy, gowdie n jewel.

gouk see **gowk¹, gowk²**.

goule n throat.

goupin see **gowpin**.

gouthart adj in a fright.

govance n good breeding.

gove. golf n/v gaze; stare.

gow n blacksmith; smith.

gowan n daisy.

gowd see **goud**.

gowden see **gouden**.

gowf n golf.

gowfba n golfball.

gowfer n golfer.

gowff n/v strike.

gowfstick n golf club.

gowk¹, gouk n cuckoo; fool, simpleton; April fool.

gowk², gouk v stare vacantly.

gowk-like adj stupid-seeming.

gowk-spit n cuckoo-spit.

gowl n/v howl; yell.

gowlie adj scowling.

gowp n ache; gulp; stare. • v gape; gulp.

gowpin, goupin n hollow of the hand.

gowpinful n double handful.

gowst n gust.

gowster n outburst; swaggerer.

gowstie adj desolate; gusty; tempestuous; vast; wasted.

grabbie adj covetous.

grabble n grab; grasping. • v grab.

gracie adj devout; virtuous; well-behaved.

gracious adj outgoing.

gradawa n graduate.

grafel v grovel.

graff¹ adj coarse.

graff² n grave.

graid see **graith**.

grain¹ n/v groan.

grain², grane n branch; stem.

graip n fork; pitchfork. • v fork.

graipple v grapple.

graisle v crackle.

graith, graid, grait n apparatus; belongings; harness; equipment; goods; machinery; tools; medicine; wealth. • v prepare, make ready; harness.

graithin n outfit; trappings.

graithlie adv carefully.

gralloch v disembowel.

gramarye n magic.

gramloch adj miserly.

gramlochlie adv graspingly.

gramshoch adj coarse.

gran adj excellent; grand.

granbairn n grandchild.

grandery n grandeur.

grandochter n granddaughter.

grane see **grain**.

granfaither n grandfather.

gran-wean n grandchild.

grange n corn farm.

granit adj forked.

granmither n grandmother.

grannie n granny.

grannie's mutch n snapdragon; columbine; old-fashioned girl.

gransher n great-grandfather.

granzie n barn.

grashloch adj boisterous.

gratis adj gratuitous.

gravat, grauvat n cravat; muffler; scarf.

graveyaird n graveyard.

gravy n sauce.

gray adj grey.

graybeard n pitcher; stone bottle.

greable see **greeable**.

great adj boastful.

gree n step; degree; prize; pre-eminence; supremacy. • v agree; conciliate; correspond.

greeable, greable adj agreeable; harmonious; peaceable.

greeance, greement n agreement; assent; concord; harmony.

green¹ adj young; youthful. • n backyard.

green², grene v crave; yearn, long.

greenichie adj greenish.

greenin n craving.

green lintie n greenfinch.

greet, greit n cry. • v cry; lament; weep.

greetie *adj* weepy.

greetin *n* lamentation.

greetin-faced *adj* moaning.

greetin-fou *adj* maudlin.

greice *see* **grice**.

greit *see* **greet**.

gremmar *n* grammar.

grene *see* **green²**.

gresp *n/v* grasp.

gress *see* **girse**.

gret *adj* great.

grew *n* greyhound.

grice, greice *n* pig.

grie *n* gradation.

grieve *n* farm bailiff; overseer.

grilse *n* young salmon.

grim *adj* roan.

grip *n* mastery. • *v* catch; capture; seize.

grippie *adj* mean, parsimonious.

grippiness *n* avarice; meanness.

grippitt *adj* avaricious.

grisk *adj* avaricious; greedy.

grist *n* girth.

grit *adj* great.

groatie buckie *n* cowrie.

groats *npl* husked oats.

groff, grofe *adj* obscene; strident; vulgar; rough.

groncie *adj* fine.

groof *n* belly.

grooflins *adj* prone.

groose *n* grouse (bird).

groosie *adj* coarse-faced.

grosset, grosart *n* gooseberry.

grosset-bush *n* gooseberry bush.

grouk *v* watch over.

grounch *v* grunt.

ground mail *n* burial rent.

ground lair *n* burial plot.

grounge *see* **grunge**.

growe *v* develop; grow.

growl *n* grumbler.

grown-up *adj* overgrown.

growp *v* grope.

growthe *n* growth; vegetation; weeds.

growthie, growthy *adj* fertile; humid; lush; thriving; weed-infested; well-grown.

growthieness *n* fertility.

grudge *v* squeeze.

grue¹ *n* half-frozen water.

grue² *adj* horrible; trembling. • *n* horror; revulsion; tremor. • *v* shudder; creep.

grugous *adj* grizzly.

gruishie *adj* gross.

grumlie *adj* grumbling.

grumly *adj* muddy.

grummle *n/v* grudge; grumble.

grumph *n* grumbler; grunt. • *v* grumble; grunt.

grumphie *adj* grumpy; ill-natured.

grumple *v* feel; palpate.

grun *n* basis; farmland; ground; text.

grun-ebb *n* low tide.

grunkle *n* snout.

gruns *npl* lees; sediment.

grunsel *n* groundsel.

grunstane *n* grindstone.

grunzie *n* mouth; snout.

grup *n/v* grip.

grupe *n* dung trench.

grush *n* grit. • *v* crush; squash.

grushie *adj* thick.

gruslins *npl* intestines.

gryce *n* pig.

gryce *n* claw.

gryfe *n* claw.

gryking *n* dawn.

gub *v* beat.

gubbing *n* beating.

guddle, ginnle *n* mess; slovenly person. • *v* catch in the fingers.

gude *see* **guid**.

gudelie *see* **guidlie**.

gudeman *see* **goodman**.

gudewife *see* **guidwife**.

gudge *n* gouge; dislodge.

gudgie *adj* short and thick.

guess *n* conundrum; riddle.

guff *n* aftertaste; smell; savour; stench.

guffle *v* puzzle.

guid, gude, gweed *adj* good; in-law. • *n* good; (*pl*) livestock.

guidal *n* guidance.

guid bit *n* long time.

guid-brither *n* brother-in-law.

guid-dochter *n* daughter-in-law.

guide *v* control; govern; handle; organise; **guide yersel** behave.

guider *n* manager.

guideship *n* guidance; treatment.

guid-faither *n* father-in-law.

guid-fowk n fairies.
guid-gaun adj flourishing.
guidlie, guidly, gudelie adj good-humoured; goodly; godly. • adv properly.
guidman, goodman, gudeman n proprietor; farmer; husband.
guidliheid n goodliness.
guid-mither n mother-in-law.
guid-sister n sister-in-law.
guid-son n son-in-law; stepson.
guidwife, goodwife, gudewife n farmer's wife; wife; housewife; landlady; matron.
guidwilled adj zealous.
guidwillie adj benign.
guid words n prayers.
guiltful adj guilty.
guise n masquerade. • v disguise.
guiser, gysar n one in disguise or wearing a mask.
gulder, guldar n threat.
gullet n gully.
gulliegaw v gash.
gullion n marsh; morass.
gully n large knife.
gullygaw n brawl.
gulpin n raw fellow.
gulsach n jaundice.
gum n condensation; rancour.
gumbile n gumboil.
gummle adj indistinct.
gump n ninny.
gumple n excess.
gumption n common sense; pluck.
gun n pipe for tobacco.
gundie adj greedy.
gunkie n dupe.
gunner v gossip.
gurk n fat short person.
gurl n gale; gurgle. • v gurgle.

gurlie, gurly adj gnarled; gurgling; savage; surly; stormy.
gurr n/v growl.
gurthie adj corpulent; heavy; oppressive.
guschet see **gushet**.
guse n goose.
gushel n dam; sluice.
gushet, guschet n gusset; gore of skirt.
gust n flavour; taste. • v taste.
gustie, gusty adj appetising; savoury; tasty.
gustless adj tasteless.
gut n gout.
gutcher n grandfather.
guts n glutton.
gutser n bellyflop.
gutsie, gutsy adj gluttonous; voracious; greedy.
gutsin n overeating.
gutsiness n gluttony; greed.
gutter n mire.
gutterbluid n guttersnipe.
gutters npl puddles; dirtiness.
guttie¹, gutty adj corpulent; pot-bellied; gross; thick.
guttie² n rubber; catapult.
guttle v guzzle.
gweed see **gude**.
gyf see **gif²**.
gyle-hoose n brew-house.
gymp v gibe; taunt.
gynour n engineer.
gype adj keen; hungry.
gyping adj open-mouthed.
gyrth see **girth**.
gysar see **guiser**.
gyte, gite adj daft; crazy, mad; inflamed; lovesick. • n lunatic.
gyter n drivel; driveller.

H

ha¹ v have.
ha² n hall; house; mansion.
haaf n sea.
haaf-net n bag net.
haar n fog, mist; hoarfrost.
haarie adj foggy, hazy, misty.
habber v stutter.

habbergaw n hesitation.
habbie adj stiff-jointed.
habbie-horse n hobby-horse.
habble¹ n perplexity; slovenly person. • v confuse.
habble² v snap, growl.
habblie adj big-boned.

hace *adj* hoarse.

hachel *n* slut.

hachle *see* **hauchle**.

hack¹ *n* adze; muck-rake • *v* chop, cut up, roughen.

hack² *n* chap.

hack³, heck *n* wooden frame, rack.

hackit *adj* cracked.

hackle *n* cockade; cock's neck feathers.

hack stock *n* chopping block.

hackum-plackum *adv* even-steven.

had *see* **haud**.

haddie *n* haddock.

haddin *n* house; possession.

ha'door *n* front door.

hae *v* have; take; credit (believe/think); **hae an ee in** covet; **hae an ee till** desire; **hae wi** go with.

haem-houghed *adj* knock-kneed.

haet *n* least thing.

haffet, haffit *n* sidelock; temple; side of the head.

hafflin *adj* half-grown.

hafless *adj* destitute.

haft *n* dwelling.

hag¹ *n* bank.

hag² *n* stroke; notch. • *v* cut, cut down, strike; fell (a tree).

hage, haig *n* hedge.

hagg *n* broken peaty ground.

haggart *n* nag.

hagger *n* small rain.

haggerdash *n* disorder.

haggersnash *n* offal.

haggerty-taggerty *adj* ragged.

haggis *n* offal and oatmeal pudding.

haggle *v* mar.

hagglie *adj* rough.

haggs *see* **hagg**.

hagman *n* woodcutter.

haif-knab *n* bourgeois.

haig *see* **hage**.

haigle¹ *v* haggle.

haigle² *v* walk with difficulty.

haik *v* drag.

hail¹ *adj* able-bodied, healthy. • *v* heal.

hail², haill, hale *adj* entire, whole, total. • *adv* quite. • *n* the whole.

hail³ *npl* pellets.

hail-heidit *adj* unharmed, unhurt.

haill *see* **hail²**.

haillie *adv* wholly.

hailscart *adj* scot-free, unscathed.

hailsome *adj* medicinal.

hailstane *n* hailstone.

haimert *see* **hameart**.

haimmer *n/v* hammer.

hain, hane *v* conserve, reserve, save; stock.

hainch *n* haunch; lameness. • *v* leg-up.

hainches *npl* haunches.

hainer *n* frugal person, saver.

haingle *adj* slack.

haingles *npl* influenza.

hainin *n* economy.

haining *n* hedging.

hainins *npl* savings.

haip *n* heap, mass. • *v* heap.

hairm *n* harm. • *v* harp on, nag.

hairp *n* harp.

hairse *adj* hoarse.

hairst *n* harvest.

hairster *n* harvester.

hairst mune *n* harvest moon.

hairt *n* heart.

hairth *n* hearth.

hairy *n* prostitute.

hairy hutcheon *n* sea urchin.

hairy-tail *n* trollop.

haisome *adj* wholesome.

haister *v* speak on impulse.

hait¹ *n/v* heat. • *adj* hot.

hait² *n* atom; speck.

haithen¹ *adj* incomprehensible, inconceivable.

haithen² *n* heathen.

haithen³ *n* gneiss (rock).

haivel *n* conger eel.

haiveless *adj* meaningless; shiftless.

haiver, haver *v* babble; pretend to be busy.

haiverel *n* lounger.

haiverin *adj* nonsensical.

haivers *npl* babble; drivel.

haizer *v* bleach.

hald *see* **haud**.

hale¹ *v* haul, pull up.

hale² *see* **hail²**.

hale and feer *adv* altogether.

halflin, halfling *see* **hauflin**.

halflins *see* **hauflins**.

halidom *n* holiness.

halie, haly adj holy.

haliket adv headlong.

hallach adj crazy.

hallan n screen wall.

hallanshaker n sturdy beggar.

hallion n clown; rascal.

hallockit n tomboy, hoyden. • adj tomboyish.

hallop v skip about.

hallow n/v/adj hollow.

hallyoch n jabberings.

hals, hawse see **hause**.

halsbane n collarbone.

haltand adj haughty.

halth n health.

haly see **halie**.

ham n bacon.

hame n home.

hameart, hamart, haimert adj domestic; home-grown; native.

hame-bred adj homely.

hame-comin n return.

hame-drachtit adj home-loving; homesick.

hame-gaun n burial; death.

hamelie adj domestic, homely; familiar; kindly.

hamelt adj indigenous; plain.

hameower adj unaffected; vernacular.

hames n collar.

hamesucken n assault on a householder.

hame-through adv straight homewards.

hamewith adv homewards.

hammle v walk unsteadily.

hamp v stumble, stutter.

hamperit adj cramped.

hamshoch n bruise, misfortune.

han¹ n event.

han², hand n hand; clever performer; handwriting; business; job; help; direction; fuss. • v hand.

han-ban n cuff.

hanch v champ; gobble.

handclap n moment.

handfast v betroth.

handfasting, hanfastin n betrothal, unblessed marriage.

hand-hap n chance.

handie¹ adj adaptable, amenable.

handie² n milk pail.

handless see **hanless**.

handsel, hansel n seasonal gift. • v inaugurate; celebrate.

handselling n inauguration.

hane see **hain**.

hanfae n handful.

hanfastin see **handfasting**.

hangie n executioner, hangman.

hangit-faced adj villainous.

hanigle adj workshy.

hank¹ n influence.

hank² n skein. • v fasten, loop.

hankie n bucket.

hankle v tie up.

hanless, handless adj fumbling, incompetent, inefficient, clumsy.

hanlessness n incompetence.

hanlin n piece of work.

hannie¹ adj light-fingered.

hannie² n milk pail.

hannle, haunle n handle.

han ower heid adv indiscriminately.

hanplane n plane for wood.

hansel see **handsel**.

hansh, haunsh v snap at.

hant¹ n/v haunt.

hant² n custom; habit; practice, wont.

hantie, hanty adj convenient, handy.

hantle n large number.

hanwaled adj choice; hand-picked.

hanwrite n handwriting, penmanship.

hap¹ n blanket, cloak, cover; mat, rug • v clothe, drape, wrap; hide.

hap² n hip.

hap³ n/v hop.

happenin adj casual.

happer n hopper.

happergaw v sow seed unevenly.

happity adj hopping.

happy adj lucky.

hapshackle n/v fetter.

harberie n lodging.

hard adj raw; strong. • adv firmly. • n hardship.

hard-handed adj mean.

hardin adj made of rough cloth.

hardlins adv hardly.

hard neck n effrontery, presumption.

hard-neckit adj brazen.

harebell n bluebell.

hareshaw, hareshard n harelip.

hark v listen; whisper.

harl, harle *n* drag; roughcast. • *v* drag; rake together; trail; roughcast.
harled *adj* roughcast.
harm *n* distress.
harn[1] *n* brain.
harn[2] *n* coarse linen; sackcloth.
harnes[1] *npl* armour.
harnes[2] *npl* brains.
harnless *adj* brainless.
harn-pan *n* skull.
harra *n/v* harrow.
harrie *v* pillage.
harschip *see* **hership**.
harsk *adj* harsh, bitter.
hartful, hartlie *adj* cordial.
has *v* abuse, ill-treat.
hasart *adj* hoary.
hash *v* afflict, deface, destroy; munch; harass, overwork.
hashie, hashy *adj* careless, slipshod, slovenly.
hask *v* cough up.
haskie *adj* stale.
hass[1] *n* throat.
hass[2] *v* kiss.
hassie *n* confused heap.
hastard *adj* ill-tempered.
hastern *adj* early.
haste ye back! *interj* come back soon!
hatesome *adj* hateful.
hatrent *n* hatred.
hatry *adj* dishevelled.
hatter *n* assortment, irregular heap. • *v* gather in a crowd; hector.
hattert *adj* flustered, distraught.
hauch *n* callus.
hauchle, hachle *v* walk with difficulty.
haud, had, hald, hauld *n* sanctuary; dwelling; support, prop. • *v* hold; keep, contain, maintain; prop; **haud at** persevere in, persist; **haud awa** go away; **haud a wee** stop for a moment; **haud by** pass by; **haud doon** oppress; **haud in aboot** repress, restrain; **haud on** keep up; **haud oot** exclude, keep out; **haud oot o langer** amuse; **haud wi** own up to; **haud wide o** avoid; **haud yer wheesht** shut up.
hauden-doon *adj* oppressed.
hauder *n* container.
haudin *n* holding.

hauf *adj* half; semi-detached. • *n* division, half; whisky measure • *v* bisect; halve; **hauf and snake** divide equally.
hauf an hauf *n* whisky and beer.
hauf-bred *adj* crossbred.
hauf-cock *adj* tipsy.
hauf-gaits *adv* halfway.
hauf-jackit *adj* halfwitted.
hauf-licht *n* half-light.
hauflin, halflin, halfling *n* adolescent, boy; halfwit. • *adj* adolescent, half-grown; intermediate.
hauflins halflins *adj* partly. • *adv* half.
haufroads *adj/adv* halfway, midway.
hauf-yokin, ten-hours'-bite *n* morning pause in ploughing.
haugh[1] *n* riverside pastureland.
haugh[2] *see* **hoch**.
haugull *n* sea wind.
haukit *adj* white-faced.
hauld *see* **haud**.
haulm[1] *n* stalk.
haulm[2] *see* **holm**.
haun *see* **han**.
haunle *see* **hannle**.
haunsh *see* **hansh**.
haup *v* swing to the right.
hause, hals, hawse *n* narrow part, defile; neck. • *v* embrace.
hausebane *n* collarbone.
haut *n* halt; limping.
have *v* heave.
haveless *adj* feckless.
haver *see* **haiver**.
haveril *n* babbler.
havers *see* **haivers**.
havings, havins *npl* behaviour.
haw *adj* green or pale blue. • *n* hollow.
haw-buss *n* hawthorn bush.
hawk *n/v* hack.
hawkie *n* cow.
hawkit *adj* foolish; white-faced.
hawse *see* **hause**.
hawy *adj* heavy.
hazel oil *n* caning.
hazelraw *n* lichen.
hazy *adj* feeble-minded.
he *n* male; man.
heading *n* scorn.
headlins *adv* headlong.
headrigg *n* turning area for plough.

heague v butt.

heally v abandon.

hearer n churchgoer.

hearing n lecture; scolding.

hearken v hear, eavesdrop, listen.

hearkener n listener.

heart v encourage.

heartscald n heartburn.

heartsome adj merry.

heather-ask n lizard.

heather-bleater n snipe.

heather-cow n heather besom.

heather lintie n twite.

heather-lowper n countryman.

heave v rise.

heavenlie adj divine.

heavy n bitter beer.

hech interj indication of contempt.

hechle v breathe hard; **hechle and pechle** puff and pant.

hecht n promise, pledge • v raise in price; heighten; name.

heck see hack³.

heck-door n door between a kitchen and byre.

heckle n criticism. • v hook; cross-question; storm.

heckle-pins n tenterhooks.

hedder n heather; ling.

hedderie adj heathery.

hedder-reenge n hydrangea.

hedger n hedgehog.

hedinful adj scornful.

hee, hey adj high. • v raise.

heefer n heifer.

heeld v lean.

heelie adj disdainful • n affront; pique; slight. • v affront.

heeligoleerie adj topsy-turvy.

heely adj arrogant.

heepy n fool.

heestie adj hasty.

heez pron his.

heeze n assistance. • v dignify, exalt, extol; elevate, lift, raise.

heff n resting-place, environment. • v dwell.

heft n handle, haft.

heftit¹ adj accustomed.

heftit² adj flatulent.

heich adj high, tall; haughty; overween-

ing. • adv disdainfully; haughtily; loudly; proudly. • n eminence.

heich-heidit adj arrogant, condescending.

heich-kilted adj immodest.

heichmaist adj highest.

heicht¹ n altitude, height; summit. • v heighten.

heicht² adj promised, engaged to.

heid¹ n head; top; summit. • adj principal. • v behead, decapitate.

heid² n issue, point of discussion.

heid³ n heat.

heidban n waistband.

heid bummer n manager.

heider n header.

heid-heich adv confidently.

heidie, heidy adj headstrong, impetuous, rebellious; intelligent, brainy.

heidmaist adj chief; topmost.

heidsman n leader.

heidy see heidie.

heiffle v have intercourse with.

heil, heill n health.

heild v cover, hide.

heily adj proud.

hein-shinn'd adj with heavy shinbones.

heiranent adv concerning this.

heir downe adv here below.

heirly adj honourable, noble.

heirship, heirskap n inheritance.

heis v hoist.

heist n haste. • v hasten.

heiven n heaven.

heivenlie adj heavenly.

hellicat n hell-cat, demon.

helmy adj rainy.

helpender adj auxiliary. • n assistant.

helplie, helplyk adj helpful, obliging.

helter n/v halter.

hemmins npl leather shoes.

hempe n shoot.

hempie, hempy adj romping. • n rogue.

hen n dare. • v withdraw.

hench v limp.

hender v hinder.

hen-hertit adj cowardly.

henner n feat.

hen-pen n chicken dung.

hen-taed adj pigeon-toed.

hen-wifie n poultry woman.

herbour *n* harbour; port.
herd, hird *n* cattle herdsman, shepherd.
hereawa *adv* hereabouts, in this area.
here's tae ye *interj* cheers!
heriot *n* landlord's claim to part of a deceased tenant's estate.
herison *n* hedgehog.
heritour *n* heir.
herk *v* hark.
herie *n* imp.
herling *n* trout.
hern *n* heron.
herness *n* harness.
herr *n* hair.
herrie *v* harry, harass; pillage, ravage; **herrie oot** evict, expel.
herrin *n* herring.
herrin hake *n* hake.
herrin hog *n* grampus.
hersel, hirsell *n* mistress, female head of house. • *pron* herself.
hership, harschip *n* plundering.
hersum *adj* strong, harsh.
hert *n* heart. • *v* hearten.
herten *v* embolden.
hertenin *n* encouragement.
hert-glad *adj* delighted.
hert-hale *adj* organically sound.
hertie *adj* genial, hearty; liberal.
hertilie *adv* heartily.
hertill *adv* hereunto.
hertless *adj* discouraging, disheartening.
hert-likin *n* affection.
hert-peetie *n* compassion.
hert-roastit *adv* exasperated.
hert-sair *adj* grief-stricken.
hert's care *n* anxiety.
hert-scaud *n* heartache; repulsion.
hertsome *adj* encouraging; satisfying.
hervy *adj* poor-looking.
hesp[1] *n/v* clasp; hasp.
hesp[2] *n* hank.
het *adj* fermenting; hot, warm.
hetful *adj* hot.
het pint *n* hot whisky drink.
het-skinn'd *adj* thin-skinned.
het-skinnt *adj* fiery.
hettle *adj* fiery.
heuch, heugh *n* coalmine; precipice; ravine; crag.

heuk-bone *n* rump-steak.
hey[1] *n* hay.
hey[2] *see* **hee**.
hey-fowk *n* hayfork.
hey-sned *n* scythe.
hiccory *adj* ill-humoured.
hicht *n* altitude.
hichtit *adj* infuriated.
hick[1] *n/v* hiccup.
hick[2] *v* haggle.
hiddin *n* fastening, hinge.
hiddle *n* huddle. • *v* hide.
hiddlie *adj* sheltered.
hidie *n* hide-and-seek.
hidie-hole *n* hiding place.
hidin *n* secrecy.
hidlins *adj* secret, surreptitious. • *adv* secretly, surreptitiously.
hidwise *adj* hideous.
Hielan *adj/n* Gaelic; Highland.
hielan, hieland *adj* highland; green, naive; unskilled; hospitable.
Hielander *n* Highlander.
Hielans *n* Highlands.
high-bendit *adj* ambitious; dignified.
high heid yin *n* boss, leader.
hilch[1] *n* brow of a hill.
hilch[2] *v* hobble.
hill *n* peat bog, pithead.
hillheid *n* hilltop.
hill-run *adj* hilly.
hime *n* hymn.
himlane *adv* on his own.
himsel *pron* himself.
hin *adj/n* back.
hindberry *n* raspberry.
hinder *see* **hinner**.
hinderen, hinderend, hinend *see* **hinneren**.
hind-head *n* back of the head.
hine, hyne *n* haven, harbour.
hinend *see* **hinderen**.
hing *v* hang. **hing doun** dangle; **hing in** persevere; **hing on** bide; **hing tae** join in; **hing the pettit lip** sulk. • *n* lean.
hinger *n* curtain.
hingers *npl* hangings.
hingin *adj/n* hanging.
hingin-like *adj* poorly, sick looking.
hingin-luggit *adj* abashed, dejected, downcast.

hingle *v* loiter.

hing-on *n* tedium.

hing-thegither *adj* clannish.

hink, hynk *v* be in doubt.

hinkum *n* sneak.

hinmaist *adj* final, hindmost, ultimate. • *adv* finally. • *n* close (conclusion).

hinmaist day *n* Judgement Day.

hinner, hinder *adj* latter. • *n* obstruction. • *v* hinder, delay; linger.

hinnerance *n* hindrance.

hinneren, hinderen, hinderend *n* back, backside, extremity; hindquarters; last part; refuse, leavings.

hinnie, hinny *n* honey, darling. • *adj* sweet.

hinniesickle *n* honeysuckle.

hint¹ *n* moment, chance.

hint² *adj* hind, rear. • *n* rear. • *prep* behind.

hint-haun, hint-hand *adv* behindhand, tardy.

hintside foremaist *adv* backwards.

hint-the-haun *adj* backward.

hip *n/v* hop. • *v* omit, pass over; hop.

hippertie-skippertie *adj* frisky.

hippin *n* nappy.

hippitie *adj* lame, limping. • *adv* lamely.

hir *pron* her.

hirays *n* ready money.

hirch *v* shiver.

hird *see* herd.

hirdum-dirdum *n* mirth.

hirdy-girdy *n* confusion.

hire *n* titbit.

hireman *n* male servant.

hireship *n* service.

hirne *n* corner, recess.

hirple *v* hobble, limp.

hirsel¹ *n* flock, sheep flock. • *v* flock; **hirsel yont** move along.

hirsel² *v* shrug.

hirself *see* hersel.

hirst¹ *n* accumulation.

hirst² *n* hilltop, ridge; wood.

hissel¹ *n* hazel.

hissel² *pron* himself.

hist *n* haste. • *v* hasten.

histie *adj* dry.

hit *pron* it.

hitch *n* loop.

hite, hyte *adj* avid, keen; enraged.

hither-an-yon *adj* estranged.

hive¹ *v* swell.

hive² *n* haven, harbour.

hivie *adj* well-off.

hivvie *adj* heavy.

hizzie *n* hussy, girl.

hoachin *see* hoatchin.

hoaliday *n* holiday.

hoam *v* spoil in cooking.

hoaspital *n* hospital.

hoast, hoist *n* cough.

hoatchin, hoachin, hotchin *adj* restless; overrun, seething, teeming; infested, swarming.

hobble *v* bob.

hobleshow *n* fuss, pother.

hoburn sauch *n* laburnum.

hoch, hough, haugh *n n* thigh, hamstring, hock.

hochle *v* dodder, shamble; copulate.

hockerty-cockerty *adv* piggy-back.

hod *v* hide.

hodden *adj* country-style.

hodden-grey *adj* grey-coloured cloth.

hoddins *npl* child's stockings.

hoddle, hodle *v* waddle.

hodgel *n* dumpling.

hoeshins *npl* stockings without feet.

hog, hogg *n* young sheep. • *v* pollard.

hogget, hoggie *n* hogshead.

hogglin and bogglin *adj* unsteady.

hogling *n* pig.

Hogmanay *n* New Year's Eve, last day of the year.

hois *n* hose, stockings.

hoist *see* hoast.

hoit *n* clumsy person.

hoker *v* sit broodingly.

hole *n* puddle.

holl *v* dig, hollow.

hollin *n* holly.

holm, haulm *n* river bank; uninhabited islet.

holt¹ *n* wood.

holt² *v* stop.

holyn *n* holly.

Holy Willie *n* sanctimonious person.

homologate *v* corroborate.

homyll *see* hummel.

honest *adj* estimable, honourable.

honest-like *adj* decent.

honesty *n* decency, respectability; decorum, propriety; honour.

hoo¹ *adv* how; why.

hoo² *v* hoot.

hooch *v* whoop. • *interj* hurrah!

hoodie *see* **huide.**

hooivver *adv* however.

hook *n* sickle.

hool *n* husk.

hoolet *n* owl.

hoolie *see* **huilie.**

hoose, hoosie *n* house, apartment. • *v* house.

hoose-en *n* gable.

hoose-fast *n* housebound.

hoosehadder *n* householder.

hoosehaddin *n* housekeeping.

hoose-heat *adj* house-warming.

hoosie *see* **hoose.**

hoot¹ *v* flout, pooh-pooh.

hoot², hoots *interj* pshaw.

hoozle *v* perplex.

hope *n* hill; hollow among hills; narrow haven.

hope kist *n* bottom drawer.

hopple *n* hobble.

horn¹ *n* prow.

horn² *v* denounce.

horn-dry *adj* bone-dry.

hornie *adj* sexually excited.

horny golach, horny goloch *n* earwig.

horoyally *n* singsong.

horsecouper *n* horse dealer.

horse gowan *n* ox-eye daisy.

hort *v* maim, hurt.

hose *n* socket.

hostler *n* innkeeper.

hot¹ *n* hat.

hot², hott *n* small, loose heap.

hotch *n/v* hitch. • *v* jerk away.

hotchin *see* **hoatchin.**

hotchpotch *n* mutton with broth.

hothoose *n* hothouse.

hott *see* **hot².**

hotter *n* jolting; quiver; seething mass; swarm. • *v* bump about; crowd together; simmer; jolt; seethe; toddle. • *adj* shaking.

hottle *n* hotel.

houd *v* wriggle, float.

houff *see* **howff.**

houffie *adj* snug.

hough¹ *adj* unhealthy.

hough² *see* **hoch.**

houghmagandie *n* sex.

houk¹ *n* hulk, big ship.

houk² *see* **howk.**

houp *n* mouthful, taste.

houre *see* **howre.**

houstrie *adj* bad (of food).

hove¹ *v* expand, swell.

hove² *v* throw, fling.

hoven *adj* blown up.

hover *v* delay, pause.

how *see* **howe.**

howd *v* assist at childbirth.

howdie *n* midwife.

howdle *v* crowd together.

how-dumb-deid *n* dead of night.

howdyin *n* midwifery.

howe, how *adj* hollow; deep; concave. • *n* hollow, cavity, depression, valley; hoe; hood; mound. • *v* hoe. • *adj* concave; deep; deep-set; famished; guttural; intense; sunken.

howe o the fit *n* sole of the foot.

howe o winter *n* midwinter.

howf, howff, houff *n* public house; haunt; burial place, cemetery; den; shelter. • *v* frequent.

howfing *adj* mean, shabby.

howk, houk *v* dig. • *v* dig, excavate, prise out; penetrate into; rummage, unearth, uproot.

howker *n* digger.

howmet *n* little cap.

hownabe *conj* howbeit.

howp *n/v* hope.

howpful *adj* hopeful.

howphyne *n* darling.

howre, houre, hure *n* whore.

howsoon, howsune *adv* as soon as.

howtowdie *n* non-laying hen.

hoy¹ *n* heave.

hoy² *v* hail, greet.

hoy³ *v* hurry.

huck *v* haggle.

hud *v* hold.

hudd *n* hod.

hudderie *adj* tawdry.

hudderin *adj* flabby.
hudder on *v* throw on.
huddry *adj* sluttish.
hudge *v* accumulate.
hudgemudgin *adj* whispering.
hud-neuk *n* corner by the fire.
hue *n* small portion.
huff *v* disappoint.
huid *n* hood.
huide, hoodie *n* carrion crow; hooded crow.
huidie craw *n* sinister-looking person.
huidit *adj* hooded.
huif *n* hoof.
huik *v* consider.
huil, hule *n* covering; skin; pericardium; pod. • *v* hull, husk.
huilie, huly, hoolie *adj* slow. • *adv* gently; slowly.
huird *n/v* hoard.
huist *n* heap.
huldie *n* nightcap.
hule *see* **huil**.
hulgie *adj* humped.
hull *n* hill.
hullerie *adj* raw damp.
hullion *n* wealth.
huly *see* **huilie**.
hum¹ *n* drone.
hum² *n* sham.
humest *adj* uppermost.
humfish *v* surround.
humlock *n* hemlock; hogweed.
hummed *adj* frustrated.
hummel, homyll *n* hornless male deer. • *adj* without horns.
hummelt *adj* polled.
hummer *v* murmur.
hummle *adj/v* humble.
humour *n* pus.
humoursome *adj* humorous.
humph *n* hump; humpback; taint. • *v* lug.
humphed, humph'd¹ *adj* hunched.
humphed, humph'd² *adj* fetid, bad-smelling, putrid.
humphie, humphy *adj* tainted, unpalatable.
humple *v* limp.
humstrum *n* fit of temper.
hun *n/v* hound.
hunchie *n* hunchback.

hunder *n* hundred. • *adj* hundred, hundredth.
hune *v* stop, delay.
hunger *v* famish.
hungert *adj* peckish, hungry, starved.
hunk *n* slut.
hunker *v* sit, squat; **hunker down** squat.
hunker-bane *n* femur; thigh-bone.
hunkers *n* hams; haunches.
hunker-slide *v* prevaricate.
hurcheon *n* hedgehog.
hurdie, hurdy *n* hip.
hurdies *npl* backside, buttocks.
hure *see* **howre**.
hurkle-bane *n* hipbone.
hurl¹ *n* drive in a carriage or car, ride; surge. • *v* drive; hurtle; be driven; push along; ride; wheel.
hurl² *n* death rattle.
hurl-barra *n* wheelbarrow.
hurlie *n* barrow.
hurloch *adj* cloudy.
hurlygush *n* spurting out.
hurthy *adv* promptly.
hurtsome *adj* hurtful; injurious; noxious.
husband *n* farmer.
hush *n* gush, abundance, whisper.
hushel *n* worn-out implement.
hushie, huzz *v* lull to sleep.
hushie-ba *n* lullaby.
hushlochy *adj* hurried.
hussie, huzzy *n* needlecase, sewing kit.
hut¹ *n* small heap.
hut² *pron* it.
hutch *n* creel for coal.
huttit *adj* hated.
huv *v* have.
huzz *see* **hushie**.
huzzy *see* **hussie**.
hwll *n* ululation.
hynd-wynd *adv* straightforward.
hyne¹ *adv* hence; late.
hyne² *see* **hine**.
hyne-awa *adj* far away.
hynk *see* **hink**.
hyple *v* go lame.
hypothec *n* mortgage.
hypothecate *v* mortgage.
hyste *n/v* hoist.
hyte *see* **hite**.

I

i *see* **in.**

icker *n* ear of corn.

Idalian *adj* Italian.

idder *see* **ither.**

idleset *adj* idle. • *n* idleness; laziness; unemployment.

ieasing *n* childbed.

ieroe *n* great-grandchild.

ignorant *n* ignorant person.

iie *n/v* oil.

ilie *adj* oily.

ilk¹, eik *pron* each; every. • *n* same; **ilk ane** all and sundry; everybody; **ilk ither** one another.

ilk² *n* same name, place, nature or family.

ilka *pron* each; every. • *adj* every; **ilka day** every day; **ilka sae lang** now and again; **ilka year** annual.

ilkaday *n* weekday.

ill *adj* evil; wicked; counterfeit; cruel; depraved; harmful; ineffective; infamous; noxious; profane; unkind; unskilled; unwholesome. • *adv* badly; wickedly. • *n* evil; wickedness; injury; mischief; wrong; malice.

ill-dreid *n* apprehension.

ill-faur'd *adj* ugly.

ill-gi'en *adj* ill disposed.

ill-aff *adj* badly off; poor.

ill-colourit *adj* discoloured.

ill-come *adj* ill-egitimate.

ill-contriven *v* disobedient.

ill-contrivit *adj* badly behaved; contradictory.

ill-curponed *adj* bad-tempered.

ill-daein *adj* licentious, dissipated. • *n* misconduct; misdemeanour; wrongdoing.

ill-daer *n* evildoer, malefactor.

ill-deedie *adj* mischievous; undisciplined; unruly; wicked.

ill-deein *adj* wrong.

ill-ee *n* evil eye; longing.

ill-farran *adj* unkempt.

ill-fashioned *adj* ill-mannered.

ill-faured *adj* discourteous; ill-mannered; offensive; shabby; ugly.

ill-gabbit *adj* foul-mouthed.

ill-gaited *adj* naughty; wicked.

ill-gate *n* bad habit.

ill-gates *n* mischievousness.

ill-gotten *adj* ill-egitimate.

ill-guidit *adj* mismanaged.

ill-hertit *adj* malevolent.

ill-intendit *adj* ill-disposed.

ill-kindit *adj* cruel; hostile; inhuman.

ill-laits *npl* bad manners.

ill-less *adj* guiltless, innocent.

ill-likit *adj* unpopular.

ill-mou'd *adj* abusive; impolite; insolent; rude.

ill-name *n* disrepute.

ill-paid *adj* regretful.

ill-pit *adj* hard-pressed.

ill-scrapit *adj* bitter.

ill-set *adj* disobliging; evill-y disposed.

ill-settin *adj* clumsy.

ill-shakken *adj* ungainly.

ill-speakin *adj* slanderous. • *n* aspersion; calumny.

ill-thing *n* devil.

ill-thochit *adj* nasty-minded.

ill-thriven *adj* undernourished; scraggy.

ill-tongue *n* slander; swear-words.

ill-tonguit *adj* abusive; slandering.

ill-trickit *adj* tricky.

ill-wared *adj* wasted.

ill-waured *adj* ill-spent.

ill-will- *n* disfavour; hatred; hostility; malice. • *v* hate.

ill-will-ed *adj* averse.

ill-will-ie *adj* grudging; spiteful; vindictive.

ill-yokit *adj* incompatible.

immedant *adj* immediate.

immedantly *adv* immediately.

immis *adj* changeable.

imp *n* shoot. • *v* graft.

impidence *n* cheek; impertinence.

impident *adj* impertinent.

implement *n* fulfilment.

impless *n* pleasure.

importable *adj* unbearable.

importance *n* means of support.

impouerit *adj* poor.

improbation *n* confutation; disproof.

improve v disprove.

in prep during; on; with. • adv inside; within; at home; on good terms; **in-about** close to; **in a hurry** unexpectedly; **in-ouer and out-ower** backwards and forwards. • v go; come; put, push, get in. • n entrance.

inawn v owe.

inbearing adj meddlesome; officious.

inbring v bring in; import.

inby, inbye adj inner; low-lying. • adv inside, indoors; close to.

incarnet adj carnation-coloured.

inch n island.

income n arrival; newcomer; abscess.

incomer n intruder; immigrant.

incoming adj ensuing; succeeding.

incontinent adv immediately.

indick v indict.

indiscreet adj rude.

indisgestion n indigestion.

indraught n customs duty.

induct v instal.

indwaller n inhabitant.

indwell v reside in.

infa n junction.

infang v cheat.

infar, infare n entertainment at home.

infeft v invest.

infeftment n investiture.

infield n land under cultivation.

infortune n misfortune.

ingaan adj ingoing.

ingan n onion.

ingang n access; entrance; lack.

ingangs npl intestines.

ingate n access.

ingaun n entering; entrance.

ingetting n collection.

ingine n engine, machine; faculty, talent; ingenuity.

ingle n fire; fireside.

ingle-neuk n chimney corner; fireside corner.

inhabile adj inadmissible.

inhauden adj pent up.

injuiry n inquest.

injure v insult.

inkfish n cuttlefish; squid.

inklin n inclination; intuition.

inkneed adj knock-kneed.

inks n tidal land by a river.

inlaik n lack; reduction. • v do without; die.

inlat n bay; cove; inlet; avenue; concession; opportunity.

inlyin n confinement.

inn n habitation.

innerlie adj inland; snug; fertile; neighbourly; affectionate; compassionate; likeable; sympathetic.

innin n introduction; reception.

inower adv inside. • prep inside.

inpit n contribution.

inquire at v consult.

inseat n farm kitchen.

insense v convince; enlighten; **insense intae** instil.

insicht n furniture; implements.

insist v prolong; persevere; **insist for** insist on; **insist in** proceed with.

insnorl v implicate; inveigle; involve.

insteid prep instead.

instructions npl brief.

intae prep into; in; within.

intak n ground taken in from moorland; eating; narrowing of a wall, offset. • v take in.

interdict n injunction. • v prohibit.

inthrow adj the fireside. • prep by means of.

intil prep into. • v enter.

intimmers n mechanism; workings; consort.

invade v assail; assault; attack.

invite n invitation.

inwey adj inward.

inwith adv within; on good terms with.

Irisher n Irishman.

irne, airn n iron.

iron fit n last (in shoemaking).

iron man n winch; pylon.

irons npl surgical instruments.

irritancy n nullification.

irritate v nullify.

is adj this. • conj as. • pron this.

ish n expiry; issue, exodus.

it prep at. • pron that.

ither, idder adj other. • pron other.

itherwhere adv elsewhere.

itherwhiles adv other times.

itherwise adv otherwise.

itsel *pron* itself.
iver *adj* upper. • *adv* ever.
iver *adv* ever; **iver an on** continually.
iverie *adj* every.
iverlie *adv* constantly.

ivernow *adv* just now.
ivnoo *adv* forthwith.
iz *pron* me.
izel *see* **eizel**.

J

jab *v* pierce.
jabart *n* sick or dying animal.
jabbit *adj* weary.
jabble *n* agitation; bewilderment; disturbed water.
jabloch *n* weak liquor.
jabot *n* necktie.
jachelt *adj* blown about.
jack *n* privy.
jack-easy *adj* easy-going.
Jacob's ladder *n* belladonna; deadly nightshade.
jadstane *n* white pebble.
jaffled *adj* jaded.
jag *n* fatigue; leather bag; injection; prick; prickle; thorn. • *v* prick; puncture.
jagget *n* full bag.
jaggie *adj* prickly; thorny.
jags *see* **jaugs**.
jaicket *n* jacket.
jaikie *n* jackdaw.
jaip, jape *v* mock.
jairble *v* spill; sprinkle.
jairblins *npl* dregs.
jalouse *v* conjecture; deduce; imagine; presume; speculate; suspect.
jamb *n* projection; wing.
jammed *adj* preoccupied.
jamph¹ *v* tire out.
jamph² *n* banter; jeer; mockery. • *v* banter; gibe; jeer; jilt.
jandies *n* jaundice.
jangle *v* prattle.
janitor, jannie *n* caretaker.
jank *v* fob; trifle; **jank off** run off.
Januar *n* January.
jape¹ *n* toy; trinket.
jape² *see* **jaip**.
jarg *n* grating noise.
jargle *v* cry shrilly.
jasp *n* jasper; particle; spot.

jass *n* throw.
jaud *n* nag, horse.
jaudie *n* stomach of a hog.
jaugs, jags *npl* saddle bags.
jauk *v* fit loosely; slack.
jaunder *v* talk idly.
jaunt *v* taunt; jeer.
jaup, jawp *n* breaker; surf; dash of water. • *v* fatigue; (*water*) rebound as waves; **jaup the watter** waste one's efforts.
jaupie *adj* splashy.
jaupin fou *adj* brimming.
jaur *n* jar.
jaurnoch *n* filth.
jaw *n* wave; mass of water or other liquid; coarse talk. • *v* spurt; surge.
jaw-box *n* sink, basin.
jaw-hole *n* sewer; sump; drain.
jaw-lock *n* lockjaw.
jawp *see* **jaup**.
jawther *v* talk frivolously.
jeck *v* discard; neglect.
jeck-easy *adj* indifferent.
jedge *n* gauge.
jee *n* swerve. • *v* budge; displace; move; swerve.
jeeg *n* jig. • *v* jig; taunt.
jeeger *n* eccentric.
jeel *n* chill; frostiness. *v* chill; freeze; congeal; set.
jeelie *n* jam; jelly.
jeelie jaur *n* jamjar.
jeelie neb *n* bloody nose.
jeelie piece *n* jam sandwich.
jeelous *adj* jealous; envious.
jeest¹ *n/v* jest.
jeest² *n* joist.
jeet *n* jet.
jelly *adj* upright; worthy.
Jennie *n* country girl.
Jennie a'thing *n* female storekeeper.
Jennie-hunner-legs *n* centipede.

Jennie-langlegs *n* daddy-longlegs, crane-fly.

Jennie-nettle *n* nettle.

Jennies *npl* calipers.

Jessie *n* sissy.

jeve *n* nudge; shove.

jevel *v* joggle.

jibber *n* silly talk.

jibbings *npl* last drops at milking.

jibble *v* spill.

jick *v* dodge.

jig *v* play the fiddle; dance.

jiggin *n* dancing.

jigot *see* **gigot**.

jigs *npl* capers.

jile *n* jail; prison. • *v* jail.

jiler *n* jailer.

jillet *n* flirt; giddy girl.

jilp *v* spurt; throw water on.

jimmy *adj* spruce; trim.

jimp¹, gimp *adj* sparing. • *adv* scarcely; scantily; sparingly. • *v* curtail; scrimp.

jimp² *adj* neat.

jimpit *adj* short.

jine *n/v* join.

jiner *n* joiner.

jing *n* jingle. • *v* jangle; jingle.

jink¹ *n* chink; cranny.

jink² *n/v* dodge; trick; zigzag.

jinker *n* lively girl.

jint *n* joint.

jirg *n/v* creak.

jirk¹ *v* unship stealthily.

jirk² *see* **chirk**.

jirkinet *n* bodice.

jirt *v* squirt.

jisk *v* caper.

jist *adv* just.

jizzen-bed *n* childbed.

jo *n* lover, sweetheart.

joab *n* job.

joater *v* wade through mire.

job *n/v* jab.

jobbie1 *adj* prickly.

jobbie2 *n* turd.

Jock *n* rustic.

Jockie *n* countryman; gipsy.

Jock Tamson's bairns *npl* human race, humankind.

jockteleg *n* clasp knife, folding knife.

joggle *v* move shakily.

Johnny a'thing *n* male storekeeper.

Johnsmas *n* Midsummer Day.

joice *n* juice.

jokie *adj* jocular, jovial.

jollock *adj* fat and jovial.

jonick *adj* fair, just; genuine; honest; impartial; veritable. • *n* fair play; justice.

joogle¹ *n/v* joggle.

joogle² *v* juggle.

jookerie *n* juggling.

jordan *see* **jourdan**.

jore *n* mixture; mire.

jorram, jorum *n* rowing song; chorus; drinking vessel.

joskin *n* farmworker.

jots *npl* odd jobs.

jotter *n* exercise book, notebook; dawdler; odd-jobs man.

jotterie *n* odd or dirty work.

jottin *n* memorandum.

jottle *v* feign business.

joug *n/v* jug.

jougs *npl* pillory.

jouk, jowk, juke *n* curtsy; meander. • *v* curtsy; dodge; duck; cower; flinch; deceive; dupe; trick; elude, evade; play truant; wince.

jouker *n* deceiver.

joukerie *n* deceit; double-dealing; evasion.

joundie *v* jog with the elbow.

jourdan, jordan *n* chamberpot.

jow *n* peal; swell. • *v* toll, peal, ring; move from side to side.

jowel *n* jewel; precious stone.

jowk *see* **jouk**.

jubish *adj* dubious.

judgement *n* sanity; wits.

juffle *v* walk hastily.

juffles *npl* worn shoes.

juggins *npl* rags.

juggle *v* shake.

Juin *n* June.

juke *see* **jouk**.

jum *adj* cold; reserved.

jummle *n/v* jumble; muddle.

jumpie *n* bodice.

jumpin raip *n* skipping rope.

jumzie *n* something that is too large.

jundie *n/v* jog; push; shove; trot.

junk *n* chunk.

junt *n* large piece of something.
jupe *n* tunic.
jurmummle *v* crush.
jurr *n* servant girl.

justify *v* punish by death.
justrie *n* justice.
juxt *adv* next to.
jyple *n* ill-dressed person.

K

kaa *see* **kay**.
kabe *n* rowlock.
kackie *v* excrete.
kae *v* invite.
kail, kale *n* cabbage; dinner.
kail blade *n* cabbage leaf.
kailwife *n* female greengrocer.
kailworm *n* caterpillar.
kailyard, kailyaird *n* back garden; kitchen garden.
kaim *n* comb. • *v* comb; **kaim down** strike with the fore-hooves.
kain *n* penalty; rent.
kair *n* puddle.
kaithe *v* show oneself.
kale *see* **kail**.
kame *n* low ridge; crest of a hill; comb. • *v* climb; comb, rake.
kar *see* **ker**.
kartie, kertie *n* pubic louse.
katy-handed *adj* left-handed.
kauch *n* bustle.
kavel, cavel *n* mean fellow.
kay, kaa *n* jackdaw.
keave *v* toss the horns threateningly.
kebar *n* rafter.
kebbock, kebbuck *n* cheese.
keck *v* go back on a bargain; faint.
keckle *n/v* chuckle; cackle; chortle.
keech, keich, keigh *n* excrement, faeces. • *v* defecate.
keechin *n* fermented but undistilled liquor.
keek¹ *n* malicious person.
keek² *n* peep. • *v* spy; peep.
keeker *n* black eye; peeping Tom.
keekhole *n* peephole; spy-hole.
keek o day *n* sunrise.
keel¹ *n* coastal sailing vessel.
keel² *n* crayon.
keelick *n* anger.
keelie¹ *n* kestrel.
keelie² *n* lout, ruffian; slum-dweller.

keeling, keiling *n* large cod.
keelivine *n* black-lead pencil.
keen *adj* enthusiastic; eager.
keep *v* care for; tend; sustain; **keep shoatie** keep watch; **keep tryst** fulfil an engagement.
keepie-in *n* detention.
keep-up *n* upkeep.
keestless *adj* tasteless.
keezlie *adj* barren.
keich *see* **keech**.
keiling *see* **keeling**.
keiltch *v* hoist up.
keind *adj* kind, sort.
keip *see* **kep**.
keir *v* drive.
keitchin *n* kitchen.
keks *npl* pants.
kelpie *n* water spirit, water sprite.
kelt *n* salmon after spawning.
kelter *v* undulate; heave up.
kelties *npl* children.
kemp *n* champion; warrior. • *v* combat; compete; contend; strive; vie.
ken *n* comprehension; knowledge. • *v* know; recognise.
kenable *adj* apparent, obvious; blatant.
kendle *see* **kennle**.
kene, keyne *adj* daring.
kengude *n* lesson.
kenmairk *n* brand, sheepmark.
kennin *n* acquaintance; hint; apprehension; recognition.
kennle, kendle, kinnle *v* kindle; ignite; bring forth.
kennlin *n* kindling.
kenspeckle *adj* conspicuous; familiar; prominent; well-known.
kent *adj* known.
kep¹ *n/v* cap.
kep², keip *n* catch; chance. • *v* intercept; encounter; parry; prevent; keep; retain; **kep again** turn back.

kep-a-gush n splay-footed person.

ker, kar adj left.

kerbit adj peevish.

ker-haundit adj left-handed.

kern n foot soldier.

ket¹ adj irate. • n carrion.

ket² n fleece.

ketach n left hand.

kethat n cloak.

kettle n cooking pot; picnic.

ketty adj matted.

keuchle n cough.

key v lock.

keyne see kene.

keytch n/v toss.

kibble adj strong; active.

kick n habit; novelty.

kicky adj gaudy.

kiffle, kighle n ticklish cough.

kill n kiln.

killick n seaman.

killywimple n gewgaw.

kilogie n kiln fire.

kilt, quelt n pleated form of Highland dress. • v tuck up.

kilter v fettle.

kiltie n boy in a kilt; soldier.

kiltit adj tucked up.

kim adj frolicsome; keen.

kimmen, kimmond n milk pail.

kimmer n gossip.

kin adj native. • n extraction; kind, lineage; relation; variety.

kinch n loop; noose; problem.

kinchin n child; kid.

kindly adj congenial; natural; normal.

kink v struggle for breath.

kink-hoast n whooping cough.

kinnen n rabbit.

kinnle see kennle.

kinred adj kindred.

kinrick n kingdom; realm.

kinsh v tighten a rope by twisting.

kintle v fondle.

kintra adj of the country; rustic. • n country; district; region.

kip¹ n haste.

kip² v take another's property.

kip³ n peak.

kippage n ship's company.

kipper v cure fish.

kippit adj turned-up.

kipple n couple.

kir adj cheerful; amorous.

kirk n church.

kirk-fowk n congregation.

kirkin n first appearance of a married couple in church.

kirkstile n churchyard gate.

kirkyaird, kirkyard n churchyard; graveyard.

kirn adj rummaging. • n churn; messy work; pottering. • v churn; mill around.

kirn dollie n corn doll.

kirnel n kernel.

kirnie n cheeky lad.

kirn milk n buttermilk.

kirr adj complacent.

kirstal n crystal.

kirsten v baptise. christen.

kirstenin n christening.

kirstie n whisky jar.

kis conj because.

kist n chest, coffer; thorax. • v store.

kistit adj dried up.

kitchen, kitching n solid foods; seasoning. • v flavour, spice.

kitchenless adj bland.

kitchie v live in.

kith n acquaintances.

kittie n kittiwake.

kittit adj deprived.

kittle adj adept; ticklish; tricky; intricate; fickle, unpredictable. • n feat; stimulus; tickle. • v arouse, enliven; bring forth; tickle; perplex; tease; titillate; tune.

kittlie adj itchy; precarious; sensitive.

kittlin n kitten.

kizen v shrink.

kizzen n cousin.

klippert n shorn sheep.

knab n hillock; pretentious person; small laird.

knack n/v snap; taunt.

knackety adj egoistic.

knackie, knacky adj adroit; facetious; skilful; witty.

knaggie adj with bulges.

knap¹ n knob; hillock; protuberance; kneecap.

knap², knop n blow, tap, slight stroke; bite; morsel. • v rap, strike; pat; cleave; speak in an English way.

knappel n clapboard.

knappie adj bumpy.

knappin hammer n stone hammer.

knarlie adj knotted.

knaw n male child.

kneef, kneif adj active.

knewel n crossbar.

knible adj nimble.

knicht n knight.

knick n/v click.

knidder v keep under.

knidget n mischievous child.

knit v unite.

knitch n/v bundle.

knock n clock; hill; knoll.

knog n something or someone short and stout.

knoit n hunk. • v gnaw.

knooff v chat.

knop see **knap²**.

knot n cloudberry; flowerbed; node. • v lump.

knotless adj futile, ineffective; aimless.

knottie adj lumpy.

knowe n knoll, little hill.

knuckle v give way, submit.

knudgie adj squat and strong.

knurl n dwarf; knob.

knuse v cuddle; press with the knees or knuckles; pummel; squeeze.

kow n goblin.

kowk v retch.

koyt v beat; flog.

kweerichin adj unskilful.

kye n cattle.

kye time n milking time.

kyle n sound, strait.

kyle n strait.

kyles npl ninepins, skittles.

kyloe n Highland black cow.

kypie n left-hander.

kyte n belly.

kythe v appear; show; practise; demonstrate; reveal.

kythin n manifestation.

kytie adj corpulent.

L

laa n law.

lab n portion. • v pitch, toss.

labber v soil.

laborin n tillage.

lab-sidit adj inclinded to one side, lop-sided.

lach, lauch n/v laugh.

lacht n fine; penalty.

lachter¹ n laughter.

lachter² n lecher; clutch of eggs; layer.

lack, lak n blame; disgrace; fault. • v slight; reproach.

lad n boy; boyfriend; son; youth.

laddie n boy; young lad.

lade n millrace.

lade-sterne n lodestar.

lad o pairts n promising youngster.

ladry n rabble.

lady's fingers n cowslip.

lady's thummles n foxglove.

laffy adj soft.

laft n loft.

lag adj lingering; slow.

laggery adj dirty.

laggin n edge.

laich, laigh adj inferior; low. • n basement. • v lower; delay.

laich room n cellar.

laid n/v load.

laidner n larder.

laidron n rascal, reprobate; slattern.

laif n loaf.

laigh see **laich**.

laik¹ n linen cloth.

laik² v leak.

laily adj lowly.

laip v lap.

lair¹ n place for lying down; burial place.

lair² n marsh. • v sink.

lair³, lare, lear n doctrine; dogma; learning.

laird n lord; landowner; chief.

lairdie n small landowner.

lairdlie adj august; lordly; aristocratic.

lairge adj benevolent; copious; numerous; innumerable; large; lavish.

lairie *adj* boggy.

lairn *v* learn.

lairstane *n* gravestone, headstone, tombstone.

laist *adj/adv* last. • *n* the last. • *v* hold out; last.

lait, lete *n* manner; gesture.

laith, lathe *adj* loathsome; reluctant. • *n* loathing; scorn. • *v* detest, loathe.

laitherin *adj* lazy.

laithful *adj* disgusting, horrible.

laithlie *adj* abhorrent; foul; loathsome.

laithsome *adj* detestable.

laitless *adj* uncivil.

laits *n* behaviour.

laive *v* throw water.

lak *see* **lack**.

lake *v* heed.

laldie *n* chastisement.

lall *n* shiftless person.

lallan *adj* of the Lowlands. • *n* lowland.

Lallans *n* Lowland speech, Scots.

lamb's tongues *n* mint.

lame *adj* earthen. • *n* pottery, earthenware.

lament *n* elegy.

lameter *n* cripple.

lammer *n* amber.

lammie *n* lamb.

lamp *v* belabour; trounce; stride.

lamper eel *n* lamprey.

lamping *adj* trouncing.

lan *n* land.

lance *n* lancet, scalpel.

lanch, lench *n/v* launch.

land *n* tenement house.

landart *adj* country.

landlash *n* heavy rain.

landlouper *n* unsettled person, rover.

land o the leal *n* heaven.

landward *adj* rural, rustic.

landways *adv* by land.

lane¹ *n* slow stream; rivulet.

lane² *adj* lone; alone; solitary.

lanelie, lanely *adj* lonely.

lanesome *adj* lonely.

lang¹ *adj* long; tall; great.

lang² *v* long for, yearn.

lang³ *prep* along.

lang-board *n* long table.

lang-chaftit *adj* lantern-jawed.

lang-drauchit *adj* scheming.

langel *v* entangle.

lang-heidit *adj* profound; sagacious.

langis, langins *prep* along.

langle *n/v* hobble.

lang-lugged *adj* sharp-eared.

lang-nebbit *adj* long-nosed; pedantic; prying.

langour *n* boredom.

langrin *adv* at length.

lang-shankit *adj* long-legged.

langsum *adj* slow.

lang syne *adv* long since. • *n* long ago.

lan-moose *n* vole.

lans *v* throw out; spring forward.

lant *v* deride; jeer, mock.

lap *n* coil. • *v* surround; embrace.

lapper *v* besmear; clot, curdle.

lapron *n* young rabbit.

lapster *n* lobster.

larach *n* base; site; building site.

larbour *adj* lazy.

lare *see* **lair³**.

larges *n* liberality.

larick *n* larch; lark.

larie *n* laurel.

larrie *n* lorry.

lash *v* fall; pour.

lass *n* girl; sweetheart; maid.

lassie, lassikie *n* young girl; girlfriend.

lass-like *adj* girlish.

lass o pairts *n* promising youngster.

lassock *n* little girl.

lastie *adj* durable.

lat *v* allow, let, permit, suffer; **lat be** cease; **lat doon** drop; **lat gird** let fly; **lat ken** divulge; **lat licht** acknowledge; **lat see** indicate; **lat wit** proclaim.

latch¹ *n* mire; wheel; rut.

latch² *v* procrastinate.

late *v* heat metal.

lathe *see* **laithe**.

lathron *adj* lazy.

latron *n* latrine, privy.

latter *adj* lower.

lauch *see* **lach**.

laugh *v* own.

laught *n* law.

lavatur *n* washing vessel.

lave¹ *n* rest, remainder, residue.

lave² *v* bail.

lave-luggit *adj* droop-eared.
lavendar *n* washerwoman.
laverock *n* lark; skylark.
law[1] *adj* low.
law[2] *v* litigate, sue.
law[3] *n* tumulus.
law-board *n* ironing board.
lawbor *n* labour.
lawbor *v* labour.
lawer *n* attorney, lawyer.
lawin *n* bill for drink.
lawin-free *adj* scot-free.
law plea *n* lawsuit.
lax *n* salmon.
lay[1] *v* put; form; plant; **lay aff** hold forth; **lay at** strike at; **lay by** incapacitate; **lay in** turn up; **lay the brain asteep** contemplate.
lay[2] *n* lathe.
lay-aff *n* harangue; rigmarole.
lay-fittit *adj* flat-footed.
laylock *n* lilac.
lea[1], **ley** *adj* fallow; infertile; barren. • *n* unploughed land; grassland.
lea[2] *v* leave.
leader *n* tributary.
leading *n* provisions.
leadsman *n* pilot.
leaf *n* segment.
leager *v* encamp.
leal *adj* chaste; loyal; honest; law-abiding. • *adv* loyally.
lealtie *n* allegiance, loyalty.
leam[1], **leem**, **leme** *n* gleam; glow; light; ray; sunbeam. • *v* gleam; glow; shine; blaze.
leam[2] *v* shell nuts.
lean *v* recline.
leap[1] *n* waterfall.
leap[2] *v* burst open.
lear *see* **lair**[3].
learn, **leern** *v* instruct; teach.
leash *v* lash; tie together.
least *conj* lest.
leasumlie *adv* lawfully.
leath *v* loiter.
leather, **ledder** *n* hide. • *v* thrash.
leave *n* dismissal.
lebbers *npl* slobberings.
leche *v* cure.
leck[1] *n* slab.

leck[2] *v* leak.
ledder *see* **leather**.
leddiness *adj* ladylike.
leddy *n* lady.
leddy-launners *n* ladybird.
leddy's purse *n* shepherd's purse.
lee *n/v* fib, lie.
leech *n* doctor.
leed *n/v* strain.
leefow *adj* lonely.
leegen *n* legend.
leelang *adj* livelong.
leem *see* **leam**.
leenge *v* slouch.
leep *v* heat; burn; parboil.
leepit *adj* pampered.
leerie *n* lamp; lamplighter.
leern *see* **learn**.
leesome *adj* balmy; pleasant; shady.
leet *n* list. • *v* nominate; list.
leeve *v* live; permit; **leeve aff** live on.
leevin *n* subsistence.
leeze, leis *v* be lease to; **leeze me** is dear to me.
leg *v* run.
leg-bane *n* shinbone.
leggat *n* invalid stroke in golf.
leggums *npl* gaiters; leggings.
legim *adv* astride.
leglin *n* milk-pail.
leid[1] *n* language; theme.
leid[2] *n* lead.
leif[1] *n* leave, permission.
leif[2] *v* believe.
leind[1] *v* stay.
leind[2] *see* **lend**[2].
leiper *n* basket-maker.
leis *see* **leeze**.
leish *adj* athletic.
leishin *adj* tall and active.
leist *v* incline, tilt.
leister, lister *n* spear; fish spear. • *v* spear.
leisum *adj* lawful; warm.
leit, let *v* pretend.
lekame *n* corpse.
lell *v* take aim.
lemane *n* sweetheart.
leme *see* **leam**.
lempit *n* limpet.
len *n* loan. • *v* lend; deliver.
lench *see* **lanch**.

lend¹ *n* loan.
lend², **leind**, *v* dwell.
lendis *npl* buttocks.
lenth *n* distance; height; length; stature. •
  v lengthen.
lep *v* go rapidly.
lerk *v* shrivel.
les, **less** *conj* unless. • *adj* fewer. • *n*
  lease.
lest *adj* last, final. • *adv* last. • *n* • the last.
  • *v* last, endure.
let¹ *n* hurdle. • *v* reckon; expect; dismiss;
  let aff break wind; **let o'er** swallow; **let
  on** mention.
let² *see* **leit**.
let-abee *conj* not to mention.
lete *see* **lait**.
letter *n* writ.
letteron *n* writing desk.
leuk *n* look; survey. • *v* look; inspect; survey; view; **leuk ower** look after;
  watch; **leuk til**, **leuk till** observe; behold; look at.
leuk see! *interj* look here!
leven *n* lawn.
lever *adv* rather.
levin *n* lightning; sunlight.
lew *adj* lukewarm. • *v* cool.
lewder *v* batter; move heavily.
lewer *n* lever.
ley *see* **lea**.
liam, **lyam** *n* string; thong.
liart *adj* grey-haired.
lib *v* castrate; geld; neuter.
libart *n* leopard.
libbet *adj* neutered.
libel *n* indictment; treatise.
licent *adj* accustomed.
licht *adj* bright, light; dizzy; merry. • *n*
  light; enlightenment. • *v* mitigate; temper.
lichten *v* alleviate; brighten; light;
  lighten.
lichter *v* unload; deliver.
licht-hertit *adj* light-hearted.
lichtlie *adv* lightly. • *v* despise; scorn;
  slight; underrate; undervalue.
lichtlieness *n* contempt.
lichtlifie *v* deprecate.
lichtsome *adj* agile; carefree; cheering;
  enlivening; delectable.

lick *v* hit; beat; hurry.
lickerie *n* liquorice.
lickit *adj* thrashed.
licklip *adj* fawning, wheedling.
lickma-dowp *n* sycophant.
lid *n* leaf.
lidder *adj* sluggish.
lide *v* thicken.
lie *n* bed.
lief *adj* dear, beloved; willing. • *n* beloved.
liefsome *adj* desirable.
liege *n* subject; vassal.
lieutenand *n* lieutenant.
lifieness *n* vivacity, liveliness.
lift¹ *n* sky.
lift² *n* encouragement; whip-round; card-
  trick; coal-seam; swell. • *v* cheer; collect; pick up; steal; arrest; serve; **lift an
  lay** pick and choose.
lifter *n* cattle rustler.
liftie *adj* dirty and sticky.
lifting *n* removal.
lig¹ *n/v* lie.
lig² *v* fall behind; lodge; make love to.
liggat *n* self-closing gate.
ligger-lassie *n* camp-follower.
lik¹ *adj* appropriate, apt; like; likely,
  probable. • *adv* approximately. • *v*
  fancy; like.
lik² *see* **lyke**.
likand *adj* pleasing.
likewark *n* limekiln.
liking *n* pleasure.
likly *adj* competent. • *n* chance; likelihood.
lilt *n* song; tune; rhythm. • *v* sing out.
lily *n* narcissus.
limb o the deil *n* mischievous person.
lime *n* mortar.
limestane *n* limestone.
limmer *n* gangster; rogue; hussy; prostitute.
limn *n* replica; likeness.
limner *n* painter, portrait-painter.
linch *v* limp.
lind *n* lime tree.
line *n* account; betting slip; note; prescription.
linens *npl* underclothing.
lines *npl* certificate.

ling¹ n gait; line.

ling² n tall thin grass.

lingel¹ n shoemaker's thread.

lingel² v tie firmly; hobble.

linget n linseed.

lingit adj flexible.

link¹ n skip. • v walk smartly.

link² n vertebra.

linkie adj sly.

links¹ npl locks of hair; sandy ground by the sea, dunes; golf course.

links² npl sausages.

linn, lynn n waterfall, cataract.

lin-pin n linchpin.

lint¹ v rest, relax; wink.

lint² n flax.

lintel n mantelpiece.

lintie n linnet; pipit.

lip n chip in a blade, etc; brink; edge. • v taste.

lippen v depend; entrust; look after; expect.

lippening adj occasional. • n expectation.

lipper adj leprous. • n leper.

lire, lyre n flesh.

lirk¹ n crease; rumple. • v crease, rumple.

lirk² v lurk.

lish adj athletic.

lisk n flank; groin.

liss n stopping, cessation. • v stop.

lissance n respite.

lissens n release; cessation.

list¹ adj agile.

list² v enlist; recruit.

lister see **leister**.

lit n dye. • v dye; colour; blush.

lite n excrement.

lith¹ n joint; division; section; segment. • v disjoint.

lith² v listen.

lithe adj calm, tranquil; kind; gentle. • n stillness; shelter; lee; soften; thicken.

lither adj lax, lazy.

lithesome adj affectionate; genial; mild.

lithin n thickening.

lithrie n mob.

little ane n child.

little-boukit adj deflated; insignificant; small.

littlie adj rather small.

liver adj sprightly.

lizour n pasturage.

loags npl stockings without feet.

loamy adj lazy.

loan¹ n provisions; wages.

loan², loaning n enclosed way; avenue; lane; cow path.

loave v put on sale.

loch n lake.

lochan n small lake.

locker adj curled; curly.

lockerie adj rippling.

locket n belch.

lockfast adj secured. • n lock and key.

lockman n executioner.

loddan n puddle.

lodesman n pilot; steersman.

lo'e see **luve**.

loff n praise.

loggerin adj soaked.

loit n turd.

loll v mew.

long lie n lie-in.

loo see **luve**.

lood adj loud.

loof see **luif**.

loofie see **luifie**.

loom n diver; fog; haze; mist.

loon, lown n boy, lad; stripling; scallywag, scamp; lecher.

loonder n wallop, whack. • v strike out; wallop, whack.

loonderin adj thrashing.

loop n bend, winding.

loopie adj shifty.

loorie adj overcast.

loose n louse.

loosies npl lice.

loosome adj lovable; lovely.

loot v yield.

lootch n stoop.

lordship n royalty.

lose, loss n praise.

losh interj lord!

loss¹ v lose, mislay; unload.

loss² see **lose**.

lotch n snare. • v jog.

louch n cavity.

loue, love v praise.

lounlie adj sheltered.

loup see **lowp**.

loupen-steek *n* broken stitch.
lour *n* lure.
lourd *adj* dull; surly.
louse *see* **lowse**.
lout *v* bow down.
lout, lowt *v* stoop.
louthshouther'd *adj* round-shouldered.
lovanentie! *interj* dear me!
love *see* **loue**.
lovie *n* lover.
low *v* haggle; stop.
lowden *v* calm; die down; moderate; reduce; subdue.
lowe *n* fire; flame; radiance. • *v* burn; rage; flare.
lown[1] *adj* serene; peaceful; still; sheltered; windless; undemonstrative. • *adv* peacefully. • *n* calm; peace; silence; peaceful place. • *v* tranquillise.
lown[2] *see* **loon**.
lownd *adj* quiet.
lowp, loup *n* jump, leap. • *v* bound, jump, leap; pop; spring; **lowp aff** alight, dismount; **lowp on** mount; **lowp the kintra** emigrate.
lowpin-on stane *n* mounting stone.
lowrie *n* fox. • *adj* foxy.
lowse, louse *adj* dishonest; immoral; lawless; licentious; loose; loose-fitting; unfastened; unsettled. • *v* detach; knock off; let go; release; undo, unbind.
lowsen *v* loosen; untie.
lozen *n* pane of glass.
lozenger *n* lozenge.
lozenit *adj* glazed.
lozent *adj* criss-crossed.
lubbard *n* lout; coward.
lubbertie *adj* lazy.
luck *v* prosper; succeed.
lucken *adj* locked up. • *v* lock.
lucken-brow'd *adj* close-browed.
luckie *n* old woman.
luck-pock *n* lottery.
lucky *adj* ample.
lucky poke *n* lucky dip; raffle.
ludge *n/v* lodge.
ludger *n* lodger.
ludgin *n* lodging.
luely *adv* softly.
luf *see* **luve**.

lufrent *n* affection.
lufsum *see* **lusome**.
lug *n* ear; fin; flange; flap. • *v* cut off the ears.
luggie *n* small wooden dish.
lugmairk *n/v* earmark.
luif, loof *n* palm; paw.
luifie, loofie *n* smack on the hand.
luim *n* implement; instrument; loom.
lum *n* chimney; chimney stack; funnel.
lumbagie *n* lumbago.
lum can, lumheid *n* chimney pot.
lum hat *n* top hat.
lummed *adj* thwarted.
lunk, lunkie, lunkit *adj* lukewarm; (*weather*) close.
lunkhole *n* hole in a dyke for sheep.
lunt[1] *n* match, light; column of smoke. • *v* puff out smoke.
lunt[2] *v* walk fast.
lunyie *n* loin; hip.
luppen sinnon *n* ganglion.
lurdane *n* fool.
lusome, lusum, lufsum *adj* lovely.
luss *n* dandruff.
lusty *adj* beautiful; pleasant.
lusum *see* **lusome**.
lute *n* sluggard.
luthrie *n* lechery.
luve, luf, lo'e, loo *n/v* love.
luve-bairn *n* bastard, love-child.
luve-blink *n* loving look.
lyam *see* **liam**.
lyardly *adv* sparingly.
lyart *adj* grey; silvery; grizzled; multicoloured.
lyflat *adj* deceased.
lyin siller *n* ready cash.
lyke, lik *n* corpse.
lykly *adj* good-looking.
lyksay *adv* like as.
lymfad, lymphad *n* galley.
lynn *see* **linn**.
lyomons *npl* feet.
lype *n* crease.
lyre *see* **lire**.
lyte *n* short time.
lyter *v* loiter.
lythe[1] *n* pollack.
lythe[2] *n* shelter.
lythocks *n* meal poultice.

M

ma¹ *pron* my.
ma² *see* mair.
maa, mae *n/v* bleat, baa.
maad *see* maud.
macer *n* mace bearer; drinking cup.
mach *see* maich.
mache *v* strive.
machine *n* vehicle.
machle *v* be busy doing nothing.
macht *n* strength.
mack *adj* neat.
macklack *adv* clatteringly.
mackrel *n* pimp.
mad *adj* annoyed; indignant.
madderam *n* folly; hilarity; insanity.
made on *adj* simulated.
made tie *n* bow-tie.
made up *adj* elated.
mae¹ *see* mair.
mae² *see* maa.
maese *v* allay.
magg *v* steal.
maggie *n* magpie.
maggotie *adj* whimsical.
maggs *npl* gratuity.
magink *n* oddity; queer-looking person.
magistrand *n* final-year undergraduate.
mags, maigs *npl* hands.
maich, mach *n* son-in-law.
maichless *adj* feeble.
maid *n* maggot.
maiden *n* corn dolly; guillotine; spinster.
maid-in-the-mist *n* navelwort.
maig *v* handle roughly.
maighrie *n* money; valuables.
maik, mayock *n* equal; peer.
maikless *adj* matchless.
mail *n* mark, stain; tribute.
mail-free *adv* rent-free.
mail gairden *n* market garden.
mailie *n* pet ewe.
main *adj* low-class.
mainner¹ *n* manner.
mainner² *n* fertiliser, manure. • *v* ferti-
    lise, manure.
mainnerlie *adj* mannerly.
mainners *npl* manners.
mains *n* home farm.

mainto *n* obligation.
mair¹, ma, mae *adj* more. • *adv* more;
    moreover.
mair² *n* sheriff's officer.
Mairch *n* March.
mairch *n* border, boundary, frontier; line;
    march. • *v* be bounded by; march;
    mairch wi adjoin.
mairchant *n* customer.
mairch dyke *n* boundary wall.
mairch-stane *n* landmark.
mairriage *n* marriage; matrimony.
mairry *v* marry.
mairtin *n* martin.
mairtyr *n* martyr. • *v* wound.
mais'd *adj* overripe.
maist *adj* major; most. • *adv* most.
maister *n* master; boss; director.
maister an mair *n* autocrat.
maistlie, maistly, maistlins *adv* most of
    all, mostly; especially; largely.
mait¹ *adj* weary.
mait² *n* flesh, meat; sustenance; diet. • *v*
    cater; feed.
mait-lik *adj* well-fed.
mait-rife *adj* abounding in food.
maitter *n* affair; matter. • *v* matter.
major-mindit *adj* high-minded.
mak *v* compose poetry; avail; make; set,
    thicken; mak a bauchle o ridicule;
    mak a fashion o pretend to do; mak a
    rue repent; mak for look like; prepare
    for; mak in with ingratiate; mak murn
    fur bewail; mak o cherish; mak on pre-
    tend; simulate; mak siccar ensure;
    mak to approximate; mak up remuner-
    ate; mak weel get on, succeed.
makar *n* poet.
makint *adj* confident.
makly *adj* seemly. • *adv* equally.
mak-on *n* impostor; make-believe.
malagrooze *v* disarrange.
male *see* meal.
malegrugrous *adj* grim.
malice *n* illness.
malifice *n* sorcery.
malison *n* curse; malediction.
malky *n* razor.

mallat v feed.

mallduck n fulmar.

malvesie n malmsey.

mam n mum.

mammie n mummy.

mamp v nibble.

man see **maun**.

man-body n adult.

mand n payment.

mandrit adj tame.

mane n complaint; dirge. • v console; pity; bemoan.

mang v stupefy; hurt.

mangle v press smooth.

mangyie n hurt.

manheid n manhood.

maniable adj able to be handled.

manish v cope; manage.

mank v blemish; maim; mar.

mankit adj corrupt; mutilated.

manly adj human.

manner v mimic.

mannie n little man; captain, skipper.

manrent n homage.

manritch adj masculine.

manse n minister's house.

manswear v perjure.

manswearing n perjury.

mansworn adj perjured.

mant, maunt n impediment. • v stutter.

manteel n mantle.

manter n stutterer, stammerer.

mantie-maker n dressmaker.

mappit adj thick-headed.

mar, marr n obstruction; injury; disadvantage. • v mutilate; obstruct.

marbel adj feeble.

marbles npl taws.

marbyr n marble.

march see **mairch**.

mare n mason's hod.

margulyie v spoil.

marischal n steward, marshal. • v marshal.

marish adj marshy.

mark n importance. • v note.

markit adj distinguished; notable.

marled adj variegated.

marlie adj mottled.

marmaid n mermaid.

maroonjous adj outrageous.

marr see **mar**.

marrot n guillemot.

marrow, marra adj equal. • n companion; spouse; consort; match. • v match; equal.

marrowless adj incomparable; matchless; unequalled; unmarried.

mart n winter provisions.

martlet n martin.

masar, mazer n drinking cup.

masel pron myself.

mashie n golf club.

mashlach adj mingled.

mashlin n mixed grain.

mask n mesh. • v brew; infuse; enmesh.

maskin adj brewing.

maskin-pat n teapot.

massacker v batter; maul; mutilate.

massie adj boastful; self-important.

massymore, massimore n dungeon.

matit adj spent.

mattle v nibble.

mauch n marrow, pith; maggot.

mauchless adj helpless; powerless.

maucht n strength.

mauchy adj dirty.

maud, maad n grey shepherd's plaid.

maugre n ill-will. • prep despite. • v dominate; master; spite.

mauk n maggot.

maukin n hare; young girl.

maukit adj filthy; maggoty.

maum v steep.

maumie adj full-bodied; luscious; mellow; ripe.

maun, man v aux must.

maun, man² v accomplish, effect; control.

maunder v jabber.

maundrel n chatterer.

maunner v maunder.

maunt see **mant**.

maut n/v malt.

mautman n maltster.

mavis n thrush, song thrush.

maw n mallow.

maw¹ n/v mew, miaow.

maw² n seagull.

maw³ v mow; scythe.

mawer n mower.

mawsie adj strapping. • n hard woman.

mawten v malt.
may n maid; girl.
maybe n possibility.
mayock see **maik**.
maze[1] n measure of herrings.
maze[2] n astonishment.
mazer see **masar**.
meal, male n oatmeal; flour made from oats or barley.
meal-ark, meal kist n meal chest.
mealie pudding n oatmeal pudding.
mealock n crumb.
mean adj scraggy.
mear n mare.
measelt adj blotchy.
meath n maggot.
meat-rife adj abounding in food.
mebbe adv maybe; perhaps; possibly.
meble n moveable object.
meckant adj mischievous.
mede n meadow.
mediciner n physician.
meduart n meadow-sweet.
meeth[1] adj modest.
meeth[2] see **meith**[2].
meethless adj inactive.
meeths npl bodily action.
meg n flipper.
megrim n whim; preposterous idea.
meik v tame, humble.
meikle, mekyl adj big; great. • adv much.
meir n mare.
meis, mese v mitigate.
meisel v crumble.
meith[1] n mark; boundary marker; feature; landmark. • v mark boundaries of.
meith[2], **meeth** adj sultry.
meithie adj maggoty.
meiths npl boundary.
mekyl see **meikle**.
melder n quantity of meal ground at a time.
meldrop n drip.
mell[1] n club; hammer. • v hammer.
mell[2] v amalgamate; mix; blend; consort; meddle.
melt n milt, sperm; spleen; tongue.
meltith n meal.
mem n madam.
memerkin n something very small.
memmit, memt adj related; allied.

mend v atone; fatten; reform.
mends npl amends; atonement; compensation; damages; reparation; penance.
mene n meaning; moaning. • v bemoan; intend.
meng v become mixed.
mengie n collection.
mense n discretion; etiquette; common sense; hospitality; honour; tact. • v treat respectfully. • v adorn; grace.
menseful adj discreet; courteous; intelligent; polite; sensible.
menseless adj boorish; silly; grasping; extortionate.
mention n trifle.
menye, meynie n followers.
mercat n market; commerce.
mercat cross n market cross.
merch see **mergh**.
merchan n merchant; shopkeeper.
merciable adj merciful.
merciall adj martial.
merciment n mercy.
mercury n barometer.
mere n boundary; sea.
mergh, merch n marrow, pith.
merk n mark; silver coin. • v mark.
merle n blackbird.
merrit adj married.
merry dancers n northern lights, aurora borealis.
merry-hine n dismissal.
merse n fertile land among hills.
mervie adj rich, mellow.
mervil adj inert.
mese see **meis**.
message boy n errand boy.
messages adj shopping; purchases; errands.
messan n small dog, mongrel.
metal n roadstone.
mete v paint.
mett n measure; measurement.
mettle adj mettlesome; sturdy.
Mey n May.
Mey bird n whimbrel.
meynie see **menye**.
mi pron my.
micht n might.
michtie adj mighty; stately; scandalous; disgraceful; shameful.

mid n midst. • prep midst.

midden n dung heap; bin; compost heap; rubbish dump.

midden bree n effluent.

midden hole n hole for dung.

middle v interfere, meddle.

middlin adj medium; moderate; tolerable. • adv fairly; tolerably.

middlins adv moderately.

midgie, midge, mudge n gnat.

midnicht n midnight.

mids adj middle. • n centre; compromise.

miff n petulant fit.

mildrop n snot; froth.

milk-hoose n dairy.

mill¹ n snuff-box.

mill² n fight. • v beat, drub.

millart n miller.

millstew n mill dust.

milltrowse n mill sluice.

milner n dweller by a mill.

milygant n false person.

mim adj affected; prim, prudish, mealy-mouthed; restrained. • adv primly.

mim-mou'd adj mincing; affectedly modest.

min adj less.

mince n minced meat.

minch n minced meat. • v mince.

mind v remember; recall; remind; intend.

minding n keepsake; memory; souvenir.

mine n level.

mine ain pron my own.

mines pron mine.

ming¹ v mix; confuse.

ming² n bad smell. • v give off a bad smell.

minging adj smelly; stinking.

minikin adj very small.

mink n noose; entanglement; matrimony.

minnie n mother; female parent of an animal; minnie's bairn mother's pet.

minnon n minnow.

minnonette n mignonette.

mint n aim, purpose; attempt; feint. • v hint; aim; attempt; allude; feint; intend; plan; utter; mint at speak of.

minute n dot.

minuwae n minuet.

miraculous adj loutish.

mird v make advances to; meddle; jest; mird wi deal with.

mire-duck n mallard.

mirk n black; obscure; dark. • adj dark; gloom. • v darken.

mirken v darken.

mirkie, mirky adj merry. • adv merrily; pleasantly.

mirkin n nightfall.

mirklins adv in the dark.

mirksome adj gloomy; murky; sombre.

mirky see mirkie.

mirlie adj speckled.

mirligoes n dizziness.

mirls n measles.

mirrot n carrot.

misanswer v disobey.

misbehadden adj improper; out of place; unbecoming.

misca v decry; denounce; disparage; mispronounce; slander.

miscairry v miscarry.

miscaw v miscall; revile.

mischancie adj unfortunate.

mischant n evildoer. • adj wicked.

mischanter n disaster.

mischief n wicked person; misfortune.

mischieve v be hurt.

mischievious adj mischievous.

miscomfit v displease; offend.

miscontentit adj dissatisfied.

misdoubt n doubt. • v doubt; mistrust.

misert adj miserly. • n miser.

misfall, misfare v miscarry.

misfault n misdeed.

misfortunate adj luckless.

misgae v fail; miscarry; miss; let down.

misgoggle v spoil.

misgrugle v rumple.

misguide v abuse; waste; mismanage.

mishannle v maim; mangle.

mishanter n disaster; misfortune; mishap.

misharrit adj unhinged.

misk n coarse grassland.

misken v be ignorant of.

misleard adj rude, slatternly; deluded.

mislearit adj misinformed.

mislearnit adj erroneous.

mislippen v distrust; neglect; overlook; disappoint.

mismae v disturb.
mismaggle v spoil.
mismak v shape wrongly.
mismarrow v mismatch.
mismarrowed adj ill-assorted.
misperson v abuse.
misred adj complicated.
miss, mys n fault. • v avoid; escape; fail; **miss yersel** v miss something.
missaying n calumny, lie.
misset v displease.
missionar n preacher.
misslie adj solitary.
mistaen adj mistaken; misunderstood.
mistak, mistaik n misapprehension; mistake. • v mistake; transgress; neglect.
mistell v misinform.
mister v need.
mistimeous adj unpunctual.
mistlie adj solitary.
Mistress n Mrs.
mistrow v suspect.
mistrowing n distrust.
mistryst v seduce; fail to meet.
mith v may.
mither n mother.
mitle v eat away.
mittens npl woollen gloves.
mittle v hurt.
mixit, mixt adj fuddled; tipsy.
mixter-maxter adj heterogeneous; motley. • n concoction; confusion; hotch-potch; mixture.
mizzer n/v measure.
mizzle¹ v/n muzzle.
mizzle² v disappear; melt away.
moach v rot.
moch¹, mogh n moth.
moch², mochy, moich adj moist.
mochie¹ adj moth-eaten.
mochie² adj muggy.
mochre v hoard.
mockrif adj sardonic; scornful.
mode n courage.
moderate v preside.
modgel n noggin.
modren n modern.
mody, mudie adj bold.
moggan n sleeve; footless stocking.
mogh see **moch¹**.
moich see **moch²**.

moider v knock insensible.
moidert adj dull.
moil n hard labour.
moilie n unhorned bullock; mild person.
moister n moisture.
mollat n bridle bit; curb.
molligrant adj whining.
moloss adj loose.
molten v melt.
mon see **mun**.
Monanday n Monday.
mone v take notice of.
moneth n month.
monie, mony adj many.
moniefeet n centipede.
moniment n monument; laughing stock.
moniplied adj manifold.
moniplies npl tripe.
Mononday n Monday.
month o muins n eternity.
mony see **monie**.
moo see **mou**.
moodie adj brave.
moog n mug.
mool¹, moul n chilblain.
mool² n slipper.
mool³ n mould. • v crumble; **mool wi** dally with.
moolder v moulder.
mooldin n moulding.
moond n mound.
moose n mouse.
moose-fa n mousetrap.
moose wab n cobweb, spider's web.
moot¹, mute n hint; insinuation. • v insinuate; whisper; say; divulge; fritter.
moot², mout n moult. • v decay.
mooth¹ adj misty.
mooth² see **mou**.
moothie n mouth organ.
mootie adj parsimonious.
mootle v nibble.
morn n morrow, tomorrow.
mornin n morning.
morning n morning tipple.
morn's morn n tomorrow morning.
morn's nicht n tomorrow night.
morroch v soil.
mortal adj dead drunk.
mort-claith, mortcloth n pall.
mort-heid n death's head; turnip lantern.

moss *n* bog, marsh; moor; peat bog; swamp.

moss aik *n* bog oak.

moss-bummer *n* bittern.

moss-hag *n* peat working.

mossie *adj* boggy; swampy.

mosstrooper *n* bandit.

most *n* mast.

mosted *adj* crop-eared.

mote¹ *n* flaw.

mote² *n* embankment.

moth *adj* warm.

mothie *adj* unaired.

mou, moo, mooth *n* mouth; blade. • *v* mention; tell.

mou-ban *v* articulate.

moudie *see* **mowdie**.

moul *see* **mool¹**.

mounth *n* mountain.

moup *n* nibble.

mou-poke *n* nosebag.

mouser *n* moustache.

mout *see* **moot²**.

mouten *v* dissolve.

mouter *v* fret.

moutit *adj* reduced.

movir, mure *adj* mild.

mow *v* copulate.

mowar *n* mocker.

mow-bit *n* morsel.

mowch *n* spy.

mowdie, moudie *n* mole; mole-catcher.

mowdiehill *n* molehill.

mowdieskin *n* moleskin.

mowdieworp *n* mole.

mowdiewort *n* intriguer; recluse; slow-witted or underhand person.

mowe *n* dust.

mowp *v* nibble.

moy *adj* gentle.

moyen *n* foreknowledge; forewarning; prescience; mediation. • *v* induce; recommend.

moyt *adj* many.

mozie, mozy *adj* decayed.

muck *n* dung; clutter. • *v* shift dung; clean.

muckflee *n* dung-fly.

muckle *adj* great; big; large; mature; much; **muckle big** huge, vast. **muckle mou'd** wide-mouthed. • *adv* much.

muckle coat *n* overcoat.

muckle kirk *n* parish church.

mud *n* stud.

muddle *v* grub; overturn.

mudge¹ *n* motion; movement. • *v* shift; move.

mudge² *see* **midgie**.

mudgeons *npl* frownings.

mudgins *npl* movements.

mug, muggle *v* drizzle.

muggart *n* mugwort.

mugger *n* crockery seller.

muggy *adj* drizzly; tipsy.

muid *n* mood.

muild *n* soil.

muilder *v* putrefy.

muin¹ *n* goldcrest.

muin² *n* month; moon.

muir *n* heath, moorland; common.

muirburn *n* heath-burning.

muith *adj* oppressively hot; warm, misty.

mulberry *n* whitebeam.

muldes, mools *npl* dust.

mule *n* mould.

mulk *n/v* milk.

mulkin steel *n* milking stool.

mull¹ *n* headland.

mull² *n* canister.

mull³ *n* mill.

mull⁴ *n* lip.

muller *v* crumble.

mulock *n* crumb.

multi *n* high-rise flat.

mum¹ *n* mutterer.

mum² *adj* tingling from cold, numb.

mummie *v* mumble.

mump *v* mimic; shuffle, loaf; mope; mumble; mutter.

mumple *v* retch.

mun, mon *n* man.

munge *v* mumble.

munk *v* diminish.

munkrie *n* monastery.

munsie *adj* contemptible.

munt *n* mount. • *v* mount; adorn.

muntain *n* mountain.

muntin *n* trousseau.

munts *npl* fittings.

murdie-grups *n* belly-ache.

murgeon *n* grimace; murmur. • *v* grimace, mock.

murky *n* dark.
murl *v* disintegrate; pulverise.
murlie *n* small object.
murlin *n* fragment.
murmell *v* protest.
murmichan *n* bugbear.
murmuration *n* murmur.
murn *v* complain; mourn.
murning *n* mourning.
murnings *npl* mourning clothes.
murr *n* purr.
murther *n* murder. • murder; bedevil;
    persecute.
murtherer *n* killer, murderer.
musall, mussall *n* veil. • *v* veil.
mush *n* muttering.
musicker *n* musician.

musk *n* moss.
mussel scaup *n* mussel-bed.
must *n* mould.
mustart *n* mustard.
muster *v* talk volubly.
mutch *n* woman's headdress.
mutchit *n* brat.
mutchkin *n* pint.
mute *see* **moot**[1].
muther *n* great number.
muve *v* move.
myance *n* wages.
mynde *n* mine. • *v* undermine.
mype *v* talk too much.
myrkest *adj* rottenest.
mys *see* **miss**.
mystir *adj* necessary.

N

na[1] *conj* but; than.
na[2] *see* **nae**.
nab *n* peg; smart stroke.
nabal *adj* churlish; grasping. • *n* miser.
nacket *n* pert or precocious child; insig-
    nificant person.
nacketie, nackety *adj* compact.
nackit *adj* bare.
nadkin *n* bad smell.
nae, na *adj* no. • *pron* not any. • *adv* no;
    not; **nae bother** easily; **nae doot**
    doubtless; **nae ornar** unusually; **nae**
    place nowhere.
naebodie *pron* nobody.
nae-canny *adj* unnatural.
nae-fair *adj* unfair.
naegait *adv* in no way.
nae-in *adj* absent-minded; daydreaming.
nae-richt *adj* simple-minded.
nae see by *v* favour.
naet *n* nought.
naethin *n* nothing.
nae-weel *adj* unwell, indisposed.
nae-wicelik *adj* bizarre.
naffing *n* idle chat.
nag[1] *n* peg.
nag[2] *v* strike; taunt.
naig *n* horse.
nail *v* clinch.
nain *adj* own.

naipkin *n* handkerchief; napkin.
nairra-nebbit *adj* bigoted, prejudiced;
    sharp-nosed.
naistie *adj* nasty.
naither, naitherans, nather *conj* neither.
naitral *adj* natural.
naitur *n* nature.
nakit *adj* bare; naked, nude.
nam *v* seize hold of.
namecouth *adj* famous.
namelie, namely *adj* noted; notable; fa-
    mous.
nane *adj* no; none. • *pron* none; not any.
nap *n* milk vessel.
naperie *n* table linen.
naperie press *n* linen cupboard.
nappit *adj* ill-humoured.
nappy, nappie *adj* heady, foaming; tipsy.
    • *n* ale.
nar *adj* close, near. • *adv* near; nearly.
    • *conj* nor. • *prep* close by, near.
narby *adj* nearby.
narr *v* snarl.
narrer *adv/prep* nearer.
narrest *adv/prep* nearest.
narvis *adj* Norwegian.
na-say, nay-say *n* contradiction; denial;
    refusal; veto. • *v* deny; veto.
nash *v* prate.
nar-side *n* left side.

nat adv not.
natch n/v notch.
nate adj exact; neat; trim.
natheless adv notwithstanding.
nather see **naither**.
natter adj nagging. • v nag; rant.
nattle v nibble.
naturaill adj lawful.
natural philosophy n physics.
nauchle n dwarf.
naukie adj wheezing.
naur adj near.
nawiss adv nowadays.
nay-say see **na-say**.
ne¹ adv near.
ne² conj neither.
ne³ v neigh.
neaphle n trifle.
near adj niggardly. • adv almost; narrowly; nearly.
nearaboot prep near.
near cut n short cut.
near-gaun adj niggardly.
near-han, nearhand adj near, close; neighbouring.
neb n beak, bill; nose; face; nib; tip; pinpoint; projection; nosy person. • v pry.
nebbie adj nippy; nosy.
nebbit adj beaked.
nece n granddaughter.
necessar adj essential; necessary.
necessars npl necessaries.
necessitat v necessitate.
neck n collar. • v embrace.
neck-break n ruin.
ned n tearaway; yob.
nedeum n gnawing pain.
nedmist adv undermost.
neebor see **neibor**.
needcessitie n necessity; need.
needful adj indigent; needy.
neef n difficulty.
neemit n dinner.
neep n swede, turnip.
neep-cutter n turnip slicer.
neep-heid n blockhead.
neep-lantern n turnip lantern.
neepshaw n turnip top.
Ne'erday n New Year's Day; New Year gift.
neese v sneeze.

neeshin v be on heat.
neesing n sneezing.
neet n nit.
neet n nit; miser.
neeze n sneeze.
neff n nave; hand.
neffit n dwarf.
neffow v take in handfuls.
negleck n/v neglect.
neibour, neebor n neighbour; counterpart; bedfellow; mate; partner.
neibourheid n neighbourhood.
neibourlik adj neighbourly.
neibours adj much alike.
neich v approach.
neid n need.
neidforse n necessity.
neiffar see **niffer**.
neipert n neighbourliness.
neipsie adj prim.
neir, neyr n kidney.
neist adj next; nearest.
neithers prep notwithstanding.
neive see **nieve**.
nem n/v name.
nerby adv nearby.
nere hand adv nearly.
nere til prep close to.
nervish adj nervous.
ness, nes n bluff, headland, promontory.
nestie adj nasty. • v befoul, foul.
net n caul.
nether¹ adj lower; under.
nether² n adder.
nether end n backside.
nethmaist, nethmost adj lowest; undermost.
nettlie adj ill-humoured.
netty n wool-gatherer.
neuk n alcove, recess, corner; nook.
neukit adj crooked.
nevel, nevell n punch. • v pummel, punch.
nevelling n fisticuffs.
nevilstane n keystone.
nevin v name.
nevoy n grandson; great-grandson; nephew.
nevoy n nephew.
new¹ adv newly.
new² v curb.

newfangle n innovation.
new-farran adj newfangled, novel.
newin n novelty.
newings npl news.
newis, newous adj greedy for.
newlins adv newly, recently.
newmost adj nethermost.
newous see **newis**.
newse v talk over the news.
next adj next but one.
neyr see **neir**.
nib n nip; pinch; pencil-point. • v pinch.
nibbie n shepherd's crook.
nibbit n sandwich.
nice adj simple.
nice-gabbit adj faddish about food.
nicher v neigh, whinny.
nicht n night.
nichtingale n nightingale.
nicht mutch n nightcap.
nick v catch; cut off; drink heartily; snip.
nicket n small notch.
nickle n knuckle.
nicknackie adj skilful.
nicks, nix v set up a mark.
nickstick n tally.
nickum n scallywag.
nicky-tams n trouser ties below the knees made of string or leather.
nicniven n chief witch.
nidder v depress; pinch.
niddle v work uselessly with the fingers.
nidge n nudge.
nid-noddin adj dozing; nodding.
nidge v nudge; squeeze through.
nidgel n fat youth.
nief n female bondservant.
nieve, neive n fist.
nieveful n fistful.
nieves npl fisticuffs.
niffer, neiffar n barter; exchange. • v bargain; barter; exchange; trade.
niffnaffs npl trifles.
niggar n miser, niggard.
nimmle adj nimble.
nimness n neatness.
nineteent adj nineteenth.
nint adj ninth.
nip n pungency; pinch; notch; advantage; fragment; piece. • v cheat; steal; catch; constrict; smart.

nipcaik n secret eater.
nip-lug n acrimony; backbiting; squabbling.
nippers npl pincers.
nippit, nippie, nippy adj niggardly, cheese-paring, miserly, avaricious; brusque, bad-tempered; narrow-minded; terse; tight-fitting.
nippity adj jerky.
nippy-sweety n bitter person.
nipscart n mean person.
nirb n stunted thing.
nirl n crumb; dwarf. • shrink; diminish; pinch with cold.
nirled, nirlie adj stunted.
nit n nut.
nitch n bundle; notch.
nither[1] adv nether.
nither[2] v shrivel; be cold.
nitherie adj feeble-growing.
nithering adj biting.
nithert adj shrivelled.
nittles npl new horns.
niver, nivir adj never. • adv never; **niver heed** never mind.
nix see **nicks**.
nixie n water nymph.
nixt, nixtin adj next.
nizwise adj perceptive.
nizzlin adj miserly.
no adv not.
no-able adj unfit.
no-bad adj satisfactory.
nocht, nochtis n nothing; naught.
nochtie adj puny.
nock n notch; clock.
nocket n midday meal.
noddle n head; brain.
noddy n cab; coach.
nodge n/v nudge.
nog n knob; peg.
noggie n drinking cup.
noise v clown.
noisome, noyous adj noisy.
noit v beat.
noitled adj drunken.
noll n push. • v strike with the knuckles.
nolt, nout n black cattle.
nolt-hird n cattle herd.
noo adv now.
nooadays n nowadays.

noof, nuff *adj* neat.
noop *n* cloudberry.
nor[1] *adv/conj* than.
nor[2] *n* north.
no-richt *adj* abnormal; unwell.
norie *n* notion.
norlan *adj* northern.
norlander *n* northerner.
norlin *adj* northerly.
norlins *adv* northwards.
normost *adj* northernmost.
Norn *n* language of the Northern Isles.
northart *adj* northern.
northart *adv* northwards.
nosethirl *n* nostril.
nosewiss *adj* keen-smelling.
nost *n* noise; chatter.
note *v* use.
noteless *adj* unnoticed.
notour *adj* infamous, notorious.
nourice, nouris *n* nurse; foster-mother. *v* nourish.
noust *n* landing place.
nout *see* **nolt**.

now *n* top of the head.
no-weel *adj* ailing.
no-wise, no-wyse *adj* weak in the head; deranged.
nowmer *v* count.
nowt *n* nothing.
noy *v* annoy.
noyit *adj* vexed.
noyous *see* **noisome**.
nuce *adj* destitute.
nuff *see* **noof**.
nuin, nune *n* noon.
nummer *n/v* number.
numptie *n* nitwit.
nune *see* **nuin**.
nuse *v* knead.
nyaff *n* insignificant or pert person. • *v* yelp.
nyaffing *adj* idle; insignificant.
nyarr *v* fret.
nyatter *v* chatter.
nyle *n* navel.
nyse *v* beat; thump.
nyte *v* deny.

O

o, oan *prep* of; on.
oam *n* air, atmosphere; aroma; condensation; shimmer.
obefore *adv* before.
obeisance *n* subjection.
objeck *n* object; article. • *v* object.
object *n* witless person.
obleegement *n* favour; obligation.
obleis *v* bind; oblige.
obscure *adj* secret.
observe *n* observation, remark.
obset *v* repair.
obtemper *v* obey.
ochone *interj* alas.
ocht *n* ought. • *pron* anything.
ocker *n* usury.
ockerer *n* moneylender.
odds *n* consequence; change.
oder *conj* either.
odious *adj* excessive, intense.
odoure *n* nastiness.
odsman *n* chief arbiter.
oe, oo *n* grandchild.
o'er *see* **ower**.

offcome *n* apology.
offer *n* projecting bank.
off-faller *n* apostate.
offgoing *n* death.
offish *n* office.
offisher, officiar *n* officer; court official.
offset *n* recommendation.
ogart *n* pride.
ogertful *adj* squeamish.
olick *n* tusk.
olie *n* oil.
olight *adj* nimble.
oliphant *n* elephant.
olite *adj* ready.
omast *adv* uppermost.
on-beast *n* monster.
onbraw *adj* ugly.
on brede *adv* wide open.
oncome *n* approach, attack, development, progress.
oncost *n* overheads.
onder *adv* under.
onding *n* downpour; fall of snow; attack, onset, onslaught.

oneith *adj* uneasy. • *adv* with difficulty.

onfa *n* snowfall; coming on of night.

onfeel *adj* unpleasant.

onfrack *adj* lax.

on fur yersel *adj* independent.

ongae *n* progress.

ongauns *npl* behaviour, goings-on, happenings, procedure.

on-hanger *n* hanger-on.

on hecklepins *adj* anxious.

onie, ony *adj* any.

onie ane, onie yin *adj* anyone.

oniebodie *n* anybody.

onie gait *adv* in any place.

onie how, onie road *adv* anyhow.

oniething *pron* anything.

oniewey, onieways *adv* anyhow; anywhere.

onkennable *adj* unknowable.

onker *n* portion of land.

onlay *v* superimpose.

onless *conj* unless.

onlouping *n* mounting of a horse.

onlyf *adj* alive.

on-marrows *adj* sharing.

on-nettles *adj* uneasy.

on-past *adj* not having passed.

onpit *n* array, costume.

onsettin *adj* ugly. • *n* attack.

onstead *n* farm building.

ontak *n* job.

ontakkin *n* enterprise.

onter *v* rear.

on the road *adj* pregnant.

on till *adv* well nigh to.

ontray *v* betray.

ontron *n* evening meal.

onwaiting *n* attendance, service. • *adj* attending.

ony *see* **onie.**

oo¹ *n* wool.

oo² *n* oyster.

oo³ *v* woo.

oo⁴ *pron* we.

oo⁵ *see* **oe.**

ooen *adj* woollen.

oof *n* wolf.

oof-lookin *adj* stupid-looking.

ooglie *adj* ugly.

ooie *adj* woolly.

ook, oulk, owlk *n* week.

ooklie *adj* weekly.

ool¹ *n* owl.

ool² *v* bully, ill-treat.

oo-mill *n* tweed mill.

oop¹ *adv/prep* up.

oop², wup *v* bind.

oor¹ *n* hour.

oor² *pron* our.

oorie *adj* chilly, frozen, shivery; eerie, uncanny; miserable-looking; raw.

oorlich *adj* out of sorts.

oorsels *pron* ourselves.

oos *n* fluff.

oosie *adj* fluffy; furry.

ooslie *adj* slovenly.

oot *see* **out.**

ooth *n* value.

oowen *adj* woollen.

ooy *see* **ooie.**

open *n* gap, opening.

open tae *adj* available.

opo-pogo-eye *n* gobstopper.

oppone *v* oppose.

or *adv* before; rather than. • *conj* before, lest. • *prep* before.

oranger *n* orange.

ord *n* mountain ridge.

ordeen *v* destine; ordain.

orders *npl* paraphernalia.

ordinar, ornar *adj* ordinary; humdrum, routine.

ore *n* grace; favour.

oreeginal *adj* original. • *n* origin.

orf *n* puny individual.

orison *n* oration.

orlang *n* full year.

ornar *see* **ordinar.**

orp *v* fret.

orphant, orpheling *n* orphan.

orpit *adj* proud.

orra, orrow *adj* abnormal; eccentric, odd, quaint; irregular; miscellaneous; nondescript; spare, occasional; unemployed, unmatched; leftover.

orrals, orras, orrows, orts *npl* bits and pieces, odds and ends; leftovers, remains, scraps.

orraman *n* odd-jobs man.

ort *v* throw away.

orts *see* **orrals.**

oshen *n* mean person.

ostend v show.
ostleir n innkeeper.
ostrye n inn.
othir adj other.
oubit n caterpillar.
ouder n light haze.
ouer see **ower**.
oufdog n wolf-dog.
oughtlins adv any extent.
ougsome adj horrid.
oulk see **ook**.
our v awe.
ourlop see **owerloft**.
ouster see **oxter**.
out, oot adj outlying; outside. adv out; completely. • v turn out; expend, issue, divulge.
outa, oota, ootae, ooten adv/prep out of.
outaboot adj out of the way; outdoor. • adv out of doors.
outbearing adj bullying.
outbreaker n criminal.
outby, ootby adj out of doors, outlying. • adv outwards; outside. • n outskirts.
outca n cattle pasture.
outcast n quarrel.
outcome n emergence; end product; escape; produce; production; profit.
outcoming n exit.
outcuissen n outcast.
outerlie adj offshore.
outerlin n black sheep.
outfall n dispute.
outfield n unmanured arable land.
outforth adv henceforth.
outgait n exit.
outgang n exit; expense; outlay.
outganging n going out.
outgaun adj ebbing.
outgie n expenditure.
outherans adv either.
outish adj showy.
outlabour v exhaust (of soil).
outlak prep except.
outlan adj exotic; remote. • n outcast, alien; outlying land.
outlat n outlet.
outler n beast that remains outside.
outlin adj alien. • n foreigner; outlaw.
outly adv fully.
outmaist adj outermost.

outon adv by and by.
out ower adv over; **oot ower the lugs** adj absorbed.
outpit v emit; send out; throw out.
outrake n expedition.
outray v treat disgracefully.
outred v extricate; finish off.
outredding n rubbish.
outrel n alien; incomer; newcomer; stranger.
outricht adv outright.
outrig n array, costume, dress, garb.
outrinning n expiry.
outroom n outer room.
outset n arrangement, display, layout; beginning, publication.
outshot n pasture land; extension.
outspeckle n laughing stock.
outstrikin n eruption.
out through adv right through.
outwaile n rubbish.
outwair v expend.
outwan adv outwards.
outward adj unkind; reserved.
outwark n outside work.
outwith adv beyond; opposed to; outside; outwards; abroad; away from. • prep beyond.
outwittins adv without knowing.
over see **ower**.
ovies npl overall.
ovven n oven.
owdience n audience.
owe adj owing.
ower, o'er, ouer, our, over adv excessively; over; too. • prep over. • v get over, recover from.
owerance n ability; dominion; supervision.
owerby adv just beside, over.
owercast adj overcast.
owercome n chorus; theme. • v overcome; recover.
owerend v turn over.
owerest adj highest.
owerfa'in n point of childbirth.
owerflete v overflow.
owergaffin adj clouded.
owergang, owergae v go over; give up; elapse; infest, overrun, dominate, exceed, surpass, oppress.

owerhaile, owerhale, owerharl v oppress; overtake; overlook.

owerhaun, owerhan n upper hand; victory.

owerheld, owerhede adv without distinction. • n average. • adj untidy, careless.

owerhelld v cover over.

owerhing v overhang.

owerhip v skip over.

owerhye v overtake.

owerin n remains.

oweritious adj careless; excessive. • adv too much.

owerlay n cravat, necktie.

owerleuk v overlook.

owerlie adj facile; unconventional. • adv carelessly, casually.

owerloft, ourlop n upper deck.

owerman, owersman n inspector; overseer; umpire; ruler.

owermeikle, owermuckle adj over much; too much.

owermest adv topmost.

owermonie adj too many.

owermuckle see owermeikle.

owernown n afternoon.

owerplus adj surplus.

owerpooer v overpower.

owerrad adj too hasty.

owerrate v overrate.

owerrax v overreach.

ower-richt adj awry.

owerrid v traverse.

owerrin v overrun.

owersailzie v build above a close.

owersee v oversee, supervise.

owerset v defeat; translate.

owersettin n translation.

owershot n excess.

owersile v cover.

owersman see owerman.

owerstap v overstep.

owertaen, owertane adj overcome, overtaken.

owertak v accomplish in a hurry; overtake.

owerthraw v overthrow.

owerthrough adv across the country.

owertill adv above, beyond.

owerturn n turnover.

owerword n frequently repeated word; refrain.

owg v shudder.

owlk see ook.

own v favour.

owrie adj chilly.

owrn v adorn.

owse[1] n ox.

owse[2] v bail.

owsen n oxen.

owt n/pron anything.

owthor n author.

oxter, ouster n armpit. • v elbow, jostle; take by the arm.

oxterful n armful.

oxter-pooch n breast pocket.

oyce n sea inlet.

oyl-dolie n olive oil.

oyne n oven.

oynte v anoint.

oyss n custom; use.

P

paak, paik v beat.

paal n post.

pabrod n pot lid.

Pace, Pasch, Pask n Easter.

pace[1] n peace.

pace[2] n weight.

Pace egg n Easter egg.

pack[1] adj familiar.

pack[2] n conspiracy.

pack[3] n property.

packald n pack.

packet n pannier.

packhouse n store.

packlie adv familiarly.

packman n pedlar.

paction n bargain, collusion, covenant.

pad n path, track. • v go on foot; trot along.

padder v tread.

paddist n footpad.

paddit adj well-trodden. • v trample down.

paddock n sledge.

Paddy's mairket n shambles, untidy place.

pade n toad.

paffle adj allotment.

paichled adj exhausted.

paid n path.

paiddle v paddle.

paidle n hoe. • v paddle; trample; tread down.

paidlin n ainless.

paik[1] n trick.

paik[2] see **paak**.

paikie n prostitute.

pail n hearse.

pallace n palace.

paile n canopy.

pailie adj deformed.

pailin n paling.

painch, pench n abdomen, belly; paunch.

painches n bowels; entrails; tripe.

pains n rheumatism.

paintrie n painting.

paip[1] n pip.

paip[2] n pope.

pair n set.

paircel n group.

paircel n parcel. • v parcel.

pairish n parish.

pairk n park.

pairl n pearl.

pair o cairds n pack of cards.

pairt n part; quota. • v part; sever; share.

pairtie n party.

pairtless adj free from.

pairtlie adj partly.

pairtner n partner.

pairtsay n joint venture.

pais n retribution.

paithment n pasture; pavement.

paitrick n partridge.

palaver n claptrap; idle chatter; ostentatious behaviour.

palaverin adj ostentatious.

pale v cut into.

palie adj pallid.

pall[1] n bollard; pillar, pole.

pall[2] v baffle, frustrate.

pall[3] v strike with the fore-hooves.

pallach n porpoise.

pallet n ball, globe; float.

palmander n pomander.

palmer v straggle from place to place.

paltrie n trash.

palyard n lecher.

pam n knave.

pan[1] n cranium, skull.

pan[2] n valance.

pan[3] v match.

panash n panache.

pand n pledge; pawn.

pander v drift, trail from place to place.

pandit adj pawned.

pan drop n mint imperial.

pandrous n pimp.

pandy n stroke of the tawse on the hand.

pane n fine cloth.

panel n accused, defendant; prisoner; dock (of court).

pang adj full. •v cram; throng.

panged adj compressed.

pangful adj crammed.

panst adj cured.

pantener adj rascally.

pantoun n slipper.

pant-well n covered well.

pap[1] n woman's breast.

pap[2] n sea anemone.

pap[3] v move about quickly; shoot.

pap[4], **pawp** v beat; dab.

pape see **paip**.

papingo n parrot.

pap-milk n breast-milk.

pap o the hass n uvula.

pappant adj wealthy.

papple v bubble up.

par v fail.

paraffin n get-up.

parafling n evasion.

paraleese v paralyse.

paraleesis n paralysis.

parawd n parade, procession.

parbrake v puke.

pare v impair.

pareeshioner n parishioner.

parigal adj equal.

parische adj from Paris.

park[1] n field, open ground; wood.

park[2] v rear.

parkie n park-keeper.

parle n speech.

parpane *n* wall, partition.

parrach *v* crowd together.

parritch *n* porridge.

parritch-time *n* breakfast hour.

parroch *n* paddock.

parrock *v* shut up.

parry *v* equivocate.

partan *n* sea crab.

parteeclar *adj* particular, exceptional; hygienic • *adv* particularly. • *n* confidential.

parteetion *n* partition.

particularity *n* detail, idiosyncrasy.

partnerie *n* partnership.

partrick *n* partridge.

Pasch, Pask *see* **Pace.**

pass[1] *n* aisle; pace; team.

pass[2] *v* forgive, pardon.

passage *n* corridor.

passments *n* braid.

pass-ower *n* omission.

past a *adj* beyond belief; intolerable.

pastance *n* pastime.

paster *n* pasture.

past mendin *adj* incorrigible; irreparable.

pat *n* pot.

pat-bool *n* pot handle.

pate *n* peat.

patent *adj* ready.

pat-fit *n* pot-leg.

pathlins *adv* by a steep path.

patience *n* passion.

patientful *adj* submissive; long-suffering.

patter[1] *v* beat down, trample.

patter[2] *v* move quickly; repeat in a low voice.

pattle *n* ploughman's stick.

pattren, pattron *n* pattern.

pauchle *n* swindle. • *v* embezzle; pilfer.

pauchtie *adj* haughty, self-important; saucy.

pauge *v* prance.

paukie *see* **pawky.**

paulie *adj* feeble.

paut *v* stamp menacingly; kick.

paveelion *n* pavilion.

pavie *n* lively motion.

paw *n* pa, dad.

pawis *n* parts in music.

pawk *n* wile.

pawkery *n* cunning, guile.

pawkie[1] *n* woollen mitten.

pawkie[2]**, pawky, paukie** *adj* astute, roguish, shrewd; humorous, flirtatious. • *n* flirtation.

pawmer *n* palm tree.

pawn[1] *n* pawnshop.

pawn[2] *n* peacock.

pawn[3] *v* foist.

pawnd *n/v* pawn.

pawp *see* **pap**[3].

pawrent *n* parent.

pawt *v* finger; paw.

pay *v* satisfy; drub.

paycock *n* peacock.

paye *n* paving.

payment *n* pavement.

payne[1] *adj* pagan.

payne[2] *v* be at pains.

paysie *n* peahen.

peak *v* squeak.

peakit *adj* peaky.

peanie *n* hen turkey.

pearie *n* humming top.

pearl *v* purl.

pearlin *n* pearlstring.

pearlins *n* lace.

pea-splittin *adj* petty.

peat bree *n* peaty water.

peat-caster *n* peat-cutter.

peat-castin *v* peat-cutting.

peat-corn *n* peat dust.

peat-creel *n* peat basket.

peat-hag *n* peat working.

peat lowe *n* peat fire.

peat moss *n* peat bog.

peat-pat *n* peat trench.

peat-reek *n* peat smoke.

pech, pechle *n* panting breath. • *v* breathe; gasp, puff and pant.

pechan *n* stomach.

pechie *adj* asthmatic, breathless.

pechts *npl* Picts.

pedder *n* pedlar.

pee *v* urinate, soak by urination.

peeble *n* pebble.

peecifee *v* pacify.

peedie *adj* little, tiny.

peeins *n* urine.

peek *n/v* cheep.

peel¹, peil *n* palisade, stockade.
peel² *n* pill.
peel³ *n* pool.
peel⁴ *v* equal.
peeled egg *n* windfall.
peelie *adj* thin.
peelie-wallie, peely-wally *adj* colourless, pale, sickly-looking.
peel-ringe *n* skinflint.
peen¹ *n* apex; peak; pin; hammer point. • *v* pin.
peen² *n* pane.
peenge *v* complain; pine.
peenie, pinnie *n* apron, pinafore.
peep *see* **pepe**.
peepy-show *n* cinema.
peer¹ *n* pear.
peer² *v* equal.
peerie *adj* sharp-looking; timid; small.
peerie heel *n* stiletto heel.
peerieweerie, peeriewirrie *adj* minute, very small.
peesie-weesie *adj* sharp-featured.
peesweep, peewee, peeweet *n* lapwing; peewit.
pee-the-bed *n* dandelion.
peetifu *adj* pitiable.
peever *v* piss; wet.
peevers *npl* hopscotch.
pegil *n* dirty housework.
peg off *v* go off.
pegrall *adj* paltry.
peifer *v* whimper.
peikthank *adj* ungrateful.
peil *see* **peel¹**.
peild *adj* bald.
peilour *n* thief.
peisled, pyslit *adj* comfortably off.
pelcher *n* mullet.
pell *n* soured buttermilk.
pellet *n* pelt.
pellock¹ *n* bullet.
pellock² *n* porpoise.
peltrie *adj* trashy.
pen¹ *n* conical hill.
pen² *n* plume, quill; stalk, stem.
penceful' *adj* conceited.
pench *see* **painch**.
pend *n* arch; covered entryway; vaulted passageway.
pendit *adj* arched.

pendle *n* pendant; earring; pendulum.
penge *v* droop.
penkle *n* rag, fragment.
penny-bridal *n* wedding where the guests pay for the entertainment.
penny-fee *n* earnings.
penny-pig *n* piggy-bank.
penny-wheep *n* small beer.
penseful *adj* pensive; wistful.
pensie *adj* pompous, self-important; responsible.
pent *n* paint. • *n* paint; paintwork.
pentit *adj* painted.
pep *n* cherry-stone.
pepe, peep *n* chirping.
perdue *adj* driven to extremes.
perdurabil *adj* lasting.
perfit, perfite *adj* perfect. • *adv* perfectly. • *v* consummate; finish.
perish *v* dissipate; polish off.
perite *adj* skilled.
perjink *adj* fastidious, prim. • *adv* fastidiously, primly.
perk *n* clothes rail.
perlicket *n* scrap.
perlie *n* little finger.
permusted *adj* scented.
perneurious *adj* scrupulous.
pernickitie, pernickety *adj* cantankerous; touchy; precise in little things.
perpen, perple, perplin *n* partition.
perr *n* pair.
perrakit *n* chattering child.
pershittie *adj* precise.
persil *n* parsley.
perskeet *adj* unappreciative.
pest *n* plague. • *v* pester; plague.
pet¹ *v* anger; take offence.
pet², pettle *v* fondle.
peugh *interj* pshaw!
peughle *v* try feebly to do something.
peuther *v* canvass; solicit.
pewl *n* complaint. • *v* complain; **pewl at** pick at (food).
pewther *n* pewter.
pewtherer *n* worker in pewter.
pey¹ *n* pay. • *v* pay for; remunerate.
pey² *n* pea.
pey³ *n* beating, punishment. • *v* punish.
pey bree *n* pea soup.
peyne *v* forge.

peyzart *adj* miserly.

philabeg *n* kilt.

photie *n* photograph.

phrase, phraise *v* wheedle, talk up. • *n* cant; delusion; gush.

phrasie *adj* effusive, fulsome, gushing.

pibroch *n* bagpipe music.

picher *n* pickle.

picht *n* pith, force.

pick¹ *n* pitch, bitumen.

pick² *v* pitch, hurl.

pick³ *v* peck.

picken *adj* pungent.

pickerel *n* dunlin.

picket *adj* shrunken.

picket weer *n* barbed wire.

pickie-fingered *adj* thievish.

pickle¹ *see* **puckle**.

pickle² *v* commit small theft.

pickman *n* miner.

pickstaff *n* pike.

pick-thank *adj* ungrateful.

picter *n* picture.

picter hoose *n* cinema.

pie, pye *v* pry.

piece¹ *n* sandwich, packed lunch.

piece² *n* space.

piece box *n* packed lunch box.

piece break *n* tea break.

pie-hole *n* eyelet.

pig *n* earthenware pitcher; moneybox.

piggerie *n* earthenware pottery.

pight *adj* pierced.

pikary *n* pilfering.

pike *n* pick. • *v* pick, gather; spike.

pikie *adj* barbed, spiked.

pik-mirk *adj* pitch dark.

pilch *adj* thick.

pile¹ *n* blade.

pile² *v* propel.

pilget *v* quarrel.

pilgrimer *n* pilgrim.

pilin *n* fence.

pilk *v* peel, shell, husk.

pillions *npl* rags.

pilliwinks *npl* thumbscrews.

pillowbere *n* pillowcase.

pilyie *v* pillage.

pinch *v* lever.

pinchers *npl* pincers, pliers, tweezers.

pine *n* affliction, suffering.

piner *n* labourer.

pingle *v* strive.

pingle-pan *n* pan.

pinglin, pingling *adj* meticulous, toilsome. • *n* difficulty.

pink¹ *v* trickle, drip, splash.

pink² *n* primrose.

pinkie *n* little finger.

pin leg *n* wooden leg.

pinner *n* elaborate headdress.

pinnie *see* **peenie**.

pinnit *adj* suffering from diarrhoea.

pint *n/v* point.

pintit *adj* punctilious; punctual.

pintitlie, pintitly *adv* accurately; punctiliously; punctually.

pintle *n* penis.

pint-stoup *n* two-quart measure.

pipe¹ *n* acorn.

pipe² *n/v* flute.

pipe major, pipie *n* pipe-band leader.

pipe-riper *n* pipe cleaner.

piper's news *n* old news.

pipes *n* bagpipes.

pippen *n* doll, puppet.

pirl *n/v* coil, curl, eddy. • *v* roll; stir with a long rod; twirl.

pirlicue *n* conclusion.

pirlie *adj* crisp; curling, curly.

pirlie-pig *n* piggy-bank.

pirn *n* bobbin, reel.

pirr¹ *n* tern.

pirr² *v* flow; ooze out.

pirrie *adj* neat.

pirzie *adj* conceited.

pish *n* piss, urine. • *v* piss, urinate; **pish doon** *v* rain.

pish-pot *n* chamberpot.

Piskie *n/adj* Episcopalian.

piskie *adj* dry.

pit¹ *n* colliery; dungeon.

pit² *v* put; **pit aboot** disconcert, distress; **pit aff** waste time; **pit airms an legs tae** embellish; **pit at** proceed against, prosecute; **pit by** lay aside; make do; **pit doon** murder; **pit fae** prevent, put off; **pit in yer spuin** interfere; **pit on** impress; **pit oo ane's ee** supplant; **pit ower** achieve; consume; defer; survive; sustain; swallow; **pit tae yer haun** help; **pit the brain asteep** meditate; **pit**

the heid on head-butt; **pit throu hauns**
investigate; **pit throu hauns o deal**
with.

pital n rabble.

pit bing n pit heap.

pit-mirk adj pitch-dark.

pit-on n insincerity, pretence.

pitten-on adj affected, insincere.

pixie n fairy.

pizen n poison.

place n estate; **place o haud** retreat.

plack n small coin.

placket n placard.

plackless adj moneyless.

plagium n kidnapping.

plaid, plaidie n Highland outer dress.

plaidin n tartan.

plaig n toy.

plain adj blatant.

plaine v show.

plainen n linen.

plain loaf n batch loaf.

plainstane n pavement.

plaint n protest.

plaister n plaster. • v plaster; mess about.

plane tree n sycamore.

plank n/v cache. • v dump.

plantin n copse, grove, plantation, woodland.

plash¹ n plaice.

plash² n/v splash. • v cascade.

plashin adj soaking, squelching.

plat¹, plet adj due, direct.

plat² adj flat. • n cowpat.

plat³ n landing.

platch v tread noisily.

play¹ n pastime, sport. • v amuse oneself;
play fair hornie play fair; **play the rig
wi** hoax; **play wallop** tumble over.

play² v boil hard.

play-feir n playfellow.

playock n plaything, toy.

playrife adj playful.

plea n enmity; discord.

pleat n pigtail, plait.

plede, plead v debate; quarrel.

pledge v toast.

pleen n objection.

pleep¹ n redshank.

pleep² v peep.

pleesure n pleasure. • v content, satisfy.

plenish v furnish, supply.

plenishin, plenishings, plenishment n
furniture, furnishings.

plenteous adj complaining.

plenty adj many. • n proportion.

plep n something weak and feeble.

pleppit adj creased.

plesance n pleasure.

plet¹ n/v plait; pleat.

plet², pletten v rivet.

plet³ see **plat¹**.

plettie n balcony.

plettiestanes npl pavement.

pletty n landing.

pleuch, pleugh n/v plough.

pleuchie, pleughie n ploughman.

pleuch-sock n ploughshare.

pleuch-stilt n plough-handle.

pleugh see **pleuch**.

plinkin adj tinkling.

pliskie n plight; practical joke.

plit n turned earth.

pliver n plover.

plodge v squelch.

plook, plouk, pluke n pustule, pimple.

plookie adj pimpled.

ploom n plum.

ploom damas n prune.

plore v play in mud.

plot n swelter. • v pluck; scald; swelter.

plotcock n devil.

plot-het adj scalding.

plottie n punch, hot drink.

plottit adj meagre; plucked-looking.

plouk see **plook**.

ploussie adj plump.

plout v splash.

plouter v flounder, splash noisily.

plowd n waddle.

plowp n/v plop.

plowt¹ n clodhopper.

plowt² n plunge. • v plunge; dump.

plowt³ n potted meat.

plowter n muddy place. • v dabble, potter; wade.

plowterie adj rainy, showery.

ploy n action; escapade; business, enterprise, scheme, undertaking.

pludisome adj dogged.

pluff¹ n blast; puff. • v puff out; blast; explode; set on fire.

pluff² *n* pad.

pluffie *adj* fleshy, puffy.

plug *n* charge.

pluke *see* **plook**.

plum *n* deep river pool.

plumb *adj* plump.

plummer *n* pommel.

plump *n* cloudburst; cluster; plopping noise. • *v* rain.

plumper *n* plunger.

plumrock *n* primrose.

plunk¹ *n* popping noise. • *v* put down, set down.

plunk² *v* play truant; shirk.

plunker *n* truant.

ply¹ *n* plight, state.

ply² *n* fold, strand. • *adj* thickness.

plype *n* plunge. • *v* plunge; paddle; tumble in water.

poach *v* mess about; mush.

pock *see* **poke**.

pockarred *adj* pock-marked, scarred.

pockmantie *n* travelling bag.

podle *n* tadpole.

poffle *n* small piece of land; farm.

poind *n* useless person.

poinding *n* seizure.

poiner *n* digger of turves.

poinies *npl* gloves.

point *n* state of the body.

pointed *adj* exact.

pointit *adj* exacting.

poisonable *adj* poisonous.

poist *v* gorge.

poke, pock *n* bag; paper bag; pouch.

pokey hat *n* ice-cream cone.

poldach *n* flood plain, marshy ground by a river.

policy, policies *n* laid-out parkland around a house.

polis *n* police.

polisman *n* policeman.

polist *adj* artful.

polypoke *n* polythene bag.

pome *n* poem.

pomp *v* pump.

poo *n* crab.

pooch *n* pouch; pocket; finances. • *v* pocket.

poochle *adj* self-assured, self-confident.

pooer *n* power.

pook, puik *v* pull; pluck; strip.

pookit *adj* plucked; lean; threadbare.

pooks *npl* new feathers; downy feathers.

poop *n* turd.

poopit *n* pulpit.

poor *n* deluge. • *v* pour.

poorfae *adj* powerful.

poorie *n* cream/milk jug; oilcan.

poorins *npl* dregs.

poortith *n* poverty.

pooshin *n*/*v* poison.

pooshinable *adj* unpleasant.

pooshinous *adj* poisonous.

poot *v* pout.

poother *n*/*v* powder.

pootherie *adj* powdery.

pootie *adj* miserly.

pootrie *n* poultry.

Pope's eye *n* rump steak.

popil *n* poplar.

pople *v* bubble up; boil.

pork *n* prod; • *v* prod; gore.

porkepik *n* porcupine.

porridge *n* oatmeal boiled in water.

port¹ *n* gateway.

port² *n* tune.

portie *n* mien; behaviour.

pose *v* deposit.

posie *n* garland.

posnett *n* moneybag, skillet.

poss, pouss *v* push.

postie *n* postman.

post-sick *adj* bedridden.

pot, pott *n* pit; pond.

potch *v* toy with one's food.

potent *adj* wealthy.

poticary *n* pharmacist.

pott *see* **pot**.

potted heid, potted hoch *n* potted meat.

potterlowe *n* pulp.

pottie *n* putty; small pot.

pottle *adj* potful.

pou *n*/*v* pull. • *v* extract.

pouder, pouther *n* dust; powder.

poullie *n* pullet.

pound *n* pond; reservoir.

pounse *v* carve; emboss.

poupit *n* pulpit.

pour *n* rainfall.

pourie *n* jug.

pousie *n* hare; cat.

pouss¹ *n* push.

pouss² *see* **poss.**

poust *n* strength.

pouster *n* situation.

poustie *n* authority; control.

pout¹ *n* young partridge or fowl.

pout² *v* poke; start up.

pouter *v* rummage blindly.

pouther *see* **pouder.**

pouzle *v* search about; puzzle.

povereese *v* impoverish.

povie *adj* snug.

pow *v* head, poll.

powart *n* tadpole.

powe¹ *n* pothole.

powe² *n* skull.

powk *n/v* poke.

powl *n* crutch; pole.

pownie *n* pony.

powsowdie *n* mash; sheep's-head broth.

poy *v* work hard.

poyntal *n* pointed dagger.

praan *n* prawn.

praicious *adj* precious.

praisent *n* gift, present.

pran, prann *v* compress, pulp, hurt.

prang *n* prong.

prap *n/v* prop, support. • *n* target.

prat *n* trick. • *v* trick; **prat wi** tamper.

pratful *adj* tricksy.

prattick *see* **prottick.**

preachin *n* sermon, service.

pree *v* taste; experience; **pree the lips o** kiss.

preein *adj* tasting, sample.

preek *v* be well turned-out.

preen *n* pin; fishing hook. • *v* pin.

preenack *n* pine needle.

preen-cod *n* pincushion.

preenheid, preinheid *n* pinhead.

preese *n/v* press.

prek, prik *v* gallop.

prent *n/v* print.

prentar, prenter *n* printer.

prent-buik *n* printed book.

prentice *n/v* apprentice.

prescribe *v* lapse.

prescription *n* lapse.

preser *v* preserve.

preses, presies *n* president; spokesman; chairperson.

press *n* cabinet, cupboard.

prest *adj* ready.

prestable *adj* enforceable; payable; practicable.

pretense *n* plan.

pretty, protty, proty *adj* elegant; manly; handsome. • *v* neatly made.

pretty dancers *n* northern lights.

prevade *v* neglect.

preve *adv* privately.

prevene *v* come before.

preves *npl* proofs.

prick¹ *n* wooden skewer.

prick² *v* stampede.

prickie *adj* prickly.

prick-ma-dentie *adj* affected, over-refined.

prideful *adj* snobbish, vain, arrogant.

prie *v* taste; **prie one's mou'** take a kiss.

prif *v* entreat.

prig *v* bargain, haggle, plead.

priggin *adj* pleading.

prik *see* **prek.**

prime¹ *v* drink heavily.

prime¹ *v* fill.

primp *n* prig. • *v* take on prudish airs.

primpie *adj* dressy.

primpit *adj* affected, elaborate.

primsie *adj* demure, old-maidish.

principal *n* original.

prink *v* deck; titivate.

prinkie¹ *adj* flamboyant.

prinkle² *npl* pins and needles. • *v* prickle.

prison *v* imprison.

privative *adj* exclusive.

privie, privy *n* privet.

process *npl* legal papers.

proclaim *v* publish.

procurator fiscal *n* prosecutor.

prod¹ *n* injection; prick.

prod² *n* waster.

proddle *v* prick.

production *n* exhibit.

profession *n* sect.

profit *n* yield.

profite *adj* proficient.

prog *n/v* poke, prick, prod; jab; puncture.

progger *n* pricker.

projeck *n/v* project.

proker *n* poker.

pron *n* bran.

prood see **proud**.
proop v fart.
prop n cork, plug, stopper.
propone v propose, suggest.
prospect n spyglass.
pross v show off.
prossie adj neat.
protest v demand.
prottick, prattick n undertaking, practice; dodge.
protty, proty see **pretty**.
proud, prood adj pleased; proud; higher, sticking out.
proudness n pride; swollenness.
provoke n pest.
provokshin n provocation; temptation.
provost n civic leader, mayor.
prowan n provender.
pruif n proof.
pruive v prove; test, try.
pry n trash.
ptarmigan n white grouse.
pu v pull.
public n inn.
publis v confiscate.
publisht adj plump.
pucker n perplexity.
puckle, pickle n small amount; grain of corn; granule.
puddin n pudding.
puddle v muddle along.
puddock n frog; toad.
puddock cruddles npl frogspawn.
puddock stuil n mushroom; toadstool; fungus.
pudge n small house.
pudget n short fat person.
pudgie adj podgy.
pudick adj chaste.
pug n monkey.
puggie¹ n kitty; fruit machine.
puggie² n monkey.
puggie nut n peanut.
puidge n hovel; hut, shed.
puik see **pook**.
puil n pool.
puir adj poor.
puir-hoose n workhouse.
puir-sowl n poor fellow.
puirtith n poverty.
puist¹ adj snug.

puist² v criticise.
pul n/v pull.
pulder n powder.
pule n puff of smoke. • v puff out smoke.
pullie n turkey.
pultie n short knife.
pump v fart.
pumphal v pen.
pumpin n flatulence.
pun¹, pund n pound.
pun² v pound.
punce n thrust.
punct n point.
pund¹ v impound.
pund² see **pun¹**.
pundar n man in charge of impounding stray cattle.
punler n forester.
punye, punge v sting; pierce.
puppie n poppy.
puppie show n puppet show.
purfelt adj wheezing.
purk n pork.
purl¹ n dried cow dung.
purl² n seam stitch in knitting.
purlicue n flourish in writing.
purlicues npl whims, fancies.
purpie n purple.
purpie-fever n typhus.
purpir adj purple.
purpose adj neat, exact. • n efficiency; tidiness.
purposelik adj businesslike, methodical.
pursue v litigate; persecute.
pursuer n plaintiff.
pursy adj short and stout.
puslick n dried cowpat.
putt¹ n jetty.
putt², put n recoil. • v pulsate; throw a heavy stone.
putt an row n exertion.
putt-stane n keystone.
pyat n magpie.
pyat-horse n piebald horse.
pye see **pie**.
pyke n prickle.
pykepurs n pickpocket.
pykit adj emaciated-looking.
pyle n javelin; arrow.
pyles npl grains.
pyne n pain.

pynit *adj* dried, shrunk.
pynt *v* paint, disguise.
pyotie *adj* piebald.

pyslit *see* **peisled**.
pyster *v* hoard.

Q

quaich *n* drinking bowl.
quaid *adj* evil.
quaif *n* coif, headdress.
quaik *v* quack; wheeze.
quailye *n* squall.
quair *n* book, literary work.
quaist *n* rogue.
quait *see* **quate**.
quak *v* quake.
qual *n/adj* twelve.
qualifee *v* qualify.
qualify *v* authenticate.
qualim *n* ruin.
quall *v* abate.
quantite *n* size.
quarnelt *adj* angled.
quarran *n* leather shoe.
quarrel¹ *n* stone quarry.
quarrel² *v* reprove.
quart *n* gallon.
quarter *n* quarter pound.
quasi-delict *n* negligent action.
quate, quat, quait *adj* calm, quiet; docile; private; free. • *adv* quietly. • *n* quiet.
quatelike *adj* calmly.
quaten *v* quieten.
quave *v* zigzag downwards.
quaw *n* marsh.
quay *imper* come away!
quean, queyn, quine *n* young woman.
queed *n* tub.
queel *v* cool.
queem *v* fit exactly.
queemly *adv* neatly.
queen o the meedow *n* meadowsweet.
queer *see* **queir**.
queerie *n* odd person.
queers *npl* odd news.
queet¹ *n* ankle.
queet² *n* guillemot.
queir, queer *n* choir; chorus; chancel.
queit *n* coot.
quelt *see* **kilt**.
quenry *n* abundance of bad women.

quent, queynt *n* wile. • *adj* strange; cunning.
querd *n* fish tub.
quern *n* fowl's gizzard.
quernell *adj* square.
quernie *adj* granular, granulated.
querty, quirty *adj* lively.
quey *n* young cow.
queyn *see* **quean**.
queynt *see* **quent**.
quha *pron* who.
quhaip *n* goblin.
quham *n* dale; hollow.
quhaye *n* whey.
quheef *n* fife.
quhich *v* whizz.
quhid *v* stir.
quhile *adv* at times; formerly.
quhilk *pron* which; who.
quhilom *adv* some time ago.
quhitter *v* warble.
quhow *adv* how.
quhoyne *adj* few.
quhryne *v* squeak.
quhult *n* something large.
quhyte *adj* hypocritical.
quibow *n* tree branch.
quicken *n* couch-grass.
quickenin *n* fermenting ale.
quidder *n* womb.
quietlik *adj* quiet.
quig *n* mix-up.
quile *v* rake.
quine *see* **quean**.
quinkins *npl* liquid refuse, scum.
quirk *n/v* trick.
quirkie *adj* complex, resourceful, tricky.
quirklum *n* puzzle.
quirty *see* **querty**.
quisching *n* cushion.
quitchie *adj* very hot.
quite *adj* innocent.
quither *v* quiver.
quitout *adj* cleared of debt.

quittance *n* explanation, receipt.
quo, quod *adj* said.
quoab *n* reward.
quotha *interj* forsooth.

quoy *n* enclosed land, pen.
quytcleme *v* renounce.
quyte *v* skate.

R

ra *n* roe.
raand *n* stain.
raaze *v* madden.
rabate *v* abate.
rabble *v* mob; jabber away.
rabil *n* disorderly crowd.
race *n* run.
racer *n* low woman.
rache *n* tracker dog.
rachlie *adj* dirty.
rachlin *adj* harebrained.
rachter *n* rafter.
rack¹ *n* dislocation; curling course. • *v* stretch.
rack² *n* shock. • *v* clear up.
rack³, raik *v* reckon; care.
rackel, rackle *adj* rash.
racket¹ *n* rocket.
racket² *n* stroke, blow.
rackie *adj* over-anxious.
rackin *adj* driving.
rackle¹ *n* clank; chain.
rackle² *see* **rackel**.
rackle-handit *adj* careless.
reckless *adj* reckless.
recklessly *adv* recklessly.
rackon *v* fancy; reckon.
rackonin *n* reckoning.
rad, rade *adj* afraid.
raddour *n* fear.
rade¹ *n* sea road.
rade² *see* **rad**.
rade³ *adv* rather.
radge *adj* furious; livid; obstreperous.
radgie *adj* lustful; randy.
radote *v* rave.
radoun *v* return.
rae¹ *n* cattle pen.
rae² *n* roe.
rael *adj* authentic; forthright; real.
raep *v* reap.
raff¹ *n* flying shower.
raff² *n* abundance.
raffan *adj* merry.

raffie *adj* flourishing; quick-growing; coarse.
raft *n* rafter.
rag *n* runt.
rag *v* rally.
rag *v* reproach.
ragabash, ragabuss *n* person dressed in rags, tatterdemalion.
rag-faugh, rag-fallow *n* ground prepared for cultivation.
ragger *n* ragman.
raggit *adj* ragged.
raggle¹ *n/v* wrangle.
raggle² *v* ruffle.
ragglish *adj* erratic.
ragman *n* long piece of script.
ragweed *n* ragwort.
raible *v* gabble.
raicent *adj* recent.
raichie *n* scolding. • *v* scold.
raid *n* foray.
raif *n* robbery.
raiglar *adj* regular.
raik¹ *n* helping; journey; rate, speed. • *v* journey; rove.
raik² *see* **rack³**.
rail-e'ed *adj* wall-eyed.
raill *v* jest.
raim *n* cream.
raing¹ *n* circle; ring.
raing² *n* row. • *v* line up.
rainie *v* reiterate.
raip *n* rope; clothes line.
rair *n/v* roar.
raird, reard *v* bleat.
raise, raize *v* excite; madden; enrage; inflame; infuriate.
raised *adj* overexcited.
raith *n* quarter of a year.
raither *adv* quite; rather.
raition *n/v* ration.
raivel, reavel *n* tangle. • *v* bemuse; nonplus; outwit.
raivelt *adj* incoherent, muddled; tangled.

raivlins *npl* twisted threads.
raize *see* **raise**.
rak, rawk *n* eye-rheum; scum.
rake[1] *n* accumulation. • *v* glean.
rake[2] *n* wreck.
rakles *adj* heedless.
rale *v* gush out.
ralliach *adj* choppy.
rallion *n* ragged fellow.
rally *n/v* bunch.
ramagiechan *n* large, bony person; trickster.
ramballiach, rambaleugh *adj* stormy; tempestuous.
rambarre *v* repulse.
rambusk *adj* robust.
rame *n* phrase. • *v* recite; rave; shout.
ramfeezlement *n* disorder.
ramforse *v* strengthen.
ramgunshoch, rumgunshoch *adj* rugged.
rammage *adj* rash; rough.
rammaged *adj* deliriously drunk.
rammel *adj* branchy. • *n* small branches.
rammie *n* brawl; disturbance; ructions.
rammish *adj* enraged. • *v* storm about.
rammle *n* spree. • *v* ramble.
ramp[1] *adj* riotous; rank; strong.
ramp[2] *v* romp; sport; rage.
rampage *v* play.
rampageous *adj* furious.
ramplor *n* rambler; rover.
ramps *n* ramsons, wild garlic.
ramsh[1] *adj* rank.
ramsh[2] *v* guzzle.
ramshachled *adj* loose.
ramstam *adj* devil-may-care; obstreperous; precipitate; rash. • *adv* rashly; rudely; slapdash. • *n* reckless person.
ramstamphish *adj* hasty.
ramstougar *adj* hard; quarrelsome.
ran *n* strip.
rance *n* prop. • *v* brace; prop up; fill.
rancel *v* search for stolen goods.
rancie *see* **ransie**.
rand *n* stripe.
rander *n* conformity; restraint; dripping. • *v* ramble in speech.
randers *npl* idle rumours.
randie *adj* aggressive; riotous. • *n* woman; loose or quarrelsome woman.

randit *adj* streaked; striped.
randon *v* flow straight.
randy *adj* belligerent; vagrant.
randy-beggar *n* threatening beggar.
rane *n* demand. • *v* rant; repeat; **rane doun** speak ill of.
rangale, rangel *n* rabble, mob; heap.
rank *adj* strong.
rannoch *n* bracken.
rannygill *adj* bold.
ransackle *v* ransack.
ransh, runsh *v* gobble.
ransie, rancie *adj* red, ruddy.
ransoun *n* ransom.
rant *n* frolic; song; romp. • *v* revel; romp.
ranter[1] *n* order; orderliness.
ranter[2] *n* rover.
ranter[3] *v* darn; sew.
rantin *adj* roisterous; uproarious; high-spirited.
rantle-tree *n* fireplace beam.
ranty *adj* cheerful; tipsy.
rap *adj* instant.
rap *n* cheat; rake.
rap *n* rape vegetable.
rap *v* drop; **rap on** bump against.
rap an stow *adv* root and branch.
rape *adv* hastily.
raploch, raplach, raplock *adj* common; crude; undistinguished; homespun. • *n* coarse cloth.
rapple *v* grow quickly, shoot up.
rapt *n* robbery; thievery.
rapture *n* paroxysm.
rare *v* roar.
rase *v* pluck.
rash[1] *n* rush; reed.
rash[2] *adj* agile.
rashen *adj* of rushes.
rasp *n* birthmark; mole; raspberry.
rat *n/v* scratch; wrinkle; rut; groove.
ratch *v* tear roughly away.
ratch't *adj* ragged.
rate[1], **ratt** *n* file of soldiers.
rate[2] *v* beat; flog.
rath *adj* savage-seeming.
ratt *see* **rate**[1].
rattle *n* crash; chatterbox; speech burr. • *v* crash; talk volubly; **rattle up** put together.
rattle-bag *n* rumourmonger.

ratton n rat.

ratton-fa n rat-trap.

rauchan n grey plaid.

rauchle adj (person) blunt; grim.

raucie, rausie adj coarse.

raucking n harsh squeaking.

raucle adj stern; uncouth; unrefined.

raugh v reach.

rauky adj misty.

raun n fish roe.

rauner n female salmon.

rausie see **raucie**.

rave¹ n dream.

rave² v rape.

ravel¹ n balustrade; parapet; railing.

ravel² v twist thread; wander in speech.

ravels npl ravelled threads.

raverie n delirium.

ravin adj ravenous.

raw¹ n row, line, file. • v align.

raw² adj damp and cold; undiluted.

rawk see **rak**.

rawly adj not fully grown.

rawmou'd adj beardless.

rawn¹ adj afraid.

rawn² n fish roe.

rax n sprain. • v stretch; extend; lengthen; reach out; crane the neck; sprain; **rax oot** stretch out; **rax ower** reach over; stretch over.

raxes npl andirons.

ray n song; military array. • v array.

razzor n razor.

reable adj legitimate.

read v interpret.

readily adv probably.

ready v cook; prepare.

reak v rig; deck; reach. • v deliver; reach.

real adj good; true. • adv exceptionally.

reale adj royal.

real Mackay n genuine article.

ream, reem, reme n cream. • v cream; skim; bubble over.

ream-cheese n cream cheese.

reamer n cream dish.

reamie adj creamy; frothing.

reamin-dish n skimming dish.

reard see **raird**.

reason n right; justice.

reavel see **raivel**.

rebaldy n vulgar talk.

rebellour n rebel.

rebig v rebuild.

rebook n/v rebuke.

reboond v belch.

rebouris adv contrary.

rebut, reboyt v repulse.

receipt n recipe.

reck n course.

recoll n reminiscence.

recourse v rescue.

rector n headmaster, principal.

recure n remedy.

recusant n refuser.

recuse v refuse.

redact v reduce.

redcap n fanged spectre.

redcoal n horseradish.

redd¹ n riddance; clearance; debris; waste, refuse. • v advise; explain; unravel; clear; arrange; put in order; rid; solve; free; vacate; **redd up** resolve.

redd² n spawn; spawning ground. • v spawn.

redder n mediator.

redd-handit adj neat.

redding, reddins n riddance; rescue.

reddour n dread.

redd-up adj tidied.

rede¹ n advice; voice. • v advise; explain; unravel; clear; discern; construe.

rede² n kind of fairy.

redland n ploughed soil.

redles adj confused.

redound v refund.

redschip n furniture; gear.

redsman n rubbish clearer.

ree¹ n enclosure; yard; hen coop; chicken run; ship dock.

ree² n small sieve, riddle. • v sieve, riddle.

reebald adj ribald.

reed conj lest.

reef n roof.

reefort n radish.

reeful adj rueful.

reegh n harbour; dock.

reek, reik n smoke; vapour. • v smoke; fume.

reekie adj smoke-filled.

reekit adj begrimed; acrid; smoke-covered; smoke-cured.

reel n circular movement; dance. • v roll.

reel-fit n club foot.

reel-rall adj topsy-turvy. • n chaos; shambles.

reem see ream.

reemis, reimis, remish n din; rumble.

reenge n range; rinse. • v bustle about; rinse; clear out; explore; forage; pace; range, roam.

reepin n lean creature.

reese[1] n strong breeze.

reese[2] n flattery. • v praise.

reesie adj breezy.

reesk n rushy grass; wasteland.

reesle n rustle. • v rustle; **reesle throu** rummage.

reest[1] n roost.

reest[2] v arrest; jib; stop short.

reestie adj recalcitrant.

reeve v talk volubly.

reevin adj blazing; excitable.

reeze v fart.

reezie adj light-headed; tipsy.

refer v defer; delay; hold over.

refuise n refusal. • v refuse.

regality n rights of jurisdiction granted by the crown.

regent n university professor.

regret n complaint.

reibie adj skinny.

reid adj/n red. • v redden.

reid Rab n robin.

reidsett adj placed in order.

reik see reek.

reimis see reemis.

reird see raird.

reises n brushwood.

reishlin adj rustling.

reist[1] n instep.

reist[2] v dry in the sun.

reithe adj keen.

reive, ryve v pillage, plunder, rob.

reiver n robber; bandit; raider.

rejag n smart reply.

remainder n remnant.

reme see ream.

remede, remeid n remedy; cure. • v remedy; cure; redress.

remembrie n remembrance.

rement v remember.

remish see reemis.

remorse v repent.

renchel[1] n tall thin person.

renchel[2] n/v cudgel.

rendal n land division.

renounce v surrender.

repayre v return.

repeat v refund; retrieve; call back.

repetition n repayment; restitution.

repey v reimburse, repay.

replait v try again.

replenish v refurbish, refurnish; renovate.

repree v reprove.

requare v require.

reset, resett v harbour; receive stolen goods or animals.

resetter n entertainer; fence, receiver of stolen goods.

residenter n resident.

resile v blench; flinch from; recoil; retract; withdraw.

resolve v bring to an end.

ressum n particle.

rest n remnant.

retiral n retirement.

retour n/v return.

revert v revive.

revest v clothe.

revestry n vestry.

rew n repentance, rue. • v rue.

rewell adj haughty.

rewth n pity.

rheumatise n rheumatism.

rhinns see rinns.

riach adj brindled, dappled; drab. • n dun.

ribband n halter.

ribe n stalky cabbage.

ribie adj tall and bare.

rice n sprig.

richer n/v neigh.

richt adj right; accurate; authentic; just; healthy. • adv properly; **richt oot** bluntly; **richt-lik** equitable.

richtful adj rightful.

richtify v rectify.

richtlie adv rightly.

ricket n racket.

rickle n heap, pile.

rickle o banes n skeleton.

rickler n bad builder.

ricklie adj ramshackle.

rid n red. • v redden.

riddle n sieve; shaker.

ride n copulation. • v copulate with.

rid-face n blush.

rid-faced adj ashamed.

ridin time n breeding season.

riep n slovenly girl.

rifart n radish.

rife¹ adj plentiful. • adv plentifully.

rife² n itch.

rift¹ n cleft.

rift² n/v belch.

rig, rigg n ridge; crest; ploughed drill; back; backbone, spine.

rig-bane, riggin n backbone.

rigged an furred adj ribbed.

riggin-tree n rooftree.

rigwiddie, rigwoodie adj stubborn.

rimbursin adj ruptured.

rimburst n hernia.

rimie adj frosty.

rimless adj reckless.

rimpin n lean cow.

rin n run; channel; flow; waterfall; ford; slat. • v run.

rinaboot adj roving. • n gadabout.

rind¹, rynd n hoar-frost.

rind² v dissolve by heat; melt down; render.

ring v govern; reign; rule.

ringin adj domineering; imperious; out and out.

ringit adj wall-eyed.

ringle ee n wall-eye.

ringtails npl remnants.

rink¹ n course; race; team; tournament; curling game.

rink² v rattle.

rin-knot n slip-knot.

rinnin n gist; outline.

rinns, rhinns n headland, land between two seas.

rin-wa' n partition.

rip n osier basket.

ripe v search; rifle.

rippet n mirth; uproar.

ripple v comb flax.

ripples n diarrhoea.

ripter, ripture v rupture.

rise¹, rys n branch, twig.

rise² n hoax. • v ascend; bring about.

rising adj approaching.

riskish adj wet; boggy.

risp n file, rasp. • v file, rasp; grate; saw.

rispings npl filings.

rist n/v rest; repose.

rit n incision made with a spade; groove; score; scrape. • v score; scrape.

rither n rudder.

rittocks npl melted tallow.

rive n rent; rift; rip. • v plough; tear apart; rip; cleave; lacerate; maul; reclaim.

rizzar n redcurrant.

rizzle v rustle.

rizzon n reason; **rizzon or nane** adv obstinately.

road n method; route; tack.

roadie n path; road.

roadman n carter.

roar n noise.

roarie adj garish; lurid; noisy; roaring.

roarin gemm n curling.

roastit adj toasted.

Rob Sorby n sickle.

roch, roche adj rough; unshorn.

rochel, rockel n porch, vestibule.

rochian n hooligan, ruffian, thug.

rockle n small stone.

rocklie adj pebbly.

rockman n bird-catcher.

rod n road.

rodden see roden.

rodden fluke n turbot.

rodding n sheep track.

roddoch n wretch.

roden, rodden n rowan berry.

roden tree n mountain ash, rowan tree.

roggerowse adj outspoken.

roid adj harsh.

roif n rest; peace.

rois n rose.

roist n roost.

rokelay n short cloak.

role v ply the oars.

rollar n oarsman.

rollochin adj freespoken.

romour n disturbance.

rone¹ n ice sheet.

rone², rone-pipe n drainpipe.

ronge n gnawing.

ronie adj ice-covered.

ronk *n* moisture.

ronnet *n* rennet.

roo *v* pile up.

rood, rude *n* cross.

rook[1] *n* thick mist.

rook[2] *v* deprive; cheat.

room *n* best room, parlour, sitting room.

roon[1], **roond** *adj* circular, round; size-able.

roon[2] *n* shred.

roon[3] *v* cough noisily.

roose *v* rouse.

rooser *n* watering can.

rooshel *v* hustle.

rooshoch *adj* coarse.

roossill *v* cudgel.

roost[1] *n* loft.

roost[2] *n* rust. • *v* corrode, rust.

roostie *adj* rusty.

root-hewn *adj* perverse.

roove, rufe *v* rivet; clinch.

roperie *n* ropeworks.

roplaw *n* young fox.

roseir *n* rose bush.

roset *n* resin; rosin.

rosettie *adj* resinous.

rosidandrum *n* rhododendron.

rosin *n* area of bushes.

rost, roust *n* strong current.

rotton *n* rat.

rouchled *adj* ruffled.

rouch-rider *n* horse-breaker.

roudes *n* crone.

roudoch *adj* sulky-looking.

rouk *n* mist.

roukie *adj* drizzly; foggy, misty, hazy.

roume *see* **rowme**.

roun *v* whisper.

roun o *n* nonentity.

roup[1] *n* auction sale. • *v* sell by auction.

roup[2] *n* huskiness; hoarseness. • *v* croak; cry out.

rouper *n* one who cries out.

roupie, roupy *adj* husky, hoarse.

roupit *adj* raucous.

rousing *adj* powerful.

roust[1], **rowst** *n/v* bellow; shout.

roust[2], **rowst** *v* arouse; rouse.

roust[3] *see* **rost**.

rout *v* bellow; strike.

routh *adj* plentiful. • *n* plenty.

rovie *n* slipper.

rowan *n* ash tree.

rowan *n* mountain ash.

rowchow *adj* mixed-up; revolving. • *v* tumble about.

rowe[1] *n* list, roll. *v* roll; lurch; waddle; wheel; wind; bandage; **row up** wind up; wrap up.

rowe[2] *v* row a boat.

rowie *n* bread roll.

rowk *n* rick.

rowkar *n* tale-bearer.

rowme[1], **roume** *adj* spacious. • *n* space, room.

rowme[2] *v* roam.

rowmil *v* scrape out.

rowsan *adj* fierce.

rowst *see* **roust**[1], **roust**[2].

rowt *n* lowing. • *v* bray; low; snore.

rowth *adj* bountiful; plentiful; profuse. • *n* abundance, plenty; profusion.

rowthie *adj* abundant; copious.

royat *adj* unmanageable.

royster *n* freebooter.

royt *n* rover; babbler; brutish woman. • *v* behave noisily.

rub *adj* teasing. • *n* reproof.

ruband *n* ribbon.

rubbage *n* junk, rubbish.

rubber *n* scrubbing brush.

ruch *adj* abundant, luxuriant; rank; unshorn; rough; barbarous; bawdy; ob-scene.

ruck *n* haystack; peat stack. • *v* stack up.

ruckle o banes *n* emaciated person.

ructions *npl* trouble; hullabaloo.

rudas *adj* bold; virile.

ruddock *n* redbreast.

rude *see* **rood**.

rue *v* regret.

rufe *see* **roove**.

ruff[1] *n* roll of a drum. • *v* applaud.

ruff[2] *v* disarray.

ruffie *n* brushwood torch; ruffian.

ruffill *n* loss.

rug *n* current; tide; twinge. • *v* pull; tug; **rug and rive** seize and take away.

ruif *n* ceiling; roof.

ruil *n* wild girl.

ruinage *n* destruction, ruination.

ruint, runt *v* make a grinding noise.

ruise n blandishments, flattery; commendation; praise. • v boast; commend; praise.

ruit n root. • v poke about; rummage.

ruive n/v rivet.

rulesum adj wicked.

rullion n leather shoe; coarse woman.

rum adj excellent; ingenious.

rumgumption n shrewdness.

rumgunshoch see **ramgunshoch**.

rumlieguff n fool.

rummage n uproar.

rummle n rumble; impetus; ruin. • v rumble.

rummlegumption n level-headedness.

rummlin adj boisterous; slapdash.

rump v crop, cut; deprive; clean out.

rumple n rump; tail.

rumple-bane n coccyx.

rumpus n disturbance.

runch n wrench. • v wrench; grind one's teeth.

runchie adj raw-boned.

rund n edge.

rung n bludgeon; stick; truncheon. • v bludgeon.

runk v bankrupt; speak ill of; deprive.

runkit adj bankrupt.

runkle n wrinkle. • v crumple; ruffle; wrinkle.

runklie adj creased, crumpled; wrinkled.

runrig n adjacent field strips of varying ownership.

runsh see **ransh**.

runt[1] n tree trunk; hard stalk; old cow; hag.

runt[2] v bounce.

runt[3] see **ruint**.

ruse v praise.

rush n boil; dysentery; rash.

rush-fever n scarlet fever.

rusk v scratch; claw.

ruskie adj stout.

ruth adj kind.

ruther[1] n rudder.

ruther[2] v storm; bluster.

rutterie n lechery.

rynd see **rind**[1].

rype v reap.

rype-pouch n pickpocket.

rys see **rise**.

ryve see **reive**.

S

sa[1] conj so.

sa[2] v say.

sab n sob. • v sob; subside.

sabbin n sobbing.

sachless adj useless.

sacket adj short; thick.

sacrify v sacrifice.

sad adj grave; steady; distressing.

sade n peat sod.

sae adv/conj so.

saem n lard.

safer[1] n sapphire.

safer[2] adv insofar.

saft adj pleasant; moist; mild; rainy; soft.

saft-eened adj soft-hearted.

saften v soften.

saftly, saftlie adv softly.

sag v press down.

saicant n second.

saicret adj/n secret.

saidle n/v saddle.

saidler n saddler.

saikless adj innocent; guileless, ingenuous; harmless; inoffensive.

sail adj awash.

sailfish n basking shark.

saill n/v seal.

saim n seam.

sain, sane n blessing. • v bless; consecrate.

saip n/v soap.

saipie adj soapy.

saiprit adj separate. • v separate; sever.

sair n sadness; sorrow; sore. • adj painful, sore; sorrowful; censorious; destructive; detrimental; distressing; grievous; hard; harmful; harsh; oppressive; pathetic; strenuous. • adv badly; cruelly, harshly; laboriously; painfully; sorely; urgently; vehemently; **sair aff** hard-up; **sair aff in a bad way**; **sair**

duin overcooked; **sair hodden doon** downtrodden; **sair made** aggrieved; **sair sought** tired out.

sairfit n emergency; rainy day.

sairgint n sergeant.

sair-heid n headache.

sairie, sairy, sary adj silly; sorry; sorrowful.

sairing n sufficiency.

sairless adj tasteless.

sairlie adv sorely.

sairness n soreness.

sairt adj surfeited.

sairy see **sairie**.

sair-yin n painful injury.

saison n/v season.

sait n bishop's see.

saithe n coalfish.

saiven adj/n seven.

saize v seize.

sake n blame.

sale, salle n palace; great room.

saler, salfatt n salt cellar.

salerife adj saleable.

salie, saulie see **soulie**.

salinis n salt pit.

salle see **sale**.

salss n sauce.

salu n health.

salve n salvo.

samelike adj similar.

samen, samin adj same. • adv together.

sammer v assort; agree.

san n sand.

sanct n saint.

sand-bunker n sand pit.

sandrach n beeswax.

sandtripper n sandpiper.

sane see **sain**.

sang n song; outcry.

sangshaw n song festival.

sangster n singer.

sanlaverock n sandpiper.

sanie n sand-eel.

sannie adj sandy.

sannie-swallow n sand-martin.

sannies n gymshoes.

sanshach, sanshauch adj disdainful; crafty.

sant v vanish.

sap n nourishing liquid.

sappie, sappy adj juicy; succulent; moist; soppy; unctuous; plump; bibulous.

sapple v steep.

sapples n lather.

sapples npl soapsuds.

saps npl sops.

sapsie adj effeminate; lenient; weak-willed.

sap-spail n sapwood.

sar v vex.

sard v rub; chafe.

sare[1] adv sorely.

sare[2] v soar; savour.

sarfe v serve.

sark, serk n shirt; shift; surplice. • v line.

sarkin n shirt cloth.

sarkless adj shirtless.

sary see **sairie**.

sasine n investiture with a title to land.

Sassenach adj English. • n English person; Lowlander.

sat n snare.

sate n seat.

Satterda, Saturnday n Saturday.

sattle v settle.

sattle-bed n divan bed.

sauch, saugh n willow.

sauchen, sauchin adj of the willow; soft; weak.

sauchning n reconciliation.

saucht n ease; quiet.

saudall n comrade.

sauf adj safe. • v save.

saufand adv except.

sauftie n safety.

saugh see **sauch**.

saul, , sawle n courage; fortitude; mettle; soul; spirit.

saulie see **soulie**.

saum n psalm.

saumon n salmon.

saunt n saint.

sauntlie adj saintly.

saur n smallest portion; taste. • v savour.

saut adj salt; expensive. • n salt. • v salt; overcharge; snub.

saut bree n salt water.

saut-dish n salt-cellar.

sauter n harridan.

sautie adj brackish; salty.

saut-watter *n* seaside.
savendie *n* sagacity.
savie *n* know-how.
saw neb *n* goosander.
saw[1] *n* salve; ointment; saying.
saw[2] *v* sow; save.
Sawbath *n* Sunday.
sawer *n* sower.
sawins *n* sawdust.
sawin-time *n* seed time.
sawistar *n* sawyer.
sawle *see* **saul**.
Sawtan *n* Satan.
sax *adj/n* six.
saxpence *n* sixpence.
saxt *adj/n* sixth.
saxteen *adj/n* sixteen.
saxteent *adj/n* sixteenth.
saxtie, saxty *adj/n* sixty.
say *n* proverb; saying; remark; speech; story. • *v* **say awa** speak one's mind; **say ower** repeat; **say thegither** agree.
sayar *n* assayer.
saye *n* bucket.
saynd *n* message; messenger.
scab *n* gross offence; itch.
scabbit *adj* bare; scabbed.
scabble *v* scold.
scad[1] *n* gleam.
scad[2] *see* **scaud**.
scadded ale *n* beer with a meal.
scaddem *n* bad smith.
scaddow *n* shadow.
scadlips *n* hot thin broth.
scaff *n* food. • *v* sponge on; swig.
scaffie *n* refuse-collector; street-sweeper.
scag *v* go rotten.
scairth *adj* scarce.
scalbert *n* villain.
scald *see* **scaul**.
scalder *n* jellyfish.
scaldie *n* non-traveller.
scale *see* **skail**.
scallion *n* small onion.
scalp *see* **scaup**.
scam *v* scorch.
scambler *n* greedy feeder.
scamp *n* swindler.
scance, scanse *n* review; survey; gleam. • *v* reflect upon; review; survey; scan; shine.

scansin *adj* glinting.
scant *n* scarcity; dearth.
scantling *n* rough sketch.
scantlins *adv* scarcely.
scapp *see* **skep**.
scar[1] *adj* wild. • *n* scare. • *v* scare; shy away.
scar[2] *see* **scaur**.
scarcelins *adv* barely; scarcely.
scarf *n* cormorant.
scarnoch *n* large number.
scarp *see* **scorp**.
scarrie *adj* bare; rocky.
scarrow *n* faint light.
scart *n* cormorant.
scart[1] *n/v* scratch; scribble.
scart[2], **scarth** *n* cormorant.
scartle *n* rake; scraper.
scartlins, scartins *npl* scrapings.
scash *v* bicker; squabble.
scat *n* loss; damages.
scatterment *n* rout.
scatterwit *n* scatterbrain.
scatterwittit *adj* scatterbrained.
scaud *v* reprimand.
scaud *v* scald.
scaud, scad *v* scald.
scaudin *n* scalding.
scaul, scald *n* scold. • *v* censure; scold.
scauling *adj* scolding.
scaum *v* singe.
scaup *n* scalp; skull; thin soil.
scaur[1] *n* bank; crag; bare hillside; precipice.
scaur[2] *n/v* scar.
scaw'd *adj* faded.
scawt *adj* mangy; scabby; scruffy.
schachle *n* weakling.
schaife *n* sheaf of arrows.
schald *adj* shallow.
schalmer *n* flute-like instrument.
schame *n/v* plan; design; scheme.
schand *adj* elegant.
scheme *n* housing estate.
schemie *n* low-class person.
scho *adj* she.
scholage *n* teacher's fees.
scholar *n* pupil.
schoolie *n* teacher.
schout *v* shoot.
sclaff *n* open-handed blow.

sclafferin *adj* slovenly.

sclaffert *n* mumps.

sclaff-fittin *adj* flat-footed.

sclait, sclaite *see* **sclate**.

sclammer *n* clamour.

sclander *v* slander.

sclatch *n* daub; smear. • *v* huddle up; daub; anoint.

sclate, sclait, sclaite *n* slate. • *v* cover in slates.

sclater *n* slater, woodlouse.

sclatrie *n* obscenity.

sclaurie *v* splash with mud; abuse.

sclave *n* slave.

sclender *see* **sclinner**.

sclenderie *n* scree slope.

sclent *v* slope; look askance.

sclenters, sclenders, sclithers *n* scree.

sclidder *n* slither; sluggard. • *v* slide inadvertently, slither.

sclidderie *adj* icy.

sclim *v* shin.

sclinner, sclender *adj* slender.

sclithers *see* **sclenters**.

scob *n* splint. • *v* sew clumsily; gag.

scobie, scoobie *v* put down.

scodge *v* drudge. • *v* drudge; pilfer.

scodgie *n* menial; scullion; suspicious character.

scoggy *adj* shady; sheltered.

scoll, skole, skull *n* drinking bowl. • *v* drink a health.

scomfish *v* smother.

scon *v* play ducks-and-drakes.

sconce[1] *n* fine; extortion. • *v* fine; jilt.

sconce[2] *n* fire screen; screen; windbreak.

scone *n* cake cooked on a girdle; **scone o the day's baking** ordinary person.

scool *n/v* scowl.

scoonrel *n* scoundrel.

scoor *adj* scouring. • *n* rush; shower. • *v* scour; purge; box on the ear.

scoorie *adj* blustery; scruffy.

scoot[1] *n* razorbill.

scoot[2] *n* spurt; squirt; water pistol. • *v* squirt; spurt.

scoot[3] *n* loose woman.

scooter, scoot-gun *n* peashooter; syringe.

score *n* fissure; cleft; weal.

scorp, scarp *v* mock.

scorrie, scorie *n* seagull.

scoskie *n* starfish.

scot *v* pay a tax.

Scotch nightingale *n* sedge-warbler.

scotch mist *n* fine rain.

scoudrum *n* punishment.

scouff *n* philanderer.

scouk *v* skulk.

scoukin *adj* skulking.

scounge *v* hunt for food.

scoup *v* leap; jump.

scoupar *n* dancer.

scour[1] *n* diarrhoea.

scour[2] *v* whip; flog.

scourie[1] *adj* shabby.

scourie[2] *adj* squally.

scout *v* squirt; suffer from diarrhoea.

scouth *n* freedom; scope; room.

scove *v* fly smoothly.

scovie *n* foppish person.

scow[1] *n* something broken in pieces.

scow[2] *n* coracle.

scowder *n* dusting of snow. • *v* scorch.

scowe *n* barrel stave.

scowf *n* bragging.

scowmar *n* pirate.

scowth *n* opportunity; potential.

scowthie *adj* commodious.

scoy *adj* ill-made thing.

scra-built *adj* made of turves.

scrae *n* worn-out shoe.

scraffle *v* scramble.

scraible *v* wangle; scrabble.

scraich *n* shriek; **scraich o day** dawn.

scrall *v* crawl.

scrammle *n/v* scramble.

scran *n* food. • *v* scrounge.

scrap *n/v* scrape; **scrap o the pen** scrawl.

scrapie *n* miser.

scrat[1], **scratch** *n* rut; mean-looking person; hermaphrodite.

scrat[2] *n/v* scratch.

scratty *adj* skinny.

scrauch *n/v* screech.

scrauchin *adj* screeching.

scrauchle *v* scramble on all fours.

scree[1] *n* debris of rocks on a hillside.

scree[2], **skree** *n* riddle; sieve.

screed *n* gash, slash, tear; scream; long

list; prose; verse. • v cry; tear; defame; lie; **screed aff** recount, relate.

screenge n lash; rub. • v rub; scourge; scrub.

screeve n graze. • v tear off.

screever n pancake.

screw[1] n shrimp.

screw[2] n shrew.

scribble v tease wool.

scribe v write.

scriddan n mountain torrent.

scrieve[1] n letter; script. • v scrape; scratch; write.

scrieve[2] v glide.

scriever n scribbler; writer.

scrift n recitation. • v declaim; exaggerate.

scrim[1] n thin coarse cloth.

scrim[2] v smack, spank.

scrimp adj insufficient; pinched; scanty; scarce. • v economise.

scrimpie adj inadequate; mean; meagre.

scrimpit adj restricted; scanty; deficient; undersized.

scrimpness n scantiness.

scripter n scripture.

scrog, scrogg n stunted bush.

scrogs, scroggs npl brushwood; scrub; undergrowth.

scroggy adj bushy; stunted.

scroll n draft; notepad.

scronach n outcry.

scroonge v scrounge.

scroppit adj sordid.

scrow n/v crowd; swarm.

scrub n scourer for pots.

scrubble n/v squabble; struggle.

scrubie n scurvy.

scruff n riff-raff.

scrug v cock (hat); **scrug one's bonnet** cock one's bonnet.

scruif n crust; film; dandruff; scurf. • v skin; touch or scrape a surface.

scruiffin n paring.

scrumple v crease.

scrunt[1] n stubby branch.

scrunt[2] v grind; plane.

scruntit, scruntie adj stunted.

scry n noise; proclamation.

scrym v skirmish.

scrymmage n skirmish.

scubble v make grubby.

scud n stroke of a rod; sudden shower. • v hit with a rod.

scuddie adj bare, naked; penurious. • n bare skin.

scuddin-stane n skimming stone.

scuddle v wear out; scrub.

scuddler n kitchen boy; maid-of-all-work.

scuds n beer.

scue v go sidelong.

scuff n graze; light touch. • v brush off; touch; graze; tarnish.

scuffie adj down-at-heel; shabby; tarnished.

scug, skug n shade; shelter; pretext; subterfuge. • v screen; shelter; shade.

scuggy adj shady.

scugry, scugwise adj covert.

scuil, scuill n school; shoal.

scuil bairn n schoolchild.

scuip n/v scoop.

sculduderie n indecency.

scult n blow with or on the hand.

scum n greedy person. • v skim.

scum milk n skimmed milk.

scuncheon n cornerstone.

scunge v scrounger. • v scavenge.

scunger n prowler.

scunner n abhorrence; loathing; antipathy; object of dislike; pest. • v disgust; loathe; shrink back; sicken; surfeit.

scunnersome adj abhorrent; distasteful; objectionable.

scunnert adj fed-up.

scur[1] n mayfly.

scur[2] n scab.

scurdie n moor stone.

scurr[1] n scoundrel.

scurr[2] v slide.

scurrie adj dwarfish.

scurryvaig n lout; vagabond.

scush n/v shuffle.

scutcher n swingle.

scute see **skute**.

scuttal n filthy pool.

scutter v bungle; botch.

scutterie adj fiddly.

scuttle-hole n cesspool.

se see **sey**[2].

seagust n spume.

sea loch *n* long narrow bay of the sea.

sea maw *n* gull.

seam o teeth *n* dentures.

seannachie *n* clan bard and historian; storyteller.

sea-pyot *n* oyster-catcher.

search *v* sift.

seath, seith *n* coal-fish.

seatter *n* meadow.

seck *n* sack.

second-handit *adj* second-hand.

second-sicht *n* power of divination.

see *v* pass; **see her ain** menstruate; **see till** care for.

seed-bird *n* wagtail.

seed-fowl *n* wagtail.

seeing gless *n* mirror.

seek *v* court, woo; ask for; aspire; bid; desire; want; look for percolate; **seek tae** strive for; **seek throu** soak through; **seekto** ask to.

seek-sair *adj* bored.

seendil, seenil *adj* infrequent; rare. • *adv* seldom.

seep *n* leakage; ooze. • *v* percolate; trickle.

seepin *adj* dripping.

seerie *adj* feeble.

seeven *adj/n* seven.

seevent *adj/n* seventh.

seeventeen *adj/n* seventeenth.

seeventie *adj/n* seventy.

seg¹ *n* rush; sedge; iris.

seg², seyg *v* fall down; sink; subside.

seggle *adj* abounding in sedge.

segster *n* sexton.

sei *v* see.

seil¹, seile, sele *n* happiness; bliss; fortune; prosperity; success.

seil² *v* strain.

seildyn *adv* seldom.

seilful *adj* blissful; fortunate; propitious; successful.

seilie, seily *adj* blessed; happy.

seir, sere *adj* several.

seirie *adj* haughty.

seissle *v* confuse.

seith *see* **seath**.

sel *n/pron* self.

selchie, selcht *see* **selkie**.

selcouth *adj* strange.

sele *see* **seil¹**.

seleck *v* select.

self *adj* same; **self an same** identical; selfsame.

selkie, selchie, selcht *n* seal.

sellack, sellock *n* small fish.

sellarie *n* salary.

sellie *adj* egotistical; selfish. • *n* selfishness.

selwyn *pron* selfsame.

sely¹ *adj* wretched.

sely² *adv* wonderfully.

semble¹ *n* parapet.

semble² *v* assemble.

sembling *n* appearance.

semi *n* second-year undergraduate.

semmit *n* vest.

semple, sempill *adj* simple; low-born, vulgar.

sen¹ *v* dispatch, send.

sen², sensyne *conj* since.

send¹ *n* mission; message.

send² *adv* then; thereafter.

sense *n* essence; pith. • *v* scent.

sensyne *see* **sen²**.

sentrices *npl* scaffolding.

sept *n* branch of clan.

sequestrate *v* confiscate.

ser *v* fit; satiate; serve.

sere *see* **seir**.

serge *n* taper; torch.

serk *see* **sark**.

serplins, sorplins *npl* soapy suds.

servan *n* servant.

servan chiel *n* manservant.

server *n* salver, tray.

service *adj* serving. • *n* round of drinks.

servit *n* serviette.

servitour *n* secretary; servant.

set¹ *n* attitude; build; characteristic; state; lease; trap; attack; sort, kind; seed-potato. • *v* accompany; let; lease; sit; seat; send; disgust; beset; befit; **set aff** dismiss; go away; plant out; send off; **set after** pursue; **set awa** set off; **set oot**; **set by** put aside; substitute; **set doon** plant; **set i** lay; **set on** invade; **set oot, set out** eject; put out; **set ower** ferry; **set tae** attack; set upon; **set up** stir up; **set up yer gab** speak out.

set² *adj* distressed.

set-doon *n* sit-down.
set-down *n* rebuff.
set-stane *n* whetstone.
sett *n* large cobblestone.
setter *n* leasor.
setterel, settrel *adj* squat, thickset.
setting *adj* becoming; fit.
settlement *n* testament.
settlins *npl* dregs of beer.
settrel *see* **setterel**.
Seturday *n* Saturday.
Saturday penny *n* pocket money.
seuch *n* furrow. • *v* divide.
sevendle *adj* extreme.
severals *adj* several.
sewster *n* sempstress.
sey[1] *n* armhole of a dress; beef.
sey[2], **se** *n* sea.
sey[3] *n* specimen.
seyd *n* sewer; drain.
sey daisy *n* sea-pink, sea-thrift.
seyg *see* **seg**.
seyne *v* see.
seytoon *n* seaport.
shab *v* smuggle.
shable *n* crooked sword.
shach *v* distort.
shachle *n* shuffling walk. • *v* shamble;
  shachle aff shake off.
shachlin *adj* shapeless.
shackle *n* wrist.
shackle-bane *n* wristbone.
shae[1], **shee** *n* shoe. • *v* shoe.
shae[2] *pron* she.
shae pint *n* shoelace.
shaft *n* handle.
shag *n* barley chaff.
shaif *n* sheaf.
shair *adj* sure.
shairp *adj* gritty; sharp. • *n* sharpening.
shairpen *v* sharpen.
shairplie *adv* sharply.
shak *n* shake. • *v* shake; **shak a fa** wrestle; **shak a fit** dance.
shaker *n* quaking grass.
shall *n* scale; shell. • *v* shell.
shalla *adj/n* shallow.
shalloch *adj* abundant.
shalt, shaltie *see* **sheltie**.
shalter *n* shelter.
sham[1], **shaum** *n* leg.

sham[2] *v* strike.
shamble *v* stretch the limbs; writhe.
shame *n* pity.
shammle *v* dislocate.
shan *adj* no-good.
shane *v* heal.
shangie[1] *adj* meagre.
shangie[2] *n* shackle; chain; washer.
shangles *npl* handcuffs.
shank *n* leg; handle, shaft; coal pit; knitter; stalk; stem. • *v* travel on foot; dig a
  coal pit; knit; **shank aff** set off.
shanks' naig *n* walking.
shannach *n* Hallowe'en fire.
shantieglan *n* knife-grinder.
shap *n* shop.
shape *n* attitude; posture.
share *v* pour off; separate liquids; shear.
shargar *n* scraggy or stunted person.
sharins *npl* remains after sharing.
sharn *n* animal dung.
sharny *adj* covered with dung.
sharrachie *adj* chilly.
sharrow *adj* bitter-tasting.
shatter *v* chatter.
shaul, shawl *adj* shallow.
shaum *see* **sham**[1].
shaup *n* husk; pea pod. • *v* pod.
shaupie *adj* lank.
shave, sheave *n* slice. • *v* slice; sow.
shavie *n* trick.
shaw[1] *n* wood, copse, thicket; woodland;
  flat land at the base of a slope.
shaw[2] *n* show. • *v* show; display; trim.
shawl *see* **shaul**.
shaws *npl* stalks.
shear, sheer *v* reap; divide.
shearer *n* reaper.
shears *npl* clippers; sheep-shears.
sheave *see* **shave**.
sheckle *n/v* shackle.
shed *n* hair parting; division of land. • *v*
  divide; separate.
shedda *n/v* shadow.
shedding *n* parting of the ways.
sheddings *npl* crossroads.
shee *see* **shae**.
sheemach *n* pack-saddle.
sheen *v* shine.
sheer *see* **shear**.
sheiling *n* summer hut.

shell n husk. • v husk grain; **shell down** shell out.

sheltie, shalt, shaltie n small horse; Shetland pony.

shelvie adj shelving.

shent adj destroyed, ruined.

sherk n shark.

sherp adj piquant.

shethe n whet stick.

sheuch, sheugh n ditch; drain; trench; furrow. • v dig a ditch, etc.

shew v sew.

shewin n needlework, sewing.

shewster n needlewoman.

shew-up n closure.

shidder n/v shudder.

shiel n shield.

shiemach adj malevolent.

shiffle v shuffle.

shift n removal. • v change places.

shilcorn n blackhead.

shilfa n chaffinch.

shill¹ adj chilly.

shill² adj shrill.

shilped adj timid.

shilpie n timid person.

shilpit, shilped adj insipid; sickly-coloured; fearful, timid; emaciated; haggard; lanky; puny; sour.

shim n horseshoe.

shinty n ball and stick game; hitting stick.

shire v pour off; purify.

shirie adj watery.

shirles npl peat turves.

shirp v shrivel.

shirpet adj thin; tapering.

shirragh adj acrid.

shirrif, shirra n sheriff.

shirrot n divot.

shirrow n shrew; termagant, virago.

shite n excrement. • v excrete, shit.

shither n/v shudder.

shitten adj dirtied; contemptible.

shivereens npl smithereens.

shochle v stagger.

shochlin adj waddling.

shod n tag.

shoddie n little shoe.

shog n jog; sway. • v jog; sway; keep going.

shoggie-shoo n seesaw.

shooders n coat-hanger.

shoogieboat n swingboat.

shoogle¹, shuggle n ice floe; blood clot.

shoogle², shuggle v jolt; push; joggle; jolt. • v joggle; jolt; push; rock.

shooglie, shoogly adj shaky; unstable; wobbly.

shool see **shuil**.

shoon npl shoes.

shoot v push out.

shore¹ n jetty; pier; quay.

shore² v count; threaten; offer.

short n jiffy.

short an lang adv briefly; summarily.

shortbread n solid cake of flour and butter.

shortcome n deficiency; shortage; flaw.

shortie n shortbread.

short i the trot adj short-tempered.

shortlins adv shortly.

shorts npl flax and straw refuse.

short-set adj stocky.

shortsome adj amusing; enjoyable; entertaining.

shortsyne adv lately.

shot n plot of land; catch of a net; flow.

shot-about adv turn about.

shottle, shuttle n drawer; compartment.

shouder, shouther n shoulder.

shouder heid n shoulder joint.

shoughie n short, bandy-legged person.

shour n shower.

shout v birth.

shouther see **shouder**.

shoutin n childbirth.

showd v waddle; swing on a rope.

showers npl throes, pangs of childbirth.

showl v distort.

shreed n shred.

shrood n shroud.

shuet n suet.

shuggar n sugar.

shuggie v swing from side to side.

shuggle see **shoogle¹, shoogle²**.

shuil, shool n/v shovel.

shuilie adv surely.

shuir adj sure.

shuit¹ n/v suit.

shuit² n bulge. • v avalanche; bulge; shoot.

shullin n shilling.

shunky n toilet bowl.

shurlin n new-shorn sheep.

shuts npl shutters.

shuttle see **shottle**.

shuve v shove.

shyle v make a wry face.

sib adj akin; alike; related by blood; similar. • n kin; blood relation.

sibness n affinity; relationship.

sic, sich adj such; **sic an sae** alike; **sic lik** similar; suchlike. • adv so; **sic lik** likewise; similarly.

siccan adj such kind of; certain.

siccar, sicker, sikker adj secure; certain.

sich¹ n/v sigh.

sich² see **sic**.

sicht n sight; scrutiny; vision; pupil. • v sight; scrutinise; determine sex of animal.

sichtless adj sightless.

sicker¹ adj dependable, reliable; firm, secure; stable; steady; wary. • adv securely. • v make sure; fix; secure.

sicker², sikker see **siccar**.

siddle v sidle.

side adj hanging low; **side for side** alongside.

sidelegs n sidesaddle.

sidelins adj sidelong; sloping. • adv alongside; aside; indirectly.

sideweys adj sideways.

signet n seal.

sik v seek.

sike n stream; filter; soil. • v filter; soil.

sile¹ n ceiling.

sile², syle v blindfold; circumvent; strain.

sill n foundation beam.

siller adj silver.

siller adj silver; relating to money. • n silver; currency; money.

siller-fish n pout.

sillerless adj penniless.

sillert adj monied.

silly adj lean; frail; fearful; flimsy.

simmer n summer.

simmerset n somersault.

simpliciter adv unconditionally.

simulate adj pretended.

sin¹ n sun.

sin² n son.

sin³ adv/conj since.

sinacle n vestige.

sincere adj grave.

sinder v diverge; divide; part; thin.

sindle adv seldom.

sindry adj assorted; various; distinct; diverse; sundry. • adv separately.

sing n/v singe.

singit-like adj puny.

singlar adj unarmed.

sink n mineshaft; soggy ground.

sinnen n sinew.

sinnerie adv asunder.

sinse n sense.

sinsyne adv ago; since.

sinwart adv sunwards.

sipe, sype n spring (of water); dreg. • v distil.

siplin n sapling.

sipper n supper.

sipple v sip.

sirple v sip; sip repeatedly.

sist v cite; stop.

sit v stop growing; shrink; sink down.

sitable adj suitable.

sit-doon n job.

site, syte n grief.

sithe n satisfaction; atonement.

sithean n fairy hill.

sithes npl chives.

sitten adj stewed.

sitten-doon adj chronic.

sitting-doon n marriage settlement.

sittrel adv peevish.

siven n raspberry.

siver n covered drain.

skaddens n turf.

skaenie n twine.

skaff, skaffie n small boat.

skag n drugs; heroin.

skaik n coating. • v force apart.

skail adj scattering. • v break up; disband; ; disperse; leak out; rout; scatter; spill.

skail, skaill, scale n skimming dish. • adj scattering. • v disperse; scatter; empty; overflow; dismiss.

skailin n dispersion.

skaillie n blue slate.

skaillie-burd n writing slate.

skaillie-pen *n* slate pencil.

skailwin *n* hurricane; tornado.

skainie *n* string.

skair *v* splice.

skaith *n* hurt, injury; loss; misfortune; damage; damages. • *v* damage; hurt, injure.

skaivie *adj* hare-brained.

skalk *n* morning tumbler of whisky.

skalrag *adj* dishevelled.

skarrach *n* flying shower.

skate *n* paper kite.

skavie *n* mishap.

skean, skene *n* short knife.

skean-dhu *n* stocking knife.

skean-ochle *n* armpit knife.

skech *adj* scrounging. • *n* sponger. • *v* appropriate; filch.

skechin *adj* prowling.

skee *n* small house.

skeebroch *n* very lean meat.

skeeg¹, skig *n* small fragment.

skeeg², skeg *v* lash; spank.

skeel *n* skill.

skeelie, skeely *adj* skilful.

skeer *adj* agitated; restive; unstable. • *v* alarm.

skeet, skeitch, sketch *n/v* skate.

skeetcher, skeitcher *n* skater.

skeg *see* **skeeg²**.

skeich *adj* coy; ebullient. • *v* animate; shy.

skeir *adj* pure; holy.

skeitch, sketch *see* **skeet**.

skelb *see* **skelf¹**.

skeldroch *n* hoar-frost.

skelet *n* skeleton.

skelf¹, sklb *n* flake; scale; splinter; thin person. • *v* flake.

skelf² *n* shelf.

skellet, skellat *n* bell; rattle.

skellie¹ *adj* cross-eyed; slanting. • *n* squint; error. • *v* squint; look askance.

skellie² *n* reef.

skellie-eed *adj* squint-eyed.

skelloch¹ *n* loud cry; scream. • *v* cry out; scream.

skelloch² *n* charlock.

skellum *n* scamp.

skelp *n* stroke; blow; slap, smack; large portion; slab; squall. • *v* spank; beat

fast; move quickly; gallop; skip along; tick.

skelpie *n* naughty child.

skelping *n* thrashing; whipping; hiding.

skelter *v* scurry; scutter; scuttle.

skelve *n/v* slice; layer.

skelvy *adj* layered.

skemmel *v* scramble; stagger.

skemmels *n* meat market.

skemmling *adj* shambling.

skene *see* **skean**.

skep, scapp *n* beehive; basket.

skep-bee *n* bee.

skerry *n* tidal rock.

sket *adv* hastily.

sketch *see* **skeitch**.

sketchers *n* saw-horse.

skeugh *see* **skew**.

skevrel *v* totter around in circles.

skew, skeugh *n* twist. • *v* twist; skew; splay; squint; differ.

skew-fittit *adj* splay footed.

skewl *v* distort; turn aside.

skeyld *n* surf.

skibe *n* mean person.

skice *v* make off; slip away.

skid *v* slide; squint.

skiddie *adj* slant.

skiddle *v* slop; slosh.

skiff, skift *v* move smoothly; skip; brush against.

skiffie *n* coal tub; flying shower.

skift *see* **skiff**.

skiftin *n* skirting board.

skig *see* **skeeg¹**.

skiggle *v* spill.

skill *n* reason; sense; approval.

skilt *v* swill.

skilting *n* drinking hard.

skimmer *v* flicker; shimmer.

skimmering *adj* glimmering.

skin *n* particle.

skink¹ *n* shin of beef; soup.

skink² *n* drink. • *v* decant.

skinkle¹ *n* small portion. • *v* spill.

skinkle² *n* shining. • *v* sparkle.

skinnymalink *n* skinny person.

skip *n* captain.

skippit *adj* peaked.

skire *adj* pure; mere.

skirgiffin *n* half-grown girl.

skirl *n* crackle; scream; shrill cry. • *v* cry shrilly; scream; shriek; **skirl up** sing loudly.

skirlie *n* flurry.

skirl-in-the-pan *n* sizzling.

skirl-nackit *adj* stark naked.

skirp *n* pellet. • *v* mock; splash.

skirrivaig *v* run about wildly.

skirt *v* elope.

skit *n* vain creature, chit. • *v* flounce; prance.

skite¹ *n* skid; jollification; ricochet. • *v* skid, slide; rebound; strike off.

skite² *n* excrement; nasty person. • *v* excrete forcibly.

skitter *n* diarrhoea. • *v* excrete liquid matter.

skitterful *adj* suffering from diarrhoea.

skitterie *adj* trifling.

skive *v* cut into slices; shave; transfix.

skivet *n* blacksmith's shovel.

sklaik *v* smear.

sklaitie *adj* smeared.

skleet *adj* smooth.

skleff *adj* shallow; thin; flat-chested.

sklent *adj* oblique. • *n* cant, incline; slope. • *v* slant; slope; squint; swerve.

skleter *v* scamper.

skliff *n* scuff; scree. • *v* scuff.

skliffer *n* layer.

sklinter *v* splinter.

sklout *n* cow dung.

skloy *n* slide. • *v* slide; skate.

sklyte *v* slip.

skole *see* **scoll**.

skook *n* skulking person. • *v* skulk.

skoosh *n* jet of fluid, spurt; lemonade.

skoosh-car *n* tramcar.

skoosher *n* sprinkler.

skow *n* coracle.

skrae-shankit *adj* with long thin legs.

skrank *adj* skinny.

skran-pock *n* beggar's wallet.

skree *see* **scree**².

skreek *n/v* screech.

skreenge *n* lash; loose woman. • *v* scourge; search for.

skreich o day, skreigh o day *n* daybreak, dawn.

skrift *n* recital from memory. • *v* make up; fib.

skrimmish *n/v* skirmish.

skrine *n* unboiled sowens.

skrinkie *adj* lank; shrivelled.

skrow *n* shrew; scroll; slight shower.

skrumpilt *adj* shrunken.

skrunkit *adj* pinched; shrivelled.

skrunkle *v* shrink.

skrunt *v* make a grating noise.

skrunty *adj* raw-boned.

skry *v* cry; proclaim.

skube *n* draught of drink.

skudler *n* master of ceremonies.

skug *see* **scug**.

skull *see* **scoll**.

skurriour *n* scout.

skute, scute *n* lout. • *v* walk flat-footedly.

sky *n* daylight; shadow; ridge of a hill; light in the sky before sunrise and after sunset. • *v* look about; look while shading the eyes; shade; **sky up** clear up.

skybald *adj* worthless. • *n* useless person; lazy horse.

skybrie *adj* bad; useless. • *n* thin light soil.

skyme *v* gleam with reflected light.

skynk *v* serve out liquor.

skype *n* worthless person.

skyrie *adj* gaudy.

skyte *n* nasty type; throwing out. • *v* throw out.

skytle *v* move from side to side.

sla *v* slay.

slab *v* eat greedily.

slabber *n* slobber; slovenly person. • *v* slaiver; slobber.

slack¹ *n* opening between hills.

slack² *n* slackening. • *v* cease.

slackstate *n* mess.

slade, slaid *n* hollow; den.

sladge *n* slovenly person.

slae¹ *n* slow-worm.

slae² *n* sloe.

slae³ *n* blackthorn.

slae-black *adj* black as the sloe.

slag *n* morass. • *v* make moist; **slag up** gobble up.

slaggie *adj* soft; thawing.

slaid *see* **slade**.

slaiger *n* mud; dollop of soft stuff. • *v* waddle in the mud.

slaik *n* lick. • *v* bedaub; lick.
slaik, slake *n* something hidden; hoard.
  • *v* carry off and eat in secret.
slain *n* steep wooded slope.
slaip *adj* sleek.
slaipie *n* mean person; plate-licker.
slair *v* smudge.
slairg *n* dollop of semi-sticky stuff.
slairg *v* bedaub.
slairt *v* mess about; outdo; outstrip.
slairy *v* smear.
slaister, slyster *n* messy person; slops.
  • *v* do in a bungling way.
slaisterie, slaistery *adj* messy; mired.
slaister-kyte *n* mucky feeder.
slait[1] *adj* sluttish.
slait[2] *v* level; abuse; maltreat.
slake[1], **slaik** *n* river weed.
slake[2] *see* **slaik**.
slam *n* share of ill-gotten gain.
slammach *v* seize.
slammikin *n* slut.
slamp *adj* pliant; supple; slim.
slanger *v* linger.
slank *adj* thin.
slap, slop *n* break; dollop; gap; narrow
  pass; breach in a wall.
slapper *n* large object.
slappin *adj* big; strapping.
slarry *v* besmear.
slash *n* slush. • *v* kiss wetly; work in wet
  or mud.
slashie *adj* slushy.
slatch *n* slattern. • *v* dabble in mire;
  move heavily.
slate *v* let loose.
slater *n* woodlouse.
slauchter *n* carnage; bloodshed; slaughter. • *v* slaughter.
slaukie *adj* slimy.
slaupie *adj* indolent.
slavers *n* saliva.
slaw *adj* slow.
slawlie *adv* slowly.
slay-worm *n* slow-worm.
sled *n* sledge; sledge driver.
slee, sle *adj* expert; sly; well-made;
  wise. • *adv* slyly. • *v* slip; steal craftily.
sleech *v* coax.
sleek *n* silt; slime; sleet. • *v* slink.
sleekie *adj* sleety; deceitful.

sleekit *adj* smooth; plausible; shining;
  sleek; artful; smooth-tongued; underhand; deceitful, crafty.
sleekitness *n* artfulness.
sleelie *adv* slily.
sleenge *v* lounge.
sleep *v* lapse; **sleep in** oversleep.
sleeper *n* dunlin; foundation beam.
sleeperie *adj* sleepy, somnolent.
sleesh *n* slice.
sleeth *n* sluggard.
sleif *v* slip.
slepe, slip *n* sleep.
slepery *see* **slippery**.
slerp *v* expectorate; salivate; spit.
sletch *n* slime.
sleuch *see* **slouch**.
sleuth[1] *n* sloth.
sleuth[2] *v* neglect; loiter.
slew *v* tilt.
slewit *adj* sleeved.
slibbie *adj* slippery.
slicht[1] *adj* slight; worthless.
slicht[2] *n* cunning; sleight. • *v* jilt; abandon; contrive.
slid, slide *adj* slippery.
slidder *adj* unstable. • *n* slip. • *v* defer;
  delay.
slidderie, sliddery *adj* disloyal; evasive;
  fraudulent; smooth-tongued; uncertain; unreliable; loose.
slide *see* **slid**.
slidness *n* slipperiness.
slieve-fish *n* cuttlefish.
sliggy *adj* cunning; talkative.
slike, slik *n* slime.
slim *adj* slight; naughty. • *v* work carelessly.
slimmer *adj* delicate.
sling *v* walk with long steps.
slinger *v* reel; totter.
slink *adj* long; slender; thin. • *v* deceive.
slinkie *adj* long; slender.
slinkin *adj* deceitful; creeping.
slip *n* breach; miscarriage. • *v* abort.
slip[1] *n* overdress; teenage girl.
slip[2] *see* **slepe**.
slipbody *n* camisole.
slipe *n* runner. • *v* slide; move easily.
slipper, slippar *adj* slippery. • *n* slipperiness.

slippery, slepery *adj* causing sleep.

slippie *adj* slippery.

slipshod *adj* with shoes but no stockings.

slite *v* rip apart; slit.

slitter *n* mess; messy or untidy person; dribbler. • *v* eat messily.

slitterie *adj* messy; sloppy.

slive *n* sliver.

sloan, sloun *n* envious person.

sloap *n* slut.

sloat *n* greedy person.

sloch[1] *n/v* slough.

sloch[2] *v* do something carelessly.

slochan, slocher *n* clumsy or awkward person.

slock *n* strong drink. • *v* quench; douse; moisten; extinguish; appease.

slocken, slokin *v* celebrate; allay; slake, quench.

slockener *n* thirst-quencher.

slogan, slughorn *n* war cry; rallying cry.

slogger *v* slop up with a spoon.

sloggerin *adj* slovenly; trailing.

sloggy *adj* slimy; marshy.

slogie *n* nightgown.

sloit *n* slovenly person.

slokin *see* **slocken**.

slomie *adj* distended.

slong *n* sling.

slonk *n* ditch. • *v* wade through.

sloom *v* slumber, unsettled sleep; slump; waste away decay.

sloonge *n* layabout. • *v* idle, loaf, lounge; souse.

sloonger *n* idler, loafer.

sloosh *n* dash; sluice.

sloot *n* sluttish person.

slop[1] *n* tunic.

slop[2] *see* **slap**.

slope *v* idle; shirk.

sloper *n* shirker.

slork *v* walk through slush; eat noisily.

slorp *n* slurp. • *v* slurp; lap.

slorping *adj* tawdry.

slot *n/v* bar; bolt.

slotter *v* waste one's time.

slottery *adj* drowsy; inert.

slouch, sleuch, slug *n* deep ravine.

sloum *n* scum.

sloun *see* **sloan**.

slounge *n* splash; sneaky person. • *v* fall in with a splash; lounge about hoping for food.

sloupe *n* silly person.

slubber *n* drool, slobber; sloppy food. • *v* bespatter; drool, slobber; do something carelessly.

slug *see* **slouch**.

slughorn *see* **slogan**.

slug road *n* road through a narrow pass.

slummish *v* trifle away one's time.

slump[1] *n* estimate; remnant. • *v* lump together.

slump[2] *n* marsh; dull thump.

slumpie *adj* marshy.

slung *n* tall lank dunce.

slunken *adj* lank and lean.

slurich *n* soft sloppy food.

slush *n* odd-job worker.

slutch[1] *n* hanger-on.

slutch[2] *n* sludge.

slute *n* slow lazy creature.

slutter *n* slop.

slutterie *adj* sluttish.

slutterin *adj* snoring.

sly *n* slide. • *v* come up silently.

slype *n* coarse person; wet furrow. • *v* slip; strip off.

slyster *see* **slaister**.

slyte *v* sharpen, whet; move easily.

sma *adj* small; narrow; of low station. • *n* small amount.

smachry *n* trash.

smack *v* speed.

smad *v* stain. • *n* small stain.

smaik *adj* small. • *n* puny person.

smairt *adj* alert; smart.

smalie *adj* little; puny.

smas *n* small change.

smash *v* shiver; beat hard.

smashin *adj* large; excellent.

smatchet *n* small man.

smatter *v* deal in trifling things; batter; smash.

smatters *npl* trifles.

smeddum *n* common sense; courage; drive; energy; liveliness.

smeeg *n* kiss.

smeek, smeik *n* smoke. • *v* smoke; fumigate; suffocate.

smeekie, smeikie *adj* smoky.

smeekit *adj* smoke-stained.

smeerless *adj* uninteresting.

smeerless *see* **smerghless**.

smeeth, smeth *adj* smooth.

smeik *see* **smeek**.

smelt *see* **smolt**[1].

smergh *n* marrow; vigour; vitality.

smerghless, , smeerless *adj* languid; vapid; feeble.

smervy *adj* savoury.

smeth *see* **smeeth**.

smeuch *n* fumes; smoke.

smewy *adj* savoury.

smiddle *v* smuggle; work by stealth.

smiddy *n* blacksmith's shop, forge.

smikker *v* smile enticingly.

smird *v* gibe.

smirikin, smurachin *n* hearty kiss.

smirk *n/v* smile.

smirkle *n* smile; suppressed laugh.

smirl *n* trick.

smirr *n* hazy rain.

smirtle *n/v* smirk.

smit[1] *n* blemish; smudge; smut; contagion; infection. • *v* contaminate; pollute; taint.

smit[2] *n* clashing sound.

smitch *n* stain; speck; slur.

smittle, smittral, smittin *adj* infectious; contagious.

smocher *v* breathe with difficulty.

smochie *adj* stifling; stuffy; sultry.

smoit *n* obscene talker.

smolt, smelt *n* salmon fry.

smoo *n* placid smile.

smooder *v* smoulder.

smook *v* sneak-thieve.

smookie *adj* pilfering.

smool *v* secure by underhand means.

smoor *v* damp; quench; put out; smother; suppress; obscure.

smoorich *n* cuddle; kiss. • *v* caress; hug.

smoost *v* burn away gradually.

smore *v* extinguish.

smore, smure *v* smother with smoke; choke.

smot, smote *n/v* stain.

smottrit *n* stained.

smoupsie *n* stripling; lad.

smout[1] *adj* clear; mild.

smout[2] *see* **smowt**.

smoutie *adj* sooty.

smoutter *v* eat little but often.

smowt, smout *n* small person; young child; small creature.

smuchtie *adj* fuggy.

smudder *v* smother.

smuddoch *n* smoky fire.

smudge, smue *n* suppressed laugh. • *v* laugh secretly, smirk; simper.

smug *v* embrace amorously.

smugly *adj* amorous.

smuik *n* fumes.

smuik *v* smoke.

smuil *v* go sneakily.

smuir *n* cloud.

smuist *v* smoulder; smoke.

smuister *v* smother.

smuith *adj* smooth.

smuithlie *adv* smoothly.

smulachin *adj* puny-looking.

smule *v* wheedle; curry favour.

smult *v* crop short.

smurachin *see* **smirikin**.

smuragh *n* peat dust.

smure *see* **smore**.

smurr *n* drizzle.

smush[1] *n* burning smell; state of liquefaction.

smush[2] *v* bruise.

smushle *v* drizzle.

smutchack, smytch *n* impish boy.

snab *n* brow of a hill.

snabbin *n* cobbling.

snack[1] *adj* quick; acute.

snack[2] *n/v* snap.

snackie *adj* full of tricks.

snag *n* broken branch. • *v* hack off branches; chide.

snag, snagger *v* snarl.

snaggy *adj* sarcastic.

snaik *v* sneak.

snail *n* slug.

snap *adj* smart. • *n* snack; brittle biscuit. • *v* eat hurriedly.

snapper *v* stumble.

snappert *adj* tart; hasty.

snappit *adj* abrupt.

snappous *adj* quick-tempered.

snappy *adj* sharp in business.

snar *adj* tart.

snare *adj* prudent.

snarre *adj* severe.

snash *n* crude talk. • *v* talk crudely.

snash-gab *n* prating.

snashters *npl* junk food; pastries; sweets.

snauchle *v* loiter.

snaw *n/v* snow.

snaw brue *n* meltwater.

snawfleck *n* snowflake; snow bunting.

snawie *adj* snowy.

snaw-pouther *n* fine snow.

snawsel *adj* snow-covered.

snear, sneer *v* hiss; snort.

sneck¹ *n* latch; bolt. • *v* latch; bolt; shut; **sneck aff** switch off; **sneck up** lock up.

sneck² *n* cut; incision; notch; dip. • *v* cut into, incise; notch; prune; lop.

sneck³ *v* snatch; steal.

sneck-drawer *n* two-faced person, deceiver.

sneck-drawing *adj* crafty; stealthy. • *n* craftiness.

snecks *npl* railway points.

sned *n* shaft of a scythe.

sned *n* cut. • *v* prune, lop, trim; truncate; castrate.

sneddins *npl* prunings.

sneel *v* snivel.

sneep *see* **snip¹**.

sneer *see* **snear**.

sneesh, snish, snush *n* snuff. • *v* sneeze.

sneeshin-mill *n* snuffbox.

sneg *v* snip; chop off; cut off; interrupt.

sneist, sneest *n* contempt; sneer; taunt. • *v* treat with disdain.

sneistie, sneisty *adj* contemptuous; sneering; uncivil.

sneith *adj* smooth; polished; refined. • *n* smoothness.

snell *adj* keen, biting; sharp; severe, austere; acrid; acrimonious; bitter; high-pitched, piercing; pungent; rigorous; sarcastic; tangy; violent. • *adv* eagerly; keenly; severely.

sneyster *v* cauterise; roast.

snib *n* bolt; door-catch; fastener. • *v* bolt; cut; geld.

snibbit *adj* cut short; trimmed.

snicher *n/v* snigger; titter.

sniffel *v* be slow in action.

snifflin *adj* procrastinating.

snift *n* sniff.

snifter *n* severe blast; tot of strong drink. • *v* sniff; snuffle; snore.

snip¹, sneep *n* dazzling.

snip² *v* stumble slightly.

snipe *n* let-down. • *v* defraud.

snippie *adj* sharp-tongued; tart.

snippit *adj* snub.

snippy *n* kettle; teapot.

snirk, snork *n* snort. • *v* snort; wrinkle one's nose.

snirl *v* sneeze.

snirt *n* snort. • *v* breathe snortingly.

snish *see* **sneesh**.

snisty *adj* saucy; rude.

snite *v* snuff; extinguish.

snivel *v* breathe hard through the nose.

snocher *n* snore.

snochter-dichter *n* handkerchief.

snocker *v* snort.

snod *adj* lopped; pruned; neat; tidy; compact; level; snug. • *v* prune; neaten.

snodge *v* walk sneakily.

snog *v* jeer.

snoick *adj* virgin; watertight.

snoit *v* blow one's nose with one's finger and thumb.

snoke, snook, snowk *v* sniff at; scent; smell; hunt.

snool *v* submit.

snoot *n* detective; snout.

snoove *v* walk or move steadily.

snoovin *adj* sneaking.

snoozle *v* nuzzle; sleep.

snork *see* **snirk**.

snorl *n* kink; difficulty; scrape; dilemma.

snorlie *adj* knotted; twisted.

snosh *adj* fat and contented.

snot, snottie *n* dunce.

snotter *n* snot. • *v* breathe congestedly through the nose.

snotterbox *n* nose.

snotterie, snottery *adj* runny-nosed.

snotters *npl* snot; melted candlewax.

snottie¹, snotty *adj* abrupt; brusque; curt; huffy.

snottie² *see* **snot**.

snouthie *adj* dark and rainy.

snowk *see* **snoke**.

snubbert *n* loose knot.

snude *see* **snuid**.

snuffie *adj* sulky.

snuffiness *n* sulkiness.

snug *n* stroke; push. • *v* push; butt.

snuid, snude *n* hairband; snood, fillet with which a woman's hair is bound up.

snuil *n* lazy person. • *v* give in; submit; rebuff.

snuk, snuke *n* small headland.

snurkle *v* knot.

snurlie *adj* knotty.

snush *see* **sneesh**.

snype *n* punch; blow. • *v* punch.

snysters *npl* cakes; titbits.

snyte *v* walk feebly.

so *v* pour oil on water.

soakie *adj* plump.

soam *see* **sowme**.

sober, sobir *adj* spare; frugal; poor; mean; weak.

soc, sock *n* right to hold a baronial court.

socher *adj* lazy. • *v* take good care of oneself.

socht *adj* exhausted; tired.

sock¹ *n* ploughshare.

sock² *see* **soc**.

sod¹ *n* turf of peat.

sod² *adj* firm steady.

sod³ *adj* sad.

sodger *n* soldier.

sodie *n* soda.

sodie-heid *n* silly person.

soft *adj* moist; rainy.

soke *v* slacken.

solan *n* gannet.

sold¹ *n* money; ingot.

sold² *v* solder.

sole *n* sill; subsoil.

solid *adj* sane.

solist *adj* careful; anxious.

some *adv* some extent; somewhat.

somegait *adv* somehow.

someplace *adv* somewhere.

someway *adv* somehow.

sonce *n* prosperity.

Sonday *n* Sunday.

sonk¹ *v* talk drivel.

sonk² *n* grassy seat.

sonnet *n* ditty.

sonse *n* luck.

sonsie, sonsy *adj* lucky; good-humoured; pleasant-looking; attractive; buxom; capacious; lucky; sociable; substantial; appealing.

soo *n* sow¹.

soo¹ *v* smart.

soo² *see* **sow**.

sooch *v* swill.

soogh *n* copious draught.

sook, souk *n* flatterer; sycophant. • *v* suck; seep; breast-feed, suckle; ingratiate; **sook in wi** suck up to.

sooker *n* sucker.

sookie *adj* ingratiating; suckling. • *n* spoilt child; clover.

soom *v* swim.

soon¹ *adj* near; quick; direct.

soon² *adj* sound; orthodox.

soon³ *n* noise, sound.

soon⁴, sound *n* swoon, faint; spin.

soop *n* sweep, brush.

sooper *n* brush.

soople *adj* agile, lithe, supple. • *adv* nimbly.

soor, sour *adj* acid, bitter; sour.

soordook *n* buttermilk; yoghurt.

soor-faced *adj* sour-looking.

soor-lik bodie *n* miserable-looking person.

soormilk scone *n* buttermilk scone.

soormou'd *adj* sulky.

soorock, sourock *n* sorrel.

soor plooms *npl* sour grapes.

soosh, sush *v* beat; flog.

sooth¹ *n* south.

sooth², suth *adj* true. • *n* truth; honesty.

soother *v* calm; soothe.

soothfow *adj* honest.

soothlan *adj* southern.

sooth-moother *n* mainlander.

sop *n* crowd.

sope *v* become weary.

sord *n* crossbar in a gate.

sorn, sorne *v* billet oneself; make requisition.

sorner *n* beggar.

sornie *adj* parasitic.

sorple *v* scrub.

sorplins *see* **serplins**.

sorra *n* menace; sadness; sorrow.

sorraful *adj* sorrowful.

sort *v* adjust; arrange; fit out; equip; chastise; castrate; mend; nurse; provide for.

sosh *adj* sociable; bibulous.

soss *v* fall flat.

sot *n* fool.

sotter *n* crackle; colony of insects. • *v* cluster; saturate; simmer; sputter.

sotterie *adj* soggy.

sottle *v* make a bubbling sound.

souch, sough *adj* breathing; equable; silent; deserted. • *n* rustling; whistling sound; melody; equanimity; feeling; scandal; style; timbre. • *v* breathe heavily, especially in sleep; make a sound like the wind; rustle; drone; **souch awa** breathe your last.

soud *n* quantity.

souder, souther, sowder, sowther *v* allay; cement; confirm; endorse; patch up; strengthen; unite; solder.

soudie *n* gross, heavy person.

soudly *adj* soiled.

souf, souff *v* sleep disturbedly.

souft *adj* exhausted.

souk *see* **sook**.

soukit *adj* exhausted.

soulie, salie, saulie *n* silent mourner.

soum *n* sum; measure of pasture land.

soun *adj* smooth; level.

sound *see* **soon**[4].

soup *v* sob; grow weary; sweep.

souple *adj* flexible; pliant.

sour *see* **soor**.

sourd *n* sword.

sourock *see* **soorock**.

sourse *v* rise.

souse *adv* heavily. • *v* thrash.

souter, soutar *n* shoemaker. • *v* cobble.

souterin *n* shoemaking.

souther *see* **souder**.

southron, suthron *adj* southern; English. • *n* English; southerner; English person.

soutt *v* sob.

sover, sovir *adj* secure.

sow, soo *n* haystack. • *v* stack.

sowce *n* flummery.

sowder *see* **souder**.

sowe *n* winding sheet.

sowens, whinkens *npl* flummery.

sowff *n* sleep, slumber; wheezing.

sowlpit *adj* drenched.

sowme, soam *n* harness chain.

sowp[1] *n* rain. • *v* drench.

sowp[2] *v* sup.

sow-siller *n* hush money.

sowther *see* **souder**.

soy *n* silk.

spaad *n* spade.

space *n* pace; kind; sort.

spae *n* prediction; prophecy. • *v* forecast; foresee; predict; prophesy.

spaeman *n* seer, soothsayer.

spaewife *n* fortune-teller, soothsayer.

spag *n* paw.

spaig *n* skeleton.

spaik, spake *n* perch; spoke.

spaikit *adj* spoked.

spail, spale *n* chip; lath; taper.

spailings *npl* shavings.

spain *see* **spean**.

spaingie *n* cane.

spairge *v* dash; spatter with liquid, spray.

spait *see* **spate**.

spake *see* **spaik**.

spald *see* **spaul**.

spale[1] *v* melt.

spale[2] *see* **spail**.

spaller *v* sprawl.

span[1] *n* hand-span. • *v* grasp.

span[2] *v* harness horses to a vehicle.

spang *n* bound; leap; pace; span. • *v* flick; leap; span.

spang-new *adj* brand-new.

spank *v* sparkle; shine; move smartly; travel fast.

spanker *n* one who walks smartly.

spankering *adj* nimble.

spankie, spanky *adj* spirited; sprightly.

spar *n* rung. • *v* close with a bolt.

spare[1] *adj* barren.

spare[2] *n* slit; fly opening in trousers.

spargeon *v* plaster.

sparginer *n* plasterer.

spark *n* spot; blemish; small particle of liquid; raindrop. • *v* soil; bespatter.

sparkie *adj* quick-witted.

sparkle *n* spark.

sparpell v disperse.

sparragrass n asparagus.

spars, sparse adj widespread; sprawling. • v spread.

spartle v kick about; move unexpectedly; leap.

spat n place; spot.

spatch n large spot.

spate, spait n flood; heavy deluge; torrent; rise.

spatril n note.

spattle n small flood.

spaul, spald n shoulder; joint; limb.

spave v spay.

spaver n spayer, castrator.

spavie n spavin in horses.

spayn v grasp.

speak n comment; pronouncement; speech; statement; subject; topic; scandalmongering. • v order; **speak a word tae** admonish; advise; **speak back** reply, retort.

spean, spain v wean.

spean fae v separate from.

speaning n weaning.

specht n woodpecker.

speck n blubber.

speckie adj bespectacled.

spede v speed; be successful.

speeder n penny-farthing; spider.

speel¹ n break; spell. • substitute.

speel², spele, spiel n/v climb.

speeler n crampon.

speendrif n spindrift.

speengie rose n peony.

speer see **speir**.

speerit n spirit.

speeritie adj energetic; spirited; vivacious.

speer-wundit adj out of breath.

speet n skewer; spit.

speg n wooden pin.

speice n pride.

speik n speech.

speir, speer, spere n inquiry; query; question. • v ask; inquire; query; interrogate; probe; consult; request; **speir at** question; **speir for** ask after; propose; **speir oot** research; trace; track down.

speiring adj inquisitive; questioning. n

interrogation; investigation; probe; proposal.

speirings npl tidings; news; inquiries.

spek v speak.

speld v expand; slice open; spread out.

spelder v pull apart; spreadeagle; thrash about.

spelding n dried haddock.

spele see **speel²**.

spelk n splint. • v splint; splinter.

spell n tale. • v tell; narrate; blaspheme.

spence, spens n larder; inner part of house.

spend n spring jump.

spend v spring gallop.

spendrif adj extravagant.

spendrif n spendthrift.

spendrife adj prodigal.

spenn v button up.

spens see **spence**.

spentacles npl spectacles.

spere see **speir**.

sperfle v squander.

sperk n/v spark.

speshie n species.

speug, spilgie n tall, meagre person.

spice n blow; thwack; pepper. • v hit; pepper.

spice-box n pepperpot.

spicy adj peppery; proud.

spiel see **speel²**.

spile¹ n bung; spigot.

spile² v spoil.

spilgie see **speug**.

spilk v shell peas.

spilkins npl split peas.

spill, spyll v destroy; perish.

spin n tale. • v progress.

spindle-shankit adj long-legged.

spink n pink.

spinkie adj slim; agile.

spinnie n spinning wheel; spindle.

spinnie v shoot out.

spintle adj lean; thin.

spire¹ v dry up; wither.

spire² n partition wall.

spirie adj slender.

spirl v rush about.

spirlie adj slim; spindly. • n slender person.

spirling n smelt; small trout.

spirtle see **spurtle**.

spiry adj hot and dry.

spit n light rain.

spite n vexation. • v provoke.

spits, spittins npl spittle.

spittal n hospice.

spitten n puny creature.

spitterie adj spurting irregularly.

spittins see **spits**.

spittle n spit.

splairge n splutter. • v splash; splatter; splutter; vilify.

splairgin adj spluttering.

splash fit n splay foot.

splatch n big messy thing; splodge.

splatter adj sprinkling. • v scatter; spatter, sprinkle; splash noisily.

splay n squabble. • v flay.

splechrie n furnishings.

spleet n/v split.

spleet-new adj new.

spleiter n blot.

splenner v stride.

spleuchan n purse; pouch for tobacco.

spleuter v burst out.

splinder n/v splinter.

split n rift.

split-new adj new.

sploit v spout; spatter.

splore n drinking bout; exploit; frolic; jollification; spree; rumpus. • v flaunt; show off.

splung v carry off in secret.

splunt, sproag, sprunt v go courting in the dark.

splute v exaggerate.

spoach v poach.

spoacher n poacher.

spodlin n toddler.

sponsible adv admissible.

spoonge n sponge; hungry hanger-on.

spoot, spout n spout; marshy spring. • v spout.

spootcher n bailer.

spootfish n razor-fish.

spoot-gun n popgun.

sporne v stumble.

sporran n Highlander's leather purse or pouch.

spousin adj of a bride.

spout see **spoot**.

spoutie adj conceited.

spoutroch n thin ale; bad drink.

sprachle v flail; sprawl.

sprack adj lively.

sprackle v clamber.

spraich n shriek. • v cry out; lament.

spraing n long stripe; tint. • v tint.

sprangle, sprattle v struggle free.

spreath n foray; raid; wreckage.

spreckelt, spreckled adj speckled; spotted; variegated.

spreckle n/v fleck; speckle.

spree adj sprightly; spry; trim. • n sport; merriment.

spreed, spreid n spread. • v spread; diffuse.

spreith n/v plunder.

sprend, sprent n leap; spring; clasp; hole. • v spring forward.

spreul, sprewl n struggle. • v sprawl; struggle.

sprig n headless nail.

spring n cheerful dance tune; reel.

springald n youth, stripling.

springall adj adolescent.

sproag see **splunt**.

sproosh, sprush adj brisk; spruce; neat. • v spruce.

sproot n/v sprout.

sprose n ostentation. • v make a show.

sprosie adj vain.

sprot n reed; withered stump or stalk.

sprug, spug n sparrow.

sprunt see **splunt**.

sprunt v sprint.

sprush[1] n spruce (tree).

sprush[2] see **sproosh**.

spudyoch n sputtering; sparking.

spue v billow.

spug see **sprug**.

spuile, spule n spool; shuttle.

spuin, spune n spoon.

spuinful adj spoonful.

spule see **spuile**.

spulper n rumour-monger.

spulyie n booty, loot, plunder; depredation; jetsam. • v devastate, lay waste; sack, plunder.

spune see **spuin**.

spung n stringed purse; fob. • v pick pockets.

spunk n spark; match; small fire; spirit. •
v perk; **spunk oot** leak out; **spunk up**
revive.

spunkie n will-o'-the-wisp.

spur n scrape.

spurdie n house sparrow.

spure v investigate.

spurtle, spirtle n stirring stick.

spy v pry.

spyauck n example.

spyll see **spill**.

spyn v glide.

spynner v run or fly swiftly.

squaich n/v scream.

squaik n/v squawk; squeak.

square-wricht n joiner.

squash v splash water.

squat v smack.

squatter¹ v squander.

squatter² see **swatter**.

squattle v sprawl.

squeeb n squib.

squeef n disreputable person.

squeel n school.

squerr adj square.

squibe v topple over.

squile n/v squeal.

squint adj/adv oblique; askew.

squirb v skim.

squirbile adj ingenious.

squirl n flounce; trimming.

sruif n surface.

sta n bore; stall. • v bore; satiate.

stab n stake.

stab and stow adv completely.

stacher v totter.

stack n column of rock; peat stack.

stacket n wooden wall.

staff n walking stick.

staffage adj obstinate; hard to swallow.

stage n informal trial; the bar. • v accuse
without formal trial; put on trial; **stage
about** saunter.

staggie n young stag.

staggrel n staggerer.

staig n horse; gelding; stallion.

staignant adj stagnant.

stalk v accommodate.

staill see **stale**.

staincheon n stanchion.

stainyell n wagtail.

stair n staircase.

stairge v walk solemnly.

stairt n beginning; debut. • v begin, commence.

staive n/v sprain.

stake an rice adj sketchy.

stale, staill n body of armed men; prison;
foundation of haystack.

stalker n huntsman.

stallanger n stallholder.

stalwart adj brave.

stam v stamp.

stame n steam.

stamfish adj sturdy.

stammagust n disgust at food.

stammer v falter; stagger; trip.

stammle v stumble upon.

stammygaster v bewilder, flabbergast;
shock.

stamp n trap.

stan see **stand**.

stance n site; station. • v station.

stanch, stanche v assuage.

stanch-girss n yarrow.

stand, stan, staun n goal; stall; stand;
water bucket. • v cost; stand; obey;
take place; **stand o'er** remain unpaid;
stand up hesitate.

standart n table leg.

standing stane n monolith.

stane n stone; millstone; testicle. • v
stone.

stane an lime n masonry.

stane-cast n stone's throw.

stane-chack n wheatear.

stane-chakker n stonechat.

stane-clod n stone's throw.

stane-deid adj stone-dead.

stane-dumb adj totally silent.

stane-knapper n stonebreaker.

staners n shore gravel.

stanewark n stonework.

stane-wod, stane-wud adj stark mad.

stang¹ n sting; pang; wound. • v sting.

stang² n long pole.

stang o the trump n livewire.

stanie adj rocky; stony.

stank n stagnant pool; moat; open drain;
swampy area. • v fill, satisfy.

stankie n water-hen.

stannerie adj gravelly.

stannert n standard.

stannin graith n unmovable fixtures.

stap[1] n stave.

stap[2] n stop, cessation; step; surfeit. • v stop; step; block, obstruct; cram; gorge; pack; plug; stuff.

stap-bairn n stepchild.

stap-faither n stepfather.

stapin v thrust into.

stap-mither n stepmother.

stappack n meal mixed with water.

stappil, stapple n stopper.

stappin n stuffing.

stappin-stane n stepping stone.

stappit adj stuffed.

stapple[1] n staple.

stapple[2] n pipe stem.

stapple[3] see **stappil**.

stare adj stiff.

starglint n shooting star.

stark adj strong; potent; durable. • adv energetically.

starn[1], **sterne** n star.

starn[2] n stern of ship.

starnie, starny adj starry. • n little star.

starnlicht n starlight.

starrach adj bleak.

start n moment. • v startle; run about wildly.

starty adj skittish.

stashie see **stushie**.

station agent n station master.

sta'tree n tethering stake.

staumrel adj half-witted.

staun see **stand**.

staup n long step. • v step.

stave v push; shove.

stavel v blunder on; stumble.

staver v saunter.

staw n aversion; surfeit. • v cloy; have enough of.

stawsome adj nauseous; wearisome.

stay, stey v dwell, live, reside; lodge.

stead, sted v place; furnish.

steading, steiding n farm buildings; out-buildings; building site.

steak see **steek**.

steamie n public laundry.

stech n heap; crowd; atmosphere. • v cram; confine; puff, be out of breath.

stechie adj stiff; stiff-jointed.

steck n rick; stack. • v stack.

sted see **stead**.

steek[1], **steak, steik** v shut, close; clench; attach.

steek[2] n stitch. • v stitch; embroider; gore.

steek[3] n baton; staff; stick.

steel[1] n steep wooded hillside; handle; stool.

steel[2] n steelyard.

steelie n ball bearing.

steelrife adj overbearing.

steepit adj sodden.

steer[1] n commotion, stir. • v stir, bestir;.

steer[2] v meddle with; molest; pester;.

steer[3] see **stere**.

steer-tree n plough handle.

steg[1] n gander.

steg[2] v stalk.

stegh n glut.

steid n impression; imprint; track; trail. • v place; track.

steiding see **steading**.

steik[1], **steke** v pierce.

steik[2] see **steek**[1].

stell[1] n covert; shelter; prop; river pool. • v fix; place; set up; prop; halt; load.

stell[2] n still. • v distil.

stellar n distiller.

sten, stend n bound, spring. • v spring; rise.

stench adj inflexible; rigid; uncompromising.

stend see **sten**.

stenloch n coalfish.

stennis n sprain.

stent[1] adj stretched out. • v stretch; extend; draw out; tauten.

stent[2] n levy; tax. • v levy; tax; assess.

stent[3] n fixed task. • v stint; stop; restrain; allocate; allot; apportion.

stenter n clothes prop.

step aside v err.

sterde, sterdy adj strong.

stere, steer v govern; plough over.

sterk adj stark.

sterne see **starn**.

stert n beginning; start. • v begin; start; stick up.

sterve v starve.

steug n thorn, prickle.
stevin n voice; ship's prow.
stew n stench, stink. • v stink.
stew¹ v rain slightly.
stew² see **stue**.
stewart, steward n royal deputy or representative.
stewartry n territory under the rule of a steward; jurisdiction.
stey¹ adj steep.
stey² see **stay**.
stibble n stubble.
stibbler n stubble gatherer.
stibblie, stibbly adj stubbly.
stichlie adj fibrous.
stick¹ n obstacle; slight hindrance; stoppage. • v stop in the middle; bungle; fail; **stick in** persevere; **stick up tae** confront.
stick² see **steek²**.
stickin adj unsociable.
stickit adj embedded; failed; unfinished; unable to continue.
stickle v scruple.
sticks and staves npl rack and ruin.
sticky-fingert adj light-fingered.
sticky-willie n cleavers.
stiddie n anvil.
stieve adj firm; immobile; resolute; rigid; stiff; sturdy; thick; trusty; potent. • adv stably; staunchly; stiffly.
stievlie adv firmly.
stife n smoky smell.
stiffen v starch.
stiffenin n starch.
stile v place; set.
still adj morose; reserved. • still n pause. • adv nevertheless; **still an on** always; nevertheless; yet.
stilp, stilt v go on crutches.
stilpin adj striding.
stime n fraction; jot; vestige. • v peer.
stimpart n fourth part.
sting n punt pole; thatching pole.
stinge adj stiff; hard.
stinkin Tam n tansy.
stinnell n sharp pain.
stint v cease, stop; pause; droop.
stirk n year-old bullock.
stirkie n little stirk.
stirkin adj wounded; stricken.

stirlin n starling.
stirra n stout young person.
stitch n furrow, drill.
stith adj steady.
stitter n/v stutter.
stitter v stutter.
stivage adj stout; strong.
stivet n short stout man.
stivey n quantity of glutinous food.
stoan n suckers; stems. • v put out suckers.
stoater n beauty.
stoatin adj beautiful.
stob n splinter; stump; post, pole. • v fence; pierce.
stobbed, stob-feathered adj unfledged.
stobbie adj spiky.
stock n block. • v become hard; branch out.
stockie n cheese sandwich.
stocking n springing stems; livestock.
stodge v plod; stump.
stodger n plodder.
stodgie adj sulky.
stog¹ n tree stump. • v walk heavily.
stog² n sharp instrument; splinter. • v pierce.
stoggie adj rough.
stoich n bad air; smoke reek.
stoichert adj over-dressed.
stoit, stoiter n/v lurch, stagger; totter.
stok v thrust.
stok swerd n pointed sword.
stole, stowl n stalk of corn.
stoll n safe place. • v place in safety; ambush.
stolum n large broken-off piece.
stonkerd adj sullen.
stoo see **stow**.
stook n shock of corn. • v put into shocks.
stookie n plaster, stucco; effigy; stupid person.
stooks, stugs npl backward-pointing horns.
stool n stems from a single root.
stoom v frown.
stoop n ally, supporter; prop; post, gatepost.
stoor see **stour**.
stoot¹ adj robust; stout.

stoot² v stutter.

stoot³ see **stuit**.

stooth v plaster.

stootherie n larceny, theft.

stoot-hertit adj stout-hearted.

stoothin n lathing and plastering.

stor adj severe.

store n sheep or cattle.

store farm n stock farm.

stormcock n missel-thrush.

storm window n projecting roof window protected by slates.

stot¹ n blockhead.

stot² n/v stammer.

stot³ n young bull or ox.

stot⁴ v bounce; walk bouncily; bustle; rebound; stumble; stop.

stotter n totter. • v stumble.

stoun, stound¹ n period; instant; while; ache; pang; throb. • v ache; throb.

stoun, stound² n stunned state, stupor. • v resound.

stoun, stound³ v astound, bewilder.

stoup n pot, pitcher, tankard.

stoup an roup adv lock, stock and barrel; completely.

stour¹, stoor n agitation; commotion; battle; strife; flying dust; spray; gush; blizzard, snowstorm. • v gush; spray; rise in foam; rush; **stour aboot** move quickly.

stour² adj stern.

stourie adj dusty.

stourie-fit n incomer.

stourie lungs n pneumoconiosis; silicosis.

stourreen n warm drink of beer and oatmeal.

stouth n theft.

stouth and routh n abundance.

stouthrie n provision; furnishing.

stove n stew. • v steam; stew.

stow, stoo v crop; lop.

stowe v feed; stow.

stowed adj crowded; packed.

stowen n glutton.

stowfie adj dumpy.

stowl see **stole**.

stowlins, stownlins adv furtively, stealthily.

stown adj stolen.

stowp n flagon.

stra, straa, stray n straw; trifling thing.

strabble n dangling object.

stracht, straucht adj straight. • adv straight; straightaway. • n straight road. • v smooth out; straighten.

stracht-forrit adj straightforward.

strack adj strict.

strae n straw.

strae daith n natural death.

straik n excursion; seizure; streak; stripe. • v stroke; anoint; level; streak; stripe; **straik hands** join hands.

strait adj close-fitting; tense. • v straighten; tighten.

strake adj struck.

stramash n disturbance; brawl; clamour; accident; disaster; fury; uproar; wreckage.

strammel n straw.

stramp adj trampling. • n stamp; tread. • v stamp; tramp, tread; stump along; trample on; beat down.

stramullion n strong masculine woman.

strand n coast, shore.

strang adj strong; virulent.

strange adj self-conscious.

stranglie adv strongly.

strap v string together.

strapper n groom.

strath n wide river valley; dale.

strathspey n dance and tune.

straucht see **stracht**.

stravaig n roaming. • v amble; roam, wander; ramble idly; gad, gallivant.

stravaiger n aimless wanderer.

strawn n gutter.

stray see **stra**.

streamer v streak.

streamers npl aurora borealis.

streek, streik n speed; exertion. • v stretch, stretch out; lay out; question; **streek doun** lie flat.

streekit adj stretched.

streel, strule v urinate forcibly.

streen n/v strain.

streend see **streind**.

streetch n/v stretch.

streich adj stiff; affected.

streik see **streek**.

streikin adj tall; agile.

streind, streend *n/v* sprain.

strenie *adj* lazy.

strenth *n* stamina; strength.

stress *v* put to inconvenience.

striak *n* sound of the trumpet.

strick¹ *adj* rapid. • *n* rapid part of a stream.

strick² *adj* strict.

strick³ *v* strike.

stricklie *adv* strictly.

striddle *n* stride. • *v* bestride, straddle; stride.

stride-legs, stridelins, stridlins *adv* astride.

striffin *n* membrane.

strik *n* infestation.

strin, strind *n* descent.

strin², strinn *n* stream; running water.

string *v* hang by the neck.

stringin *n* lace.

strinkle, strinkil *v* strew; sprinkle.

strinn sse **strin²**.

strintle *n* rivulet.

strip¹ *n* belt of trees; chevron.

strip² *see* **strype**.

strip³ *n* stirrup.

strippings *npl* last of a cow's milk.

strippit *adj* striped.

stritchie *adj* sluggish.

striven *adj* on bad terms; at loggerheads.

strodd, strodge *v* stride out.

stron *n* beach; shore.

stronachie *n* stickleback.

strone *n* urination. • *v* spout; piddle, urinate.

strood *n* worn-out shoe.

stroonge *adj* gruff.

stroop *n* water tap.

strooshie *n* squabble.

stroot *adj* stuffed full.

stroozle *v* struggle.

strop *n* treacle.

stroul *n* fibre found in food.

strounge *adj* harsh-tasting.

stroup *n* spout of pump or kettle.

stroupag *n* pot of tea.

stroupie *n* small penis.

strouth *n* force; violence. • *v* compel.

strow *n* shrew.

strowbil *adj* stubborn.

strowd *n* silly song.

strucken *adj* stricken.

strucken up *adj* turned to stone.

strule *see* **streel**.

strum¹ *n* fuse.

strum² *n/v* sulk.

strumming *n* giddy feeling; loud murmuring noise.

strungie *adj* sullen.

strunt¹ *n* strong drink.

strunt² *v* affront; strut, swagger.

strunt³ *n* spar.

struntit *adj* offended; piqued.

strunty *adj* shrunk.

stry *v* overcome.

strynd, strynde *n* kindred; spring.

strype, strip *n* stream.

stubblin *adj* short and thickset.

stubie *n* bucket.

study, stuthie *n* anvil.

stue, stew *n* dust.

stuff¹ *n* corn, grain; vigour, mettle.

stuff² *v* become breathless; supply.

stuffet *n* lackey.

stuffie *adj* game, plucky.

stug¹ *n* thorn; stump; rawboned woman.

stug² *n* spike; stab. • *v* stab.

stuggen *n* obstinate person.

stuggy *n* uneven stubble.

stugs *see* **stooks**.

stuil *n* stool.

stuir *n* penny.

stuit, stoot, stut *v* prop; support.

stult *n* stilt.

stumfish *adj* strong-growing.

stummle *n/v* stumble.

stump *n* blockhead. • *v* walk on one leg.

stumpie *adj* one-legged.

stumpit *adj* stumpy.

stunk *n* stake.

stunks *n* ill-humour.

stunner *n* large foolish man.

stupit *adj* dense, stupid.

stuppie *n* wooden bucket.

sture *adj* hefty; strong; rough.

sture at *v* be annoyed with.

sturken *v* recuperate.

sturne *n* trouble.

sturoch *n* mixed milk and meal.

sturt *n* annoyance. • *v* molest; vex.

sturty *adj* troublesome.

stushie, stashie *n* fuss; commotion,

hubbub; uproar; quarrel, row; turbulence; tumult;.

stut¹ *n/v* stammer, stutter.

stut² *see* **stuit.**

stuthie *see* **study.**

styan *n* stye.

stye *v* climb.

styme *n* glimpse. • *v* see indistinctly.

stymie *n* short-sighted person.

styte *n* nonsense.

subfeu *v* sublease.

subite *adj* sudden.

subject *n* property.

subset *n/v* sublease, sublet.

subsist *v* stop.

substancious *adj* powerful.

succar, succur *n* sugar.

succre *v* sweeten with sugar.

sucken *adj* legally bound.

suckies *npl* clover blossoms.

suckler *adj* suckling.

suddard *n* soldier.

suddart *adv* southwards.

suddent *adj* sudden.

suddentlie *adv* suddenly.

suddenty *n* suddenness.

suddle, suddil *v* soil, sully.

Sudreys *n* Hebrides.

suenyng *n* dreaming.

suerd, swerd *n* sword.

suffer *v* delay; be patient.

sufficient *adj* substantial.

suffrage *n* prayer for the dead.

sugarallie *n* liquorice sugar.

sugg *v* move heavily.

suggan *n* heavy coverlet.

suggie *n* young sow.

suggyre *v* suggest.

suilk *see* **swilk.**

suin *adj* imminent. • *adv* soon; **suin or syne** sooner or later.

suinest *adj* quickest.

suit¹ *n* soot.

suit² *n* bevel. • *v* sue for.

suith *adj* honest.

suithfast, suthfast *adj* true; trustworthy.

sukert *n* sweet.

sulk it *v* be sulky.

sullige *n* soil.

sully *adj* silly.

sulyeart *adj* bright; clear.

sum *adj* some.

sumdeil *adv* somewhat.

sumhin *pron* something.

summer *v* pasture cattle in summer.

summer-coutts *npl* heat shimmerings.

summer-sob *n* summer storm.

summons *n* writ.

sump *n* mine shaft.

sumped *n* soaked.

sumph *n* half-witted person, oaf. • *v* be in a stupor.

sumphish *n* doltish.

sunblink *n* sunbeam.

sundoon *n* sunset.

sunk *n* turf seat.

sunkan *adj* sullen.

sunket *n* delicacy; lazy person.

sunkets *npl* provisions.

sunkie *n* low stool.

sunyie¹ *n* excuse; delay.

sunyle² *v* care.

sup *n* small quantity of liquid; beverage; dram. • *v* booze; eat with a spoon.

superior *n* landlord.

supersault *n* somersault.

supir *v* sigh.

suppable *adj* palatable.

supplie *v* supplicate.

suppois *adv* although.

suppoist *n* supporter.

suppone *v* suppose; hope.

suppowall *n* support.

suppriss *n* oppression. • *v* suppress.

surcoat *n* under-waistcoat.

surfeit *adj* immoderate; intemperate; over-priced.

surpeclaithe, surples *n* surplice.

surprise *v* be surprised.

sush *see* **soosh.**

suskit *adj* threadbare.

sussie *adj* careful. • *n* care. • *v* trouble.

sute¹ *n* sweat.

sute² *adj* sweet.

suth *see* **sooth.**

suthfast *see* **suithfast.**

suthron *see* **southron.**

sutten *adj* stunted.

suwen *v* wait upon; follow.

swa *n* sway.

swabble *n* long stick; tall thin person. • *v* thrash.

swabblin stick n cudgel.
swack[1] adj plentiful. • n large quantity. • v drink deep; blow hard.
swack[2] adj agile; lithe; pliant.
swacken v make pliant.
swackin adj tall; clever; active.
swad n swede.
swag v sag; swing.
swage v quiet.
swagger v stagger.
swaible n swab. • v mop; swab.
swaif n kiss.
swaip adj slanting.
swaird n sward.
swaish adj full-faced; benign.
swaits see **swats**.
swak awa v decay; wither.
swale adj plump.
swall[1] v distend; inflate; swell.
swall[2], **swally** v swallow; devour.
swallen adj swollen.
swallin adj swelling.
swalme n tumour.
swalter v flounder.
swam n large quantity.
swamp adj thin.
swampie n tall thin person.
swander v swoon.
swane, swayn n young person.
swank n slender.
swankin adj athletic.
swankle v make a slurping sound.
swanky adj active; celver.
swap[1], **swaup** n pod of young peas.
swap[2] v draw; throw; strike. • adv forcibly.
swap[3] n cast of features.
swar n snare.
sware, swire n neck; saddle between hills.
swarf, swerf v faint; stupefy.
swarm v abound.
swarrach n disorderly heap.
swartback n great black-backed gull.
swarth n fainting fit; sward; exchange.
swarve v incline to one side.
swash adj broad-built; fuddled. • n fat person; swagger. • v swell.
swashy adj broad-built; fuddled.
swatch adj cursory. • n excerpt; pattern; specimen.
swathel n strong man.

swats, swaits n new ale; beer.
swatter, squatter v move quickly through water.
swattle v cudgel.
swaukin adj hesitant.
swaul v swell.
swaup see **swap**[1].
swaver v walk feebly.
swaw n ripple; wave; billow. • v make waves; ripple.
sway[1] n chimney rack for pot-hooks.
sway[2] v tilt.
sway[3] n swathe of grass.
swayl, sweal v swaddle.
swayn see **swane**.
sweal[1] n twist; whirl. • v twist; whirl round; melt away.
sweal[2] see **swayl**.
sweart see **sweir**.
swech n trumpet.
swechan n rushing of water.
swecher, swescher n trumpeter.
swecht n momentum.
swedge n blacksmith's chisel.
swedgin n violence.
swee n inclination to one side; pot-hanger. • v move something aside.
sweeg see **sweig**.
sweek v do properly.
sweel n swill. • v swill; swathe; wash in a stream; wash down; swallow.
sweem n/v swim.
sweer[1] n expletive; swear word. • v swear.
sweer[2] see **sweir**.
sweerie n swear word.
sweerie-words n swear words.
sweet n stress; sweat. • v perspire; sweat.
sweetie n sweet, sweetmeat, confection; sweetheart.
sweetie bottle n sweet-jar.
sweetieman n confectioner.
sweetie poke n bag of sweets.
sweeties npl confectionery.
sweetie shop n sweet shop.
sweetie-stan n sweet-stall.
sweetiewife n confectioner; gossipy person.
sweetin adj sweaty.
sweet pan drop n peppermint.
sweg n large quantity.
sweig, sweeg n guttering candle.

sweill n swivel. • v move in a circular direction.

sweirt, sweart, sweert adj lazy, workshy; slow; difficult; hesitant; hovering; irresolute; loath; reluctant; unwilling.

sweirtie n indolence, lethargy, sloth; disinclination; reluctance.

sweich, swelchie n seal; whirlpool.

swell n bog.

swelly v swallow.

swelt v die; swoon.

swelth adj voracious.

sweltrie adj sweltering.

swerd see **suerd**.

swerf see **swarf**.

swey n/v sway; swerve.

swick adj clear of. • n deception; fraud; trick; charlatan, swindler. • v bluff; cheat; deceive; swindle.

swickerie adj swindling. • n trickery.

swicky adj deceitful.

swidder v hesitate.

swiff n/v whizz.

swig v turn suddenly.

swilk, suilk adj such.

swill v swaddle.

swine arnit n oat-grass.

swine-mait n pigswill.

swine's-saim n hog's lard.

swing n stroke.

swinge n clash.

swingle v separate flax.

swingler n flax beater.

swing-rope n hawser.

swink v toil; work hard.

swipe v move circularly; give a swinging stroke.

swipper adj nimble.

swire see **sware**.

swirk v spring up.

swirl n twirl.

swirlie adj contorted; frizzy; knobby; knotty. • n frizz. • v frizz.

swith, swyth adj swift. • adv as soon as; swiftly, quickly, speedily; **swith wi virr** adj vehement.

swither n hesitation; indecision; perplexity; quandary. • v be hesitant; fluctuate; vacillate.

swither² n/v swelter.

swithering adj vacillating; hesitant.

swithnes n speed.

swordsliper n sword-maker.

sworl n swirl.

swuff v breathe whistlingly.

swurd n sword.

swurl n/v swirl.

swyke v make to stumble.

swypes n yeasty beer.

swyth see **swith**.

sybie n spring onion.

sye n/v filter.

syle see **sile²**.

sylin n ceiling.

syll v cover.

syllab n syllable.

synd¹ n appearance.

synd² v rinse; wash; drink.

syndings npl slops.

syndrely adv afterwards; since; severally. • conj seeing.

syne¹ adv afterwards; ago; directly after; thence; thereafter; therefore; thereupon. • conj since.

syne² n rinse. • v rinse; **syne oot** wash out.

syneteen n/adj seventeen.

syning-glass n looking glass.

sype¹ v drip-dry.

sype² see **sipe**.

sypins npl oozings.

syre n sewer.

syte see **site**.

syth n strainer.

sythens adv although.

T

ta adj this.

ta and fra adv to and fro.

taave v toughen.

taavin, tawin n wrestling.

taberner n innkeeper.

tabetless, tapetless adj benumbed; heedless.

tabets, teppits npl bodily feelings.

tablet¹ n reliquary.

tablet² see **taiblet**.

tabrach n rotting animal food.

tach, tatch v arrest.

tacht, taght adj tight; taut.

tack¹ n lease.

tack² n loose grip.

tacket n boot or shoe nail; hobnail.

tackety n hobnailed.

tackie adj blundering, clumsy.

tackle n arrow.

tacksman n lease-holder; senior tenant.

taddy n tadpole.

tade see **taid**.

tae¹ prep to. • adv too; **tae the fore** adj surviving.

tae² n toe; prong, tine; tea.

taen¹ adj embarrassed; surprised.

taen² v pt took; pp taken; **taen doun** emaciated; **taen up wi** preoccupied.

taen³, tane n the one contrasted with the other.

taen-awa n changeling.

taenhauf n one half.

taff n toff; ostentatious person.

taff-dyke n turf dyke.

tafferel adj thoughtless.

taffie n toffee, treacle toffee.

taffil n table.

taffle v tire.

tag n shoe fastening; lace. • v wane; tie.

tag an rag n every bit.

taggit adj white-tailed.

tagglit adj harassed.

taght see **tacht**.

taibetless adj numb.

taiblet, tablet n sugar toffee., fudge.

taickle n/v tackle.

taid¹, tade, taud n sheep tick; toad; small child.

taid², taud v manure.

taidrel n puny creature.

taidstule n mushroom.

taigle v bamboozle, confuse; detain; delay; entangle; hamper; mix up.

taiglesome adj hindering; tedious; time-consuming; tiring.

taik v tack (in sailing).

taiken n token.

taikning n signal.

tail, tale n account; reckoning; retinue; end; backside.

tail-toddle n sex.

tailye n bond. • v entail.

taing, tang adj straight; tight. • n handle slot; prong, tine; tongue of land.

taint n proof.

taip n tapestry.

tair v bray.

taird n contemptible creature; taunt.

tairge v scold severely.

tairm n term.

tairt n tart.

taissle v blow about; stir up.

taist¹ n sample.

taist² v grope about.

taistrill n grubby girl.

tait, tate n small piece; lock of hair.

taith see **tath**.

taiver v wander.

taivers npl tatters.

taiversum adj tiresome.

taivert adj wearied.

tak n capture; catch; disposition; prize. • v take; pledge; lease; **tak a lend of** make a fool of; **tak aff** drink up; **tak doon** debilitate, weaken; dilute; **tak in aboot** take control of; **tak in** leak; meet; **tak leg** bail; retreat; decamp; run away; **tak o** resemble; **tak on** affect; chaff, joke; **tak on haun** undertake; **tak oot** enrol; **tak tellin** need reminding; **tak tent** notice; **tak tent o** beware of; watch; **tak the gate** set off home; **tak the road** set off, set out; **tak up** comprehend; reopen; rise; **tak wi** acknowledge; allow; admit.

take n state of mind.

takie adj long-lasting.

takin n pinch.

talbert n sleeveless garment.

tale see **tail**.

talent n desire; purpose.

talla n tallow.

tallie lamp n miner's lamp.

tallon talloun n tallow. • v pitch; caulk.

tammachless adj eating little.

tammie n beret.

Tammie norrie n puffin.

tammil v scatter.

tammock n hillock.

tammy-nid-nod n chrysalis.

Tam o Shanter n beret.

tandle n bonfire.

tane *see* **taen**.

tang *see* **taing**.

tanghal *n* bag.

tangis *see* **tangs**.

tangit *adj* iron-rimmed.

tangle[1] *n* icicle.

tangle[2] *n* seaweed.

tangle[3] *adj* tall; feeble.

tanglewise *adj* slender.

tangs, tangis *npl* tongs.

tannle *see* **tawnle**.

tantersome *adj* exasperating.

tantrums *npl* high airs.

tap *adj* excellent; first-rate. • *n* top; crest; forelock; tip. • *v* beg, cadge.

tap-coat *n* topcoat.

tape *v* use sparingly.

taper-tail *adj* topsy-turvy.

tapetis *n* tapestry.

tapetless *see* **tabetless**.

tapisht *adj* lurking.

taploch *n* wild girl.

tappietoorie *n* turret.

tappin *n* crest; top.

tappit *adj* crested; topped; tufted.

tappit-hen *n* quart measure; large wine bottle.

tapsalteerie *adj/adv* topsy-turvy; upside down; higgledy-piggledy.

tapsman *n* drover; foreman.

taptaes *npl* tiptoes.

taptee *n* eager anticipation.

tapthrawn *adj* stubborn.

tar-buist *n* tar box.

tardie *adj* peevish.

targat *n* tatter; tassel. • *v* edge with tassels.

targe *n* harridan. • *v* beat; reprehend.

targed *adj* shabby.

tarlies *n* lattice.

tarloch *adj* weak; peevish; eating little. • *n* troublesome woman.

tarmanick *n* turmeric.

tarrow *v* delay; haggle.

tarry-breaks, tarry-breeks *n* sailor.

tarry-fingered *adj* thievish.

tartan *adj* of the tartan. • *n* striped and check-patterned cloth.

tartle, tertle *v* recognise; discern; **tartle at** look at in surprise.

tartuffish *adj* sulky.

tarveal *v* fatigue.

tary *v* distress.

tash *n* discredit; dishonour; stigma; stain. • *v* soil, stain; injure; upbraid; discredit; dishonour; fatigue; **tash about** throw carelessly.

tashful *adj* dishonourable.

tashie *adj* unkempt, untidy.

task *n* angel; spirit.

tasker *n* pieceworker.

taskit *adj* wearied.

tassie, tass *n* cup, goblet.

taste *v* tipple.

tatch[1] *n* fringe; fastening.

tatch[2], **tach** *v* fix lightly.

tatch[3] *see* **tatch**[1].

tate *see* **tait**.

tath, taith *n* animal dung; luxuriant grass. • *v* apply manure.

tatshie *adj* ill-dressed.

tattie, tawtie *n* potato.

tattie bannock *n* potato cake.

tattie bing *n* potato clamp.

tattiebogle *n* ragamuffin; scarecrow; scruff.

tattie bree *n* potato soup.

tattie-champer *n* potato masher.

tattie-creel *n* potato basket.

tattie-deevil *n* potato digger.

tattie-howker *n* potato gatherer.

tattie-howkin, tattie-liftin *n* potato harvest.

tattie-pairk *n* potato field.

tattie-parer *n* potato peeler.

tattie-peelin *n* potato skin.

tattie-pit *n* potato pit.

tattie-ploom *n* potato seedbox.

tattie-poke *n* potato bag.

tattie-scone *n* potato scone.

tattieshaws *n* potato leaves.

tattrel *n* rag.

taucht *n* melted tallow.

tauchy *adj* greasy.

taud *see* **taid**[1], **taid**[2].

taulch, taugh *n* tallow.

taupie, tawpie *n* foolish woman.

taupin *n* tap root.

taur *n/v* tar.

taurie *adj* tarry.

taut *v* mat; tangle.

tautit *adj* matted; shaggy.

taw¹ *n* fibre.

taw² *n* rolling marble; difficulty. • *v* suck hard; make tough.

tawan *n* reluctance.

tawbern *n* tabor.

tawie *adj* tame.

tawin *see* **taavin**.

tawm *n* fit of ill humour.

tawnle, tannle *n* balefire, bonfire.

tawpy *adj* slovenly.

tawse, taws, taz *n* punishment strap; whip. • *v* whip.

taxatour *n* assessor.

taxt *n* tax.

taynt, taint *v* convict.

tayntour *n* witness in law.

taz *see* **tawse**.

tazie *n* playful girl.

teal¹, teil *n* busybody.

teal², tole *v* wheedle.

tealer *n* wheedler.

tea-haun *n* tea-drinker.

tear *n* comic; wag. • *v* gust; labour hard; **tear intae** assault, attack.

tearin *adj* energetic.

tea-skiddle *n* tea party.

teaz *n* golf tee.

teazle *v* tease; vex.

tedd *adj* ravelled.

tedder *n* tether, tethering rope. • *v* tether.

tee¹ *n* peg or little heap of sand on which golfers set the ball for the first stroke. • *v* set up a golf ball.

tee² *adv* too.

teedle *n* make mouth music.

teedy *adj* ill-humoured.

teeger *n* tiger.

teel *v* cultivate; till.

teem *v* deluge; gush; stream.

teen *n* chagrin; grief. • *v* provoke.

teename *n* nickname.

teenge *n* colic; tinge. • *v* tinge.

teep *n* category; type.

teepid *adj* tepid.

teepit *adj* kept on short allowance.

teeple *n* light touch. • *v* touch lightly.

teesie *n* fit of passion.

teet, tete *n* stolen glance. • *v* peep.

teethache *n* toothache.

teethrife *adj* toothsome.

teethy *adj* crabbed.

teicher, ticher *n* tiny drop. • *v* ooze slightly.

teight *adj* tired.

teil¹, tele *v* cultivate the soil.

teil² *see* **teal¹**.

teind, tyne *n* spark; tithe. • *v* kindle.

teinds *npl* tithes.

teir *adj* tiresome. • *n* fatigue.

teirful *adj* exhausted.

teist *n* handful.

tele *see* **teil¹**.

teleland *n* arable land.

telisman *n* farmer.

tell *v* count.

teller *n* accountant cashier.

telling *n* admonition; warning.

telt *v* told.

temp *v* tempt.

temper *v* put into order.

tenchis *npl* taunts.

tend¹ *v* attend; support.

tend² *see* **tent³**.

tender *adj* sickly, poorly; beloved. • *adv* weakly.

tenement *n* house incorporating several dwellings, flats.

ten-hours'-bite *see* **hauf-yoking**.

tenon *n* tendon.

tenor *n* tenon.

tent¹ *adj* watchful. • *n* attention; care; heed; notice. • *v* attend; observe; heed; pay attention; tend; stretch out.

tent² *n* field pulpit.

tent³, tend *adj/n* tenth.

tentie *adj* attentive; heedful; observant; watchful.

tentily *adv* carefully.

tentless *adj* careless; heedless; inattentive.

teppits *see* **tabets**.

terce *n* third part.

tercian *n* cask.

tere *adj* tender.

teribus *interj* war cry of Hawick.

term day *n* quarter day.

terne *adj* fierce.

ternish *v* tarnish.

terr *v* tear.

terrel *adj* terrible.

terrible *adv* extremely.

terrie *n* terrier.

terrification *n* terror.

terse *n* debate.

tersel *n* table companion.

tert *n* tart.

tertiam *n* third part of a butt of wine.

tertian *n* third-year undergraduate.

tertle *see* **tartle**.

testificate *n* passport; testimonial.

testit *adj* bequeathed.

testoon *n* silver coin.

testor *n* bedcover.

tete *see* **teet**.

teth *n* temper.

tether *v* confine; restrain; tie.

tetherfaced *adj* cross-looking.

teuch[1] *n* draught of liquor.

teuch[2] *adj* tough; dry.

teuchit, teuchat *n* lapwing.

teuchter *n* country person; boor; Highlander.

teud *n* tooth.

teudle *n* tooth of a rake. • *v* insert a tooth.

teug, tug *n* rope; halter; tug. • *v* tug.

teuk, took *n* aftertaste.

teukin *adj* quarrelsome.

tew *v* toughen; fatigue; overpower.

tewel *n* tool.

teym *v* empty.

teyne *adj* furious. • *n* rage. • *v* irritate.

tha, they *pron* these.

thack *n/v* thatch.

thack an raip *n* comforts.

thacker *n* thatcher.

thackit biggin *n* thatched cottage.

thackless *adj* roofless.

thae *adj/pron* these, those.

thaft *n* rowing bench, thwart.

thaim *pron* them.

thaimsels *pron* themselves.

thain *see* **thane**[2].

thairm *n* belly; gut.

thairm-band *n* catgut string.

thairms *npl* intestines.

thame *see* **theme**.

than *adv/conj* then.

thane[1] *n* noble; provincial leader.

thane[2], **thain** *adj* undercooked, rare.

thankful *adj* praiseworthy.

thankrif *adj* grateful.

tharf *v* need.

that *adv* so.

the[1] *adj* this.

the[2] *v* prosper.

the[3] *see* **thee**.

thede *n* nation.

thee, the, they *n* thigh.

theedle, theevle *n* stirring stick.

theek *v* thatch.

theeking *n* thatch.

theevle *see* **theedle**.

thegither *adj* concerted. • *adv* together.

theik, thek *v* cover; roof.

theme, thame *n* bonded servant.

then *conj* than.

thenk *v* thank.

thereaway *adv* thereabouts, about there.

there-ben *adv* in there.

therefrae *adv* from there.

therein *adv* indoors.

thereout *adv* outside.

theretill *adv* thither.

therteen *adj/n* thirteen; thirteenth.

thesaure *n* treasure.

thesaurer *n* treasurer.

thetes, theads *npl* drawing ropes.

thew *n* custom; manner; quality.

thewit *adj* disciplined.

thewles *see* **thowless**.

they *see* **tha**; **thee**.

thick *adj* intimate; thickset.

thiefie *adj* disreputable; furtive.

thig, thigg *v* ask; beg; plagiarise.

thiger, thiggar *n* parasite; beggar.

thigging *n* begging.

thight *adj* watertight.

thilse *adv* else.

thimber *adj* gross; heavy.

thin *adj* annoyed; unfriendly.

thine, thyne *adv* thence.

thinefurth *adv* henceforth.

thing *n* amount; public meeting; affairs of state.

think on *v* devise.

thir *pron* these.

thirdsman *n* arbitrator; referee.

thirl *n* hole. • *v* perforate; drill; bore; pierce; bind; thrill; tingle; furl; enslave.

thirlage, thirldome *n* thraldom.

thirled tae *adj* obsessed.

thirling *adj* very cold.

tho *adv* then; at that time.

thocht¹ n belief; care; thought; disquiet, unease; tiny amount.

thocht² conj although.

thochtbane n wishbone.

thochtie, thochty adj anxious; attentive; grave; thoughtful.

tholance n toleration.

thole n endurance; patience; tolerance. • v suffer, bear, endure, put up with; tolerate; **thole throu** pull through.

tholeable adj bearable, tolerable.

tholemoodie, tholmude adj patient.

tholesum adj bearable.

tholnie n toll.

thon adv yon, yonder. • pron that; those; yon.

thonder adj/adv yonder.

thoom, thoomb see **thoum**.

thoosan adj/n thousand.

thor n imprisonment.

thorough adv through.

thorow adj thorough. • v clean.

thorrows npl troubles.

thort adj transverse. • adv athwart; transversely.

thorter, thortour prep/adv across. • v contravene; oppose; thwart.

thoum, thoom, thoomb, thowm n thumb; **aside yer thoum** fumblingly.

thout v sob.

thowe, thow n/v thaw.

thowl, thowel n rowlock.

thowless, thewles adj inactive; inert; lethargic; sluggish; unprofitable; useless; tasteless.

thowlessnes n inactivity.

thowm see **thoum**.

thra, thro, throuch adj eager; brave; obstinate. • n eagerness.

thrab n/v throb.

thrae adj backward; reluctant; stiff.

thraft adj surly.

thrain v go on about something.

thraip v thrive.

thrait n threat. • v threaten.

thram v prosper, thrive.

thrammel n binding rope. • v wind; reel.

thrang adj crowded; numerous; close; familiar with; busy; active. • n crowd; throng; busyness. • v throng; press.

thrangitie n pressure.

thrapple n windpipe; throat; Adam's apple. • v strangle; throttle.

thrash¹ n rush.

thrash² v thresh.

thrashel n threshold.

thratch v grasp convulsively.

thrave n twenty-four sheaves of corn; considerable quantity.

thraw n anger; brief moment; pang; contortion; convulsion; distortion; drawback; perversity; quarrel; setback; stubbornness; throe; throw; tilt. • v wreath; wrench; oppose; throw; contort; defy; discolour; pervert; purse; quarrel; sling; snag; twist; wring; **thraw up** grow quickly.

thrawart adj forward; perverse; adverse; cross-grained; stubborn, obstinate; distorted; intractable; perverse; pigheaded; reluctant; self-willed; stubborn; twisted; wry.

thrawn-gabbit adj peevish.

thrawn-mou'd adj wry-mouthed.

thrawnness n perversity; stubbornness.

threap n affirmation; argument; controversy; dispute; quarrel; row; swingletree; tradition. • v affirm; allege; argue; assert; browbeat; carp; dispute; exhort; harp; insist; nag at; quarrel; reiterate; row; **threap at** urge.

threapin n insistence.

threapment n assertion.

three-neukit adj three-cornered.

threep, threpe n firm belief.

threeple adj/v treble; triple.

threeplet n triplet.

three-taed adj three-pronged.

threft adj reluctant; perverse.

threid n thread.

threne n popular saying.

threpe see **threep**.

threswald, threshwart n threshold.

threte n/v throng; crowd.

threttene adj/n thirteen.

threttie, thretty adj/n thirty.

thrid see **trid**.

thrie adj/n three.

thriest n constraint.

thrieveless adj negligent; thriftless.

thrife n prosperity.

thrifite n moneybox.

thrift *n* employment; work.

thriftless *adj* profitless.

thrimle *v* press; squeeze; wrestle.

thrimp *v* press.

thring *v* hoist; shrug. • *v* hoist; press.

thrinter *n* three year-old beast.

thrissil *n* thistle.

thrissle cock *n* missel thrush.

thrissly *adj* irritable.

thrist[1] *n/v* thirst.

thrist[2] *n* thurst; pressure; difficulty. • *v* thrust; spin; trust.

thrister *n* thirsty person.

thristy *adj* thirsty.

thrive *n* success.

thro *see* **thra**.

throch[1] *n* sheet of paper; short book.

throch[2] *adv* through.

throck *n/v* crowd.

throll *n* hole.

throstle *n* song thrush. • *v* warble.

throu, throwe *prep* across; during; through; by; by authority of.

throuch[1] *n* faith; credit.

throuch[2] *v* carry through; pierce.

throuch[3] *see* **thra**.

throu-come *n* ordeal.

througang *n* thoroughfare.

through-gawn *adj* persevering; enterprising; go-ahead.

through *adj* thorough.

throughal *adj* frugal.

throughbearin *n* livelihood.

throughither *adj* disorderly; disorganised.

through-pit *n* activity; capacity; production; output.

through-pittin *n* cross-examination.

throuither, through-other *adj* all over the place.

throuitherness *n* inefficiency; muddleheadedness.

throw *v* twist.

throwder *adj* chaotic; unmethodical.

throwe *see* **throu**.

thruch-stane *n* grave slab.

thrum[1] *n* thread; perverse streak.

thrum[2] *v* purr.

thrummer *n* poor musician.

thrump *v* press; push.

thrunland *adj* rolling.

thrush *n* rush. • *v* fall; tumble; cleave.

thrustle *n* thistle.

thry *adj* cross; perverse.

thryft *v* thrive.

thud *n* wheedling. • *v* wheedle.

thummle *n* thimble.

thummles *npl* raspberries.

thumper *n* large individual.

thumpin *adj* great.

thunner *n* thunder.

thunner-an-lichtenin *n* lungwort.

thunner-plump *n* thunder shower.

thus-gate *adv* in this way.

thwankin *adj* overcast; cloudy.

thyne *see* **thine**.

tice, tise, tyse *v* attract; entice; coax.

tichel *n* quantity; something kept in secret.

ticher[1] *v* snigger.

ticher[2] *see* **teicher**.

tichle *v* join hands.

ticht *adj* able; competent; hard-up; parsimonious; tight. • *adv* neatly, tidily; tightly. • *v* shut tight.

tichten *v* tighten.

tick *n* grain, granule.

ticker *n* dot; point.

ticket *n* shabby or untidy person.

tickle *v* puzzle.

tickler *n* problem; puzzle.

ticklie, tickly *adj* puzzling.

tid *n* occasion; season; proper time.

tiddie *adj* cross-tempered.

tide *n* ocean, sea.

tidie *see* **tydie**.

tie *n* trick.

tied *adj* inevitable.

tiend-free *adj* free of tithes.

tiff *v* spit out.

tift[1] *n* state, condition. • *v* arrange.

tift[2] *n* quarrel.

tift[3] *v* drink down.

tifter *n* quandary.

tiftie, tifty *adj* petulant; touchy; quarrelsome.

tig *n* touch; light tap; game of tag; fit of ill humour. • *v* touch lightly; dally.

tiggy *adj* pettish.

tigher *v* titter; ooze out.

tig-taggin *n* haggling.

tig-tire *n* suspense.

tike¹, tyke n dog, mongrel; boor, churl.
tike² n ticking for bed.
till¹, til prep to; until; while.
till² n clay.
till³ v entice.
tillie¹ adj clayey.
tillie² n ship's tiller.
tillie-clay n unproductive clayey soil.
tillie-pan n pan, skilled.
tilt adj snatched.
timeaboot, timeabout adv alternately.
timeous adj opportune.
timetaker n plotter; lier in wait.
timmer¹ adj bashful.
timmer² adj tuneless, unmusical;
  wooden. • n timber. • v beat; **timmer up**
  get on briskly with.
timmerman n carpenter.
timming n coarse woollen cloth.
timorsome, timorsoum adj fearful;
  nervous; timid, timorous.
timpan see **tympan**.
tin n accent.
tinchel n closing circle of hunters.
tindle n tinder.
tine see **tyne**.
tingle n jingle. • v jingle; ring; tinkle.
tink¹, tinker, tinkler n itinerant trader;
  gipsy; tinker.
tink² v rivet.
tinnel n watermark.
tinnie n can; small bowl; tinsmith.
tinsal see **tynsaill**.
tint n indication.
tip¹ v tap.
tip² see **tup**.
tipper v walk on tiptoe.
tipper-tapper v totter.
tipperty adj unstable.
tippet n halter; small fragment.
tippie, tippy adj fashionable, stylish.
tire n fatigue; tiredness; weariness.
tirl¹ n breeze. • v veer.
tirl² n sharp stroke on a musical instrument.
tirl³ v uncover; strip; undress.
tirless n grating; grill; lattice; trellis;
  turnstile.
tirlie n winding path.
tirr¹ v tear; snarl.
tirr² adj crabbed. • n bad-tempered child.

tirr³ v denude, strip, undress.
tirran, tyrane adj tyrannical. • n despot,
  tyrant.
tirrivee, tirravee n fury, rage; tantrum.
tische n girdle.
tise see **tice**.
tishie n tissue.
tissle n/v tussle.
tit¹ n/v jerk.
tit² n nipple; teat.
tither adj additional. • n other.
tithing n tidings.
titlin n runt.
titly adv speedily.
tittie, titty n sister.
titup n trigger.
tizzle v stir up.
to adj shut.
toalie n round bannock.
toam v rope.
toath see **toth**.
tobacco fleuk n sole.
toby n valve.
tocher n dowry. • v bestow a dowry.
tocherless n without a dowry.
tocum n approach.
tod n fox; ivy bush.
toddle, todle n unsteady walk; stroll;
  child. • v walk unsteadily; totter; stroll;
  waggle; ripple.
toddy n hot whisky and water.
todgie n small cake.
tod-hunt n foxhunt.
tod's turn n dirty trick.
to-fa n close; end.
tofall n lean-to.
tofore adv/prep before.
to-gang n meeting.
togersum adj tedious.
toighal n parcel.
toir¹ v beat.
toit² n fit of illness or temper.
tokie n small child.
tolbooth n jailhouse; town hall.
toldour n cloth of gold.
tole see **teal²**.
toll, toll-bar n turnpike.
tollie n toll-keeper.
to-look n prospect.
tolor n state; condition.
tolter adj precarious; unstable. • v totter.

tome¹, tom *n* fishing line.
tome² *v* draw out.
tommack *n* hillock.
tomshee *n* fairy hillock.
to-name *n* additional name.
tongue *v* chide.
tongue-be-trusht *adj* outspoken.
tongue-ferdy *adj* talkative.
tongue-raik, tongue-rake *n* loquacity; fluency.
tongue-tackit *adj* dumb; tongue-tied.
tonnoched *adj* wrapped in a plaid.
tontine *n* annuity shared by several subscribers.
toober¹ *n* quarrel.
toober² *v* beat; strike.
tooch *n* shot.
toog *n* tussock.
toohoo *n* insipid person.
took *see* **teuk**.
tool *n* towel.
toolyie *n* brawl. • *v* fight.
toom *adj* empty; vain; unprofitable.
toom-skinn'd *adj* hungry.
toon *n* hamlet.
toon *n* town.
toon hoose *n* town hall.
toonsers *npl* townspeople.
toon yett *n* main street.
toop *see* **tup**.
toopikin, toopick *n* pinnacle.
toor *n* tower.
toorie *n* pompom; tassel; topknot.
toosh *n* bedgown.
toosht *n* tuft.
tooshtie *n* bunch.
toot¹ *interj* pooh.
toot² *n* tippler. • *v* drink up.
toot³ *v* trumpet.
tooter *n* horn; trumpet.
toothful *n* mouthful.
toottie *n* drunkard.
toottle *v* mutter.
top *v* tap.
tope *v* oppose.
topper *n* something excellent.
topster *n* tapster.
to-put *n* addition; add-on.
to-putter *n* taskmaster.
tore *n* saddle pommel.
torett *n* muffler.

torfeir *n* hardship.
torfel *v* pine away.
torie, tory *n* grubworm; contemptible small person.
tork *v* torture.
torne *n* tower.
torpit *n* turpentine.
torter *n/v* torture.
tortie *n* tortoise.
tory *see* **torie**.
tosh *n* neat; trim. • *v* tidy; smarten; **tosh up** dress up.
tosie, tousy *adj* tipsy; warm; snug.
tosiness *n* snugness.
tost *v* tease; vex.
tot¹ *n* aggregate.
tot² *n* toddler. • *v* totter.
total *adj* teetotal.
totch *n* jerk. • *v* toss; rock.
toth, toath *n/v* manure.
tother *adj* other.
toth-fauld *n* dung pit.
tottie *n* toddler, tot. • *v* take tottering steps.
tottle *v* bubble; toddle.
touch *v* apply the assent to an act of Parliament; **touch up** remark on.
touchbell *n* earwig.
touk¹ *n* stroke; drumbeat.
touk² *n* tuck; protective wall. • *v* tuck.
toun *n* town; farm buildings.
tounder *n* tinder.
toun-gate *n* street.
toun-raw *n* town's rights.
toup *n* dolt.
tour¹, toure *n* turn.
tour² *v* speed.
tour-aboot *adv* alternately.
touse *v* dishevel; rumple; knock about; pull about; tease.
tousie *adj* disordered; rough; rowdy. • *n* contest. • *v* rumple; handle roughly.
touslie *adj* ruffled.
touss *v* confuse.
toustie *adj* testy.
tousy *see* **tosie**.
tout *n* copious draught of drink. • *v* drink; drink up, empty.
touther *v* put into disorder.
toutherie *adj* disordered.
toutle *v* tipple.

tove v issue; stream out; soar; smoke strongly; talk easily.

tovie adj tipsy; babbling.

tovise v flatter.

tow¹ n hemp; flax.

tow² n cable, rope, cord; cage.

tow³ v give way; perish; fail.

towar n rope-maker.

towdy n backside.

towerick n summit; eminence.

towerist n tourist.

towin v toss about.

towl n toll. • v clang; knell; toll.

towt n indisposition.

towtherie adj dishevelled.

toxie, tozie adj tipsy.

toy n woman's headdress.

trachelt adj harassed; overwhelmed; overworked; troubled.

trachle, trauchle n drudgery; nuisance; exertion; mess; encumbrance. • v afflict; drudge; toil; draggle; trail; dishevel, bedraggle; encumber, burden.

trachlesome adj exhausting.

track¹ n feature; trait; tract.

track² n trench. • v break in.

track-boat n canal boat.

trackit, trakit adj tired out.

trackpot, truckpot n teapot.

trad n track; course.

trade n corporation.

tradesman n handicraftsman.

trae¹ adj stubborn; hard to teach.

trae² see **tray**.

traffeck n trade; dealings; intercourse; communication; traffic. • v trade; deal; traffic.

trag n trash.

traget, trigget n trick.

tragullion see **tregallion**.

traicherous adj treacherous.

traicle n molasses; treacle.

traik n wanderer; trudge; mutton. • v wander idly; tramp; straggle; be in declining health.

traikit adj fatigued.

traison n treachery; treason.

traissle v tread down.

traist, trest adj loyal; faithful. • n trust. • v trust.

traisty adj loyal; faithful.

traisure n treasure.

tram n shaft of a cart; beam; leg.

tramort n corpse.

tramp n stamp. • v stamp; tread down; **tramp claes** wash clothes by treading.

tramper n vagrant.

trams npl legs.

trance n aisle; corridor; lane.

trance door n inner door.

tranont, trawynt v march fast in secret.

transack n negotiation; transaction. • v transact.

translate v transfer.

transport v move a minister from one charge to another.

trantle n deep rut.

trantle-hole n dumping hole.

trantles npl small things; toys.

trap n ladder.

trappin n edging; ribbon, tape; trimming.

trash v maltreat.

trash o' weet n heavy rainfall.

trashy adj rainy.

trat n crone.

tratour n traitor.

trattil, trattle v babble.

trauchle see **trachle**.

traveller n roving tinker.

travise n stable.

travish v sail backwards and forwards.

trawart adj perverse.

trawynt see **tranont**.

tray, trae n trouble.

treat v regale.

tred n trade. • v track; trail; trade.

tree n barrel.

tree-clout n wooden heel on shoe.

treeple v beat time.

treesh v coax.

treeshin n courting.

tree-speeler n tree-creeper.

tregallion, tregullion n assortment.

treilie adj chequered.

trein adj of wood.

treit, trete v entreat.

trek adj diseased; dying.

tremmie v quaver; tremble.

tremmlin tree n aspen.

trenkets see **cuddie heels**.

tress¹ n trace.

tress² n trestle.

trest adj trusty.
tret adj long; well-proportioned.
trete see **treit**.
trevaille n retinue.
trew v believe; trust.
trewbut, trewage n tribute.
trews npl long narrow trousers.
tribble n ailment; disease; tribulation; trouble.
tribblesome adj troublesome.
tricker n trigger.
tricky adj artful.
trid. thrid adj third. • n third part. • v divide in three.
trie n stick.
triffle[1] n trefoil.
triffle[2] n trifle.
trift n industry; thrift.
trig adj active; dapper, neat, trim; orderly; tidy; well-made. • v neaten.
trigget see **traget**.
triggin n decking out.
trigle v trickle.
trigness n neatness.
trim v thrash.
trimmer, trimmie n low woman.
trindle v trundle.
trine n drinking match.
tring n series.
trink n channel; gutter; drain; runnel; rut; sea-filled pool.
trinket adj rutted.
trinkle v tingle.
trinnle n wheel.
trip n flock.
trist adj sad.
trive v thrive.
troch n trough.
trock, trog n barter; small talk; rubbish; old clothes; worthless stuff.
trocker n small trader.
trod n footstep.
troddle, trootie, trutle v trot, canter.
trodge v trudge.
trog see **trock**.
trogger n old-clothes dealer.
troke n odds and ends; association; bargain; barter; deal; chore, task; merchandise; pedlar's wares; trash; truck. • v associate; transact dubious business; bargain, barter; hobnob; truck.

troker n bargainer; dealer.
trokes npl trinkets.
troll[1] n goblin.
troll[2] n horse dung.
tron n marketplace.
trone see **trowan**.
troon adj absent. • n truant. • v play truant.
troosers npl trousers.
troot n trout.
trootle see **troddle**.
tross, trouss v pack up; truss.
troth n verity.
trotters npl sheep's feet.
trotties npl sheep dung.
trouss see **tross**.
trove n turf.
trow[1] n river vale; conduit, channel; troll; devil.
trow[2] v believe.
trowan, trone n mason's trowel.
trowie adj sickly.
trowless adj faithless.
trowth n truth.
truaghan n down-and-out.
truan n trowel.
truckpot see **trackpot**.
trudder n lumber, junk.
trudge-back n hunchback.
trudget n trick; soldering paste.
truelins adv truly.
truff n trick. • v steal.
truff dyke n turf wall.
truist n trust.
trullion n crupper; silly fool.
trum n trim; order; thread.
trump n Jew's harp.
trump v fling; march; blow the trumpet.
trumpe n valueless object.
trumph n trump card.
trumpherie adj trumpery.
trumposie adj guileful.
trumpour n deceiver.
truncher n trencher.
trunnle v trundle.
trustful adj trustworthy.
trustre n butter.
truthfae adj truthful.
trutle see **troddle**.
try v vex; annoy.
trying adj distressing.

trykle n syrup.

tryne n stratagem; retinue.

trypal n ill-made person.

tryst n agreement to meet; appointment; assignation; date; covenant. • v agree to meet; meet; convene; betroth.

trysting place n meeting place.

trystit adj engaged.

tuack, tuach n small hillock.

tucht n vigour.

tuck n riverside jetty.

tuckie adj disabled.

tue, tued adj tired.

tuff n tuft.

tuffing n tow; oakum.

tuffle v ruffle.

tug see teug.

tuggle v pull jerkily.

tuigh n suspicion.

tuil n tool; utensil.

tuilyie see tulyie.

tuim, tume adj empty; unoccupied; vacant; idling; lean; vain; unprofitable. • n void; midden. • v empty; pour out; drain; evacuate.

tuim-handit n empty-handed.

tuim-heidit n empty-headed.

tuin n tune.

tuip see tup.

tuird n turd.

tuith n tooth.

tuithie adj acrimonious; critical.

tuive v swell; rise.

tuke n tug.

tulchan n straw-stuffed calfskin; figurehead.

tulloch n mound.

tullyie v scuffle.

tulshie n ill-favoured person.

tulyie, tuilyie n quarrel; brawl; toil; trouble. • v quarrel; brawl.

tumbler n light cart.

tumbus n large thing or person.

tume see tuim.

tumfie n dolt.

tummle n/v tumble.

tummock n hummock.

tunch n/v nudge.

tune n accent; intonation; dialect; disposition; temper; mood; twang. • v adjust.

tunie adj moody.

tup, tip, toop, tuip n ram.

turbot n halibut.

turchie adj short; thick.

turcume n matted dirt.

tures npl turfs.

turf n peat.

turk adj truculent.

turkas, turkes npl pincers.

turken v harden.

turlie n whirligig.

turn n duty; piece of work; rebuff. • v become.

turnscrew n screwdriver.

turntail n fugitive.

turr n turf.

turs, turss v pack up in a bundle.

tursable adj portable.

turse n bale; truss. • v adjust; bale; truss.

tush v pooh-pooh.

tushilago n coltsfoot.

tushlach n dried cowpat.

tusk at v pull at.

tusker, tuskar n peat cutter.

tute n projection.

tutie n drunken woman.

tutor n guardian.

tutory, tutorie n tutelage; tutorship; guardianship.

twa adj two.

twa faul adj dual.

twa n two.

twa, twae n two.

twa-beddit adj twin-bedded.

twa-eed steak n kipper.

twa-fangelt adj indecisive.

twa-fauld adj two-fold; double.

twa-handit crack n dialogue.

twal adj/n twelve.

twalmonth n twelvemonth.

twaloors n midday, twelve o'clock; midday meal.

twalt, twelt adj twelfth.

twang n twinge.

twasome, twasum n pair; two in company.

twa-three n few.

tweddle n tweed cloth.

tweed n/v twill.

tweedle v twiddle.

tweel¹ n tweed cloth. • v weave.

tweel² adv truly.

tweelie *n* quarrel.
tween hauns *n* meantime, meanwhile.
tweenwhiles *npl* intervals.
tweesh *prep* between.
tweeter *v* twitter.
tweetle *v* sing.
twelt *see* **twalt**.
twicet *adj* twice.
twidle *v* circumvent.
twig *n* twitch; short pull. • *v* cut the skin in shearing; pull hastily.
twilt *n/v* quilt.
twin, twine[1] *v* separate; diverge; deprive.
twine[2] *v* writhe.
twingle *v* twine round.
twinter *n* two-year-old beast.
twintie *adj/n* twenty.
twirk *n* twitch.
twist *n* twig.
twitch *v* touch.
twittery *adj* slender.
tyce *v* move slowly.
tydie, tidie *adj* neat; plump.

tyke *see* **tike**[1].
tyke-tulyie *n* dogfight.
tyld *n/v* cover.
tylor *n* tailor.
tymber *n* helmet crest.
tymbrit *adj* crested.
tympan, timpan *n* raised central section of a house.
tynd *n* spark.
tyne, tine *v* lose; miss; forfeit; be lost; perish.
tyner *n* loser.
tyning *n* losing.
tynsaill, tinsal *n* forfeiture.
tynt *adj* lost.
typin *adj* laborious.
tyrane *see* **tirran**.
tyrement *n* interment.
tyse *see* **tice**.
Tyseday *n* Tuesday.
tyte[1] *n* quick pull. • *v* totter; snatch; pull.
tyte[2] *adj* direct.
tyttar *adv* rather; sooner.

U

ubit *adj* dwarfish.
udal *adj* held by succession; without charter.
udaller *n* land-holder.
ug *v* abhor, loathe; exasperate.
ùgertfow *adj* squeamish.
uggit *adj* upset.
ugin *adj* maddening.
ugsome, ugsum *adj* grisly, gruesome, horrible.
uilie, ule, ulie *n/v* oil.
uilie pig *n* oil jar.
ulk *n* week.
ull *adj* ill.
umast, umaist *adv* uppermost.
umbersorrow *adj* hardy, rugged.
umbeschew *v* to avoid.
umbeset *v* surround on all sides.
umbre *n* shade.
umost *adj* uppermost.
umquhile *adj* deceased, former, late. • *adv* sometimes; former.
umrage *n* umbrage.
undauntit *adj* undaunted.

unalik *adj* different, unlike.
unawaurs *adv* unawares.
unball *v* unpack.
unbauld *adj* humble.
unbekent *adj* unknown.
unbesit *n* monster.
unbiddable *adj* uncounsellable.
unboding *adj* unpromising.
unbowsome *adj* implacable, obstinate.
uncairdly *adv* carelessly.
uncanny, uncannand, wancanny *adj* dangerous; malignant, mischievous; ominous; supernatural. • *n* danger.
unce *n* ounce.
unchance *n* mischance.
unchancie, unchancy, wanchancie *adj* dangerous, risky; inauspicious, ill-fated, unlucky.
unco[1], **unclie,** *adv* extremely, very.
unco[2] *adj* eccentric; odd; strange.
unco fowk *n* strangers.
uncoft *adj* unbought.
unco guid *n* moral persons.
uncoist *n* expense.

uncolins *adv* oddly.

uncome *adj* not arrived.

unconess *n* eccentricity, strangeness.

uncos *npl* news; rarities.

uncouthy *adj* dreary, inhospitable.

unct *v* anoint.

unction *n* auction.

undecent *adj* indecent.

undeemous *adj* immense; incalculable.

undegest *adj* rash, premature.

underly *v* undergo.

undighted *adj* (cloth) not dressed.

undo *v* cut off.

undoch *n* puny creature, runt.

unegall *adj* unequal.

uneith *adv* with difficulty.

unerdit *adj* unburied.

unfandrum *adj* bulky.

unfankle *v* disentangle.

unfarran, unfarrant *adj* unmannerly; unsophisticated; senseless; stupid.

unfeil *adj* uncomfortable.

unfeiroch *adj* feeble.

unfleggit *adj* unafraid.

unforlatit *adj* unforsaken, not afraid.

unforsain'd *adj* undeserved.

unfree *adj* without liberties of a burgess.

unfreelie *adj* cumbersome.

unfreen *n* enemy, opponent.

unfreenship *n* animosity, ill-will.

unfrugal *adj* lavish.

ungand *adj* unbecoming.

ungeir'd *adj* naked.

ungrate *adj* ungrateful.

unhanty *adj* inconvenient.

unhearty *adj* uncomfortable.

unheild *v* uncover.

unhele *n* pain.

unhertsome *adj* cheerless; melancholy.

unhine, unhyne *adj* extraordinary.

unhit *adj* unnamed.

unhonest *adj* dishonest.

unhyne *see* **unhine.**

unkennin *adj* ignorant.

unkensome *adj* unknowable.

unkent *adj* unfamiliar, unknown, unobserved.

unlach *n* crime.

unlatit *adj* undisciplined.

unlaw *n* crime. • *v* fine.

unleif *adj* unpleasant.

unleill *adj* dishonest.

unlo'esome, wanliesome *adj* unlovely.

unmensefu *adj* without manners.

unmoderly *adj* unkindly.

unnest *v* dislodge.

unooforament *adj* uncomfortable, unpleasant.

unplenished *adj* unfurnished.

unpurpose *adj* awkward.

unquart *n* sadness.

unraivel *v* unravel.

unreason *n* injustice, iniquity.

unrede *adj* cruel.

unricht *adj* unjust. • *n* injustice.

unrude *adj* impure.

unrufe *n* trouble, toil.

unsaucht *adj* disturbed.

unsiccar *adj* insecure.

unsnarre *adj* blunt.

unsneck *v* unlatch.

unsned *adj* unpruned.

unsonsie *adj* unlucky.

unswack *adj* stiff.

untented *adj* unwatched.

untenty *adj* inattentive.

unthrifty *adj* unfriendly.

untill *adv* unto.

untimeous *adj* unseasonable.

untowtherlie *adj* unwieldy.

untraist *adj* unexpected.

untraisty *adj* faithless.

untrig *adj* slovenly.

untrowable *adj* incredible.

untynt *adj* not lost.

unwar *adj* unwary, unawares.

unwashen *adj* unwashed.

unweel *adj* ailing, sickly.

unweelness *n* ill-health, sickness.

unwerd, unweird *n* unlucky fate.

unwicelike *adj* indiscreet, imprudent.

unwinne *adj* extreme.

unwittins *adv* inadvertently.

up *adj* excited; grown-up. • *adv* open.

upbig *v* build up.

upbrak *n* dispersal.

upbring *n* training.

upbuller *v* boil up.

upby *adv* upstairs, up the hill.

upcast *n* taunt. • *v* be overcast, cloud up.

upcome *n* outcome; promising appearance; growth; upshot.

updaw v dawn.
upfessin n upbringing.
upfuirdays adj up before sunrise.
upgang n ascent.
uphaud n maintenance. • v guarantee; hold up; uphold, vouch for; support.
uplands adj of the country, rustic.
uplif n elation.
uplift v collect.
upliftit adj elated.
upmak n compensation; composition; fabrication; invention. • v atone; supply a want; compensate.
upmakar n storyteller; composer.
uppil v clear up.
uppil aboon adj clear overhead.
uppins adv little way up.
uppish adj aspiring.
uppittin, upputting n accomodation, lodging, quarters; erection.
upricht adj upright.
upset[1] n admission to trades guild.
upset[2] v refund; repair; recover from.
upset price n minimum price at auction.
upsetting adj uppish.
upsides adv on equal footing with.
upsittin, upsitten adj callous; indifferent; listless.

upstannin adj basic.
upsteer v hearten.
upsteerin n stimulation.
upstirring n excitement.
upsun adv after sunrise.
uptak n apprehension; understanding. • v collect.
uptaking n exaltation.
upthrou adj upland. • n inland.
upthrough adv higher up; upwards.
upwart adj upward.
upwith adv upwards.
up wi, up with adv even with; as good as.
ure[1] n heat; haze; mist; sweat.
ure[2] n ore; clay soil; reddish colour.
urf n stunted child.
urisum adj frightful.
urluch adj frail.
urn v torture.
ury adj furred, clammy.
us pron me.
usche v issue.
use n interest; usury; occasion. • v frequent; be accustomed to.
useless adj unable.
uterance n extremity.
utmaist adj utmost.
uz pron us.

V

vaick v attend to.
vaig n wandering; travel. • v wander.
vaiger n mercenary soldier.
vaigin, vaiging adj vagrant. • n idle strolling.
vail v bow down.
vailye n value. • v appraise; value.
vairriage n carriage.
vairty see **verty**.
vairye see **vary**.
vake v watch.
valabil adj available; valuable.
vale[1] n worth.
vale[2] v descend.
valient n value of a property.
valise n saddlebag.
valour n value.
vamper v show off.
vandie adj proud. • n conceited person.

vane n vein.
vanit adj veined.
vant v want.
vantose n cupping glass.
variant adj variable.
varlot n servant, minion.
vary, vairye v rave.
vassalage n great achievement; valour.
vauce v stab; kill.
vaudie adj vain; gaudy.
vauntie adj proud; boastful.
vawse n vase.
veage n jaunt, outing, voyage.
veef adj brisk.
veem n heavy sweat; trance.
veir, ver n spring.
vele, veyl n whirlpool; strong current.
velvous n velvet.
venesum adj venomous.

vennel, wynell *n* alley.
vent *n* flue; speed. • *v* sell; emit.
venust *adj* beautiful; pleasant.
vera *see* **verra.**
vere *n* goblet.
vergelt, wergelt *n* ransom.
verger *n* orchard.
verilies *adv* verily.
verra, vera *adv* very.
verrayment *n* truth.
verter *n* virtue; medicinal power.
vertesit *n* virtue; virginity.
vertue *n* thrift.
verty, vairty *adj* early.
vesie, visie *v* visit; take aim.
vetcher *n* suspicious character.
veug *n* sexual intercourse.
vex, wex *v* be sorry; aggrieve.
veyl *see* **vele.**
vice *n* voice. • *v* voice.
viciat *adj* defective.
victual *n* grain.
victualler *n* corn factor.
vieve *adj* vivid.
vilcous *adj* immoral.
vilipend *v* slight; vilify.
vindict *n* vengeance.
violer *n* violinist.
vire *n* arrow.
virl *n* ferrule.
virr *n* force; momentum.
virrock *n* corn on foot.

vise *n* fracture.
visie *see* **vesie.**
vision *n* nonentity; thin person.
visite *v* examine; survey.
vitious *adj* fierce; fiery.
vivers *npl* food.
vivual *adj* alive.
vizzy *n* view.
voar *n* spring.
vodder *n* weather.
vode *adj* empty.
voe *n* fjord, long narrow inlet.
vogie, vokie *adj* proud; vain; jolly.
voice *n* vote.
voicer *n* voter.
vokie *see* **vogie.**
volage *adj* giddy.
volish *v* vaunt.
volt *see* **vult.**
vome *v* puke.
vomiter *n* emetic.
voo *v* vow.
voostie *adv* proudly.
vote *n* vow. • *v* devote.
vourak *n* wreck.
voust *n*/*v* boast.
vouth *n* prosecution.
vouthman *n* outlaw.
vowt *n* countenance; vault; cellar. • *v* vault.
vult, volt *n* aspect.
vung *v* move with a buzzing sound.

W

wa¹ *adv* away.
wa² *n* wall, dyke.
waal *v* weld.
waasp *n* wasp.
waat, waut *n* weal.
wab *n* web.
wabbit *adj* careworn; exhausted; weary; wan; weak.
wabble *v* wobble.
wabblie *adj* watery.
wab-fittit *adj* web-footed.
wabster *see* **webster.**
wace *n* wax.
wachle *n* wobble. • *v* move to and fro.
wacht¹ *n* watch; sight.

wacht² *n* swig. • *v* drink, quaff.
wack, wak *adj* moist.
wad¹, wed *n* pledge, security; wager, bet; forfeit. • *adj* wedded. • *v* pledge; wager, bet; wed.
wad² *n* black lead; graphite.
wad³ *n* cotton wool.
wad⁴ *v* wade. • *adj* wading.
wad⁵ *see* **wald².**
wadd *n* woad.
wadder *n* weather.
waddin *n* wedding.
waddin braws *npl* wedding clothes, trousseau.
wadge¹ *n* wedge. • *v* wedge, chock.

wadge² v brandish.

wadset n handing over of land rights to a creditor. • v alienate heritable property.

wadsetter n holder of property under wadset.

wady adj vain.

wae n woe; **wae's me** interj alas, woe is me.

waebegane adj woebegone.

waeful adj woeful.

waese n bundle of straw.

waesome adj woeful.

waff, waif¹ adj aroma, odour; ailment; wave; whiff. • v blow; flap; fan; wave; shake.

waff, waif² adj low-class; stray; strayed. • n waif.

waffie adj rascally; vagrant. • n vagabond.

waffinger n vagabond.

waffle adj inert; pliable. • v rumple; shilly-shally; waver.

wafflie adj volatile.

waff-like adj shabby.

waft n weft.

wag v beckon; brandish; **wag awa** carry on.

wa-gang, wa-gaun n leave-taking; departure. • adj departing.

wag-at-the-wa' n clock with an open pendulum.

wage n pledge; pawn. • v wield.

waggle n bog.

waghorn n liar.

wa-girse n watercress.

waible v walk unsteadily.

waide v infuriate.

waiggle n/v waggle; waddle.

waik¹ adj weak.

waik² n/v watch.

waile n wand; rod.

waim see **wame**.

wain n wagon.

waingle v flutter; wave.

wainscot n felled oak.

waint¹ n glimpse.

waint² v turn sour.

waintit n soured.

wair¹ n pillow slip.

wair² v spend.

wairn v warn.

wait on v await.

waite v blame.

waiter n gatekeeper.

waith¹ n clothing.

waith², wayth n wandering; hunting.

waithman n hunter.

wak see **wack**.

wake v wander; be idle.

wakness n damp; humidity.

wakrif adj sleepless.

walcome n/v welcome.

wald¹ n plain; ground.

wald², wad v would.

wald³ v wield; govern.

wald⁴ see **well²**.

wale n choosing; choice; veil. • v choose; select.

waler n selector.

walgan n wallet.

walie, waly adj excellent. • n good fortune.

walin n selection.

wall n well; spring of water; whirlpool. • v well up; **wall up** boil up.

wallach v talk in a roundabout way.

wallae n/v wallow.

wallan adj drooping; withered. • v wither.

waller n moving crows.

wallidrag n feeble person; weakest nestling.

wallie¹, wally adj beautiful; strong; made of china; ornamental; tiled. • n porcelain; glazed tile.

wallie², wally, wallet n valet.

wallie dug n china dog.

wallies npl false teeth; intestines; finery.

wallie tile n tile.

walloch n vigorous dance.

wallock n lapwing.

wallop n heartbeat. • v gallop; move fast.

wallow v fade; wither.

wally see **wallie¹; wallie²**.

walsh, welsche adj insipid; tasteless.

walt¹ n welt.

walt² v thump.

walter, wolter n welter; upset. • v welter; wallow; overturn.

walth n plenty; wealth.

waly¹, wawlie n toy.

waly² see **walie**.

walycoat n under-petticoat.

wamb *see* **wame**.

wamble *v* move unsteadily.

wamblin *n* puny child.

wame, wamb, waim, weam *n* belly, stomach; womb.

wameful *n* bellyful.

wame-ill *n* bellyache.

wamfle *adj* limp. • *v* flap, flutter.

wamfler *n* lecher.

wamie *adj* portly.

waminess *n* corpulence.

wammle, wample *n* wallow. • *v* coil; undulate; wallow; wriggle.

wampish *v* fluctuate; move to and fro; wave.

wamyt *adj* big-bellied; pregnant.

wan¹ *n* one.

wan² *adj* deficient; dark, gloomy; tin.

wan³ *see* **wand**.

wan-bane *n* cheekbone.

wancanny *see* **uncanny**.

wanchance *n* peril.

wanchancie *see* **unchancy**.

wand, wan *n* fishing rod; switch, rod; sceptre; wicker. • *adj* made of wicker.

wand-bed *n* wicker bed.

wandocht *adj* base; despicable. • *n* puny creature.

wandrethe *n* misfortune.

wane *see* **want**.

wangrace *n* wickedness.

wanhap, wanhope, wanhowp *n* misfortune; despair.

wankill, wankle *adj* unstable.

wankish *v* twist.

wanlas *n* mistake.

wanliesome *see* **unlo'esome**.

wannis *npl* scars.

wannle *adj* agile.

wanrest *n* anxiety; uneasiness; unrest.

wanrestful *adj* unsettled.

wanrufe *n* unease.

wansonsy *adj* mischievous.

want, wane *v* defect; lack. • *v* lack; need.

wanter *n* bachelor.

wanthrift *n* extravagance; prodigality; thriftlessness.

wantin *adj* lacking; simple-minded. • *prep* without.

wanton *n* girth.

wanwordie *adj* unworthy.

wanworth *adj* valueless. • *n* price.

wanwuth *n* surprise.

wanyoch *adj* pale.

wap¹ *n* blow. • *v* throw; wrestle; fling.

wap², wup *n* bundle of straw. • *v* envelop, wrap; splice.

wapinschaw *n* weaponry display.

wap-it *v* put away.

wapnit *adj* armed.

wappen *n* weapon.

wappin *adj* enormous, gigantic, huge; monstrous.

wappit *adj* enveloped.

war¹, ware *adj* aware, conscious; wary.

war² *see* **wair**.

warand, warrand *n* surety; protection. • *v* protect.

warble *v* wriggle.

ward *n* confinement; imprisonment. • *v* imprison.

wardlie *adj* worldly.

wardour *n* prisoner; guard.

ware¹ *n* price. • *v* expend; spend.

ware² *see* **war¹**.

warehoose *n* warehouse.

waretime *n* springtime.

warf *n* dwarf.

warison *n* reward.

wark, werk, wirk *n* work; fortification. • *v* work; ache; purge; **wark on** influence.

warker *n* worker.

warkly *adj* diligent.

warld *n* world.

warldlie *adj* temporal.

warld's gear *n* worldly goods.

warliest *adj* most wary.

warlo *adj* evil. • *n* wicked person.

warlock *n* magician, wizard.

warne *v* refuse.

warnin *n* omen; portent.

warp *v* throw open; surround; weave, plait.

warple *v* intertwine; struggle through.

warrach¹ *n* knotted stick.

warrach² *v* scold.

warrachie *adj* rough; knotted.

warran *n/v* warrant.

warrand *see* **warand**.

warrandice *n* guarantee.

warray *adj* true; real.

warren *adj* of the pine tree.

warsche *see* **wersh**.

warse *adj* worse.

warsle, warsell, worsle *v* wrestle; writhe; labour; subjugate; **warsle on** struggle on; **warsle throu** get by.

warslin *adj* hard-working; struggling.

warst *adj/adv* worst.

warth *n* apparition.

warwolf *n* werewolf.

wary *v* defend; curse; execrate.

warying *n* curse.

wash, weshe *n* bevelled edge; stale urine; lye.

wash-doon *v* bevel.

washerwife, washerwifie *n* washer-woman, laundress.

washtub *n* tub for lye.

wasie *adj* sagacious.

waspit *adj* thin-waisted.

wast *n* west; left.

wastell *n* oatmeal cake.

waster¹, wester *adj* western.

waster², wester *n* three-pronged fish spear.

waster³ *v* squander.

wasterful *adj* destructive.

wasting *n* consumption (tuberculosis).

wastland, wastlins *adv* westwards.

wastle *adj* west of. • *adv* westwards.

wastmost *adj* westernmost.

wastrie *n* prodigal person.

wastrif, wastrife *adj* prodigal; wasteful.

wat¹ *v* know.

wat², wate *see* **weet**.

watchie *n* watchmaker.

watermeggie *n* dipper.

water *see* **watter**.

wath *n* ford.

wather *n* weather.

watshod *adj* with wet feet.

watter, water *n* river; water. • *v* water.

watter-brash *n* heartburn.

watter-cow *n* river spirit.

watter-craw *n* water ousel.

watter-dog *n* water rat.

watterfall *n* watershed.

wattergang *n* mill race.

wattergaw, weathergaw *n* rainbow or part of one.

watterie *n* lavatory, toilet.

watter-kelpie *n* water spirit.

watter-mouth *n* estuary.

watter-stoup *n* bucket.

wattery pox *n* chickenpox.

wattie *n* eel.

wattle *n* billet of wood.

wauch *n* wall.

wauchie *adj* sallow; swampy.

wauchle *v* shamble.

waucht *n* large draught of drink. • *v* quaff heartily.

wauge *n* wage.

wauger *n/v* wager.

waugh, wouch *adj* unpleasant-tasting.

wauk¹ *v* wake; watch.

wauk² *see* **waulk**.

waukened *adj* awake.

waukenin *n* awakening; dressing-down, reproof.

waukfere *adj* able to walk.

waukit *adj* callous.

waukrif, waukrife *adj* insomniac, wake-ful; vigilant, watchful.

waul *v* look wild.

waulie *adj* nimble.

waulk, wauk *v* tread cloth, full; shrink.

waulker *n* fuller.

waulkmill *n* fulling mill.

waumish *adj* squeamish.

wauner *v* wander.

waunert *adj* wandering.

waunnerin fowk *npl* vagrants.

waur¹ *adj* worse.

waur² *v* overcome.

waut¹ *n* border; selvedge.

waut² *see* **waat**.

wavel *v* move to and fro; wave.

waver *v* wander.

waw¹ *n* sea wave.

waw² *v* wail; caterwaul.

waxcloth *n* linoleum; oilcloth.

wayff *n* wife.

wayganging *n* departure.

waygate *n* space; room.

wayn *n* plenty.

waynd *v* change; swerve; care.

wayne *n* help; relief.

wayth *see* **waith**.

waywart *adj* wayward.

weam *see* **wame**.

wean *n* baby; child; infant; offspring.

wearful adj troublesome.

weary adj dispiriting; feeble.

weary fa' interj curse upon.

weary for v long for.

weather n storm.

weatherful, wedderful adj inclement; stormy.

weathergaw see **wattergaw**.

weave v knit stockings.

webster, wabster n weaver; spider.

weche n witch.

wecht¹ n weight. • v weigh.

wecht² n winnow; sieve. • v winnow.

wechtie adj weighty.

wechts npl scales.

wechty adj expensive; weighty.

wed see **wad¹**.

wedder n wether.

wedder see **wether**.

wedderful see **weatherful**.

wede, weid v rage.

wede-awa adj extinct.

wedgie n strange person.

weehoose n privy.

weescuil n infant school.

wee, wie adj little, small, tiny.

weed¹ n mastitis.

weed² v thin out.

weeds npl thinnings.

weegletie-waggletie adj wavering.

weeglie adj waggling; unstable.

week see **weik**.

weel¹, weil, weill adj well; healthy. • adv well; very. • interj well! • n prosperity.

weel² n eddy.

weel-daein adj affluent; well-off; proud.

weel-faured adj handsome.

weel-hained adj well-preserved.

weel-happit adj well-protected.

weel is me interj happy am I.

weel-kent adj widely known.

weel-plenisht adj well-stocked.

weel-put-on adj well-dressed.

weel-seen adj evident.

weel tae be seen adj presentable.

weel-tochert adj well-endowed.

weel-waled adj well-chosen.

weel-wared adj well-deserved; well-earned; well-spent.

weel-willie adj generous; well-meaning.

weem n cave.

ween v suspect; suppose.

weeness n smallness.

weeng n wing.

weeock n little while.

weepers npl mourning dress.

weer n wire.

weese see **weeze**.

weeshie-washie n procrastination.

weest adj depressed.

weet, wat, wate adj wet. • n rain. • v wet.

weet-ma-fit n corncrake.

weetness n wet weather.

weet yer thrapple n booze. • v booze; quench one's thirst.

weeze, weese v ooze.

weffil adj pliant.

weid see **wede**.

weif v weave.

weigh-bauk n balance.

weik, week n corner; angle.

weil, weill see **weel¹**.

wein n stain.

weir¹ n war; force. • v defend; deflect.

weir² n hedge. • v herd, drive carefully; keep in; stop; **weir in** pass; **weir intil** approach.

weir³ v wear; **weir roon** prevail upon, win over.

weird n destiny, fate; prediction. • v destine; predict, divine.

weirdful adj fateful.

weirdless adj improvident; incapable; unlucky; worthless.

weirdlie, weirdly adj sinister; happy.

weird wife n female prophet.

weiriegills npl quarrels.

weirlie, weirlik adj bellicose; warlike.

weirs npl wares.

weise v achieve by art or policy; direct.

weit v inquire.

welany n disgrace.

weld v possess.

well¹ n tap.

well², wald n/v weld.

well-grass n watercress.

well-head n spring (water).

wellit adj drowned.

welsche see **walsh**.

welt v throw.

welter v roll.

wem n stain.

wemeless *adj* blameless.

wemmyt *adj* scarred.

wendin *v* wane.

wergelt *see* **vergelt**.

werk *see* **wark**.

wernour *n* miser.

werray *v* make war on.

werrock *n* bunion; corn; verruca.

wersh, warsche *adj* acid, bitter; bland, insipid, tasteless.

wery *v* curse.

wesar *n* visor.

weschell *n* crockery.

wesely *adv* cautiously.

wesh *n/v* wash.

weshe *see* **wash**.

weskit *n* waistcoat.

wester *see* **waster**[1], **waster**[2].

wether, wedder *n* neutered ram.

weting *n* knowledge.

wevil *v* wriggle.

wex *see* **vex**.

wey[1] *n* way.

wey[2] *v* weigh.

weyes *n* weighing balance.

wez *pron* us.

wha, whae *pron* what; who.

whaak *v* quack.

wha-but-he *n* one and only; self-important person.

whack *n* cut; incision.

whae *see* **wha**.

whaisle, wheasle *v* wheeze.

whalp *n/v* whelp; pup.

wham[1] *pron* whom.

wham[2] *n* wide level glen.

whamble *see* **whummle**.

whan *adv/conj* when.

whan a' be *adv* notwithstanding.

whang *n* thong; slice; boot lace; penis; whiplash. • *v* hack in slices.

whang-bit *n* bridle.

whank *n* thump; blow. • *v* beat; flog.

whanker, whapper, whilper *n* something unusually large.

whapp *see* **whaup**[1].

whar *see* **whaur**.

whase *pron* whose.

whasomever *pron* whoever.

what *v* whet.

whaten, whatten *adv* what sort of.

whatfor *adv* for what reason.

what-like *adj* like what.

whatsomever *pron* whatever.

whatten *see* **whaten**.

whauk *n/v* whack.

whaul *n* whale.

whaum, wham *n* blow.

whaup *n* curlew.

whaup-nebbit *adj* long-nosed.

whaup[1], **whaap** *n* curlew.

whaup[2] *n* pod. • *v* pod out.

whaur, whar *adv* where.

whaur fae *adv* whence.

whaurivver *adv* wherever.

whaur till *adv* whither.

wheak, week *v* squeak.

wheasel *n* weasel.

wheasle *see* **whaisle**.

wheech *n* swipe; *n* whisk. • *v* swipe; whizz; **wheech awa** snatch away.

wheecher *n* coalman.

wheel *v* bid; pirouette.

wheem *n* caprice; fancy.

wheemer *v* mutter complaints.

wheen *n* number; quantity.

wheenge *v* whinge.

wheep *v* whistle; squeak.

wheeple *v* call like a curlew.

wheerikins *npl* buttocks.

wheerum, wheerim *n* toy; insignificant thing.

wheesht *adj* hushed. • *interj* hush! • *v* silence.

wheesk *n* gentle creak. • *v* creak gently.

wheetie *adj* mean; low.

wheetle[1] *n* duckling. • *v* cheep.

wheetle[2] *v* wheedle.

wheezie *v* blaze and crackle.

wheezle *n* wheeze; wheezing. • *v* wheeze.

wheezles *npl* asthma; bronchitis.

whew *v* whistle shrilly.

whey-bird *n* woodlark.

whey-whullions *npl* mixed oats and whey.

whickie *adj* crafty.

whid[1] *n* exaggeration. • *v* fib.

whid[2] *v* scud.

whidder *n* gust of wind; whirlwind.

whiddie *n* hare.

whiddle *v* walk lightly.

whiddy *adj* shifting.

whiff *v* blow out.

whig¹, wigg, wyg *n* clear liquid under sour cream; tea bread.

whig² *v* jog easily.

whig³, whigamore *n* Presbyterian dissenter.

whiggery *n* Presbyterianism.

whiggle *v* wriggle.

whigmaleerie *adj* gimcrack. • *n* drinking game; whim; fantastic ornament, knick-knack, trinket.

whigmaleeries *npl* frippery.

while *adv/conj/prep* until.

whiles *adv* at times; now and then; sometimes.

whilk *adj/pron* which.

whill *conj* while.

whilly, whillie *v* gull, cheat; hoax, trick.

whillybaloo *n* hullabaloo.

whillygoleerie *n* hypocrite; wheedler.

whillywha *n* wheedler; *n* wheedling.

whillywhally *v* coax; dally, loiter.

whillywhaw *adj* undependable.

whilock *n* short while.

whilper *see* **whanker.**

whiltie-whaltie *adj* in palpitation.

whimmer *v* whimper.

whimwham *n* whimsy.

whin *n* furze; gorse.

whinge *v* whine.

whinger, whinyard *n* short sword.

whink *v* bark.

whinkens *see* **sowens.**

whinner *v* whizz by.

whinnerin *adj* very dry.

whinny *adj* covered by furze or whins.

whinstane *see* **whunstane.**

whinyard *see* **whinger.**

whippert *adj* hasty.

whippy *adj* slight; contemptible.

whir, whirr *v* fly up with a whirring sound.

whirlie *n* contraption; gadget.

whirligig *n* symbol.

whirliwaw *n* whirligig.

whirret *n* blow; smack.

whish *n* whoosh; whisper. • *v* hush.

whisker *n* feather duster; broom.

whisky *n* spirit distilled from malt or grain.

whistle-binkie *n* non-payer at a penny wedding; bench-sitter.

whit *pron* what.

white *adj* unploughed. • *n* wheat. • *v* flatter; cut, pare; whittle.

white-airn *n* tinplate.

whitelie, whitely *adj* whitish; pale.

whitelip *n* flatterer.

whitemeal *n* oatmeal.

white pudding *n* pudding of meal, suet and onion.

whiter *n* whittler.

white siller *n* silver money.

whither¹ *conj* whether.

whither² *n* stroke; blow. • *v* beat.

whitie *n* whiting.

whitrat *n* stoat; weasel.

whitter *n* thing of weak growth; draught of liquor. • *v* move lightly; fritter away; speak low; patter.

whitter-whatter *n* chattering.

whittie-whattie *n* prevarication. • *v* prevaricate.

whittle *n* knife.

whittle-bealin *n* whitlow.

whon *n* worthless character.

whorle *n* small wheel.

whorle-bane *n* hipbone.

whosle *v* breathe hard.

whud *n* fib, lie.

whudder *v* make a rushing sound.

whuff *n* whiff.

whullup *v* curry favour.

whully *v* cheat.

whult *n* blow; something large.

whulter *n* whopper.

whummle, whamble *n* avalanche; downfall; upset. • *v* overturn; invert; bowl over; stir round; upset.

whumpie *n* large wooden plate.

whun *n* whin.

whun-chacker *n* whinchat.

whunlintie, whinlintie *n* red linnet.

whinstane, whunstane *n* ragstone. • *adj* hard-hearted.

whup *n/v* whip.

whuram *n* crotchet; trills and quavers.

whurken *v* strangle.

whurl *n* wheel; flywheel; whirl; whorl. • *v* whirl.

whurr *n/v* whirr.

whush *n/v* whish.

whuskie *n* whisky.

whusper *n/v* whisper.

whustle *n* siren; whistle. • *v* whistle.

whuther *conj* whether.

wi *conj* owing to. • *prep* with.

wice *adj* clever; knowing; well-informed; wise. • *v* lead; lure; manoeuvre; persuade.

wicelik *adj* becoming, seemly, fitting; proper; reasonable; rational; sagacious; sane. • *adv* sensibly.

wice-sayin *n* proverb.

wicht *adj* brave, courageous; valiant.

wicht *n* spirit.

wicht, wight[1] *adj* strong; active; clever.

wicht, wight[2] *n* man person.

wichty *adj* powerful.

wick[1] *n* naughty child.

wick[2] *n* open bay.

wicker *n* twig; short switch.

wickers *n* wickerwork.

wickit *adj* iniquitous, wicked.

widder *v* rush about.

widdershins *adv* anticlockwise; contrariwise.

widdie, woodie *n* rope made of willow; hangman's rope; gallows, gibbet.

widdle[1] *v* waddle.

widdle[2] **, wuddle** *v* make shift without great effort.

wie *see* **wee**.

wife *n* matron; woman.

wife-carle *n* house-husband.

wiffin *n* moment.

wifie *n* wife; woman.

wiflie *adj* feminine.

wifock *n* little woman.

wig *n* wall; partition.

wigg *see* **whig**[1].

wight *see* **wicht**.

wi'in *adv* within.

wild *adj* strong-tasting.

wild cotton *n* cotton-grass.

wildfire, willfire *n* marsh marigold; fire-damp.

wile[1] *adj* vile.

wile[2] **, wyle** *v* beguile; lure; win over by coaxing.

wilful *adj* willing.

wilie-coat *n* winter vest.

wilk *n* whelk.

will[1] *adj* erring; wild.

will[2] *n* desire.

will[3] *v* shall.

willcat *see* **wullcat**.

willcorn *n* wild oats.

willfire *see* **wildfire**.

willgate, wullgate *adv* misdirectedly.

willick *n* puffin.

willie *n* willow.

willie-jack *n* go-between.

willie-muff *n* willow warbler.

willie-wagtail *n* pied wagtail; water-wagtail.

willie wand *n* willow wand.

Willie Winkie *n* sandman.

willin-sweert *adj* half-willing.

willintlie *adv* intentionally.

willsome, wilsum, wullsome *adj* wilful.

willyart *adj* wild; shy.

willywha *n* cajolery.

wilshoch *adj* perverse.

wilsome *adj* desolate.

wilsum, wullsome *see* **willsome**.

wimble *n* auger.

wimble-bore *n* auger-hole.

wimple *n* complication; convolution; curl; wave; meander; ruse; wile. • *v* enfold; go in wavelets; meander, wind; squirm.

win[1] *n* wind. • *v* dry; dry in the wind; dry out; winnow.

win[2] *v* dwell.

win[3] *n* earnings; wealth. • *v* earn; gain; give; go; come; reach, attain, arrive; **win aboon** be the first; **win aff** get off; **win ahin** outsmart; **win awa** get away; go off; die, pass away; **win by** get past; **win forrit** advance; **win free** get away; **win o'er** get across; **win oot** escape; get out; **win over** surmount; **win ower** pass over; recover; **winthrow** get through; **winup** get up; stand up.

winch[1] *v* court.

winch[2] *v* wince.

winchin *adj* courting.

wind *v* exaggerate; tell stories.

winda, windae *n* window.

windae-broad *n* shutter.

windae-sole *n* window-sill.

windcuffer *n* kestrel.

winder *n* storyteller.

windle *v* walk into the wind.

windlen *n* straw bottle.
windrow *see* **winraw.**
wind-skew *n* chimney cowl.
windus *n* windlass.
windy *adj* ostentatious.
windy-wallets *n* one who farts.
wineberry *n* currant.
wingel *n* tumour.
wingle *v* wag; walk laboriously.
wink *n* moment.
winkers *npl* eyelashes.
winkit *adj* turning (milk).
winmull *n* windmill.
winning *n* pit.
winnings *npl* mineworkings.
winraw, windrow *n* long pile of drying hay or peat.
winsome *adj* merry.
wint *n* want.
winter *v* pasture animals through winter.
winter-dyke *n* clothes horse.
winterling *n* year-old cow or ox.
wintle *v* stagger.
wintrous *adj* wintry.
winze *n* curse.
wi'oot *prep* without.
wip, wyp *v* bind.
wippen *n* wrap-round binding.
wir *pron* our.
wird *n* word.
wirdie *adj* weighty.
wire *n* knitting needle.
wire *n* needle.
wirk¹ *v* herd.
wirk² *see* **wark.**
wirl *n* small person or creature.
wirlie *adj* wrinkly.
wirm *n* worm.
wirr *v* growl.
wirricow, wirriecarl *n* demon; scarecrow.
wirry *n/v* worry.
wirs, wirses *pron* ours.
wirsels *pron* ourselves.
wirth *n* worth.
wis *v* know.
wisen *v* wizen.
wisk *v* whisk.
wiss *n/v* wish.
wissel *v* exchange.
wit *n* sagacity, wisdom; sanity.
withershins *adv* anticlockwise.

wither-wecht *n* counterweight.
within eild *adj* under-age.
witter *v* inform; fight.
witterin *n* information.
wittert *adj* barbed.
wiz *pron* us.
wizzen *n* throat; trachea; life.
wizzent *adj* shrivelled.
wobat *adj* feeble.
wod¹ *adj* mad.
wod², wode *n* wood; woad.
Wodensday *n* Wednesday.
wodman *n* madman.
wodness *n* madness.
woll *n* wool.
wolroun *n* eunuch.
wolter *see* **walter.**
wolvin *adj* woven.
wolwat *n* velvet.
womple *see* **wymple.**
won *v* be able; dwell; dry.
woo *n* wool.
woodie *see* **widdie.**
woodrum *see* **wuddrum.**
wooerbab *n* lovers' knot.
woolster *n* wool stapler.
wooster *n* suitor.
wooy *adj* woolly.
wop *n* binding thread.
word *n* character; reputation.
wordie *adj* worthy.
work *v* sprain; trouble; **work wi** employ.
worl, worlin *n* puny creature.
worm *n* serpent.
worm-etten *adj* discontented.
worm-i-the-cheek *n* toothache.
worm-web *n* spider's web.
worp *n/v* warp.
worry *v* choke.
worschip *n* great deed; honour.
worset *n* worsted.
worsing *n* injury.
worsle *see* **warsell.**
worsum, woursum *n* purulence.
wort *v* waste.
worth *v* wax; become.
worts *n* part-distilled liquor.
woslie, wozlie *adj* shrivelled up.
wot *n* information.
wotlink *n* wench.
wouch¹ *v* bark.

wouch² *see* **waugh**.
woud *v* void; excrete.
wouf *n* wolf.
woursum *see* **worsum**.
wow¹ *n/v* bark; howl.
wow² *v* wave.
wowf *adj* agitated; half-mad, crazed.
wown *n* wont; custom.
wozlie *see* **woslie**.
wra *n* hiding place.
wrable *v* wriggle.
wrach *n* wraith.
wrack, wrak *n* algae; driftwood; flotsam; trash; ruin; shipwreck; wreck. • *v* demolish; ruin; wreck.
wraigh *adj* strange.
wraik *n* revenge; destruction.
wraith¹ *n* provision; food.
wraith² *adj* angry; wrathful.
wrak *see* **wrack**.
wramp *v* sprain.
wrang *adj* deformed; incorrect, wrong; unjust; improper. • *n* wrong. • *v* wrong.
wrangous *adj* ill-gotten; wrongful.
wrangouslie *adv* improperly; wrongfully.
wrangways *adv* incorrectly.
wrannie *n* wren.
wrap *n* smock.
wraple *v* entangle.
wrapper *n* dressing gown.
wrat *n* wart.
wratack *n* dwarf.
wratch *n* wretch. • *v* behave in a miserly fashion.
wrattie *adj* warty.
wread, wreath *n* cow pen.
wreak *n/v* wreck.
wreat *v* write.
wreath *n* drift; snowdrift.
wrede, wride *n* wreath.
wree *v* writhe.
wreil *v* twist; wriggle.
wreist *v* sprain.
wreth *n* wrath.
wrett *n* writing.
wreuch *n* wretchedness.
wrible *n* quaver; warble.
wricht *n* carpenter, joiner.
wride *see* **wrede**.
wrig *n* runt.

wriggle *v* wrestle.
wrik *v* wreak.
wring *n* deformity.
wrink *n* turning; trick.
wrinklit *adj* intricate.
wristie *n* muff.
writ *n* record; writing.
writer *n* attorney, lawyer, notary, solicitor.
wroken *adj* revenged.
wrongous *adj* illegal.
wrunch *n* winch.
wry *v* turn; twist.
wud *see* **wuid**.
wudden *adj* wooden.
wuddie *adj* woody.
wuddle *see* **widdle²**.
wuddrum, woodrum *n* state of confusion.
wudlins *adv* eagerly.
wudscud *n* wild boy or girl.
wuggle *n* bog.
wuid, wud¹ *adj* rabid.
wuid, wud² *n* wood.
wuiddrim *n* brainstorm.
wulk *n* periwinkle; whelk.
wull¹, wuld *adj* wild.
wull² *n/v* will.
wullcat, willcat *n* wild cat.
wullgate *see* **willgate**.
wullint *adj* willing.
wullshoch *adj* timid in courting.
wullsome *see* **wilsum**.
wult *v* wilt.
wumman *n* wife; woman.
wumman-body *n* adult.
wummle *n* gimlet.
wummle-bore *n* cleft palette.
wun¹ *n* wind.
wun² *v* win.
wunda-swalla *n* house martin.
wungall *n* sore on the foot.
wunner *n* wonder.
wunnerfae *adj* wonderful.
wunnersome *adv* wonderfully.
wunter *n* winter.
wup¹ *n* earring.
wup² *see* **wap²**.
wuppit *v* winding.
wurl *n* dwarfish person.
wurlie *adj* small; insignificant.

wurp *n* fretful person. • *v* fret; complain.
wurr *v* snarl.
wush *n*/*v* wish.
wusp *n* wisp.
wuss *n* juice.
wut *n* wit.
wutch *n* sorceress, witch.
wuther *v* wither.
wutness *n* witness.
wuzzent *adj* wizzened.
wy, wye *n* man.
wyde *n* dress; void.
wyders *n* waders.
wyg *see* **whig¹**.

wyle *see* **wile²**.
wyme *n* abdomen.
wynd¹ *n* alley; lane.
wynd² *v* turn left; separate chaff.
wyne *n* end of a furrow.
wynell *see* **vennel**.
wype *n* wreath; accidental blow.
wyr *n* arrow.
wyrrie *v* strangle.
wyte *n* blame; fault; reproach; wait. • *v*
 accuse; blame; wait; **wyte on** wait for.
wyve *v* entwine; knit; weave.
wyvin *n* knitting.

Y

yaal *n* yawl.
yaave *n* awe.
yab *n* lump of bad coal.
yabber, yabble *v* gabble.
yabblin *adj* gabbling.
yabbock *n* chatterer.
yable *adj* able.
yack *v* gabble.
yackety *adj* chattering.
yad¹ *n* piece of stony coal.
yad² *see* **yaud**.
yaddle *v* contend.
yae-time *adj* former.
yaff *v* bark; prate.
yagger *n* hawker.
yaik *v* ache.
yair, yare *n* fish trap.
yaird *n* farmyard, yard.
yairdie *n* small garden.
yairn *n* yarn.
yaised *adj* accustomed.
yald *v* yield.
yallacrack *n* altercation.
yalloch *n* shout.
yaltie *adv* slowly.
yammer, yawmer, yomer *adj* jabbering;
 • *v* jabber; shriek.
yammering *n* crying.
yamph *v* bark.
yan, yan't *adj* puny, undergrown.
yank *n* thump, sudden blow.
yanker *n* agile person.
yankin *adj* active.

yan't *see* **yan**.
yap *v* harp, nark.
yape, yaip *adj* hungry. • *v* be hungry.
yapish *adj* keen.
yaply *adv* keenly.
yare¹ *adj* ready, alert, prompt.
yare² *see* **yair**.
yark *n* blow. • *v* beat.
yarne *adv* eagerly.
yarp *v* whine; moan.
yarpha *n* fibrous woody peat.
yarr *v* snarl.
yarrow *v* earn.
yatt *n* yacht, boat.
yatter *v* fret.
yattering *n* chattering.
yattle *adj* stone-strewn. • *n* strength, fortitude.
yaud *n* nag, tired-out old mare.
yaul *v* yell.
yaul-cuted *adj* strong-ankled for running.
yauld *adj* alert.
yaumer *v* murmur.
yaup¹ *v* yelp.
yaup², yawp *adj* hungry.
yauping *adj* peevish.
yaupit *n* titmouse.
yauvins *see* **awns**.
yavil *adj* prone, flat.
yawmer *see* **yammer**.
yawp *see* **yaup²**.
yaws *n* syphilis, pox.
ye *pron* you.

yea *adv* yes.
yeald, yeld *adj* barren, infertile.
yeald nurse *n* dry nurse.
yearaul *n* yearling.
yearn *v* coagulate.
yearock *n* year-old hen.
yeattle *v* grumble.
yeck *v* hiccup. • *v* fib.
yed *n* falsehood. • *v* fib.
yeddle *adj* thick; muddy.
Yeel *see* **Yule.**
yeild *see* **eild.**
yeildins *see* **eildins.**
yeisk *v* hiccup; belch.
yeld *see* **yeald.**
yelder-e'ed *adj* evil-eyed.
yeldrick *n* yellow-hammer.
yell *v* roll (ship).
yella, yellae, yellie *adj* yellow.
yella gowan *n* buttercup; marigold.
yella lintie *n* yellowhammer.
yelloch *v* scream.
yellyhooin *adj* screaming.
yemar *n* keeper.
yeme *v* care for.
yemsell *n* keeping; custody.
yepie *n* blow.
yer *pron* your.
yerb *n* herb.
yerd *see* **yird.**
yerk *n/v* jerk. • *v* bind tightly; beat; **yerk aff** strike up.
yerker *n* heavy blow.
yerl *n* earl.
yern-bliter *n* snipe.
yersel, yerself *pron* yourself; oneself.
yester[1] *adj* last.
yester[2] *v* disturb.
yestermorn *n/adv* last morning.
yestreen *n/adv* yesterday; last night.
yet *adv* still.
yett[1] *n* gate.
yett[2] *v* pour.
yett-cheek *n* doorpost.
yettlin *n* cast iron.
yeuk, youk *n/v* itch.
yeukie[1] *adj* avid; itchy.
yevery *n* doorpost.
yield *n* compensation.
yiff-yaff *n* empty-headed talker.
yill *n* ale, beer. • *v* ply with ale.

yill-boat *n* ale barrel.
yill-cap *n* ale cup.
yill-hoose *n* ale house.
yill-wife *n* ale-wife.
yim *n* particle.
yin *adj/n* one.
yince *adv* once.
ying *adj* young.
yirb *n* herb.
yird, yerd *n* depth; earth. • *adj* stuck in the ground.
yirdfast, yerdfast *adj* deep-rooted; earthy.
yird-hungry *adj* voracious.
yirdin *n* thunder.
yirdit *adj* buried.
yirdlins *adv* along the ground.
yirlich *adj* wild.
yirm *v* whine; moan.
yirn *v* earn.
yirnin *n* rennet.
yisk *v* hiccup.
yit *conj* yet.
yivverie *adj* desirous.
ylz *pron* you.
yochel *n* bumpkin, yokel.
yock *n* yoke.
yoke *v* plough in pairs; **yoke tae** set to, engage in a dispute; start a job.
yokin *n* bout, shift, stint.
yolk *n* opaque roundel in window glass.
yoller *v* talk loudly but indistinctly.
yolpin *n* unfledged bird; young child.
yomer *see* **yammer.**
yomf *v* strike.
yon, yond *pron* those; these.
yond[1] *adv* beyond.
yond[2] *see* **yon.**
yondmost *adv* farthest.
yonner *adj* yonder. • *adv* yonder.
yont *adv* along; beyond.
yonter *adv* farther.
yontermost *adv* farthest.
yore *adj* ready, alert.
yorlin *n* yellowhammer.
youd *n* youth.
youden *adj* yielded.
youden-drift *n* wind-blown snow.
youdful *adj* youthful.
youdlin *n* young lad.
youfat *adj* small, puny.
youk *see* **yeuk.**

youlring *n* yellow-hammer.
yound *adj* opposite.
young man *n* best man.
youngsome *adj* youthful.
younker *n* nestling; youngster.
youp *n* scream.
youse, youze, youzyins *pron* (*pl*) you.
youst *n* idle chatter. • *v* talk idly.
youster *n* putrefaction.
yout *n/v* cry.
youthheid *n* youth, adolescence.
youthie, youthy *adj* youthful, juvenile, young, childish.
yove *v* talk freely, chat.
yow[1] *n* cone.
yow[2]**, yowe** *n* ewe; sheep

yowdendrift *n* blizzard, snowstorm.
yowdlin *adj* dilatory.
yowe *see* **yow**[1].
yowf *n/v* bark.
yowk *n* yolk.
yowl *n/v* wail, yell, yelp.
yowt *n/v* cry.
yowther *n* strong, bad smell.
Yule, Yeel *n* Christmas.
yule *v* observe Yuletide.
yule brose *n* fat brose.
Yule Day *n* Christmas Day.
Yule E'en *n* Christmas Eve, eve of Yule.
yuman *n* yeoman; peasant.
yunk *v* buck.
yurn *n* rennet.

English-Scots Dictionary

A

a *art* ae, ane.
abandon *v* forhoo, gie ower.
abashed *adj* abaisit, hingin-luggit.
abate *v* quall.
abattoir *n* butch-hoose.
abdomen *n* painch, wyme.
abhorrence *n* scunner.
abhorrent *adj* laithlie, scunnersome.
abide *v* bide, thole.
ability *adj* abeelitie.
abject *adj* sleekit.
ablaze *adj* ableeze.
able *adj* yable, ticht.
able-bodied *adj* hail.
abnormal *adj* no richt, orra.
abode *n* abaid.
abolish *v* elide.
abort *v* slip.
abound *v* swarm.
abounding *adj* hoatchin.
about *prep* aboot, anent.
above *prep* abuin, abune.
above-mentioned *adj* foresaid.
abreast *adv* abreist.
abroad *adv* abreed, abraid.
abrupt *adj* snappit, snottie.
abscess *n* income, bealin.
absent *adj* troon.
absent-minded *adj* forgettle, nae in.
absolute *adj* fair, black.
absorbed *adj* oot ower the lugs.
abstain *v* gae frae.
abstemious *adj* canny.
abstract *adj* abstrack.
abundance *n* rowth, feck.
abundant *adj* rowthie, ruch.
abuse *v* abuise, abeese.
abusive *adj* ill-mou'd, ill-tonguit, flyting.
accelerate *v* gie.
accent *n* tune, tin.
accept *v* accep.
access *n* ingate, ingang.
accident *n* stramash, amshach.
accidental *adj* casual.
accomodation *n* up-pittin.

accompany *v* convoy, set.
accomplish *v* get roon.
accomplished *adj* far seen.
accord *n* cord.
account *n* account, line.
accrue *v* accrese.
accumulate *v* hudge.
accumulation *n* rake, hirst.
accurate *adj* richt.
accurately *adv* pintitlie.
accuse *v* wyte, faut.
accused *n* panel.
accustom *v* brither.
accustomed *adj* yaised, heftit.
ace *n* ess.
ace of spades *n* furl o birse.
ache *n* stoun, gowp.
achieve *v* get roon, pit ower.
achievement *n* dirdum.
acid *adj* wersh, soor.
acknowledge *v* awn, lat licht, tak wi.
acorn *n* pipe.
acquaint *v* acquant, acquent.
acquaintance *n* acquantance, acquentance.
acquire *v* git.
acquit *v* free, assoilzie.
acre *n* acker, ackre.
acrid *adj* reekit, snell.
acrimonious *adj* tuithie, snell.
acrimony *n* nip-lug.
across *prep* athort, throu, thorter.
act *n/v* ack.
action *n* ploy.
active *adj* acteeve, feerie, trig, swack.
activity *n* through-pit.
actually *adv* ackwallie.
acute *adj* gleg, snack, fell.
Adam's apple *n* thrapple.
adamant *adj* positeeve.
adapt *v* adap.
adaptable *adj* handie.
add *v* eik.
addicted *adj* addikit.
addition *n* addeetion.
additional *adj* tither.

address *n/v* back, backin.
adept *adj* fell, kittle.
adequate *adj* eneuch, anew.
adhere *v* clap.
adhesive *adj* claggy, clarty.
adjoin *v* mairch wi.
adjust *v* tune, turse, sort.
admirable *adj* braw.
admit *v* awn.
admonish *v* speak a word tae.
admonition *n* telling.
ado *n* adae.
adolescence *n* youthheid.
adolescent *adj/n* (a) halflin.
adorn *v* munt, busk, mense.
adroit *adj* cannie, knackie, gleg.
adult *n* man-body, wumman-body.
advance *v* forder, win forrit.
advancement *n* forder.
advantage *n* better, nip.
adventurous *adj* aunterous.
adverse *adj* thrawart, conter.
advertise *v* adverteese.
advertisement *n* adverteesement.
advice *n* advisement.
advise *v* speak a word tae.
adze *n* eetch, hack.
affable *adj* couthie, crackie.
affair *n* maitter.
affect *v* affeck, tak on.
affected *adj* mim, pitten-on, prick-ma-dentie.
affection *n* hert-likin, fainness.
affectionate *adj* lithesome, innerlie.
affinity *n* sibness.
affirm *v* threap, uphaud.
affirmation *n* threap.
afflict *v* hash, trachle.
afflicted *adj* afflickit.
affliction *n* pine.
affluent *adj* weel-daein.
afford *v* affoord.
affront *n/v* heelie.
afloat *adv* aswim.
afoot *adv* afit, agate.
aforementioned *adj* foresaid.
afraid *adj* feart, afeared.
aft *n* eft.
after *prep* efter, ahint, back o.
afterbirth *n* cleanin.
aftermath *n* eftercome, eftercast.

afternoon *n* aifternune, efternuin.
aftertaste *n* guff.
afterwards *adv* efterwards, syne.
again *adv* agane.
against *prep* agin, gin, conter.
age *v* get up in years.
aged *adj* eildit.
agent *n* factor.
aggregate *n* tot.
aggressive *adj* randie.
aggrieved *adj* sair made.
aghast *adj* dumfoonert.
agile *adj* lichtsome, soople, swack, kibble.
agitate *v* fluffer, flocht.
agitated *adj* wowf, skeer.
agitation *n* carfuffle, jabble.
ago *adv* syne, sinsyne, abye.
agony *n* bide.
agree *v* gree, say thegither.
agreeable *adj* couthie, greeable.
agreeably *adv* condinglie.
agreement *n* greement, greeance.
ahead *prep* aheid.
aid *n* forder.
aid *v* pit tae yer haun.
ailing *adj* no weel, dowie.
ailment *n* tribble, waff.
aim *n* gley, airch. • *v* ettle.
aimless *adj* knotless, paidlin.
air *n* oam.
aisle *n* trance, pass.
ajar *adj* ajee.
akin *adj* sib, freens.
alarm *n* alairm, fleg. • *v* alairm, skeer, flichter, fleg.
alas *interj* wae's me, ochone.
alcoholic *adj* drouthie.
alcove *n* bole, neuk.
alder *n* aller, arn.
ale *n* yill, nappy.
alehouse *n* howf.
alert *adj* gleg, smairt.
algae *n* wrack.
alien *adj* fremmit, ootlin. • *n* ootrel.
alight[1] *adj* alow.
alight[2] *v* lowp aff.
align *v* raw.
alike *adj* sic an sae, sib, after ane.
alive *adj* alist, abune the muild.
all *adj* a, aw; **all kinds** orra. **all and sun-**

dry ilk ane. **all the** the hail. **all told** at a slump.

allay v souder.

allege v threap.

allegation n alleadgance.

allegiance n lealtie.

alleviate v lichten, souder.

alley n close, entry, wynd, vennel.

allocate v stent.

allot v stent.

allotment adj paffle.

allow v alloo, lat.

allude v mint.

ally n stoop.

almighty adv amichtie.

almost adv amaist, near.

alms n awmous.

aloft adv alaft.

alone adj alane, aleen.

along adv alang, yont.

alongside adv sidelins. • prep anent.

aloof adj freff, aback, abeigh. • adv aback

aloofness n abstractness

aloud adv alood.

already adv aready, areddies.

also adv an a, forby.

alter v cheenge.

alternately adv time aboot, tour aboot.

although conj albuist, alpuist.

altitude n heicht, hicht.

altogether adv athegither.

always adv aye, ayeways, still an on.

amalgamate v mell.

amaze v dumfooner.

amber n lammer.

ambition n ettle.

ambitious adj high-bendit.

amble v dander, dauner, stravaig.

amenable adj handie.

amends n mends.

amiable adj douce, couthy.

among prep amang.

amorous adj fain.

amount n amoont, thing.

ample adj lucky, fouthie.

amuse v haud oot o langer.

amusement n ploy, divert.

amusing adj pawky, shortsome.

ancestor n forebear.

ancient adj auncient.

and conj an.

anecdote n crack.

anger n birse, corruption. • v pet, fash.

angry adj wraith, atterlie.

anglicise v englify.

anguish n fash.

animal n beast.

animate v skeich.

animosity n unfreenship.

ankle n cuit, ancleth.

announce v announce.

annoy v fash.

annoyance n fasherie.

annoyed adj thin, mad.

annoying adj fashious, angersome.

annual adj ilka year.

annul v elide.

anoint v sclatch, cleester, straik.

another adj anither.

ant n eemock, emmit.

anticipate v ettle.

anticlockwise adv withershins, widdershins.

antics npl cantrips.

antipathy n scunner.

antique n auld-warld.

antiquity n eild.

anvil n stiddie.

anxiety n anxeeitie, hert's care.

anxious adj thochtie, on hecklepins.

any adj ony.

anybody n oniebodie.

anyhow adv onieways, onie road.

anyone adj onieane, onie yin.

anything pron oniething, ocht, owt.

anywhere adv oniewey.

apart adv apairt.

apartment n hoose, hoosie.

apathetic adj cauldrife, cauld-watter.

apex n peen.

apiece adv the piece.

apothecary n droggist, droggie.

appal v gliff.

appalling adj awesome.

apparatus n graith.

apparent adj kenable.

apparently adv appearinlie.

apparition n foregang, ghaist.

appealing adj sonsie.

appear v kythe.

appearance n cast.

appease v slock.

appetising *adj* gustie.
appetite *n* appeteet, cut.
applaud *v* ruff.
apple *n* aipple.
appoint *v* tryst.
appointment *n* tryst.
apportion *v* stent.
appraise *v* vailye.
appreciate *v* apprise.
apprehension *n* kennin, ill dreid.
apprehensive *adj* eerie.
apprentice *n/v* prentice.
approach *n* oncome. • *v* weir intil.
approaching *adj* rising.
appropriate *adj* lik. • *v* skech.
approve *v* appruve.
approximately *adv* lik.
April *n* Aprile.
April fool *n* gowk.
apron *n* awpron, peenie, brat.
apt *adj* lik.
arbitrator *n* arbiter, thirdsman.
arch *n* erch, airch.
argue *v* argie, argufy, threap.
argument *n* airgument, argie-bargie, threap, thraw.
aright *adv* aricht.
aristocrat *n* laird.
aristocratic *adj* lairdly.
arithmetic *n* coonts.
arm *n* airm, erm.
armful *n* oxterfu.
armpit *n* oxter.
aroma *n* oam, waff.
around *prep* aroon.
arouse *v* roust, kittle.
arrange *v* redd, sort.
arrangement *n* ootset.
array *n* ootrig, onpit.
arrears *npl* by-rins.
arrest *v* reest, lift.
arrive *v* win.
arrival *n* income.
arrogant *adj* heely, pridefu, heich-heidit.
arrow *n* arrae, arra.
arson *n* fire-raising.
art *n* airt.
artful *adj* sleekit, gleg, airtie.
artfully *adv* airtily.
artfulness *n* airtiness.
articulate *v* mou-ban.

artificial *adj* mim.
as *conj* is, alse.
ascend *v* rise.
ascribe *v* ascrive.
ash *n* ase, ass.
ashamed *adj* rid faced.
ash bucket *n* ase-backet, baikie.
ashen *adj* gash.
ashlar *n* aislar, ashiler.
ashpit *n* midden, ase-midden.
ash tree *n* esh.
aside *adv* sidelins.
ask *v* speir, ax; **ask after** ask for, speir for; **ask for** seek; **ask to** seek to.
askance *adj/adv* asklent.
askew *adj/adv* squint, asklent.
aslant *adj/adv* asklent, asclent.
asleep *adv* awa.
aspect *n* cast.
aspen *n* esp, tremmlin tree.
aspersion *n* ill-speakin.
aspire *v* seek, ettle.
aspiring *adj* ambeetious.
ass *n* cuddy.
assail *v* invade.
assault *v* invade, tear intae.
assemble *v* forgaither.
assembly *n* forgaitherin.
assent *n* greement.
assert *v* threap.
assertion *n* threapment.
assess *v* pruive, ettle.
assiduous *adj* eydent.
assignation *n* tryst.
assist *v* pit tae yer haun.
assistance *n* cast, heeze.
assistant *n* helpender.
associate *v* troke, frequent, forgaither.
association *n* troke.
assorted *adj* sindry.
assortment *n* hatter.
assure *v* asseer.
assurance *n* asseerance.
assured *adj* croose.
assuredly *adv* atweel.
astern *adv* astarn.
asthma *n* wheezles.
asthmatic *adj* pechie.
astir *adv* asteer.
astonish *v* dumfooner, bumbaze, ca the feet frae.

astonishment *n* maze.
astound *v* stoun.
astray *adv* aglee, agley.
astride *adv* stridlins, stride-legs.
astute *adj* cannie, pawkie, fell.
asunder *adv* sinnerie, abreed.
at *prep* it.
at all *adj* awa.
athletic *adj* swankin, leish, lish.
athwart *adv* thort, awkart.
atmosphere *n* oam, stech.
atone *v* mend, upmak.
atrocious *adj* awfu.
attach *v* steek.
attack *n* onding. • *v* invade, set tae, tear intae.
attain *v* win.
attempt *n/v* ettle, mint.
attend *v* tend, tent.
attendance *n* onwaiting.
attendant *n* ghillie.
attention *n* tent.
attentive *adj* tentie, eydent, thochtie.
attire *n* claes, cleedin.
attitude *n* set, shape.
attorney *n* lawer.
attract *v* tice.
attractive *adj* bonnie, sonsie.
auction *n* roup, unction.
audacious *adj* bauld.
audience *n* owdience.
auger *n* aeger, wimble.
auger-hole *n* wimble-bore.
augment *v* eik.
augur *n* fore-go.

august *adj* lairdlie.
aunt *n* aunty.
aurora borealis *n* merry dancers.
auspicious *adj* canny.
austere *adj* austerne, dour, snell.
authentic *adj* richt, rael.
authenticate *v* qualify.
author *n* owthor.
authority *n* poustie.
autocrat *n* maister an mair.
autumn *n* back-en.
auxiliary *adj* helpender.
available *adj* open tae.
avalanche *n* whummle. • *v* shuit.
avarice *n* grippiness.
avaricious *adj* grippitt, grisk, nippit.
avenue *n* inlat, entry.
averse *adj* ill-willed.
aversion *n* scunner, staw.
avid *adj* hyte, yeukie.
avoid *v* evite, miss, haud wide o.
await *v* wait on, bide.
awake *adj* waukened.
awakening *n* waukenin.
aware *adj* awaur, war.
awash *adj* sail.
away *adv* awa, wa, aback.
awe *n* dare.
awful *adj* awfie, awfu.
awkward *adj* ackwart, gawkit.
awl *n* elsh.
awn *n* baird.
awry *adv* aglee, agley, aclite.
axe *n* bullace, aix.
axle *n* aix-tree.

B

baa *n/v* maa, mae.
babble *n* blethers, haivers. • *v* blether, babble, haiver.
babbler *n* bletherskite.
baby *n* babby, bairnie, wean.
baby clothes *npl* babie-clouts.
bachelor *n* bacheleer, bachie, boy.
back *n* hin, hinneren, rig. • *adj* hin.
backbiting *n* nip-lug.
backbone *n* rig, riggin.
backdraught *n* blawdoon.

back garden *n* kailyard.
backside *n* dowp, hurdies.
backstairs *n* back.
backward *adj* backart, hint-the-haun, glaikit.
backwards *adv* back-rans, hintside fore-maist.
backyard *n* back coort, green.
bacon *n* ham.
bad *adj* baud.
badger *n* burran.

bad habit *n* ill-gate.
badly *adv* baud, sair, ill.
badly behaved *adj* ill-contrivit.
badly nourished *adj* ill-thriven.
badly off *adj* ill-aff.
bad manners *npl* ill-laits.
badness *n* ill.
bad-temper *n* crabbitness.
baffle *v* pall.
bag *n* poke, polypoke.
bagpipes *n* pipes.
bail¹ *n* caution.
bail² *v* owse, lave.
bailer *n* spootcher.
bait *n* brammel.
bake *v* byaak.
baked *adj* beukit.
baker *n* baxter, bapper.
baking plate *n* girdle.
balance *n* equal-aqual.
balcony *n* plettie.
bald *adj* bell, beld.
balderdash *n* clytach.
bale *n/v* turse.
balk *n* bauk.
ball *n* ba.
ballad *n* ballant.
ballast *n* ballish.
balmy *adj* leesome, baumy.
balustrade *n* ravel.
bamboozle *v* bumbaze, taigle.
banana *n* bananie.
band *n/v* baun.
bandmaster *n* pipe major, pipie.
bandage *n* cloot. • *v* rowe.
bandit *n* reiver, cateran.
bandy *v* giff-gaff.
bandy-legged *adj* bowlie, bowlie-leggit.
bang *n* blaff. • *v* dunner.
banish *v* bainish.
bank¹ *n* baunk.
bank² *n* baunk, hag, scaur.
bankrupt *adj* brokken, runkit. • *n* bankrout, dyvour. • *v* runk, bank-rape.
bankruptcy *n* brak.
banns *n* cries.
banquet *n* eat.
bantam *n* buntin.
banter *n/v* jamph.
bar *n* baur.
barb *n* prog.

barbed *adj* pikie, wittert.
barbarous *adj* ruch, coorse.
barbed wire *n* picket weer.
barber *n* baurber.
bare *adj* scabbit, scuddie.
barefoot *adj* barefit.
bare feet *n* baries.
barely *adv* scarcelins, barelies.
bare patch *n* blain.
bare skin *n* scuddie, skuddie.
bargain *n* block, troke, paction.• *v* troke, niffer, prig.
bargainer *n* troker.
barge *n* bairge. • *v* brainge.
bark *n/v* bouch, wow, yowf.
barley *n* bere, bigg.
barn *n* granzie.
barnacle *n* claik.
barometer *n* mercury.
barrel *n* bowie.
barrel hoop *n* gird.
barrel stave *n* scowe.
barren *adj* yeald, lea, dour, scabbit.
barrister *n* advocate.
barrow *n* barra, hurlie.
barter *n/v* troke, niffer.
base¹ *n* foond, larach.
base² *adj* dirten, wandocht.
basement *n* dunnie, laich.
bash *v* bate, ding, dunt.
bashful *adj* baushfae, blate, timmer.
basic *adj* upstannin.
basin *n* bowl, bowlie.
basis *n* grun.
bask *v* beek.
basket *n* skep, creel.
bastard *n* luve-bairn, by-start, get.
baste *v* baiss.
bat *n* backie.
batch loaf *n* plain loaf.
bath *n* dook.
bathe *v* dook.
baton *n* steek.
batter *v* lewder, massacker.
battered *adj* dashelt.
battle *n* stour, fecht.
battle-cry *n* slogan.
bauble *n* whigmaleerie.
bawdy *adj* coorse, ruch.
bawl *v* goller, yowl.
bay¹ *n* inlat.

bay[2] v bowf.
beach n stron.
beak n neb, gob, gab.
beaker n bicker.
beam n bauk, caber, blink, leam.
bear v beir, thole, bide.
bearable adj tholeable.
beard n baird.
bearded adj bairdie.
bearing n cast.
beast n baist.
beat v bate, ding, gub, dunt, bash.
beat down v patter, stramp.
beating n clearin, gubbing, badgeran.
beat time v treeple.
beautiful adj braw, bonnie, stoatin.
beautiful things npl braws.
beauty n brawness, stoater.
because conj cause, kis.
beckon v wag.
become v turn, get.
becoming adj setting, wicelik.
bed n lair, lie.
bedaub v clart, slaik.
bedeck v bedink.
bedevil v murther.
bedfellow n neibour.
bedraggle v draigle, trachle.
bedridden adj bedfast.
bedroom n chaumer.
bee n skep-bee, bumbee.
beech n buck.
beehive n skep, byke.
beef n sey.
beer n yill, swats, scuds.
beetle n clock.
beetroot n beetraw.
befall v befa, come ower.
before conj/prep afore, or, gin, till.
befoul v nestie, fyle.
befuddle v get fou.
beg v cadge, tap, beseik, prig.
beggar n thiger, sorner, gaberlunzie.
begin v stert, stairt.
beginning n stert, stairt.
begrimed adj reekit.
beguile v wile, begowk.
behave v guide yersel.
behaviour n laits, ongauns.
behead v heid.
behind adv/prep behin, ahint.

behindhand adv back, hint-haun.
behold v behaud, leuk till.
beholden adj behauden, bunsucken.
being n body.
belch n/v rift, boak.
belief n thocht.
believe v trew.
bell n skellet.
belladonna n Jacob's ladder.
bellicose adj weirlik.
belligerent adj randy.
bellow n buller. • v bellie.
bellows n bellies.
bell-rope n bell-towe.
belly n wame, painch.
bellyful n wameful.
bellyflop n gutser.
belong, belong to v belang.
belongings npl graith, goods an gear.
beloved n lief.
below adv/prep alow, ablow.
belt n tawse.
bemuse v confeese, raivel.
bench n bink.
bend n/v boo, fauld.
beneath adv/prep aneath.
benediction n blissin.
beneficial adj cannie.
benevolent adj lairge, furthie.
benighted adj benichtit.
benign adj guid-willie.
bent adj bowlie, bachled.
bequest n bequeyst.
berate v scaul.
beret n Tam o' Shanter, tammie.
berry-picking v be at the berries.
beseech v beseik, prig.
beside prep aside, forby.
besides adv forby, an a.
besiege v bely.
beslobber v slabber.
besmear v blyter, slarry.
besotted adj fond, begottit.
bespatter v slubber.
bespectacled adj speckie.
besprinkle v besplatter.
bestir v steer.
best man n young man.
bestride v striddle.
best room n room.
bet n/v bate, wad.

betide v befa.
betray v begowk.
betroth v tryst.
betrothal n hanfasting.
better-class adj bettermais.
better-looking adj better-faured.
betting slip n line.
between prep atween, atwix.
bevel n suit. • v wash doon.
bevelled edge n wash.
beverage n sup.
bewail v mak murn fur.
beware v bewaur.
beware of v tak tent o.
bewilder v stoun, stammygaster.
bewildered adj dumfoonert, bumbazed.
bewilderment n jabble.
bewitch v blink.
bewitched adj forespoken.
beyond prep ayont, beyont, ootwith.
beyond belief adj past a.
bib n brat, daidle.
Bible n the Buik.
bicker v scash.
bid n bod. • v seek, wheel.
bide v hing on.
bier n buird.
big adj muckle, meikle, sonsie.
bigot n begot.
bigoted adj begotted, nairra-nebbit.
bilberry n blaeberry.
bile n ga.
bill n (for drink) lawin; (on a bird) neb.
billow v spue.
bin n bucket, midden.
bind v bin, thirl.
birch n birk.
bird v burd.
birth v/n cleck, shout.
birthmark n rasp.
birthplace n cauf kintra, birth-grun.
biscuit n bake.
bisect v hauf.
bit n bittie; **bits and pieces** npl orrals.
bitch n bick.
bite n/v gnap.
biting adj snell, nithering.
bitter[1] adj wersh, snell, ill-scrapit.
bitter[2] n heavy (beer).
bittern n bog-bluiter.
bitter person n nippy-sweety.

bitumen n pick.
bizarre adj nae wicelik.
blab v clipe.
black adj bleck, mirk, glog. • v bleck
black and white adj chauve.
blackberry n bramble, brammel.
blackbird n blackie.
blackcurrant n blackberry.
blacken v to blecken.
black eye n keeker.
blackguard n bleckguaird.
blackhead n shilcorn.
blacking n bleck.
black lead n wad.
black pudding n bluidie puddin.
black sheep n ooterlin.
blacksmith n bruntie, gow.
blackthorn n slae.
bladder n blather.
blade n mou, pile.
blame n/v wyte.
blameless adj saikless.
bland adj wersh.
blandishments n ruise.
blanket n hap.
blaspheme v spell.
blast n pluff.
blatant adj plain, kenable.
blaze n/v bleeze.
blazing adj reevin.
bleach v haizer.
bleak adj dreich, dour, starrach.
bleat v blae, blare, maa.
bleed v bluid.
blemish n smit. • v mank.
blench v resile.
blend v bland, mell.
bless v sain.
blessed adj seilie.
blessing n sain.
blight n/v blicht.
blind n/v blin.
blink v blent.
blinkers npl blinners.
bliss n seil.
blissful adj seilful.
blister n/v blush.
blithe adj blide.
blizzard n stour, yowdendrift.
bloated adj fosie, brosie.
blob n blab.

block *n* stock. • *v* stap.
blockhead *n* stot, neepheid.
blood *n* bluid.
bloodshed *n* slaughter.
bloodshot *adj* bluidshed.
bloody *adj* bluidie.
bloody nose *n* jeelie neb.
bloom *n/v* blume.
blossom *n/v* flourish.
blot *n* spleiter. • *v* blotch.
blotch *n* tash.
blotchy *adj* measelt.
blot out *v* blotch out.
blotting pad *n* blad.
blotting paper *n* blot sheet.
blouse *n* carsackie.
blow *n* bla, chap, cloot. • *v* bla, waff; **blow out** whiff.
blown about *adj* jachelt.
blown up *adj* hoven.
blubber *v* bubble.
blubbering *adj* bubblie.
bludgeon *n/v* (to) rung.
blue *n* bew.
bluebell *n* harebell, blawort.
bluebottle *n* blue-fly.
bluetit *n* blue bunnet.
bluff[1] *n* ness.
bluff[2] *v* swick, blaflum.
bluish *adj* blae.
blunder *v* bummle.
blunder on *v* stavel.
blundering *adj* tackie, gawkit.
blunt[1] *adj* bauch (implement). • *v* fluise.
blunt[2] *adj* rauchle (person).
bluntly *adv* richt oot.
blurred *adj* blebbit.
blurt *v* blooter.
blush *n* rid face, beamer.
bluster *n/v* blouster.
blustery *adj* scoorie.
boar *n* gaut.
board *n/v* boord, buird.
boast *n/v* blaw.
boaster *n* bum, blouster.
boastful *adj* great, massie.
boat *n* bait, yatt.
boat-hook *n* bottick.
bob[1] *n* boab.
bob[2] *v* hobble.
bobbin *n* pirn.

bodice *n* jumpie.
body *n* buddie, buck.
body-snatcher *n* corp-lifter.
bog *n* moss, buggle.
bog oak *n* moss aik.
boggy *adj* mossie.
boggy ground *n* moss.
bogy *n* bogle.
bogyman *n* bowsieman.
boil[1] *n* bile, bogan.
boil[2] *v* bile.
boil up *v* bummle.
boiled sweet *n* bilin.
boiler *n* biler.
boisterous *adj* rummlin.
bold *adj* bardach, gallus.
bollard *n* pall.
bolster *n* bouster.
bolt *n/v* bowt, snib, slot.
bombastic *adj* braggie.
bond *n* band.
bone *n* bane.
bonfire *n* ball-fire.
bonnet *n* bunnet.
bonus *n* bountith.
bony *adj* beeny.
book *n* buik.
book-board *n* brod.
book-learning *n* buik-lair.
bookshelf *n* buik-buird.
boor *n* cowt, tike.
boorish *adj* menseless, coorse.
boot *n* buit.
booth *n* buith.
boot lace *n* whang.
bootnail *n* tacket.
booty *n* spulyie.
booze *n/v* sup, weet yer thrapple.
border *n* mairch.
bore *n* sta. • *v* thirl, sta.
bored *adj* seek-sair.
boredom *n* langour.
boring *adj* dreich.
borough *n* burgh.
borrow *v* get a len o.
bosom *n* bosie.
boss *n* maister, high heid yin.
botch *v* bootch.
both *pron* baith.
bother *v* bather, fash.
bottle-stand *n* gantry.

bottom *n* boddom.
bottom drawer *n* hope kist.
bough *n* beuch.
bought *v* bocht.
boulder *n* booder.
bounce *v* bunce, stot.
bound *v* boon, lowp. • *n* spang, stend.
boundary *n* mairch, meiths.
boundary-marker *n* meith.
boundary-wall *n* mairch dyke.
bountiful *adj* rowth.
bounty *n* boontie.
bouquet *n* bob, bow-pot.
bourgeois *n* haif-knab.
bout *n* yokin.
bow¹ *n* doss (eg. ribbon).
bow² *n/v* boo, beck.
bow-tie *n* made tie.
bowels *n* painches.
bower *n* bour.
bowl *n* bowlie, bicker, luggie.
bowl along *v* hurl.
bowl over *v* whummle.
bowsprit *n* bowsplit.
box¹ *n* buist.
box² *v* scoor (e.g. on the ear).
boy *n* lad, laddie, loon.
boyfriend *n* lad, cleck.
brace *v* rance.
braces *npl* galluses.
bracing *adj* caller.
bracken *n* breckan, rannoch.
brackish *adj* sautie.
bradawl *n* brog.
brag *v* blaw.
braggart *n* blouster, bletherskite.
braid *n* passments.
brain *n* harn.
brainless *adj* harnless.
brainstorm *n* wuiddrim.
brainy *adj* heidy.
bran *n* pron.
branch *n* rise, sept.
brand *n* kenmairk, buist. • *v* buist.
brand-new *adj* brent-new.
brandish *v* wag.
brash *adj* frush.
brass *n* bress.
brat *n* get.
bravado *n* braverie.
brave *adj* campie, wicht, thra.

brawl *n* rammie. • *v* tulyie.
bray *v* rowt.
brazen *adj* hard-neckit.
breach *n* slip.
bread *n* breid.
bread roll *n* bap.
breadth *n* brenth, breeth.
break *n* slap, speel. • *v* brak, brek; **break in** track; **break out** brainyell; **break up** skail.
breakdown *n* fooner.
breaker *n* jaup.
breakfast *n* brakfast.
breakwater *n* fleetdyke.
break wind *v* let aff, rift.
bream *n* braze.
breast *n* breist.
breast-feed *v* sook.
breast-milk *n* pap-milk.
breast-pocket *n* oxter-pooch.
breasts *npl* bubbies, paps.
breath *n* braith.
breathe *v* pech; **breathe your last** souch awa.
breathing *adj* souch.
breathless *adj* pechin.
breeches *n* breeks.
breed *v* cleck.
breeding season *n* ridin time.
breeze *n* tirl.
breezy *adj* blowstrie.
brew *v* mask.
brewer *n* brewster, browster.
brewing *n* browst, maskin.
briar *n* breer.
briar pipe *n* gun.
bribe *v* buy, creesh a luif.
bridesmaid *n* bestmaid.
bridge *n* brig.
bridle *n* branks.
brief *n* instructions.
briefly *adv* short an lang.
brigand *n* briganer, cateran.
bright *adj* bricht, licht.
brighten *v* lichten.
brill *n* bonnet flook.
brilliance *n* glister.
brim *n* flype.
brimming *adj* jaupin fou.
brindled *adj* riach, branit.
brine *n* brime.

bring about *v* rise.
bring in *v* inbring.
bring up *v* fess.
brink *n* lip.
brisk *adj* sproosh, gleg.
briskly *adv* gleglie.
bristle *n/v* birstle.
brittle *adj* brickle.
broach *v* mint.
broad *adj* braid.
broil *v* brile, bruilyie.
broken *adj* bracken.
broken-down *adj* fair duin.
broker *n* cowper.
bronchitis *n* wheezles.
brood *n* brod. • *v* clock.
broody *adj* clockin.
broody hen *n* clocker.
brook *n* burn, beck.
broom *n* brume, besom.
broth *n* bree.
brothel *n* bordel hoose.
brother *n* brither.
brother-in-law *n* guid-brither.
brought *v* brocht, brang.
brow *n* brae.
browbeat *v* threap.
brown *n* broon.
browse *v* brooze.
bruise *n/v* birse, breeze.
brush *n* sooper. • *v* soop.
brush against *v* skiff.
brush off *v* scuff.
brushwood *n* scrogs.
brusque *adj* nippit, snottie.
brute *n* bruit.
bubble *n/v* bibble; **bubble over** ream; **bubble up** papple.
buck *v* yunk.
bucket *n* bowie, cog.
budge *v* jee.
buffet *v* buff.
buffoon *n* fuil.
bug *n* bog.
bugbear *n* murmichan.
bugle *n* deidman's bellows.
build *n* set. • *v* big.
building *n* biggin.
building site *n* steading.
built *v* biggit.
bulge *n* bumfle. • *v* shuit.

bulging *adj* bumflie.
bulk *n/v* bouk.
bulky *adj* bouky.
bull *n* bill, boo.
bullfinch *n* bullie.
bullock *n* stirk.
bully *n* bangster. • *v* ool.
bullying *adj* bangstrie.
bulrush *n* bulwand.
bumble *v* bummle.
bumblebee *n* bumbee.
bump *n* dunch, dunt. • *v* dunt, dird; **bump about** hotter; **bump against** rap on.
bumper *n* caulker.
bumpkin *n* yochel, teuchter.
bumpy *adj* knappie.
bun *n* cookie.
bunch *n* tooshtie. • *v* rally.
bundle *n/v* bunnel, boytach.
bung *n* spile.
bungle *v* blooter, brogle.
bungler *n* fouter.
bungling *adj* fouterie.
bunion *n* werrock.
buoy *n* bowe.
buoyant *adj* gawsie.
burden *n* birn. • *v* trachle.
burdened *adj* burdenous.
burdensome *adj* burdenable.
burial *n* bural, hame-gaun.
burial ground *n* howf.
burial plot *n* lair.
buried *adj* yirdit.
burly *adj* buirdlie.
burn *n/v* birn, brenn.
burnt *adj* brunt.
burr *n* rattle.
burrow *n* bourie.
burst *n/v* brust; **burst open** leap; **burst out** spleuter.
bury *v* beerie.
bush *n* buss.
bushy *adj* bussie.
business *n* ploy.
businesslike *adj* purposelik.
bustle *n* fizz. • *v* bummle, stot.
bustling *adj* breengin.
busy *adj* thrang.
busybody *n* clishmaclaiver.
but *conj* bit.

butcher n flesher. • v butch.
butt n bowie. • v buck, dunch.
butter n freet.
buttercup n yella gowan.
butterfly n butterie.
buttermilk n soor dook.
buttocks n hurdies, dowp.
button n gornal.

buxom adj sonsie.
buy v coff.
buyer n merchant.
buzz n bum. • v bizz.
buzzard n gled.
by prep be, gin throu.
bygone adj bygane.
byway n bygate.

C

cab n noddy.
cabbage n kail, cabbitch.
cabbage leaf n kail blade.
cabin n caibin.
cabinet n aumrie, press.
cabinet-maker n caibe.
cable n tow.
cache n/v plank.
cackle v caak, keckle.
cadaver n corp.
cadet n caddie.
cadge v tap.
cage n tow.
cajole v fleetch.
cajolery n willywha.
cake n kyaak.
caked adj clottert.
cakes npl snysters.
calamity n amshack.
calculate v coont.
calf n cauf.
call v ca, cry; **call in** cry in; **call on** cry on.
calipers npl Jennies.
callous adj upsittin.
callus n hauch.
calm adj quate, lown. • n lown. • v soother; **calm down** come to.
calmly adj quatelike.
calumny n ill-speakin.
camisole n slip-body.
camomile n carmovine.
camp-follower n ligger-lassie.
campion n coo-cracker.
can n tinnie.
canal n canaul.
cancel v elide.
candid adj fair oot.
candle n caunle.

candle-end n caunle-dowp.
candlestick n carle.
cane n spaingie.
caning n hazel oil.
canister n mull.
cannonball n bool.
cant n phrase, sklent.
cantankerous adj pernickitie, cankry, carnaptious.
canter v troddle.
canvas n canass.
canvass v peuther.
cap n kep, bunnet.
capable adj feckful.
capacity n through-pit.
capacious adj sonsie.
cape n clock.
caper n/v flisk, caiper.
capers npl jigs.
caprice n wheem.
capricious adj flichtie.
capsize v coup.
captain n skip, mannie.
capture n tak. • v fang, grip.
car n caur.
carafe n cruet.
caraway n carvie.
carcass n carcidge, bouk.
card n caird (card used to comb cotton). • v caird.
card-playing n cairtin.
cards n cairds, deil's picter buiks.
card-trick n lift.
care npl thocht, tent. • v fash; **care for** keep.
carefree adj lichtsome.
careful adj cannie.
carefully adv graithlie.

careless *adj* hashie, tentless.
carelessly *adv* owerlie.
caress *v* daut, smoorich.
caretaker *n* janitor, jannie.
careworn *adj* wabbit.
carnage *n* slaughter.
carouse *v* gilravage, bend the bicker.
carp *v* threap, carb.
carpenter *n* wricht.
carpet *n* cairpet.
carriage *n* vairriage.
carrier *n* cadger.
carrion *n* ket.
carrion crow *n* huide, corbie.
carry *v* cairry, convoy, cadge; **carry on** wag awa.
cart *n/v* cairt.
carter *n* cairter.
carthorse *n* aiver.
cartilage *n* girsle.
cart-load *n* cairt-draucht.
cart-shaft *n* tram.
cascade *v* plash.
cash *n* clink.
cask *n* bowie.
cast[1] *n* swap (of someone's features).
cast[2] *v* kest.
cast iron *n* yettlin.
castanets *n* crackers.
castrate *v* lib, sort.
casual *adj* happenin.
casually *adv* owerlie.
cat *n* cheat, gib.
catgut *n* thairm.
catapult *n* guttie.
cataract *n* linn, catsherd.
catarrh *n* defluction.
catastrophe *n* stramash.
catch *n* kep, tak, sneck. • *v* nick, nip.
catechism *n* catechis.
category *n* teep.
cater *v* mait.
caterwaul *v* waw.
cattle *n* kye, baists.
cattle dung *n* sharn.
cattle man *n* herd.
cattle-shed *n* byre.
cattle-stall *n* boose.
cauldron *n* caudron.
cause *v* gar.
causeway *n* calsay.

caustic *n* cowstick.
cauterise *v* sneyster.
cautious *adj* cowshus, cannie.
cave *n* cove, gloup.
cavern *n* cove, clift.
cavil *v* cangle.
cavity *n* howe.
cavort *v* brank.
caw *v* croup.
cease *v* lat be, stint.
cede *v* gie ower.
ceiling *n* ruif.
celebrate *v* handsel, slocken.
celebration *n* foy.
cellar *n* laich room.
cement *v* souder.
cemetery *n* howf.
censorious *adj* sair.
censure *v* scaul.
centipede *n* Jennie-hunner-legs.
centre *n* mids.
certain *adj* certaint, siccar.
certainly *adv* certie.
certificate *n* brief, lines.
cessation *n* stap.
cesspool *n* scuttle-hole.
chafe *v* chaff, freet.
chaff[1] *n* caff.
chaff[2] *v* tak on (to joke).
chaffinch *n* chye.
chagrin *n* teen. • *v* chaw.
chain *n/v* cheen, chine.
chair *n* cheer.
chairperson *n* preses.
chalk *n/v* caulk.
challenge *n* brag.
chamber *n* chaumber.
chamberpot *n* chanty, pish-pot.
champ *v* hanch.
champion *n* kemp.
chance *adj* antrin. • *n* kep, likly.
chancel *n* queir.
chandelier *n* gasoliere.
change *n/v* chynge; **change places** shift.
changeling *n* taen-awa.
channel *n* trink, rin.
chant *v* chaunt.
char *n* cudding.
chaos *n* reel-rall.
chaotic *adj* throwder, tapsalterie.
chapel *n* chaipel.

character *n* farran, word, fushion.
characteristic *n* set.
charge *n* plug. • *v* chairge.
charlatan *n* swick.
charlock *n* skelloch.
chart *n* caird.
chase *v* chasie.
chasm *n* cleugh.
chaste *adj* leal.
chastise *v* chaistifie.
chat *n/v* crack, blether.
chatter *n* blethers, gab. • *v* shatter, chitter.
chatterbox *n* blether, chantie-beak.
chatty *adj* gabbie, bletherin.
cheap *adj* chape.
cheat *v* chate, begowk.
cheating *adj* chaterie.
check *n/v* chack.
cheek *n* impidence, gash,
cheekbone *n* chaft-blade.
cheeks *npl* chowks.
cheeky *adj* facie.
cheep *n/v* peek.
cheer *v* lift.
cheerful *adj* cheerisome, blithesome.
cheerfully *adv* cantily.
cheering *adj* lichtsome.
cheerless *adj* unhertsome.
cheers! *interj* here's tae ye.
cheese *n* kebbock.
cheese-paring *adj* nippit.
cheese-press *n* chessart.
chemise *n* sark.
chequered *adj* chackert.
cherish *v* mak o.
cherry *n* gean, chirrie.
chessboard *n* diceboard.
chest *n* kist, buist.
chestnut *n* chessie, cheggie.
chevron *n* strip.
chew *n/v* chow, cham.
chewing gum *n* chuggie, chuddue.
chick *n* chuckie.
chicken *n* chucken, chookie.
chicken run *n* ree.
chickenpox *n* watery pox.
chickweed *n* chickenwort.
chide *v* tongue.
chief *adj* heidmaist. • *n* laird, chieftain, himsel.
chilblain *n* mool.

child *n* bairn, wean.
childbirth *n* shoutin.
childhood *n* bairnheid.
childish *adj* bairnie.
childlike *adj* bairn-lik.
children *npl* childer.
chill *n* jeel. • *v* jeel, to daver.
chilling *adj* cauldrid.
chilly *adj* shill, chilpie.
chimney *n* lum.
chimney-corner *n* ingle-neuk.
chimney *n* lum.
chin *n* chinkie, chirle.
china *n* cheeny.
china dog *n* wallie dug.
chink *n* jink.
chip *n* spail. • *v* lip (e.g. a blade).
chirp *v* cheetle.
chisel *n* crove, cloorer.
chitchat *n* clishmaclaver.
chivalrous *adj* gentie.
chives *npl* sithes.
chock *v* wadge.
choice *n* chice. • *adj* han-waled.
choir *n* ban, queir.
choke *v* chowk.
choose *v* choice.
chop *v* champ, hack.
chop off *v* sneg.
choppiness *n* chap.
chopping block *n* hack stock.
choppy *adj* ralliach.
chops *npl* chowks.
chore *n* troke.
chortle *v* keckle.
chorus *n* queir.
christen *v* kirsten, gie a name.
Christendom *n* Christendie.
christening *n* kirstenin.
Christian name *n* given name.
Christmas *n* Christenmas, Yule.
Christmas Day *n* Yule Day.
Christmas Eve *n* Yule Een.
chronic *adj* sitten-doon.
chrysalis *n* tammy-nid-nod.
chub *n* skelly.
chubby *adj* chibbie, chuffie.
chubby-cheeked *adj* chuffie-cheekit.
chuckle *v* keckle.
chum *n* freen.
chunk *n* junk.

church *n* kirk.
churchgoer *n* hearer.
churchyard *n* kirkyaird.
churl *n* tike.
churlish *adj* carlage, nabal.
churn *n/v* kirn.
cigarette butt *n* dowt, dottle.
cinder *n* cinner.
cinema *n* picter hoose, peepy-show.
cinnamon *n* cannel.
cipher *n* ceepher.
circle *n* raing.
circular *adj* roon.
circumspect *adj* canny.
cirrus *n* gait's hair.
cistern *n* cistren.
cite *v* sist.
claim *v* awn.
clamber *v* clammer.
clammy *adj* clam.
clamour *n* stramash, sclammer.
clamorous *adj* clammersome.
clamp *n* glaun.
clandestine *adj* hidlins.
clang *v* towl.
clank *n* rackle.
clannish *adj* hing-thegither.
clapboard *n* knappel.
claptrap *n* palaver.
clash *n* swinge.
clasp *n/v* clesp, hesp.
clasp knife *n* jockteleg.
class *n* cless.
clatter *n/v* brattle.
claw *n/v* cleuk.
clay *n* cley.
clean *adj* claen. • *v* thorow, muck.
clear *adj* clair. • *v* redd.
clearance *n* redd.
clear-sighted *adj* gleg.
cleave *v* rive.
cleavers *n* sticky-willie.
cleft *n* clift, rift.
cleft palette *n* wummle-bore.
clench *v* steek.
clergyman *n* meenister, black coat.
clerk *n* clark.
clever *adj* cliver, wice.
cleverly *adv* clean-fung.
cleverness *adv* cliveralitie.
click *n/v* knick.

cliff *n* clift, craig, heuch.
climb *n* speel. • *v* clim, speel.
clinch *v* nail.
cling *v* clap.
clinging *adj* glaikit.
clinkers *npl* danders.
clip *v* cowe, dock.
clipped *adj* dockit.
clippers *npl* shears.
cloak *n* clock, hap.
clock *n* cloak.
clod *n* claut, clat.
clodhopper *n* plowt.
clog *v* clag.
clogs *npl* clampers.
cloister *n* closter.
close[1] *adj* nar, lunk.
close[2] *v* steek. • *n* hinmaist (conclusion).
close by *prep* nar.
close-fitting *adj* strait.
closure *n* shew-up.
clot *n* clat. • *v* lapper.
cloth *n* claith, cloot.
clothe *v* cleed, hap.
clothes *npl* cleas, cloots.
clothes horse *n* winter-dyke.
clothes line *n* raip.
clothes prop *n* stenter.
clothes rail *n* perk.
clothing *n* cleedin, claith.
cloud *n* clud, smuir.
cloudberry *n* knot, noop.
cloudburst *n* plump.
cloudy *adj* drumlie, cluddy.
clove *n* clowe.
cloven *adj* clowen.
cloven hoof *n* cloot.
clover *n* claver, sookie.
clown *n* hallion. • *v* noise.
cloy *v* staw.
cloying *adj* fousome.
club *n* mell.
club foot *n* reel fit.
cluck *n/v* clock.
clump *n* buss.
clumsy *adj* tackie, ill-settin.
clumsy person *n* bachle, gawk.
cluster *v* boorach.
clutch *v* claut, cleek.
clutches *npl* cleuks.
clutter *n/v* muck.

coach *n* noddy.
coagulate *v* claut.
coal *n* coll.
coal-bucket *n* baikie.
coal-cellar *n* coal-neuk.
coal-dust *n* dross, coom.
coalfish *n* saithe.
coalman *n* wheecher.
coalmine *n* heuch.
coal-seam *n* lift.
coarse *adj* coorse.
coast *n* strand.
coat *n* cot.
coat-hanger *n* shooders.
coating *n* skaik.
coax *v* fleetch.
coaxing *adj* coxy, fraikie.
cobble *v* souter.
cobbler *n* souter.
cobbling *n* snabbin.
cobblestone *n* causey stane.
cobweb *n* moose wab.
coccyx *n* rumple-bane.
cock[1] *n* cockieleerie (chicken).
cock[2] *v* scrug (a hat).
cocky *adj* croose.
cockade *n* hackle.
cockroach *n* clocker.
cocksure *adj* poochle.
codfish *n* block.
coddle *v* cuiter.
codicil *n* eik.
coerce *v* gar.
coffer *n* kist.
coffin *n* deid-kist, cauld-bark.
cognac *n* cony.
cohabitee *n* bidie-in.
coil *n* lap, pirl. • *v* pirl, wammle.
coin *n* cunyie, cross-and-pile.
coincide *v* complouter.
cold *n* cald. • *adj* coolriff, haarie.
colewort *n* curly kail.
colic *n* teenge.
collaborate *v* complouter.
collapse *v* fooner, come in.
collar *n* neck.
collarbone *n* hausebane.
collect *v* lift.
collection *n* mengie.
collection plate *n* brod.
collide *v* bairge.

collier *n* pickman.
collusion *n* paction.
colour *v* lit.
colourless *adj* fauchie, peely-wally.
colt *n* cowt, clip.
coltsfoot *n* tushilago.
columbine *n* grannie's mutch.
comb *n/v* kaim.
combat *n* fecht. • *v* kemp.
combine *v* gae thegither.
come *v* win; **come in** come by; **come together** *v* gae thegither. • **come back soon!** *interj* haste ye back!; **come on!** come awa!
comely *adj* sonsie.
comfort *n* easdom.
comforts *npl* thack an raip.
comfortable *adj* codgie, cantie.
comic *n* divert, tear.
command *n* biddin.
commence *v* stairt.
commend *v* ruise.
commendation *n* ruise.
comment *n* speak.
commerce *v/n* mercat, traffeck.
commodious *adj* scowthie.
commodity *n* gear.
common *adj* cowman, raploch. • *n* muir.
commoner *n* carle.
commonly *adj* for common.
common sense *n* mense, smeddum.
commotion *n* stushie, stour.
communication *n* traffeck.
Communion *n* the table.
compact *adj* snod, nacketie.
companion *n* compaingen, marrow.
company *n* gaitherin, clamjamphry.
compare *v* even.
comparison *n* compare.
compartment *n* shottle.
compass *n* diacle.
compassion *n* hert-peetie.
compassionate *adj* innerlie.
compel *v* gar, dwang.
compensate *v* assyth.
compensation *n* mends, upmak.
compete *v* kemp.
competent *adj* likly, ticht.
complacent *adj* kirr, bien.
complain *v* murn.
complaint *n* mane, pewl.

complete v feenish. • adj hail, fair.
completely adv fair, black, deid.
complex adj quirkie.
compliant adj bowsome.
complicated adj misred.
complication n wimple.
complicity n assession.
compliment v blaw up.
comply v complouter, come tae.
compose v clark, clink.
composed adj cannie.
composer n upmakar.
composition n upmak.
compost heap n midden.
comprehend v tak up.
comprehension n ken.
compress v pran.
compressed adj panged.
compromise v mids.
comrade n marrow, compaingen.
concave adj howe.
conceal v dern.
conceit n consait.
conceited adj big, conceitie.
conceive v cleck.
concern n fittininment.
concerning prep anent.
concerted adj thegither.
concession n conformity, inlat.
conciliate v gree.
conclude v en.
conclusion n pirlicue.
concoction n mixter-maxter.
concord n greement.
concubine n bidie-in, limmer.
concur v gree.
condemn v doom.
condensation n oam, gum.
condescending adj heich-heidit.
conduct n gate. • v conduck, convoy.
conduit n cundie.
cone n yow.
confectioner n sweetie-man, sweetie-wife (*see* gossip).
confectionery n sweeties.
conference n collogue.
confess v awn.
confident adj croose.
confidential n parteeclar.
confidently adv heid-heich.
confine v tether.

confinement n ward, inlyin.
confirm v souder.
confiscate v sequestrate.
conflict n/v fecht.
conformity n rander.
confound v confoon.
confront v stick up tae.
confuse v confeese, taigle.
confusion n mixter-maxter.
confutation n improbation.
congeal v jeel.
congenial adj kindly, couthie.
conger-eel n haivel.
congestion n closin.
congregate v forgaither.
congregation n kirk-fowk.
conjecture v jalouse.
connect v conneck.
conscientious adj eydent.
conscious n war.
consecrate v sain.
consecutive adj efter ither.
consent v gree.
consequence n eftercast.
consequences n efterins.
conserve v hain.
consider v consither.
considerable adj gey, bonnie, braw.
considerably adv gey.
considerate n considerin.
considering prep confeerin.
console v mane.
consolation n consolement.
consort v intromit, mell. • n marrow.
conspicuous adj kenspeckle.
conspire v collogue.
conspiracy n pack.
constable n polis.
constant adj close, leal.
constantly adv ivverlie, aye.
constipation n dry darn.
constrain v dwang.
constrict v nip.
construe v rede.
consult v inquire at, speir.
consume v pit ower.
consummate v perfit.
consumption n consumpt.
contact v awn.
contagion n smit.
contagious adj smittle.

contain *v* haud.
container *n* hauder.
contaminate *v* smit.
contemplate *v* lay the brain asteep.
contemporary *adj* eildins wi.
contempt *n* sneist.
contemptuous *adj* sneistie.
contend *v* kemp.
content *v* pleesure.
contented *adj* cantie, codgie.
contention *n* crinkie-winkie, airgument.
contest *n* tousle.
continually *adv* ivver an on.
continuous *adj* eend on.
continuously *adv* even on.
contort *v* thraw.
contortion *n* thraw.
contract *n/v* contrack.
contractor *n* cork.
contradict *v* conter, contrair.
contradiction *n* na-say.
contradictory *adj* ill-contrivit.
contraption *n* whirlie.
contrary *adj/n* conter, contrair.
contravene *v* thorter.
contribution *n* inpit.
contrive *v* ettle.
control *n* poustie. • *v* guide, maun.
controversy *n* threap, collieshangie.
conundrum *n* guess.
convene *v* tryst, forgaither.
convenient *adj* hantie.
converse *v* crack, confabble.
convert *v* cheenge.
convey *v* convoy, cairry.
convict *v* convick.
convince *v* insense.
convolution *n* wimple.
convolvulus *n* binwood.
convulsion *n* thraw.
cook *n* cuik. • *v* cuik, ready.
cooking pot *n* kettle.
cool *adj/v* cuil.
coop *n* ree, crib.
cooperate *v* complouter.
cope *v* manish.
coping *n* caip.
coping stone *n* caipstane.
copious *adj* lairge, rowthie.
copse *n* plantin, shaw.
copulate *v* mow.

coquettish *adj* pawky.
coracle *n* currach.
cord *n* tow.
cordial *adj* curmud, sonsie.
coriander *n* corrydander.
cork *n* prop.
cormorant *n* scart, scarf.
corn *n* stuff, werrock.
corncrake *n* craik, weet-ma-fit.
corn dolly *n* maiden, cailleach.
corner *n* cantlin, cunyie, neuk.
cornerstone *n* scuncheon.
cornflower *n* blawort.
corporation *n* trade.
corpse *n* corp, bouk.
corpulent *adj* guttie, gurthie.
correspond *v* gree.
corresponding *adj* confeerin.
corridor *n* passage, trance.
corroborate *v* homologate.
corrode *v* roost.
corrupt *adj* mankit.
cosset *v* couter, daut.
cost *n* chairge. • *v* stan.
costume *n* outrig, onpit.
cosy *adj* bien, cosh, couthy.
cot *n* beddie.
cottage *n* bothy, cot, biggin.
cottager *n* cottar.
cotton-grass *n* cat tails, bog-cotton.
cotton wool *n* wad.
cough *n* hoast. • *v* coaf; **cough up** hask.
coulter *n* cooter.
count *n/v* coont.
countenance *n* gizz.
counter *n* coonter.
counteract *v* conter.
counterfeit *adj* fause, ill.
counterpart *n* neibour.
counterweight *n* wither-wecht.
countless *adj* deemless.
country *n* kintra.
country girl *n* Jennie.
countryman *n* Jockie, heather-louper.
country person *n* teuchter.
county *n* coontie.
couple *n* cupple, kipple.
courage *n* smeddum, saul.
courageous *adj* croose, wicht.
course *n* coorse.
court¹ *n* coort.

court² v winch, gae thegither.
courteous adj hamelie, menseful.
courtesy n mense.
courting adj winchin.
courtyard n close.
cousin n kizzen.
cove n inlat.
covenant n paction, tryst.
cover n hap.
covering n hap, huil.
covet v hae an ee in.
covetous adj grabbie.
cow¹ n coo, baist.
cow² v coonger.
coward n feartie, cooard.
cowardice n cooardiness.
cowardly adj coordie, hen-hertit.
cowberries n brawlins.
cow dung n sharn.
cower v coor, jouk.
cowl n cool.
cowpat n coopat.
cowrie n groatie buckie.
cowshed n byre.
cowslip n lady's fingers.
coy adj skeich.
crab n partan.
crab-apple n craw's aipple.
crabbed adj crabbit.
crack n/v creck.
cracked adj hackit, chappit.
crackle n sotter, skirl. • v crunkle, graisle.
crackly adj crumpie, crumshie.
cradle n beddie.
crafty adj sleekit, gleg.
craftiness n sneck-drawin.
crag n scaur, craig, carrick.
cram v pang, stap.
cramp n cleeks.
cramped adj hamperit.
crampon n speeler.
cranberry n crawberry.
crane¹ n cran (bird and machine).
crane² v rax (the neck).
crane fly n Jennie-langlegs.
cranium n pan.
cranny n jink.
crash n/v rattle.
cravat n gravat.
crave v green for.
craven adj coordie.

craving n greenin.
crawl v crowl.
crayon n keel.
crazed n aff the knot, wowf.
crazy adj daft, doited.
creak n jirg. • v jirg, craik, cheep.
cream n ream, raim.
cream dish n reamer.
cream jug n poorie.
creamy adj reamie.
crease n/v cress, lirk.
creased adj runklie.
creature n craitur, baist.
credit n mense (honour). • v hae (believe/think).
credulous adj bluff.
creek n gote, geo.
creel n creil.
creep v grue.
cress n girse.
crest n tap, rig.
crested adj tappit.
crestfallen n hingin-luggit.
crevice n lirk, bore.
crib n beddie.
cricket n charker.
crimson n cramasie.
cringe v creenge, coorie.
cringing adj coorie.
crinkle v crunkle.
crisp adj crumpie, crumshie.
criss-crossed adj lozent.
critical adj tuithie.
criticise v puist.
criticism n heckle.
croak n craik. • v roup, craik, crock.
croaking adj croupit.
crochet-hook n cleek.
crockery n piggerie.
croft n craft.
crony n cronnie.
crook n nibbie.
crooked adj camshack, neukit.
croon v croodle.
crop n crap. • v rump.
cross¹ adj canshie.
cross² n/v corse.
crossbar n knewel.
crossbeam n bougar.
crossbred adj hauf-bred.
cross-examine v cross-speir.

cross-examination *n* thru-pittin.
cross-eyed *adj* skellie, gley-eed.
crossroads *npl* sheddings.
crotch *n* forkin, clift.
crotchet *n* whuram.
crouch *v* crock, coorie doon.
croup *n* chock.
crow *n* corbie, craw. • *v* craw, blaw.
crowbar *n* gavelock.
crowberry *n* crawberry.
crowd *n* crood, thrang. • *v* clamjamfrie.
crowded *adj* thrang, stowed.
crown *n/v* croon.
crow's feet *n* craw-taes.
crowsteps *n* corbie stanes.
crude *adj* coorse, raploch.
cruel *adj* ill, ill-kindit.
cruelly *adv* sair.
crumb *n* crottle, mealock.
crumble *v* crummle.
crumbly *adj* frush, bruckle.
crumpet *n* crimpet.
crumple *v* runkle, fumple.
crumpled *adj* runklie.
crunch *v* crinch, crump.
crunchy *adj* crinchie.
crupper *n* curple.
crush *v* grush.
crust *n* scruif.
crustacean *n* croy.
crusty *adj* crabbit.
crutch *n* powl.
cry *n/v* greet, yowt.
crystal *n* kirstal.
cuckold *v* cockle.
cuckoo *n* gowk.
cuckoo-spit *n* gowk-spit.
cud *n* cood.
cuddle *n* smoorich. • *v* coorie, knuse.
cudgel *n* rung.
cuff *n* han-ban, fung. • *v* fung, cloor.

cultivate *v* teel.
cultivated *adj* biggit.
culvert *n* cundie.
cumbersome *adj* unfreelie.
cunning *adj* sleekit, sliggy. • *n* slicht.
cup *n* tassie, bicker.
cupboard *n* aumrie, press.
cupboard love *n* cat-kindness.
cur *n* tike.
curb *n/v* crub.
curd *n* crud.
curdle *v* lapper.
curdled *adj* cruddie.
cure *n/v* cuir.
curio *n* ferlie.
curl *n/v* pirl.
curlew *n* whaup.
curling *n* roarin gemm.
curling game *n* rink.
curling match *n* bonspiel.
curling rink *n* rack.
curling stone *n* channel-stane.
curly *adj* pirlie.
currant *n* curran.
currency *n* siller.
current *n* rug, birth.
curse *n* butchach. • *v* ban.
cursory *adj* swatch.
curt *adj* snottie, nippit.
curtail *v* jimp.
curtain *n* hinger.
curtsy *n/v* beck, jouk.
curve *n/v* boo.
cushion *n* cushin.
custom *n* cant, haunt.
customer *n* mairchant.
cut *n* sned, whack. • *v* coll, snib, chib; **cut down** hag; **cut into** sneck; **cut off** nick, sneg; **cut up** hack. • **cut short** *adj* snibbit.
cuttlefish *n* ink-fish.

D

dab *n/v* daub, pap.
dabble *v* dauble, plowter.
dad *n* dadie.
daddy-longlegs *n* Jennie-langlegs.
daffodil *n* daffins.

daft *adj* glaikit, gyte.
dagger *n* bittock, dirk.
dainties *n* fancy breid.
dainty *adj* gentie.
dairy *n* milk-hoose.

dairymaid *n* dey.
daisy *n* gowan.
dale *n* glen, strath.
dally *v* tig.
dam *n* caul, minnie. • *v* dem.
damage *n/v* skaith, disabuse.
damaged *adj* chippit.
damages *npl* skaith, mends.
dame *n* deem.
damn *n/v* dang.
damn-all *n* deil a haet.
damned *adj* dazent.
damp *adj/n* dunk. • *v* smoor.
damsel *n* damishell.
damson *n* damasee.
dance *n* bob. • *v* birl.
dance tune *n* spring.
dancing *n* jiggin.
dancing master *n* dancie.
dandelion *n* daintie-lion, pee-the-bed.
dandle *v* daidle.
dandruff *n* scruif.
danger *n* uncanny.
dangerous *adj* uncanny, unchancie.
dangle *v* dannle, drotch.
dapper *adj* trig.
dappled *adj* riach.
dare *n* hen. • *v* daur.
daring *adj* derf. • *n* daur.
dark *n* mirk, murky. • *adj* daurk.
darken *v* mirken.
darling *n* dautie, doo.
darn *v* ranter.
dart *n/v* dairt.
darts *n* arras.
dash *n* sloosh. • *v* dad, ding.
dashing *adj* baul-daur.
date *n* tryst.
daub *n/v* sclatch.
daughter *n* dochter.
daughter-in-law *n* guid-dochter.
daunt *v* dant.
dawdle *v* daidle.
dawdler *n* jotter.
dawn *n* daakenin. • *v* daaken.
daybreak *n* daw, skreich o day.
daydream *n* dwam.
daydreaming *adj* nae in.
daylight *n* sky, daylicht.
daze *v* donner, dazzle.
dazed *adj* bumbazit.

dazzle *v* daizzle.
dazzling *adj* dazzly.
dead *adj* deid.
deadly *adj* deidlie.
deadly nightshade *n* Jacob's ladder.
dead of night *n* how-dumb-deid.
deaf *n* deef.
deafen *v* deave.
deal *n* dale, troke. • *v* dale, traffeck; **deal with** mird wi, pit throu hauns o.
dealer *n* dailer, troker.
dealings *n* traffeck.
dear *n* dautie. • *adj* lief; saut (price).
dear me! *interj* lovanentie!
dearth *n* scant.
death *n* daith, hame-gaun.
death rattle *n* hurl.
death throes *npl* deid thraws.
death-watch beetle *n* chackie mill.
debate *n/v* flyte.
debauch *v* debosh.
debauched *adj* blearit.
debilitate *v* tak doon.
debris *n* redd.
debtor *n* dyvour.
debut *n* stairt.
decade *n* daiken.
decamp *v* tak leg.
decant *v* skink.
decanter *n* cruet.
decapitate *v* heid.
decay *v* moolder, moot.
decayed *adj* mozie.
decease *v* dee.
deceased *n* corp. • *adj* umquhile.
deceit *n* deceiverie, joukerie.
deceitful *adj* sleekit.
deceive *v* jouk, swick.
deceiver *n* jouker, sneck-drawer.
decency *n* honesty.
decent *adj* dacent.
deception *n* swick, geg.
deck *v* busk, dink.
declaim *v* scrift.
declare *v* depone.
decline *n/v* dwine.
declivity *n* doonfa.
decompose *v* chynge.
decorate *v* daiker, busk.
decoration *n* decorement.
decorous *adj* douce, menseful.

decorum *n* mense, honesty.
decree *v* decern.
decrepit *adj* decrippit.
decry *v* misca.
deduce *v* jalouse.
deduction *n* afftak.
deed *n* ack.
deep *adj* howe.
deep-rooted *adj* yirdfast.
deep-set *adj* howe.
deface *v* hash.
defame *v* blad, bleck.
defeat *v* defait.
defeated *adj* defait, bate.
defecate *v* drite, keech.
defence *n* fend.
defend *v* fend, weir.
defendant *n* defender, panel.
defer *v* pit ower.
deferential *adj* patientfu.
deficiency *n* shortcome.
deficient *n* scrimpit.
defile *n* hause. • *v* fyle.
deflated *adj* little-boukit.
deflect *v* weir.
deformed *adj* pailie, wrang.
defraud *v* snipe.
deft *adj* gleg, knackie.
defy *v* thraw.
degradation *n* doon-tak, come-doon.
degrade *v* bemean.
dejected *adj* disjeckit, hingin-luggit.
delay *n* aff-pit. • *v* dring, taigle.
delectable *adj* lichtsome.
deliberate *adj* canny, delyver.
delicacy *n* sunket.
delicate *adj* dowie.
delight *n/v* delicht.
delighted *adj* hert-glad.
delightful *adj* delichtsome.
delirious *adj* deleerit.
delirium *n* raverie.
deliver *v* len, reak.
delude *v* swick.
deluded *adj* misleard.
deluge *n* poor. • *v* teem.
delusion *n* phrase.
demand *n* rane. • *v* protest.
demean *v* demain.
demeanour *n* cast.

demented *adj* gyte.
demolish *v* wrack.
demon *n* wirricow.
demonstrate *v* kythe.
demoralise *v* bemean.
demure *adj* mim.
den *n* bourie.
denial *n* na-say.
denote *v* bear.
denounce *v* misca.
dense *adj* thrang, stupit.
dent *n/v* dunt.
dentures *n* seam o teeth.
denude *v* tirr.
deny *v* na-say.
depart *v* depairt.
departing *adj* wa-gaun.
departure *n* wa-gaun.
depend *v* lippen.
dependable *adj* sicker.
deportment *n* cast.
deposit *v* pose.
depraved *adj* ill.
deprecate *v* lichtlifie.
depredation *n* spulyie.
depressed *adj* disjaskit.
depressing *adj* dreich.
depression *n* howe, glooms.
deprive *v* twin.
depth *n* yird, deepens.
deputy *n* depute.
deranged *adj* gyte.
deride *v* jamph, lant.
descend *v* gang doon.
descent *n* strin.
desecrate *v* fyle.
desert *v* gie ower.
deserter *n* fugie.
deserts *n* fairin.
deserve *v* fa.
design *v* schame.
designing *adj* sleekit.
desire *n* will, ettle. • *v* seek, hae an ee till.
desirous *adj* yivverie.
desk *n* dask.
desolate *adj* gowstie, wilsome.
despair *n* wanhowp.
despatch *see* **dispatch.**
despicable *adj* wandocht.
despise *v* lichtlie.
despite *prep* maugre.

despoil v spulyie.
despondent adj disjeckit, hingin-luggit.
despot n tirran.
destine v weird, ordeen.
destiny n weird.
destitution n puiritith.
destroy v hash.
destroyed adj shent.
destruction n ruinage.
destructive adj sair.
detach v lowse.
detail n particularity. • v condescend.
details n pl eeriorums.
detect v airt oot.
detective n snoot.
detention n keepie-in.
deteriorate v gae back.
determined adj dour, contermit.
detest v laith.
detestable adj laithsome, scunnersome.
detestation n scunner.
detriment n hairm.
detrimental adj sair.
devastate v spulyie.
develop v growe.
development n oncome.
deviate v devol.
devil n deil, Clootie.
devil-may-care adj ramstam.
devilry n deviltry.
devise v think on.
devoted adj browden.
devout adj gracie.
dew n dyow.
dexterous adj knackie.
dialect n tune.
dialogue n twa-handit crack.
diarrhoea n skitter, ripples.
diary n diet-book.
dibble n/v dimple.
die v dee, depairt; **die down** lowden.
diet n mait.
differ v skew.
different adj unalik.
difficult adj defeeckwalt.
difficulties npl adeas.
diffident adj blate.
diffuse v spreed.
dig n/v howk.
digger n howker.
digest v disgeest.

dignified adj pretty.
dignify v heeze.
dignity n mense.
dilapidated adj disjaskit.
dilatory adj aff-puttin.
dilemma n snorl.
diligent adj eydent.
dilute v tak doon.
diminish v nirl.
din n reemis.
dine v denner.
dingy adj din.
dinner n denner, kail.
dip n dook, sneck. • v dook.
dipper n water meggie, essock.
dire adj awfu.
direct adj/v direck.
direction n airt.
directly adv direck.
directly after adv syne.
director n maister.
dirge n mane, coronach.
dirt n defenn.
dirty adj clarty. • v clart.
disabled adj tuckie.
disabling adj commandin.
disadvantage n mar, affset.
disagree v cast oot.
disagreeable adj clattie.
disagreement n disagreeance.
disappear v mizzle.
disappoint v begeck.
disappointment n dashing.
disarrange v malagrooze.
disarranged adj camshachelt.
disarray v carfuffle.
disaster n stramash, mishanter.
disband v skail.
disbelieve v misdoubt.
discard v jeck.
discern v tartle.
discerning adj canny.
discharge n/v dischairge, delash.
discolour v thraw.
discoloured adj ill-colourit.
disconcert v pit aboot.
disconcerted adj taen.
disconsolate adj dowie.
discontented adj drum, worm-etten.
discord n plea.
discourage v danton.

discouraged *adj* hertless.
discouraging *adj* hertless.
discourteous *adj* ill-faured.
discover *v* fin.
discredit *n/v* tash.
discreet *adj* canny, mensefu.
discretion *n* mense.
discussion *n* communin.
disdainful *adj* heelie, sanshach.
disdainfully *adv* heich.
disease *n* tribble.
disembowel *v* gralloch.
disentangle *v* unfankle, redd.
disfavour *n* ill-will.
disgrace *n* tash.
disgraceful *adj* michtie.
disguise *v* guise.
disgust *n/v* scunner.
disgusting *adj* scunnersome. • *v* laithful.
dish *n* bowlie.
dishcloth *n* dish-cloot.
dishearten *v* disherten.
disheartened *adj* hertless.
dishevelled *adj* towtherie.
dishonest *adj* unhonest, lowse.
dishonour *n/v* tash.
dishonourable *adj* tashful.
disinclination *n* sweirtie.
disintegrate *v* murl.
disjoint *v* lith.
dislike *v* ug.
dislocate *v* shammle.
dislocation *n* rack.
disloyal *adj* slidderie.
dismal *adj* dowie, dreich.
dismiss *v* demit, skail.
dismissal *n* leave.
dismount *v* lowp aff.
disobedient *adj* coorse, ill-contriven.
disobey *v* misanswer.
disobliging *adj* ill-set.
disorder *n/v* carfuffle, dirray.
disorderly *adj* camsteerie, throughither, touther.
disorganised *adj* throughither.
disparage *v* misca.
disparagement *n* doon-tak.
dispatch, despatch *v* sen.
dispel *v* boost.
dispense *v* get by wi.
dispersal *n* upbrak.

disperse *v* skail.
dispirited *adj* dowie.
dispiriting *adj* weary.
displace *v* jee.
display *n* ootset. • *v* shaw.
displease *v* miscomfit.
dispose *v* redd.
disposition *n* tak, tune.
dispossess *v* herrie oot.
disproof *n* improbation.
dispute *n/v* aggie-bargie, threap.
disquiet *n* thocht.
disrepute *n* ill-name.
disreputable *adj* thiefie, coorse.
disrupt *v* skail.
dissatisfied *adj* miscontentit.
dissemble *v* jouk.
dissent *n/v* differ.
dissipate *v* perish.
dissipated *adj* ill-dain.
dissolve *v* mouten.
distance *n* lenth.
distant *n* adreigh, awa.
distaste *n* scunner.
distasteful *adj* scunnersome.
distend *v* swall.
distinct *adj* sindry.
distinguishable *adj* kenspeckle.
distinguished *adj* markit.
distort *v* bauchle, showl.
distorted *adj* bauchelt, thrawn.
distortion *n* thraw.
distract *v* distrack.
distracted *adj* distrackit.
distraction *n* fry.
distraught *n* hattert.
distress *n* harm. • *v* pit aboot.
distressing *adj* sair, sad.
district *n* kintra.
distrust *v* mislippen, diffide.
disturb *v* amow, distrubil.
disturbed *adj* ajee.
disturbance *n* stushie, rammie, stramash.
ditch *n* sheuch, gote.
dither *v* swither.
ditherer *n* switherer.
dithering *adj* fouterie.
ditty *n* sonnet.
divan bed *n* sattle-bed.
dive *v* dook.
diver *n* loom.

diving board *n* dale.
diverge *v* sinder, twin.
diverse *adj* sindry.
diversion *n* divert.
divert *v* entereen.
diverting *adj* shortsome.
divide *v* depert, sinder.
divine *adj* heavenlie.
division *n/v* hauf.
divulge *v* moot, lat ken.
dizziness *n* mirligoes.
dizzy *adj* licht.
do *v* dae.
docile *adj* quate.
dock *n* docken plant, panel.
doctrine *n* lair.
dodder *v* dotter, hochle.
dodge *n* prottick, evite. • *v* jouk, jink.
doe *n* dae.
dog *n* dug.
dogfight *n* collieshangie.
dogfish *n* blin ee.
dogged *adj* dour, pludisome.
doggerel *n* crambo-clink.
dogma *n* lair.
dog-tired *adj* fair duin.
dole *n* broo.
doleful *adj* dowie, doolsome.
dole money *n* broo money.
doll *n* dall.
dollop *n* slap.
dolphin *n* dunter.
dolt *n* dult.
doltish *adj* donnert.
domestic *adj* hamelie, hameart.
domicile *n* hoose.
dominate *v* owergang, maugre.
domineering *adj* ringin.
dominion *n* owerance.
donation *n* compliment.
donkey *n* cuddie.
doom *n* weird.
doomsday *n* deem's day.
door-catch *n* sneck, snib.
door-handle *n* hannle.
door-key *n* check.
door-knocker *n* chapper.
doormat *n* bass.
doorstep *n* doorstane.
doorway *n* entry, door-cheek.
dot *n* minute.

dotage *n* dottle.
dotard *n* dotterel.
dote *v* daut.
doting *adj* daft, fond.
double *v* dooble.
double-dealing *n* joukerie.
doubt *n/v* dout.
doubtful *adj* doutsome.
doubtless *adv* doutless.
dough *n* daich.
doughty *adj* douchtie.
doughy *adj* daichie.
douse *v* slock.
dove *n* doo.
dovecot *n* doocot.
down *n* doon.
down-and-out *n* truaghan.
down-at-heel *adj* scuffie.
downcast *adj* disjaskit.
downfall *n* whummle.
downhill *adv* doonwi.
downpour *n* on-ding.
downright *adj* doon-richteous.
downstairs *adv* doon the stair.
down-to-earth *adj* fair oot.
downtrodden *adj* sair hodden doon.
downwards *adv* doonwi, doon-brae.
dowerless *adj* tocherless.
dowry *n* tocher.
doze *n/v* dute.
dozen *n* dizzen.
dozing *adj* nid-noddin.
drab *adj* dreich, riach.
draft *n* scroll.
drag *n/v* harl.
dragon *n* draigon.
dragonfly *n* deil's darnin needle.
drain *n* sheuch, cundy. • *v* tuim, dreep.
drainpipe *n* rone-pipe.
dram *n* sup, droppie.
drape *v* hap.
draught *n* waff, glut.
draughts *npl* dams.
draw *v* rug (to pull/tug at sth.).
draw out *v* stent.
drawback *n* thraw.
drawer *n* shottle.
drawl *n/v* drant.
dread *n* dreid.
dream *n/v* drame.
dreamy *adj* dwawmy.

dreary *adj* dreich.
dredge *n/v* dreg.
dregs *n* poorins.
drench *v* drook.
dress *n* ootrig. • *v* hap; **dress up** tosh up.
dresser *n* bink.
dressing-down *n* waukenin.
dressing gown *n* wrapper.
dressmaker *n* mantie-maker.
dressy *adj* primpie, fussy.
dribble *n/v* dreeble.
dribbler *n* slitter.
drift *n* wreath. • *v* pander.
driftwood *n* wrack.
drill *n* furr. • *v* dreel, thirl.
drink *n* deuch, dyoch. • *v* deuch, wacht.
drinker *n* drouth.
drinking bout *n* splore.
drip *n/v* dreep.
drip-dry *v* sype.
dripping *n* rander. • *adj* seepin, droop.
drive *n* hurl, smeddum. • *v* ca, hurl.
driven *adj* drien.
driving *adj* rackin.
drivel *n* haivers, gyter.
driveller *n* gyter.
drizzle *n/v* dreezle.
drizzly *adj* roukie.
droll *adj* pawky, auld-farran.
drone *n* hum, burden. • *v* bum, souch.
drool *n/v* slubber.
droop *v* stint, penge.
drooping *adj* wallan.
drop *n* drap, blob. • *v* rap, lat doon.
droppings *n* doldies.
dross *n* drush.
drought *n* drouth.
drover *n* tapsman.
drown *v* droon.
drowned *adj* droondit.
drowse *v* dover.
drowsy *adj* droosie.
drub *v* bate.
drubbing *n* bating.
drudge *n/v* scodge.
drudgery *n* trachle.
drug *n/v* drog.
druggist *n* droggie.
drumbeat *n* ruff.
drunk *adj* fou, blootered, bevvied.
drunkard *n* drouth, drunkart.

drunkenness *n* drouthieness.
dry *adj* drouthie. • *v* dicht, win; **dry out** win; **dry up** spire, gizzen.
dryish *adj* dryachtie.
drystone wall *n* dry dyke.
dry weather *n* drouth.
dual *adj* twa faul.
dubious *adj* jubish.
duck *n* deuk, quackie. • *v* jouk, deuk.
duck pond *n* deuk's dub.
due *adj* plat.
dull *adj* dreich, dowie, dolly.
dullness *n* doufness.
dulse *n* dilse.
dumb *adj* tongue-tackit.
dumbfound *v* dumfooner.
dump *n* coup. • *v* plowt, plank.
dumpling *n* hodgel.
dumpy *adj* stowfie.
dun *n* riach. • *v* crave.
dunce *n* dobbie.
dunderhead *n* eejit.
dunes *n* links.
dung *n* muck, sharn.
dung-fly *n* muck flee.
dungeon *n* massymore.
dunghill *n* midden.
dunlin *n* pickerel.
dupe *n* jouk.
duplicate *n* dooble.
duplicity *n* joukerie.
durability *n* docher.
durable *adj* stark.
duress *n* force and fear.
during *prep* in, throu.
dusk *n* gloamin.
dust *n/v* dist. • *n* stour.
dustbin *n* bucket.
dustbin man *n* scaffie.
dusty *adj* disty, stourie.
duty *n* turn.
dwarf *n* droch, ablach.
dwarfish *adj* drochlin.
dwell *v* bide, dwall.
dwelling *n* dwallion.
dwindle *v* dreedle.
dye *n/v* lit.
dyer *n* dyester.
dyke *n* wa.
dynamic *adj* feckful, forcie.
dysentery *n* rush.

E

each *pron* ilka.
eager *adj* aiger.
eagerly *adv* snell.
eagle *n* aigle, ern.
ear *n* lug, icker.
earmark *n/v* lug-mairk.
earring *n* wup.
earwig *n* horny goloch.
earl *n* yerl.
early *adj* airlie, verty. • *adv* air, ear.
earn *v* yirn, win.
earnings *n* penny-fee.
earth *n* erd, yird.
earthenware *n* lame, pig.
earthward *adv* erthlins.
earthy *adj* yirdfast.
ease *n* easement.
easily *adv* eithlie.
east *n* aist.
easterly *adj* eastlin.
eastern *adj* easter.
eastwards *adv* eastlins.
Easter *n* Pace.
Easter egg *n* Pace egg.
easy *adj* eth.
easy-going *adj* jack-easy.
eat *v* aet.
eater *n* aeter.
eating *n* intak.
eaves *n* easin.
eavesdrop *v* hearken.
ebbing *adj* outgaun.
ebullient *adj* skeich.
eccentric *n* jeeger. • *adj* orra, unco.
eccentricity *n* unconess.
economical *adj* canny.
economise *v* scrimp.
economy *n* hainin.
ecstasy tablets *npl* eckies.
eddy *n/v* pirl.
edge *n* lip, laggin.
edging *n* trappin.
eerie *adj* oorie.
effect *n* effeck.
effective *adj* feckful.
effects *n* gear, graith.
effectual *adj* effecwal.
effeminate *adj* sapsie.

effervescence *n* fuzziness.
effervescent *adj* fuzzy.
efficiency *n* purpose.
efficient *adj* feckful, eident.
effigy *n* stookie.
effluent *n* midden bree.
effort *n* fend, ettle.
effrontery *n* hard neck.
effusive *adj* phrasie.
egotistical *adj* sellie.
eight *adj/n* aucht, echt.
eighteen *adj/n* auchteen.
eighteenth *adj* auchteenth.
eighth *adj* aucht, echt.
eighty *adj/n* auchtie.
eject *v* gie the door, set oot.
elaborate *adj* primpit.
elapse *v* owergae.
elastic *adj* elaskit.
elated *adj* made up, upliftit.
elation *n* uplif.
elbow *n* elbuck. • *v* oxter.
elder *n* eller, bourtree.
elderly *adj* eldren.
elect *v* eleck.
elegant *adj* gentie, pretty.
elegy *n* lament.
elevate *v* heeze.
elevation *n* heicht.
eleven *adj/n* eleevin.
eleventh *adj* eleevint.
elf *n* eemock.
eliminate *v* elide.
elongate *v* rax.
elope *v* skirt.
eloquent *adj* glib.
else *adv* ense.
elsewhere *adv* itherwhere.
elude *v* jouk.
emaciated *adj* shilpit.
emaciated person *n* ruckle o banes.
embankment *n* mote.
embarrass *v* gie a riddie.
embarrassed *adj* taen.
embedded *adj* stickit.
embellish *v* pit airms an legs tae.
ember *n* gleed.
embezzle *v* pauchle.

embolden *v* herten.
embrace *n* bosie. • *v* neck.
embroider *v* flourish, steek.
embroidery *n* flourishin.
emerald *n* emerant.
emergence *n* ootcome.
emergency *n* sair fit.
emigrate *v* lowp the kintra.
eminence *n* heich.
eminent *adj* markit.
emit *v* ootpit.
emphatic *adj* evendoon.
employ *v* work wi.
employees *n* fowk.
employer *n* cork.
employment *n* thrift.
empty *adj/v* tuim, oot.
empty-handed *n* tuim-handit.
empty-headed *n* tuim-heidit.
enamoured *adj* browden.
enchant *v* blink.
enchantment *n* glamour.
enclose *v* fauld.
enclosure *n* cru, fauld.
encounter *v* kep.
encourage *v* gie a lift tae.
encouragement *n* hertenin, lift.
encouraging *adj* hertsome.
encrust *v* barken.
encrusted *adj* barkenit.
encumber *v* birn, trachle.
encumbrance *n* trachle.
end *n/v* en, eyn.
endorse *v* souder.
end product *n* ootcome.
endurance *n* thole, endurement.
endure *v* thole.
enemy *n* fae, unfreen.
energetic *adj* speeritie.
energetically *adv* stark, fell.
energy *n* birr, smeddum.
enervated *adj* forfochen.
enfeebled *adj* fordwibelt.
enfold *v* wimple.
enforceable *adj* prestable.
engage *v* fee.
engaged *adj* trystit.
engaging *adj* sonsie.
engine *n* ingine.
English *adj/n* southron, Sassenach.
English person *n* southron, Sassenach.

enjoyable *adj* shortsome.
enlarge *v* eik.
enlighten *v* enlicht.
enlightenment *n* licht.
enlist *v* list.
enliven *v* kittle.
enlivening *adj* lichtsome.
enmesh *v* mask.
enmity *n* plea, unfreenship.
enormous *adj* wappin.
enough *adj/adv* eneuch.
enrage *v* raise.
enraged *adj* hyte.
enrol *v* tak oot.
ensnare *v* cleek.
ensuing *adj* incoming.
ensure *v* mak siccar.
entail *v* tailye.
entangle *v* fankle, taigle.
entanglement *n* mink.
enter *v* intil.
enterprise *n* ontakkin, ploy.
enterprising *adj* thru-gaun.
entertaining *adj* shortsome.
entertainment *n* divert.
enthral *v* blink.
enthusiasm *n* birr.
enthusiastic *adj* keen.
entice *v* tice.
entire *adj* hail.
entirely *adv* black, fair.
entourage *n* tail.
entrails *n* painches.
entrance[1] *n* ingang, ingaun.
entrance[2] *v* blink.
entreat *v* prif, fleetch.
entrust *v* lippen.
entry *n* ingang.
entwine *v* wyve.
envelop *v* wap, hap.
envious *adj* jeelous.
environment *n* heft.
enwrap *v* wap.
Episcopalian *n* piskie.
equable *adj* souch.
equal *adj/n* aqual. • *v* peel.
equally *adj* aqual, equal-aqual.
equanimity *n* souch, evenliness.
equip *v* busk.
equipment *n* graith.
equitable *adj* richt-lik.

equivocate v parry.
erect adj staunin. • v ereck, cantle.
ermine n coat-weasel.
err v step aside.
erratic adj ragglish.
erring adj will.
erroneous adj mislearnit.
error n skellie.
errand n eeran.
errand boy n message boy, eeran-loon.
errands npl messages.
erudite adj far I the buik.
erudition n buik-lair.
eruption n ootstrikin.
escape n ootcome. • v win oot, miss.
escapade n ploy.
escort n/v convoy.
especially adv earest, maistly.
essence n sense.
essential adj necessar.
estate n gear, place, scheme.
estimable adj honest.
estimate n slump. • v pruive.
estranged adj hither-an-yon.
estuary n firth.
et cetera n an siclike.
eternally adv for aye.
eternity n month o muins.
etiquette n mense.
evacuate v tuim.
evade v evite, jouk.
evaluate v comprise.
evasion n joukerie.
evasive adj slidderie.
even adj e'en, eyven.
evening n e'en, e'enin.
event n han.
ever adv aye, ivver.
every adj ilka, ivverie.
everybody n ilk ane, abodie.
everything n athings.
everywhere adv a wey, aroads.
evict v herrie oot.
evidence n evident.
evident adj weel seen.
evil adj/n ill.
evil eye n ill-ee.
evildoer n ill-daer.
ewe n yowe.
exact adj nate.
exacting adj pointit.

exaggerate v blaw.
exaggeration n whid.
exalt v heeze.
examination n examin.
examine v exemin, exem.
exasperate v fash, ug.
exasperated adv hert-roastit.
exasperating adj tantersome.
excavate v howk.
exceed v owergang, bear the gree.
exceedingly adv unco.
excel v bang.
excellent adj braw, gran, boon.
except prep excep, binna.
exceptional adj by-ornar, parteeclar.
excerpt n swatch.
excessive adj odious.
excessively adv ower.
exchange n/v niffer.
exciseman n gauger.
excite v fluffer.
excitable adj reevin.
excited adj up.
excitement n go.
exclamation n exclaim.
exclude v haud oot.
exclusive adj privative.
excrement n keech, drite, cack, geing.
excursion n straik.
executioner n hangie.
exempt v exemp.
exemption n exemp.
exercise book n jotter.
exert v fash.
exertion n putt an row.
exhaust v exoust.
exhausted adj wabbit, forfochen.
exhausting adj trachlesome.
exhibit n production.
exhort v threap.
exit n ootgang.
exonerate v free.
exotic adj ootlan.
expand v hove, come.
expect v expeck.
expectation n lippenin.
expectorate v slerp.
expedition n expedeetion.
expel v herrie oot.
expend v ware.
expense n chairge, ootgang.

experiment n prattick.
expert n deacon. • adj slee, canny.
expire v dee.
expiry n ish.
explain v expoon, rede.
explanation n quittance.
expletive n sweer.
explode v pluff.
explosion n flist.
exploit n splore, ploy.
exploration n explore.
explore v reenge.
exposed adj fusslebare.
expound v expoon.
extend v stent.
extension n eik, ootshot.
extent n boon.
extinct adj wede awa.
extinguish v slock, smore.
extol v heeze.

extort v herrie.
extortionate adj menseless.
extra adj extrae.
extract v pou.
extraction n kin.
extraordinary adj by-ornar.
extraordinarily adv forby.
extravagance n wanthrift.
extravagant adj spendrif, expensive.
extreme adj sevendle.
extremely adv unco, terrible.
extricate v howk.
exuberant adj croose, cadgie.
eye n ee.
eyebrow n broo, ee-bree.
eyelash n ee-breer.
eyelid n eelid.
eyelet n pie-hole.
eyesight n eesicht.
eyesore n derbel.

F

fabricate v feingle.
fabrication n upmak.
face n neb, face-plate.
facetious adj knackie.
facile adj owerlie.
facing prep forent.
faculty n ingine.
fad n freit.
fade v dwine, wallow.
faded adj casten.
faeces n keech, drite, cack.
fag v deave, pingle.
faggot n faggald.
fail v miss, misgae.
failed adj stickit.
failure n failzie.
faint n/v dwam, fent, fant. • adj dwamie.
faint-hearted adj fushionless.
fair adj jonick.
fairies n guid fowk.
fairly adv middlin.
fair play n jonick.
fair-sized adj dentie.
fairy n ferter, eemock.
fairy hill n sithean.
fairyland n Elfin.

fairy-ring n elf-ring.
faithful adj aefauld, feal.
fake adj fause.
fall n/v fa.
fallen adj faan.
fall out v cast oot.
fall over v coup.
fallow adj lea, ley. • v fauch.
false adj fause.
falsehood n fausehood.
falseness n pit-on.
false teeth npl wallies.
falter v stammer.
familiar adj kenspeckle.
famish v hunger.
famished adj howe.
famous adj namlie.
fan n faffer. • v waff, faff.
fancy adj fantoosh. • n wheem. • v lik.
fantastic adj pawky.
far adv faur.
far away adj hyne-awa.
far-sighted adj faur-seen.
fare n fairin. • v fa.
farewell n fareweel.
farm n/v ferm.

farmer *n* fermer, guidman.
farmhouse *n* ha.
farmland *n* grun.
farmworker *n* joskin.
farmyard *n* yaird.
farrier *n* ferrier.
farrow *n/v* ferry.
farther *adv* faurer.
farthest *adj* farrest.
farthing *n* farden.
fashion *n* fasson.
fashionable *adj* tippie.
fast *adj/adv/n* fest.
fastener *n* snib.
fastening *n* hiddin.
fastidious *adj* perjink.
fastidiously *adv* perjink.
fat *adj* creeshie. • *n* creesh.
fatal *adj* deedlie.
fate *n* fatality, weird.
fateful *adj* weirdfu.
father *n/v* faither.
father-in-law *n* guid-faither.
fathom *n/v* faddom.
fatigue *n* tire. • *v* tash, jaup.
fatigued *adj* traikit.
fatten *v* mend.
faucet *n* stroop.
fault *n* faut.
faultless *adj* perfit.
favour *n* obleegement. • *v* nae see by.
favourable *adj* canny.
fawn *v* beenge.
fawning *adj* lick lip.
fear *n* dree.
fearful *adj* timorsome, frichtsome.
fearless *adj* frichtless.
feasible *adj* faisible.
feast *n* eat. • *v* gilravage.
feat *n* kittle, henner.
featherbrain *n* sodie-heid.
feathery *adj* fuzzy.
feature *n* track, meith.
February *n* Februar.
feckless *adj* haveless.
fed-up *adj* scunnert.
feeble *adj* fecklish.
feed *v* mait, stowe.
feel *n/v* fin.
feeling *n* souch.
feet *npl* lyomons.

feign *v* fengie.
feint *n/v* mint.
felicity *n* seil.
fell[1] *adj* bang.
fell[2] *v* fooner (strike down); hag (a tree).
fellow *n* fella, chiel.
femur *n* hunker-bane.
fence *n* pilin, resetter (person). • *v* stob.
fend *v* fen.
ferment *v* barm.
fermenting *adj* het.
fern *n* firm.
ferocious *adj* fell, bang.
ferret *n* futret, foumart.
ferrule *n* virl.
ferry *n* bait. • *v* set ower.
ferry-boat *n* coble.
fertile *adj* growthie.
fertilise *v* mainner.
fertiliser *n* mainner.
fertility *n* growthieness.
fervent *adj* aiger.
fester *v* etter.
festering *adj* atterie.
festive *adj* blithe.
fetch *v* fesh.
fetid *adj* humphed.
fetlock *n* cuit.
fetter *n/v* hapshackle.
fettle *n* kilter.
feud *n* feid.
fever *n* fivver.
few *adj* fyow.
fewer *adj* less.
fib *n/v* lee.
fibre *n* taw.
fickle *adj* kittle.
fiddle *n* pauchle. • *v* to diddle.
fiddler *n* fiddlie.
fiddly *adj* fouterie, scutterie.
fidget *v* fidge, fyke.
fidgety *adj* fykie.
field *n* feedle, park.
fieldfare *n* feltie.
fiend *n* fien.
fierce *adj* fell, bang.
fiery *adj* het-skinnt.
fifteen *adj/n* feifteen.
fifteenth *adj* feifteent.
fifth *adj* fift.
fifty *adj/n* fufty.

fig 188 flight

fig *n* feg.
fight *n* /*v* fecht, faucht.
fighter *n* fechter.
figure *v* jalouse.
figurehead *n* tulchan.
filch *v* skech.
file *n* raw, risp. • *v* risp.
fill *n* fou. • *v* prime, fou.
filling *adj* fousome.
filly *n* fillock.
film *n* scruif.
filter *n*/*v* sye, sile.
filth *n* fulyie.
filthy *adj* maukit.
fin *n* lug.
final *adj* hinmaist.
finally *adv* hinmaist.
finances *npl* pooch.
find *v* fin, get.
fine *adj* braw.
finery *n* braws.
finger *v* pawt.
fingertip *n* finger neb.
finicky *adj* fykie.
fiord *n* sea loch, voe.
fir cone *n* firyowe.
fire *n* lowe.
firearm *n* firework.
firedamp *n* wildfire.
fire engine *n* the butts.
fireplace *n* chimley.
fire screen *n* sconce.
fireside *n* ingle, ingle-neuk.
firewood *n* browl.
firm *adj* sicker, stieve.
firmly *adv* hard, stievlie.
first *adj* firsten, forehand.
first-rate *adj* tap.
fish *n*/*v* fush.
fish and chips *n* fish supper.
fish, chips and peas *n* buster.
fisherman *n* fisher.
fishing hook *n* preen.
fishing net *n* buird.
fishing rod *n* wan, gad.
fissure *n* clift.
fist *n* nieve.
fistful *n* nieveful.
fisticuffs *npl* nieves.
fit[1] *adj* setting.
fit[2] *v* ser.

fitful *adj* flichtrif.
fitting *adj* wicelik.
fittings *npl* munts.
fix *v* stell, sicker.
fizz *v* bizz.
fizzing *adj* fuzzy.
fizzy *adj* fuzzy.
fjord *n* sea loch, voe.
flabbergast *v* stammygaster.
flabbiness *adv* foziness.
flabby *adj* fozie.
flag *v* fag.
flagon *n* stowp.
flail *n* frail. • *v* sprachle.
flake *n* flichan, skelf. • *v* skelf.
flamboyant *adj* prinkie.
flame *n* flam, lowe.
flange *n* lug.
flank *n* lisk.
flannel *n* flannen.
flap *n* lug, waff. • *v* flaff, waff.
flare *v* bleeze, lowe.
flash *n* gliff, glisk. • *v* glent.
flashy *adj* fantoosh.
flat *adj* plat. • *adv* flatlins. • *n* house.
flat-chested *adj* skleff.
flat-footed *adj* sclaff-fittit.
flats *npl* tenement.
flatten *v* flet.
flatter *v* flansh.
flatterer *n* sook.
flattering *adj* buttery-lippit.
flattery *n* reese, ruise.
flatulence *n* pumpin.
flatulent *adj* heftit.
flaunt *v* flird, splore.
flavour *n* gust. • *v* kitchen.
flaw *n* mote, shortcome.
flax *n* lint.
flea *n* flech, flaich.
fleck *n*/*v* spreckle.
fledgling *n* gorlin.
flee *v* flicht.
fleece *n* fleesh.
fleeting *adj* fleetful.
flesh *n* mait.
fleshy *adj* pluffie.
flexible *adj* dwaible.
flick *n* flisk. • *v* spang.
flicker *v* flaughter.
flight *n* flocht. **flight (to take to)** *v* flicht.

flighty *adj* flichty.
flimsy *adj* silly.
flinch *v* fotch, jouk.
fling *v* hove, wap.
flipper *n* meg.
flirt *n* flirdoch, jillet. • *v* gallant, glaik.
flirtation *n* dafferie, pawky.
flirtatious *adj* pawky.
flirting *adj* flindrikin.
float *n* pallet. • *v* fleet.
flock *n* paircel, hirsel. • *v* hirsel.
flog *v* flag.
flood *n/v* flude.
flooded *adj* flodden.
floor *n/v* flair.
flop *v* clap, flype.
flotsam *n* wrack.
flounce *n* squirl. • *v* flunce.
flourish *v* blume.
flourishing *adj* raffie, guid-gaun.
flout *v* hoot.
flow *n* rin, shot. • *v* fleet, pirr.
flower *n* flooer. • *v* blume.
flowerbed *n* knot.
flu *n* haingles.
fluctuate *v* swither.
flue *n* vent.
fluency *n* tongue-raik.
fluent *adj* gabbie.
fluff *n* oos.
fluffy *adj* oosie, fuzzy.
fluid *n* bree.
flurry *n* skirlie.
flush *v* reenge.
fluster *n* swither.
flustered *adj* hattert.
flute *v* pipe.
flutter *n* flaff, flichter. • *v* fluther, flichter.
fly *n/v* flee.
fly-fishing *n* fleeing.
flying *adj* fleeing.
flywheel *n* whurl.
foal *n* foichel.
foam *n/v* faem.
foaming *adj* nappy.
fob *n* spung. • *v* jank.
fodder *n/v* fother.
foe *n* fae.
fog *n* loom, haar, rouk.
foggy *adj* haarie, roukie.
foist *v* pawn.

fold *n/v* fauld.
folk *n* fowk.
follow *v* fallow.
folly *n* madderam.
fond *adj* fain.
fondle *v* culyie, daut.
food *n* fuid, scran.
fool *n* fuil, daftie.
foolish *adj* fuil-like, daft.
foolishness *n* daftness.
foot *n* fit, fuit.
football *n* fitba.
foothold *n* fit.
footling *adj* fouterie.
footpath *n* fit-road.
footprint *n* fit-dint.
footstep *n* fit-stap.
footstool *n* creepie.
foppish *adj* fussie, figgleligee.
for *prep* fir.
forage *v* reenge.
foray *n* raid, spreath.
forbearance *n* thole.
force *n* bensel. • *v* gar, dwang.
forceful *adj* forcie, fell.
forcibly *adv* swap.
ford *n/v* foord.
forearm *n* gardie.
forebear *n* forebeir.
foreboding *n* bodement.
forecast *v* spae.
forecastle *n* den.
forefinger *n* coorag.
forefront *n* forebreist.
forehead *n* foreheid, broo.
foreign *adj* furrin, elenge.
foreigner *n* ootlin.
foreknowledge *n* moyen.
forelock *n* tap.
foreman *n* foresman.
foremost *adj* foremaist.
forenoon *n* forenuin.
foresee *v* spae.
foreshore *n* ebb.
foresight *n* foresicht.
forestall *v* foresta.
forester *n* punler.
foretell *v* spae.
forethought *n* forethocht.
forever *adv* aye.
forewarning *n* moyen.

forfeit *n* wad. • *v* tyne.
forfeiture *n* forfeitry.
forge *n* smiddy. • *v* feignyie.
forgery *n* falsehood.
forget *v* foryet.
forgetful *adj* forgettle.
forgetfulness *n* forget.
forgive *v* forgie.
fork *n/v* graip.
forlorn *adj* disjaskit.
form *n/v* firm.
former *adj* yae-time, umquhile.
fornication *n* houghmagandie.
forsake *v* furhow, foreleit.
forswear *v* forsweer.
fort *n* dun, broch.
forth *adv* furth.
forthright *adj* rael.
forthrightly *adv* even oot.
forthwith *adv* the noo, ivnoo.
fortitude *n* saul.
fortnight *n* fortnicht.
fortress *n* dun, broch.
fortunate *adj* seilful.
fortune *n* forten, seil.
fortune-teller *n* spaewife.
forward1 *adj* forritsome. • *adv* forrit. • *v* forat.
forward 2 *adj* foritsome
foster-mother *n* nourice.
foul *adj* laithlie. • *v* nestie, befyle.
foul-mouthed *adj* ill-gabbit, ruch.
found *v* foon.
foundation *n* foond.
founder *v* fooner.
fountain *n* funtain.
four *adj/n* fower.
fourteen *adj/n* fowerteen.
fourth *adj* fowert.
fowl *n* fool.
fox *n* tod, lowrie. • *v* quirk.
foxglove *n* lady's thummles.
foxhunt *n* tod-hunt.
fracas *n* fraca.
fraction *n* stime.
fractious *adj* fashious.
fracture *n* vise.
fragile *adj* bruckle.
fragment *n* nip, murlin.
fragments *npl* flinders.
fragrance *n* fume.

frail *adj* dwaiblie, silly.
frank *adj* fair-spoken.
frankly *adv* fair.
frankness *n* forthiness.
frantic *adj* dancin mad.
fraud *n* cheatrie, fausehood.
fraudulent *adj* slidderie.
fray[1] *n* fecht.
fray[2] *v* faize.
frayed *adj* chattert.
freak *n* dandrum.
freckle *n* fernitickle.
freckled *adj* fernitickelt.
free *adj* quat. • *v* redd.
freedom *n* scouth.
freeze *v* jeel.
frenzy *n* frainesie.
frequent *v* howf.
frequently *adv* afen.
fresh *adj* caller.
freshen *v* caller.
fret *adj* freet. • *v* freak.
fretful *adj* fretty.
friable *adj* frush.
friar *n* freir.
Friday *n* Fraiday.
friend *n* freen, fere.
friendless *adj* freenless.
friendliness *n* freenliness.
friendly *adj* freenlie.
friendship *n* fraca.
fright *n* fear. • *v* fricht.
frighten *v* frichten, fleg, fear.
frightened *adj* frichtit.
frightening *adj* frichtsome.
frightful *adj* awfu.
frigid *adj* freff.
frill *n* frull.
fringe *n* freenge.
frippery *n* whigmaleeries.
frisk *v* flisk.
frisky *adj* hippertie-skippertie.
fritter *v* moot.
frivolity *n* dafferie.
frizz *n/v* swirlie.
frizzy *adj* swirlie.
frog *n* puddock.
frogspawn *n* puddock cruddles.
frolic *n* cantrip. • *v* daff.
frolicsome *adj* kim.
from *prep* frae, fae.

front *n* foreside.
frontier *n* mairch.
frost *n* freest.
frostiness *n* jeel.
frosty *adj* rimie, gordy.
froth *n/v* fro, fraith.
frothing *adj* reamie.
frown *n/v* froon.
frozen *adj* frozent.
frugal *adj* canny, throughal.
fruit-machine *n* puggie.
fruit-slice *n* fly cemetery.
frustrate *v* pall.
frustrated *adj* hummed.
fry *v* fryth.
fuddled *adj* mixit.
fudge *n* taiblet.
fuel *n* fire, eldin.
fuggy *adj* smuchtie.
fugitive *adj* foreloppen. • *n* fugie.
fulcrum *n* pall.
fulfilment *n* implement.
full[1] *adj* fou.
full[2] *v* waulk (cloth).
full-bodied *adj* maumie.
fullness *n* fouth.
fully *adv* fou, fullie.
fulmar *n* mallduck.
fulsome *adj* phrasie.
fumble *v* fummle
fumbling *n* fummle. • *adj* hanless.

fumblingly *adv* aside yer thoum.
fume *v* feem, reek.
fumes *n* smuik.
fumigate *v* smeek.
fun *n* dafferie, daffin.
fund *n* foon.
funeral *n* beerial.
funfair *n* the shows.
fungus *n* puddock stuil.
funnel *n* lum, filler.
funny *adj* knackie.
funny-bone *n* dirlie-bane.
furious *adj* radge.
furnish *v* plenish.
furniture *n* plenishin.
furrow *n/v* furr.
furry *adj* oosie.
further *adj/adv/v* faurer, forder.
furthermore *adv* forby.
furtive *adj* thiefie.
furtively *adv* stowlins.
fury *n* stramash, tirrivee.
furze *n* whin.
fuse *n* strum.
fuss *n* stushie, carfuffle. • *v* fizz, gae on.
fussiness *n* fykerie.
fussy *adj* fykie.
fustiness *n* foost.
fusty *adj* foostie.
futile *adj* knotless.

G

gab *v* blether.
gabble *v* yabber, raible.
gabbling *adj* yabblin.
gable *n* gavel, hoose-en.
gad *v* stravaig, traik.
gadabout *n* rinaboot.
gadfly *n* cleg.
gadget *n* whirlie.
Gaelic *adj/n* Hielan, Erse.
gaff *n* clep, gaad.
gag *n* baur.
gaiety *n* galliardness.
gain *v* win.
gait *n* ling, gang.
gaiters *n* leggums.

gale *n* gell, gurl.
gall *n/v* ga.
gallant *adj* pretty.
galley *n* gaillie.
galling *adj* chawsome.
gallivant *v* stravaig, traik.
gallon *n* quart.
gallop *v* wallop, skelp.
gallows *n* widdie.
galore *adj* rowth.
galoshes *npl* galashes.
gamble *v* gammel.
gambol *v* flisk.
game *adj* stuffie. • *n* gemm.
gamekeeper *n* gamie, ghillie.

gander *n* gainer.
ganglion *n* luppen sinnon.
gangster *n* limmer.
gannet *n* gant.
gaol *n* jile.
gap *n* slap, open.
gape *v* gowp.
gaping *adj* gawpin.
garb *n* ootrig.
garbage *n* hinneren.
garden *n* gairden.
gardener *n* gairdner.
garish *adj* roarie.
garment *n* cleedin.
garret *n* gaillie.
garrulous *adj* bletherin.
garter *n/v* gairten.
gash *n* screed. • *v* gulliegaw.
gasp *n/v* pech.
gate *n* yett.
gatepost *n* stoop.
gateway *n* gate-slap, port.
gather *v* gaither.
gathering *n* gaithering.
gaudy *adj* skyrie.
gaunt *adj* clappit.
gawky *adj* ackwart.
gawp *v* gowp.
gaze *n/v* glower, gove.
gear *n* graith.
geld *v* lib, sort.
gelding *n* staig.
gender *n* gener.
generous *adj* furthie, lairge.
genial *adj* lithesome, hertie.
genitals *npl* doddles (male), fud (female).
genius *n* genie.
genteel *adj* gentie.
gentian *n* bad money.
gentility *n* gentrie.
gentle *adj* lithe, douce.
gently *adv* huilie.
gentry *n* gentrice.
genuine *adj* genivin, jonick.
genuine article *n* real Mackay.
germinate *v* brere.
gesture *v* gester.
get *v* git; **get at** ettle at; **get away** win awa; **get by** warsle throu; **get off** win aff; **get on** mak weel; **get out** win oot;

get over git abuin; **get through** get by; **get up** win up.
get-up *n* paraffin.
ghastly *adj* gashlie.
ghost *n* ghaist.
ghostly *adj* eldritch.
giant *n* etin.
gibber *v* gabber.
gibberish *n* blethers.
gibbet *n* widdie.
gibe *n* geeg, dunt. • *v* gleek, jamph.
giblets *n* harigals.
giddy *adj* glinkit..
gift *n* compliment, praisent.
gift-horse *n* gien-horse.
gigantic *adj* wappin.
gild *v* gilt.
gilded *adj* giltit.
gill *n* gillock.
gills *npl* ginnles.
gimlet *n* wummle.
ginger *n* ginge.
gingerbread *n* gingebreid, gibbery.
gipsy, gypsy *n* Jockie, tink.
girdle *n* girl.
girl *n* lass, lassie, quine.
girlfriend *n* lassie, cleek, tairt, lumber.
girlish *adj* lass-like, cissie.
girth *n* grist.
gist *n* rinnin.
give *v* gie. **give in** to snuil; **give up** quat; **give way** knuckle.
given *adj* gien.
gizzard *n* gizen.
glad *adj* blithe.
gladly *adv* blithe.
gladness *n* blitheness.
glamour *n* glamourie.
glance *n/v* glent, glisk.
glare *n* gliff. • *v* glower (expression).
glaring *adj* glairie-fairie.
Glasgow *n* Glesca.
glass *n/v* gless.
glasses *npl* glesses.
glass-work *n* glassin.
glassy *adj* glazie.
glaze *v* glaize.
glazed *adj* lozenit.
glazier *n* glasin-wricht, glasser.
gleam *n* glim, leam. • *v* glaim, leam.
gleaming *adj* blinterin.

glean v rake.
glebe n glybe.
glebe land n glybe.
glib adj gleg-tonguit.
glide v scrieve.
glimmer n glim, stime. • v blinter.
glimmering adj skimmering.
glimpse n glim, glaff. • v get a sicht o.
glint n/v glent.
glinting adj scansin.
glisten v glister.
glistening n gleet.
glitter n/v glent.
glittering adj glaizie.
globe n pallet.
gloom n mirk; • v gloum.
gloomy adj mirksome.
glory n glore.
gloss n glaize.
glossy adj glaizie.
glove n gloove.
glow n/v glowe, leam.
glower v froon.
glue n batter.
glum adj dowie, drum.
glut n galore, stegh.
glutinous adj claggie.
glutton n guts, gorb.
gluttonous adj gutsie.
gluttony n gutsiness.
gnarled adj gurlie.
gnash v chirk.
gnat n midge, midgie.
gnaw n/v gnyauve.
gneiss n haithen.
go v gae, gang. • n smeddum; **go astray** gang agley; **go away** haud awa; **go off** chynge; **go with** hae wi.
goad n gaud, brod. • v brod.
go-ahead adj through-gaun.
goal n dale.
goat n gait.
gobbet n gabbit.
gobble v gammal, hanch.
goblet n tassie.
goblin n blackman.
gobstopper n opo-pogo-eye.
god n goad, gweed.
God-forsaken adj God-left.
godforsaken adj dreich.
godly adj gidlie.

godmother n cummer.
goings-on npl ongauns.
gold n goud.
goldcrest n muin.
golden adj gouden.
goldfinch n goldie.
golf n gowf.
golfball n gowfba.
golf club n gowfstick.
golfer n gowfer.
good adj guid, barrie.
good breeding n govance.
good-for-nothing n dae-na-guid.
good-humoured, goodly adj guidlie.
goodliness n guidliheid.
goodness! interj fegs.
goods n graith.
goosander n saw neb.
goose n guse.
gooseberry n grosset.
gooseberry bush n grosset-bush.
gooseflesh n caul creeps.
goose-grease n goose-seam.
gore[1] n gushet.
gore[2] v stick, pork.
gorge[1] n cleuch.
gorge[2] v stap.
gorgeous adj braw.
gorse n whin.
gosh! interj goshens!
goshawk n gos.
gosling n gaislin.
gossip n clavers, clack; (person) a sweetie-wife. • v blether, clatter.
gossipy adj glib-gabbit.
gouge n/v gudge.
gout n gut.
govern v guide, ring.
gown n goon.
grab n/v grabble.
grace n bethankit. • v mense.
graceful adj gentie.
gracious adj couthy.
gradation n grie.
graduate n gradawa.
grain n tick, stuff.
grammar n gremmar.
grampus n herrin hog.
granary n garnel.
grand adj gran.
grandchild n gran-bairn, gran-wean.

granddaughter *n* grandochter.
grandeur *n* grandery.
grandfather *n* granfaither, geetsher.
grandmother *n* granmither.
grandson *n* nevoy.
grant *v* gie.
granular *adj* quernie.
granule *n* tick.
graphite *n* wad.
grapple *v* graipple.
grasp *n/v* gresp.
grasping *adj* nabal, menseless. • *n* grabble.
graspingly *adv* gramlochlie.
grass *n* girse.
grasshopper *n* gerslowper.
grassland *n* meedow, ley.
grassy *adj* girsie.
grate¹ *n* chimley.
grate² *v* risp, chirk.
grateful *adj* thankrif.
gratified *adj* prood.
grating *n* tirless.
gratuitous *adj* gratis.
gratuity *n* maggs.
grave¹ *n* graff, lair.
grave² *adj* thochtie.
gravedigger *n* beadle.
gravelly *adj* chinglie.
gravestone *n* lairstane.
graveyard *n* graveyaird, kirkyaird.
gravy *n* bree.
graze *n* scuff, screeve. • *v* scuff.
grazing *n* girsin.
grease *n/v* creesh.
greasy *adj* creeshie.
great *adj* grit, gret, aul.
greatcoat *n* big coat, bavarie.
great-grandchild *n* ieroe.
great-grandfather *n* gransher.
great-grandson *n* nevoy.
greatly *adj* unco.
greed *n* gutsiness.
greedy *adj* gutsie.
green *adj* haw, hielan.
greenfinch *n* green lintie.
greengrocer *n* kailwife.
greenish *adj* greenichie.
greet *v* goam.
greeting *n* ca.
grey *adj* gray.

greyhound *n* grew.
griddle *n* girdle.
gridiron *n* brander.
grief *n* teen, dool.
grief-stricken *adj* hert-sair.
grievance *n* eelist.
grieve *v* fyke.
grievous *adj* sair.
grill *n* tirless. • *v* brander.
grim *adj* rauchle, dour.
grimace *n/v* girn.
grime *n* clart.
grimy *adj* brookie.
grin *n/v* girn.
grind *v* runch, scrunt.
grind-stone *n* grun-stane.
grip *n/v* grup.
grisly *adj* ugsome.
grist *n* girst.
gristle *n* girstle.
gristly *adj* girslie.
grit *n* grush. • *v* cramsh.
gritty *adj* shairp.
grizzled *adj* lyart.
grizzly *adj* grugous.
groan *n/v* grain.
groin *n* lisk.
groom *n* strapper.
groove *n* rit. • *v* rat.
grope *v* glaamer, growp.
gross *adj* guttie.
ground *n* grun.
groundsel *n* grunsel.
group *n* boorach, paircel.
grouse¹ *n* groose (bird).
grouse² *v* girn.
grove *n* plantin.
grovel *v* grafel.
grow *v* growe.
growl *n/v* gurr.
grown-up *adj* up.
growth *n* growthe.
grub *v* muddle.
grudge *n* grummle.
grudging *adj* ill-willie.
gruel *n* blearie.
gruesome *adj* ugsome.
grudge *n* ga.
gruff *adj* stroonge.
grumble *v* grummle, girn.
grumbler *n* growl, grumph.

grumbling *adj* grumlie. • *n* girn.
grumpy *adj* grumphie.
grunt *n/v* grumph.
guarantee *n* warrandice. • *v* uphaud.
guard *n/v* gaird.
guardian *n* tutor, curator.
guess *v* ettle, jalouse.
guffaw *n/v* gaff.
guidance *n* guideship.
guide *v* airt, ettle.
guile *n* pawkery.
guileless *adj* saikless.
guillemot *n* marrot, queet.
guillotine *n* maiden.
guiltless *adj* ill-less.
guilty *adj* guiltful.
gull[1] *n* goo (bird).
gull[2] *v* whillie (hoax/trick).
gullet *n* thrapple.
gullible *adj* fond.

gully *n* gullet, gill.
gulp *n/v* gowp, glaip.
gum *n* gam, goom.
gumboil *n* gumbile.
gunshot *n* brattle.
gurgle *n/v* gurl.
gurgling *adj* gurlie.
gurnard *n* crooner.
gush *n* stour; phrase. • *v* stour, teem; phrase.
gushing *adj* phrasie.
gusset *n* gushet.
gust *n* gowst. • *v* dad, tear.
gusty *adj* gowstie.
gut *n* thairm. • *v* gip.
gutter *n* gitter, trink.
guttersnipe *n* gutterbluid.
guttural *adj* howe.
guzzle *v* guttle, gilravage.
gymshoes *n* sannies.
gypsy *see* **gypsy.**

H

habit *n* haunt, kick.
habitable *adj* biglie.
habitation *n* inn.
habits *n* gates.
hack *n/v* hawk.
hackle *n* heckle.
haddock *n* haddie.
haft *n* heft.
hag *n* runt.
haggard *adj* shilpit.
haggle *v* haigle, argie-bargie.
hail *v* hoy
hailstone *n* hailstane.
hailstorm *n* blatter.
hair *n* herr.
hairband *n* snuid.
haircut *n* cowe.
hairy *adj* birsie.
hake *n* herrin hake.
half *adj/n* hauf. • *adv* halflins.
half-grown *adj* halflin.
half-light *n* hauf licht, gloamin.
halfpenny *n* bawbee.
halfway *adj* hauf-roads.
halfwit *n* daftie, halflins.
halfwitted *adj* hauf-jackit.

halibut *n* turbot.
hall *n* ha.
hallow *v* sain.
halo *n* broch.
halt *n/v* haut.
halter *n/v* helter
halve *v* hauf.
hams *n* hunkers.
hamstring *n* hoch.
hamlet *n* toon, clachan.
hammer *n/v* haimmer.
hamper *v* taigle.
hand *n* han, haun.
handicap *n* doon-haud.
handkerchief *n* naipkin, snochter-dichter.
handle *n* hannle, haunle. • *v* guide.
handsome *adj* braw, weel-faured.
handwriting *n* hanwrite.
handy *adj* hantie.
hang *v* hing.
hangings *npl* hingers.
hangman *n* hangie.
hank *n* hesp.
hanker *v* ettle.
haphazard *adj* antrin.

hapless *adj* donsie.
happen *v* come.
happenings *npl* ongauns.
happily *adv* blithe.
happiness *n* seil.
happy *adj* blithe.
harangue *n* lay-aff.
harass *v* hash.
harassed *adj* trachelt.
harbour *n* herbour, hine.
hard *adj* sair, coorse, dour.
hard cash *n* dry siller.
hard-hearted *adj* whunstane.
hardly *adv* hardlins.
hard-pressed *adj* ill-pit.
hardship *n* hard.
hard-up *adj* ticht, sair aff.
hard-working *adj* warslin.
hardy *adj* derf.
hare *n* bawd, donie.
harebell *n* bluebell.
hare-brained *adj* cat-wittit.
harelip *n* hareshaw.
hark *v* herk.
harm *n/v* hairm.
harmful *adj* ill, sair.
harmless *adj* saikless.
harmonious *adj* greeable.
harmonise *v* cord.
harmony *n* greement.
harness *n* herness. • *v* graith.
harnessed *adj* drachtit.
harp[1] *n* hairp.
harp[2] *v* yap, threap.
harridan *n* targe, sauter.
harrow *n/v* harra.
harrowing *adj* sair.
harry *v* herrie.
harsh *adj* sair.
harshly *v* sair.
harvest *n/v* hairst.
harvester *n* hairster.
hasp *n* hesp.
haste *n* heist, hist.
hasten *v* heist, hist.
hasty *adj* heestie.
hat *n* hot.
hatch *v* cleck.
hatchet *n* aix.
hatching *adj* cleckin.
hate *v* ill-will.

hateful *adj* hatesome.
hatred *n* ill-will.
haughtily *adv* heich.
haughty *adj* heich.
haul *n* drave. • *v* hale.
haunches *n* hainches, hunkers.
haunt *n/v* hant.
haunted *adj* boglie.
have *v* hae, ha, hiv.
haven *n* hine.
havoc *n* dirdum.
hawk[1] *n* gled.
hawk[2] *v* clocher (cough); cadge (peddle wares).
hawker *n* cadger.
hawser *n* swing-rope.
hawthorn *n* chaw.
hay *n* hey.
haycock *n* cole.
hayfork *n* hey-fowk.
haystack *n* ruck.
hazardous *adj* unchancie.
haze *n* loom.
hazel *n* hissel.
hazelnut *n* cracker nut.
hazy *adj* roukie, haarie.
he *pron* e, ei.
head *n* heid.
head-butt *v* pit the heid on, gie a Glesca kiss.
headache *n* sair heid.
header *n* heider.
headland *n* ness.
headlong *adv* haliket.
headmaster *n* rector.
head off *v* kep.
headstone *n* lairstane.
headstrong *adj* heidie.
heady *adj* nappy.
heal *v* hail.
health *n* halth.
healthy *adj* hail.
heap *n/v* haip.
hear *v* hearken.
hearse *n* pail.
heart *n* hert, hairt.
heartache *n* hert-scaud.
heartbeat *n* wallop.
heartburn *n* watter-brash.
hearten *v* hert, upsteer.
hearth *n* hairth.
heartily *adv* hertilie.

hearty *adj* hertie.
heat *n/v* hait.
heath *n* muir.
heathen *n* haithen.
heather *n* hedder.
heathery *adj* hedderie.
heave *n* hoy. • *v* have.
heaven *n* heiven, the land o the leal.
heavenly *adj* heivenlie.
heavily *adv* souse.
heavy *adj* hivvie.
hector *v* hatter.
hedge *n* dyke.
hedgehog *n* hedger.
heed *n/v* tent.
heedful *adj* tentie.
heedless *adj* tentless.
heedlessly *adv* blinlins.
hefty *adj* sture.
heifer *n* heefer.
height *n* heicht, lenth.
heighten *v* heicht.
hell *n* the ill place.
help *n* cast. • *v* pit tae yer haun.
helpful *adj* helplie.
helping *n* raik.
helpless *adj* mauchless, doless.
helter-skelter *adv* ding-dang.
hem *n* bord.
hemlock *n* humlock.
hen *n* chookie.
hence *adv* hyne.
hen-coop *n* ree.
hen-harrier *n* gled.
her *pron* hir.
herb *n* yerb.
herd *n* paircel. • *v* wirk.
herdsman *n* herd.
hereabouts *adv* hereawa.
hermaphrodite *n* scrat.
hernia *n* rimburst.
heron *n* hern.
herring *n* herrin.
herring fishing *n* drave.
herself *pron* hersel.
hesitate *v* swither.
hesitant *adj* sweirt.
hesitation *n* swither.
heterogeneous *adj* mixter-maxter.
hew *v* howk.
hiccup *n/v* hick.

hide[1] *n* leather.
hide[2] *v* hod, dern.
hide-and-seek *n* hidie.
hideous *adj* laithlie.
hiding *n* skelping.
hiding place *n* hidie-hole.
higgledy-piggledy *adj* tapsalterie.
high *adj* heich.
high-born *adj* gentie.
higher *adj* prood.
highest *adj* heichmaist.
Highland *adj* Hielan.
Highlander *n* Hielander, teuchter.
Highlands *n* Hielans.
highly *adv* unco.
high-minded *adj* major-mindit.
high-pitched *adj* snell.
high-rise flat *n* multi.
hilarious *adj* glorious.
hilarity *n* madderam.
hill *n* hull, hope, ben, law, pen.
hillock *n* cairney, knab.
hillside *n* brae.
hilltop *n* hillheid.
hilly *adj* hill-run.
himself *pron* himsel.
hind *adj* hint.
hinder *v* hinner, block.
hindering *adj* taiglesome.
hindmost *adj* hinmaist.
hindquarters *n* hinneren.
hindrance *n* hinnerance.
hinge *n* hiddin.
hint *n* moot. • *v* mint.
hinterland *n* erse.
hip *n* hap, hurdy.
hire *n* fraucht. • *v* fee.
his *pron* heez.
hiss *n* fuff. • *v* bizz.
hissing *adj* fuzzy.
hit *n/v* gowff.
hitch *n/v* hotch.
hither *adv* hereawa.
hive *n* byke, skep.
hoard *n/v* huird.
hoarder *n* gear-gaitherer.
hoar-frost *n* haar, cranreuch.
hoarse *adj* hairse.
hoarseness *n* roup.
hoary *adj* hair.
hoax *n* rise. • *v* play the rig wi.

hob *n* bink.
hobble *n* langle. • *v* hirple, langle.
hobby-horse *n* habbie-horse.
hobgoblin *n* bockie.
hobnail *n* tacket.
hobnob *v* troke, frequent.
hock *n* hoch.
hod *n* hudd.
hoe *n/v* howe.
hog *n* gaut.
hogshead *n* hogget, hoggie.
hogweed *n* humlock.
hoist *n/v* hyste, thring.
hold *n* haud. • *v* haud; **hold back** dachle; **hold forth** lay aff; **hold off** haud aff; **hold on** behaud; **hold out** laist; **hold over** refer; **hold up** uphaud.
holding *n* haudin
hole *n* thirl.
holiday *n* hoaliday.
hollow *n* hallow, haw. • *v* hallow, howk.
holly *n* hollin.
holy *adj* halie.
home *n* hame.
home farm *n* mains.
home-grown *adj* hameart.
home-loving *adj* hame-drachtit.
homely *adj* hamelie.
homesick *adj* hame-drachtit.
homespun *adj* raploch.
homestead *n* steading, fermtoon.
homeward *adv* hamewith.
honest *adj* jonick.
honestly *adv* aefauldlie.
honesty *n* aefauld.
honey *n* hinnie.
honeysuckle *n* hinniesickle.
honour *n* honesty, mense.
honourable *adj* honest.
hood *n* huid.
hooded *adj* huidit.
hoodwink *v* swick.
hoof *n* huif.
hook *n/v* cleek.
hooligan *n* rochian.
hoop *n* gird.
hoot *v* hoo.
hop *n/v* hap, hip.
hopper *n* happer.
hopscotch *n* peevers, beds.
hope *n/v* howp.

hopeful *adj* howpful.
horde *n* fleesh.
horizon *n* easin.
horizontally *adv* flatlins.
horn *n* tooter.
hornless *adj* doddy.
horrible *adj* ugsome, grue, laithful.
horror *n* grue.
horse *n* cuddie, naig.
horsefly *n* cleg.
hospitable *adj* cadgie, hielan.
hospital *n* hoaspital.
hospitality *n* mense.
host *n* thrang.
hostile *adj* ill-kindit, awkwart.
hot *n* het.
hotchpotch *n* mixter-maxter.
hotel *n* hottle.
hothouse *n* hothoose.
hot-tempered *adj* birsie.
hound *n/v* hun.
hour *n* oor.
house *n/v* hoose.
housebound *n* hoosefast.
householder *n* hoosehadder.
housekeeping *n* hoosehaddin.
house martin *n* wunda-swalla.
house-warming *adj* hoose-heat.
housewife *n* guidwife.
hovel *n* puidge.
hover *v* swither.
hovering *adj* sweirt.
how *adv* hoo.
however *adv* hooivver.
howl *n/v* gowl.
hoyden *n* hallockit.
hubbub *n* stushie.
huddle *n/v* hiddle.
huff *n* dort, fung.
huffy *adj* snottie.
hug *n* chirt. • *v* smoorich.
huge *adj* wappin, muckle big.
hulk *n* houk.
hull *n/v* huil.
hullabaloo *n* whillybaloo.
hum *n/v* bum.
human being *n* bodie.
humane *adj* cannie, couthie.
humanity *n* fowk.
human race *n* Jock Tamson's bairns.
humble *adj/v* hummle.

humbug *n* pit-on.
humdrum *adj* ornar.
humid *adj* growthie.
humiliate *v* bemean.
humiliation *n* doon-tak.
humour *n* eemir.
humourless *adj* dour.
humorous *adj* humoursome.
hump *n* humph.
humpback *n* humph.
hunchback *n* hunchie.
hunched *adj* humphed.
hundred *adj/n* hunder.
hundredth *adj* hunder.
hungry *adj* hungert.
hunk *n* knoit.
hunt *n* fork. • *v* snoke.
hurdle *n* let, flake.
hurl *v* pick.
hurly-burly *n* fizz.

hurricane *n* skailwin.
hurry *n* chase. • *v* lick, hoy.
hurried *adj* hushlochy.
hurriedly *adv* fiercelins.
hurt *n/v* skaith.
hurtful *adj* hurtsome.
hurtle *v* hurl.
husband *n* maun.
hush *n* lown. • *v* ba.
hushed *adj* wheesht.
husk *n/v* huil.
huskiness *n* roup.
husky *adj* roupie.
hussy *n* besom, limmer.
hustle *v* dreel, rooshel.
hustling *adj* forcie.
hut *n* puidge, bothy.
hydrangea *n* hedder-reenge.
hygienic *adj* parteeclar.
hymn *n* hime.

I

I *pron* aw.
ice *n* frost.
ice-cream cone *n* pokey hat.
icicle *n* tangle.
icy *adj* sclidderie.
identical *adj* self an same.
idiosyncrasy *n* particularity.
idiot *n* daftie.
idle *adj* idleset. • *v* sloonge, slope.
idleness *n* idleset.
idler *n* sloonger.
idling *adj* tuim.
idol *n* eedol.
if *conj* gin, an.
ignite *v* kennle.
ignoble *adj* foutie.
ignominy *n* tash.
ignorant *adj* far back, unkennin.
ill *adj* ull.
ill-assorted *adj* mismarrowed.
ill-bred *adj* menseless.
ill-disposed *adj* ill-intendit.
illegal *adj* wrongous.
illegitimate *adj* ill-come, ill-gotten.
ill-fated *adj* unchancie.
ill-favoured *adj* ill-faured.

ill-gotten *adj* wrangous.
ill-health *n* unweelness.
ill-humour *n* canker.
ill-looking *adj* peely-wally.
ill-mannered *adj* ill-faured.
ill-natured *adj* grumphie.
illness *n* ill.
ill-spent *adj* ill-waured.
ill-tempered *adj* crabbit.
ill-treat *v* ool.
illustrious *adj* markit.
ill-will *n* unfreenship.
imagination *n* fantice.
imagine *v* jalouse.
imbecile *adj* wantin. • *n* daftie.
immature *adj* bairnlik.
immediate *adj* immedant.
immediately *adv* immedantly.
immense *adj* undeemous.
immerse *v* dook.
immersion *n* dookin.
imminent *adj* suin.
immobile *adj* stieve.
immoderate *adj* surfeit.
immodest *adj* heich-kilted.
immoral *adj* lowse.

impact *n* dunt.
impartial *adj* jonick.
impatient *adj* fuffie.
impeccable *adj* evendoon.
impecunious *n* ill-aff.
impede *v* dachle.
impediment *n* mant.
imperious *adj* ringin.
impertinence *n* impidence.
impertinent *adj* impident.
impetuous *adj* heidie.
impetuously *adv* fiercelins.
impetus *n* rummle.
implacable *adj* unbowsome.
implement *n* luim.
implicate *v* insnorl.
impolite *adj* ill-mou'd.
import *v* inbring.
importune *v* prig.
imposing *adj* gawsie.
impostor *n* mak-on.
impound *v* pund.
impoverish *v* povereese.
impregnate *v* bairn.
impress *v* pit on.
impression *n* steid.
imprint *n* steid.
imprison *v* prison.
imprisonment *n* ward.
impromptu *adj* affluif.
improper *adj* misbehadden.
improperly *adv* wrangouslie.
improvement *n* betterness.
improvident *adj* weirdless, daeless.
imprudent *adj* unwicelike.
impudence *n* impidence.
impudent *adj* impident.
impulsive *adj* furthie.
in *prep* i.
inactive *adj* thowless.
inadequate *adj* scrimpie.
inadmissible *adj* inhabile.
inadvertently *adv* unwittins.
inattentive *adj* tentless.
inaugurate *v* handsel.
inauguration *n* handsellin.
inauspicious *adj* unchancie.
incalculable *adj* undeemous.
incapable *adj* weirdless.
incapacitate *v* lay by.
incessantly *adv* even on.

incise *v* sneck.
incision *n* sneck, whack.
incite *v* airt.
inclement *adj* coorse, weatherful.
inclination *n* inklin.
incline *n* sklent.
incoherent *adj* raivelt.
incomer *n* ootrel, stourie-fit, sooth-moother.
incomparable *adj* marrowless.
incompatible *adj* ill-yokit.
incompetent *adj* haunless.
incompetence *n* haunlessness.
incomprehensible *adj* haithen.
inconceivable *adj* haithen.
inconvenience *n*/*v* disconvenience.
inconvenient *adj* disconvenient.
incorrect *adj* wrang.
incorrectly *adv* wrangways.
incorrigible *adj* past mendin.
increase *n*/*v* eik.
indebted *adj* behauden.
indecent *adj* undecent, foutie.
indecency *n* sculduderie.
indecision *n* swither.
indecisive *adj* twa-fangelt.
indeed *adv* deed.
indentation *n* dunt.
independent *adj* on fur yersel.
index finger *n* coorag.
indicate *v* lat see.
indication *n* tint.
indict *v* indick.
indictment *n* libel.
indifferent *adj* cauld-watter, jeck-easy.
indigenous *adj* hamelt.
indigent *adj* needfu.
indigestion *n* indisgestion.
indignant *adj* mad.
indignation *n* fashery.
indirectly *adv* sidelins.
indiscreet *adj* unwicelike.
indiscreetly *adv* braid.
indiscriminately *adv* han ower heid.
indisposed *n* nae weel.
indisposition *n* towt.
indistinct *adj* gummle.
indolence *n* sweirtie.
indolent *adj* sweirt.
indoors *adv* inby, therein.
indubitably *adv* dootless.
induce *v* moyen.

indulge v cuiter, cock.
industrious adj eydent.
industry n trift.
inebriated adj fou.
ineffective adj knotless, ill.
ineffectual adj fushionless.
inefficiency n throuitherness.
inefficient adj hanless.
inept adj fouterie, weirdless.
ineptly adv aside yer thoum.
inert adj waffle.
inevitable adj tied.
infamous adj ill.
infant n bairn, wean.
infant school n wee scuil.
infatuated adj fond, daft.
infected adj atterie.
infection n smit.
infectious adj smittle.
inferior adj laich, duffie.
infertile adj yeld, lea.
infest v owergae.
infestation n strik.
infested adj hoatchin.
infirm adj dwaiblie, failed.
inflame v raise.
inflamed adj gyte.
inflate v swall.
inflexible adj stench.
influence n hank. • v wark on.
influenza n haingles.
inform v witter.
informant n author.
information n witterin.
infrequent adj seendil.
infuriate v raise.
infuriated adj hyte.
infuse v mask.
ingenious adj knackie.
ingenuity n ingine.
ingenuous adj saikless.
ingoing adj ingaan.
ingratiate v sook.
ingratiating adj sookie.
inhabit v bide in.
inhabitant n indwaller.
inheritance n heirship.
inhuman adj ill-kindit.
iniquitous adj wickit, ill.
initiate v brother.
injection n prod, jag.

injunction n interdict.
injure v skaith.
injured adj bemangt.
injurious adj hurtsome.
injury n ill, skaith.
inland n upthrou.
in-law adj guid.
inlet n inlat.
inn n howf.
inner adj inby.
innermost adj benmaist.
innkeeper n hostler.
innocent adj ill-less.
innocuous adj saikless.
innovation n newfangle.
innumerable adj lairge.
inoculation n jag.
inoffensive adj saikless.
inquest n injuiry.
inquire v speir.
inquisitive adj speering.
insane adj daft, gyte.
insanity n madderam.
insect n beastie.
insecure adj eemis, crankie.
insensitive adj dowf.
inside adv/prep inower.
inside out adj backside foremaist.
insidious adj sleekit.
insignificant adj little-boukit.
insignificant-looking adj shilpit.
insincere adj pitten-on.
insincerity n pit on.
insinuate v moot, mint.
insinuation n moot.
insipid adj wersh, fushionless.
insipid person n toohoo.
insist v threap.
insistence n threapin.
insist on v insist for.
insolence n clack.
insolent adj ill-mould.
insolvent adj astarn.
insomniac adj waukrif.
inspect v leuk.
inspector n owersman.
install v induct.
instant adj gliff. • n rap.
instead prep insteid.
instil v insense intae.
instruct v learn.

instrument *n* luim.
insubordinate *adj* camstairie.
insufficient *adj* scrimp.
insult *n* dunt. • *v* injure.
integrity *n* mense.
intelligence *n* mense.
intelligent *adj* menseful, heidie.
intemperate *adj* surfeit.
intend *v* mint, ettle.
intense *adj* howe, odious.
intensely *adv* unco.
intent *adj* eident.
intentionally *adv* willintlie.
inter *v* beerie.
intercept *v* kep.
intercourse *n* traffeck; tail-toddle (sex).
interfere *v* middle, pit in yer spuin.
interference *n* fittininment.
intermediate *adj* hauflin.
intermittently *adv* aff an on.
internal organs *n* harigals, intimmers.
interpret *v* read.
interrogate *v* speir.
interrogation *n* speiring.
intertwine *v* warple.
intervals *npl* tweenwhiles.
interview *n* collogue.
intestines *npl* ingangs, thairms.
intimate *adj* far ben. • *n* freen.
intimation *n* burial letter.
intimidate *v* coonger.
into *prep* intae, intil.
intolerable *adj* past a.
intonation *n* tune.
intoxicate *v* fill fou.
intoxicated *adj* fou.
intoxication *n* drouthieness.
intractable *adj* thrawn, dour.
intrepid *adj* campie.
intricacy *n* wimple.
intricate *adj* kittle.
intriguer *n* mowdiewort.
introduction *n* innin.

intruder *n* incomer.
intuition *n* glent, inklin.
inundate *v* flude.
inure *v* brither.
invade *v* set on.
inveigle *v* insnorl.
invent *v* cleck.
invention *n* upmak.
invert *v* whummle.
invest *v* infeft.
investigate *v* pit throu hauns.
investigation *n* speiring.
investiture *n* infeftment.
invitation *n* invite.
invite *v* inveet.
invocation *n* sain.
involve *v* insnorl.
inward *adj* inwey.
irascible *adj* crabbit.
ire *n* birse.
iris *n* seg.
Irishman *n* Irisher.
irksome *adj* fashious.
iron *n* airn. • *v* dress.
ironing *n* airnin.
irregular *adj* orra.
irregularity *n* gley.
irreparable *adj* past mendin.
irresolute *adj* sweirt.
irresponsible *adj* glaikit.
irritable *adj* crabbit.
irritate *v* fash.
irritation *n* birse.
island *n* inch.
issue *n* heid. • *v* tove.
it *pron* hit, hut.
Italian *adj* Idalian.
itch *n/v* yeuk.
itching *n* fidgin.
itchy *adj* yeukie.
item *n* eetim.
itinerant *adj* gaun-aboot.
itself *pron* itsel.

J

jab *n/v* job, prog.
jabber *v* yammer.
jabbering *adj* yammer.

jackdaw *n* cay, jaikie.
jacket *n* jaicket.
jaded *adj* forjeskit.

jagged *adj* pikie.
jail *n/v* jile.
jailer *n* jiler.
jam *n* jeelie.
jam and bread *n* jeelie piece.
jamb *n* cheek.
jamjar *n* jeelie-jaur.
jangle *v* jing.
January *n* Januar.
jar[1] *n* jaur.
jar[2] *n/v* dirl
jaundice *n* jandies.
jaunt *n* veage.
jaunty *adj* croose.
jaw *n* chaft.
jawbone *n* chaft-blade.
jealous *adj* jeelous.
jeer *n* afftak, jamph. • *v* lant, jamph.
jelly *n* jeelie.
jellyfish *n* scalder.
jerk *n/v* yerk.
jersey *n* gansey.
jest *n/v* jeest.
jet *n* skoosh, jeet.
jetsam *n* spulyie.
jetty *n* shore, putt.
jewel *n* jowel.
jib *v* reest.
jibe *n* dunt.
jiffy *n* short.
jig *n/v* jeeg.
jilt *v* begunk.
jingle *n/v* jing, tingle.
job *n* ontak, sit-doon.
jocular *adj* jokie.
jog *n/v* shog, jundie.
joggle *n/v* joogle, shoogle.

join *n/v* jine.
joiner *n* jiner.
join in *v* hing tae.
joint *n* jint.
joint venture *n* pairtsay.
joist *n* jeest.
joke *n* baur. • *v* bourd.
jollification *n* skite, splore.
jolly *adj* sonsie.
jolt *n* shoogle. • *v* hotter.
jolting *n* hotter.
jostle *v* oxter.
jot *n* stime.
journey *n/v* raik.
jovial *adj* hertie.
jowl *n* choller.
joyful *adj* blithe.
judge *n/v* jeedge.
judgement *n* decree.
Judgement Day *n* hinmaist day.
jug *n/v* joug.
juggle *v* joogle.
juice *n* joice.
juicy *adj* sappie.
jumble *n/v* jummle.
jump *n/v* lowp.
jumper *n* gansey.
junction *n* infa.
June *n* Juin.
junk *n* rubbage, clamjamfry.
junk food *n* snashters.
jurisdiction *n* stewartry.
jury *n* assize.
just[1] *adj* jonick.
just[2] *adv* jist.
justice *n* jonick, justrie.
juvenile *adj* youthie.

K

keel *v* coup.
keen *adj* hyte, gleg, snell.
keen-edged *adj* gleg.
keen-eyed *adj* gleg-eed.
keenly *adv* snell.
keenness *n* glegness.
keep[1] *n* brose.
keep[2] *v* kep, haud; **keep going** shog; **keep off** haud aff; **keep out** haud oot;

keep up haud on.
keepsake *n* minding.
keg *n* cag.
kerb *n* crib.
kerchief *n* curch.
kernel *n* kirnel.
kestrel *n* keelie.
kettle *n* snippy.
key *n* check.

keystone n putt-stane.
kick n fung. • v dump.
kick about v spartle.
kicker n funker.
kid n bairn, wean.
kidnapping n plagium.
kidney n neir.
kill v en, fell.
killer n murtherer.
kiln n kill.
kiln fire n kilogie.
kilt n philabeg.
kin n sib.
kind¹ adj couthy, canny.
kind² n kin, keind.
kindle v to kennle.
kindling n kennlin.
kindly adj hamelie.
kindred adj kinred.
kingdom n kinrick.
kink n snorl.
kipper n twa-eed steak.
kiss n smoorich. • v pree the lips o.
kitchen n keitchin.
kitchen garden n kailyard.
kite n draigon, gled.
kitten n kittlin.
kittiwake n kittie.
kitty n puggie.

knack n swick.
knave n dyvour, pam.
kneecap n knap.
kneel v cruik yer hochs.
knell v towl.
knick-knack n whigmaleerie.
knife n chib, whittle. • v chib.
knife-grinder n shantieglan.
knight n knicht.
knit v wyve, shank.
knitter n shank.
knitting n wyvin.
knitting needle n wire.
knob n knurl.
knobby adj swirlie.
knock n chap, dunt.• v chap, dunt; **knock about** touse; **knock down** ca doon; **knock off** lowse.
knocker n chapper.
knock-kneed adj in-kneed.
knoll n knowe.
knot n boucht. • v snurkle.
knotted adj snorlie.
knotty adj swirlie.
know v ken.
knowing adj wice.
knowledge n ken.
known adj kent.
knuckle n nickle.

L

laborious adj typin.
laboriously adv sair.
labour n dwang, lawbor. • v lawbor, warsle.
labourer n piner.
laburnum n hoburn sauch.
lace n stringin, pearlins.
lacerate v rive.
lack n inlaik. • v want.
lad n chiel, loon.
ladle n divider.
lady n leddy.
ladybird n leddy launners.
ladylike adj leddiness.
lag v daggle.
lair n bourie.

lake n loch, lochan.
lake-dwelling n crannog.
lamb n lammie.
lame adj hippitie, cripple.
lamely adv hippitie.
lameness n hainch.
lament n croon, coronach. • v greet.
lamentable adj awfu.
lamentation n greetin.
lamp n leerie.
lamplighter n leerie.
lamprey n lamper eel.
lancet n lance.
land n lan.
landing n plat, pletty.
landlady n guidwife.

landlord *n* superior.
landmark *n* meith.
landowner *n* laird.
lane *n* trance, loanin, vennel.
language *n* leid.
languid *adj* smerghless.
languish *v* dwine.
lanky *adj* shilpit.
lantern *n* bouet.
lantern-jawed *adj* lang-chaftit.
lap *v* laip, slorp.
lapse *n* prescription. • *v* sleep, prescribe.
lapwing *n* peewee, teuchit.
larceny *n* stootherie.
larch *n* larick.
lard *n* saem.
larder *n* spence, aumrie.
large *adj* muckle, lairge.
largely *adv* maistlie.
lark *n* laverock. • *v* daff.
larynx *n* thrapple.
lash *n* screenge. • *v* leash.
lass *n* lassie, quine.
last ¹*adj/adv/n* (the) laist, lest (final).
last 2 *v* laist, lest (endure).
last ³ *n* airon fit (in shoemaking).
last night *n* yestreen.
last part *n* hineren.
last year *n* fernyear.
latch *n/v* sneck.
late *adj* ahin, umquhile. • *adv* hyne.
later *adv* gain.
lath *n* spail.
lathe *n* lay.
lather *n* sapples. • *v* freith.
latter *adj* hinner.
lattice *n* tirless.
laugh *n/v* lach.
laughing stock *n* moniment.
laughter *n* lachter.
launch *v* lanch.
laundress *n* washerwifie.
laurel *n* larie.
lavatory *n* cludgie, watterie, wee hoose.
lavish *adj* lairge.
law *n* laa.
law-abiding *adj* leal.
lawbreaker *n* brakker.
lawless *adj* lowse.
lawsuit *n* law-plea.
lawyer *n* writer, lawer.

lax *adj* lither.
lay *v* set i; **lay aside** pit by; **lay out** streek.
layabout *n* sloonge.
layer *n* dass, skliffer, scruif.
layout *n* ootset.
laziness *n* idleset.
lazy *adj* sweirt, daeless.
lazy person *n* snuil, brochle.
lea *n* ley.
lead ¹ *n* leid.
lead ² *v* wice.
leader *n* heidsman, high heid yin.
leaf *n* blade, lid.
leak *v* leck, laik.
leakage *n* seep.
leak out *v* skail, spunk oot.
leaky *adj* gizzen.
lean ¹ *adj* pookit, tuim.
lean ² *v* heeld. • *n* hing.
leap *v* lowp.
learn *v* lairn.
learned *adj* far i the buik.
learning *n* lair, buik-lair.
lease *n* less. • *v* tak.
leather *n* ledder.
leave *n* freedom. • *v* lea, quat.
leave-taking *n* wa-gang.
leavings *npl* hinneren.
lecher *n* dyke-louper, loon.
lecture *n* lecter.
ledge *n* cantle.
lee *n* lithe.
leech *n* gell.
leek *n* foos.
lees *npl* gruns.
left *adj* car, ker. • *adv* wast.
left-hand *n* ketach.
left-handed *adj* car, ker-haundit.
left-handed person *n* corrie-fister.
leftovers *n* orts, orras.
leg *n* sham.
legal papers *n* process.
legend *n* leegen.
leggings *npl* leggums.
legs *n* trams.
leg-up *v* hainch.
leisure *n* leesure.
leisure-time *n* by-time.
lemon *n* leemon.
lemonade *n* skoosh.
lend *v* len.

length n lenth.
lengthen v rax.
lengthwise adv enlang.
lenient adj sapsie.
lest conj least.
let v lat, set; **let down** misgie; **let fly** lat gird; **let go** lowse.
let-down n snipe.
lethargic adj thowless.
lethargy n sweirtie.
letter n scrieve.
level adj snod, evenlie. • n mine. • v straik.
level-headedness n rummlegumption.
lever n lewer. • v pinch.
levy n/v stent.
lewd adj ruch.
liar n waghorn.
liberal adj hertie.
liberate v leeberate.
libertine n loon, dyke-louper.
liberty n leebertie.
library n leebrarie.
lice npl cattle, loosies.
licence n/v leeshence.
licentious adj lowse, ill-daein.
lichen n hazelraw.
lick n/v slaik.
lie n/v lee, lig.
lie-in n long lie.
lieutenant n lieutenand.
life n wizzen.
lifeless adj deid as a mauk.
lift n/v heeze.
light adj licht. • n licht, leam. • v lichten.
lighten v lichten.
light-fingered adj sticky-fingert.
light-headed adj reezie.
light-hearted adj licht-hertit.
lightly adv lichtlie.
lightning n foudrie, fireflacht.
like adj/v lik.
likeable adj fine, innerlie.
likelihood n likly.
likely adj lik.
likeness n limn.
likewise adv siclik.
liking n goo.
lilac n laylock.
limekiln n likewark.
limestone n limestane.
limit n/v leemit.

limp[1] adj wamfle.
limp[2] n/v hirple.
limpet n lempit.
limping adj hippitie. • n haut.
linchpin n lin-pin.
line[1] n mairch.
line[2] v sark.
lineage n kin.
linen n plainen, harn.
linen cupboard n naperie press.
ling n hedder.
linger v hinder.
lingering adj lag.
linnet n lintie.
linoleum n waxcloth.
linseed n linget.
lip n mull.
liquid n broo, bree.
liquor n bree, bevvy.
liquorice n lickerie.
list n leet.
listen v hark, hearken.
listener n hearkener.
listless adj fushionless.
listlessly adv davielie.
literary work n quair.
lithe adj soople, swack.
litigate v pursue.
litter n brod. • v ferry.
little adj wee, peedie, peerie. • n bittock, thocht.
little finger n pinkie.
little girl n lassock.
little man n mannie.
live v leeve, stay; **live in** kitchie; **live on** leeve aff.
livelihood n brose.
liveliness n lifieness, smeddum.
livelong adj leelang.
lively adj forcie, gleg.
livestock n gear.
livewire n stang o the trump.
livid adj blae, radge.
living n brose.
lizard n heather-ask.
loach n bairdie.
load n/v laid.
loaf[1] n laif, breid.
loaf[2] v sloonge, mump.
loafer n sloonger.
loan n len.

loath *adj* sweirt.
loathe *v* ug, laith.
loathing *n* laith.
loathsome *adj* laithlie, scunnersome.
lobby *n* entry.
lobster *n* lapster.
lobster pot *n* creel.
local *n* howff.
locality *n* airt.
lock *n* flacht. • *v* key; **lock up** *v* sneck up.
lock and key *n* lockfast.
lockjaw *n* jaw-lock.
lock, stock and barrel *n* stoup an roup.
lodge *n/v* ludge.
lodger *n* ludger.
lodging *n* ludgin.
loft *n* laft.
lofty *adj* heich.
log *n* clog.
loin *n* backsey.
loiter *v* lyter.
loiterer *n* jotter.
lonely *adj* lanelie.
long¹ *adj* lang.
long² *v* green for, glagger.
long ago *adv* lang syne.
longing *adj* awid. • *n* ill-ee.
long-legged *adj* lang-shankit.
long-suffering *adj* patientfu.
long time *adv* guid bit.
long-winded *adj* enless.
look *n/v* leuk; **look about** sky; **look after** leuk ower, lippen; **look at** leuk till; **look for** seek, **look like** *v* mak for.
look here! *interj* leuk see!
look out! *interj* min yersel!
loom *n* luim.
loop *n* kinch. • *v* hank.
loose *adj* lowse.
loose-fitting *adj* lowse.
loosen *v* lowsen.
loose woman *n* limmer, randie.
loot *n* spulyie.
lop *v* sneck.
lope *v* lowp.
lopsided *adj* lab-sidit.
loquacious *adj* gabbie.
loquacious person *n* blether.
loquacity *n* tongue-raik.
lord *n* laird.
lordly *adj* lairdlie.

lorry *n* larrie.
lose *v* loss; **lose ground** gae back.
loss *n* miss.
lot *n* awfie, awfu.
lottery *n* luck pock.
loud *adj* lood, fell.
loudly *adv* heich.
loud-mouthed *adj* glowsterin.
lounge *v* sloonge.
lounger *n* haiverel.
louse *n* loose.
lout *n* scurryvaig, filsh.
loutish *adj* coorse, miraculous.
love *n/v* luve.
lovable *adj* loosome.
love-child *n* luve-bairn.
lovely *adj* bonny, loosome.
lover *n* lovie, jo.
lovesick *n* gyte.
loving *adj* fain.
loving look *n* luve-blink.
lovingly *adv* condinglie.
low¹ *adj* laich, law.
low² *v* belloch, rowt.
low-class *adj* main, waff.
low-class person *n* keelie, schemie.
lower *adj* nether. • *v* laich.
lowering *adj* cankert.
lowest *adj* nethmaist.
lowing *adj* rowt.
lowland *n* lallan.
low-lying *adj* inby.
low-spirited *adj* disjaskit.
low tide *n* grun-ebb.
loyal *adj* leal.
loyally *adv* leal.
loyalty *n* lealtie.
lubricate *v* creesh.
luck *n* sonse.
luckless *adj* misfortunate.
lucky *adj* sonsie, canny.
lucky dip *n* lucky poke.
lug *v* humph.
lukewarm *adj* lew.
lull *n* daak. • *v* ba.
lullaby *n* hushie-ba.
lumbago *n* lumbagie.
lumber¹ *n* troke (odds and ends).
lumber² *v* trachle.
lump *n* dad, claut. • *v* knot.
lump together *v* slump.

lumpy *adj* knottie.
lunatic *n* bammer, gyte.
lung *n* buff.
lungwort *n* thunner-an-lichtenin.
lurch *n* stoit. • *v* rowe.
lure *v* wice, wile.

lurid *adj* roarie.
lurk *v* lirk.
luscious *adj* maumie.
lush *adj* growthie.
lustful *adj* radgie.
luxuriant *adj* growthie, ruch.

M

machine *n* ingine, graith.
machinery *n* graith.
mad *adj* gyte, daft.
madam *n* mem.
madden *v* raise.
maddening *adj* fashious, ugin.
madness *n* madderam.
mad person *n* gyte, bammer.
maggot *n* mauk.
maggoty *adj* meithie, maukit.
magic *n* glamour, cantrip.
magician *n* warlock.
magistrate *n* baillie.
magpie *n* maggie.
maid *n* lass, quine, servin lass.
maiden *n* dame, deem.
maid-of-all-work *n* scuddler.
maim *v* mank, mishannle.
main *adj* feck.
mainlander *n* ferry-louper, sooth-moother.
mainly *adv* fecklie.
main street *n* toon yett.
maintain *v* haud, fend.
maintenance *n* uphaud.
major *adj* maist.
majority *n* feck.
make *v* mak; **make believe** mak-on; **make do** pit by; **make for** airt for; **make much of** daut; **make off** skice; **make up to** chim.
makeshift *n* by-pit.
male *n* he.
malediction *n* malison.
malefactor *n* ill-daer.
malevolent *adj* ill-hertit.
malice *n* ill, ill-will.
malicious person *n* keek.
malignant *adj* uncanny.
malinger *v* fraik.

mallard *n* mire-duck.
mallet *n* bittle.
mallow *n* maw.
malt *n/v* maut.
maltster *n* mautman.
man *n* he, carle, chiel.
manage *v* manish.
manageable *adj* fleet.
manager *n* guider, factor, heid bummer.
managing *adj* fendie.
manger *n* foresta.
mangle *v* mishannle, massacker.
mangy *adj* scawt.
manhood *n* manheid.
manifest *v* kythe.
manifestation *n* kythin.
manifold *adj* moniplied.
manipulate *v* pauchle.
mankind *n* fowk, Jock Tamson's bairns.
manly *adj* pretty.
manner *n* mainner.
mannerism *n* ginkum.
mannerly *adj* menseful, mainnerlie.
manners *npl* mainners.
manoeuvre *v* airt, wice.
manservant *n* servan chiel.
mansion *n* ha, big hoose.
manslaughter *n* culpable homicide.
mantelpiece *n* lintel.
mantle *n* manteel.
manure *n/v* mainner.
many *adj* monie, plenty.
map *n* caird.
mar *v* mank, spulyie.
maraud *v* spulyie.
marble *n* bool, chippie.
march *n/v* mairch.
March *n* Mairch.
mare *n* mear.
marigold *n* yella gowan.

mark *n/v* merk.
marker *n* prap, cairn.
market *n* mercat.
market garden *n* mail gairden.
marketplace *n* tron.
marriage *n* mairriage.
marriage bond *n* band.
marriage partner *n* marrow.
marriage settlement *n* tocher, sitting-doon.
marrow *n* mergh
marry *v* mairry.
marsh *n* gullion.
marshal *n/v* marischal.
marshland *n* moss.
marsh marigold *n* wildfire.
marshy *adj* marish.
martin *n* mairtin.
martyr *n* mairtyr.
marvel *n/v* ferlie.
mash *n* powsowdie. • *v* champ, chap.
mashed potatoes *n* champit tatties.
masher *n* bittle.
mason *n* dorbie.
masonry *n* stane an lime.
masquerade *n* guise.
masquerader *n* guiser.
mass *n* haip, hulk.
mast *n* most.
master *n* maister. • *v* maugre.
mastery *n* poustie, grip.
mastitis *n* weed.
mat *n* hap. • *v* taut.
match[1] *n* lunt, spunk.
match[2] *n/v* marrow (equal).
matchless *adj* marrowless, maikless.
mate *n* marrow, neibour.
matrimony *n* mairriage, mink.
matron *n* wife, guidwife.
matted *adj* tautit.
matter *n/v* maitter.
mature *adj* muckle.
maul *v* massacker, rive.
maunder *v* maunner.
may *v* mith.
May *n* Mey.
maybe *adv* mebbe.
mayfly *n* scur.
mayor *n* provost.
me *pron* iz, us.
meadow *n* mede.

meadowsweet *n* queen o the mede.
meagre *adj* scrimpit.
meal *n* diet.
meal-chest *n* male-kist.
mealtime *n* diet-oor.
mealy-mouthed *adj* mim.
mean[1] *v* ettle, bear.
mean[2] *adj* grippie, scrimpit, foutie.
meander *n* jouk, wimple. • *v* wimple.
meaningless *adj* haiveless.
meanness *n* grippiness.
mean person *n* nipscart.
meantime *n* tween hauns.
meanwhile *n* tween hauns.
measles *n* mirls.
measure *n* mett, mizzèr. • *v* mizzer.
measurement *n* mett.
measuring rod *n* ellwan.
meat *n* mait, flesh.
meat market *n* skemmels.
mechanism *n* intimmers.
meddle *v* middle.
meddlesome *adj* inbearing.
mediation *n* moyen.
medicinal *adj* hailsome.
medicine *n* graith.
meditate *v* pit the brain asteep.
meditative *adj* pensefu.
medium *adj* middlin.
meek *adj* patientfu.
meet *v* kep, tryst, forgaither.
meeting *n* forgaitherin, tryst, sederunt.
meeting place *n* trysting place.
melancholy *adj* dowie, unhertsome.
mellow *adj* maumie.
melody *n* souch.
melt *v* molten, spale; **melt away** mizzle; **melt down** rind.
membrane *n* striffin.
memento *n* minding.
memorandum *n* jottin.
memorial stones *n* cairn.
memory *n* minding.
menace *n* sorra. • *v* mint.
mend *v* fettle, sort.
menial *n* scodgie.
menstruate *v* see her ain.
mention *v* mou, mint.
merchandise *n* troke.
merchant *n* merchan.
mercy *n* merciment.

merge *v* gae thegither.
merit *n* mense.
mermaid *n* marmaid.
merrily *adv* mirkie.
merry *adj* blithesome, croose.
merry-making *n* daffin.
mesh *n* mask.
mess *n* guddle, slackstate, carfuffle.
mess about *v* plaister, poach.
messy *adj* slitterie, slaisterie.
messy person *n* slitter, slaister.
messy work *n* kirn.
meteor *n* fire-flacht.
method *n* road.
methodical *adj* purposelik.
methylated spirit *n* feek.
meticulous *adj* pinglin.
mettle *n* saul.
mettlesome *adj* mettle.
mew *n/v* maw.
miaow *n/v* maw.
midday *n* twaloors.
midday meal *n* twaloors.
midden *n* coup, tuim.
middle *adj* mids.
middle-aged *adj* auld-young.
midge *n* midgie, mudge.
midnight *n* midnicht, dumb-deid.
midst *n/prep* mid.
Midsummer Day *n* Johnsmass.
midway *adv* hauf-roads.
midwife *n* howdie.
midwifery *n* howdyin.
midwinter *n* howe o winter.
might *n* micht.
mighty *adj* michtie.
mignonette *n* minnonette.
mild *adj* saft, lithesome.
mildew *n* foost.
milk *n* mulk. • *v* draw, mulk.
milking stool *n* mulkin steel.
milking time *n* kye time.
milk jug *n* poorie.
milk pail *n* bowie, hannie.
mill *n* mull.
mill around *v* kirn.
miller *n* millart.
millrace *n* lade.
millstone *n* stane.
milt *n* melt.
mimic *n* afftak.

mince *v* minch.
minced meat *n* minch, mince.
mincing *adj* mim-mou'd.
mine[1] *n* heuch.• *v* howk.
mine[2] *pron* mines.
miner *n* pickman.
miner's lamp *n* tallie lamp.
mineshaft *n* sink.
mineworkings *npl* winnings.
minister's house *n* manse.
minnow *n* minnon.
minstrel *n* bard.
mint *n* lamb's tongues.
mint imperial *n* pan drop.
minute[1] *adj* peerie-weerie.
minute[2] *n* meenit.
mire *n* clart.
mirror *n* seein gless.
mirth *n* hirdum-dirdum.
misapprehension *n* mistak.
misbehave *v* gae ower the score.
miscall *v* miscaw.
miscarriage *n* slip.
miscarry *v* miscairry, misgae.
miscellaneous *adj* orra.
mischief *n* ill, cantrip, hule.
mischievous *adj* ill-deedie, mischievious.
mischievousness *n* ill-gates.
mischievous person *n* limb o the deil.
misconduct *n* ill-daein.
misdemeanour *n* ill-daein.
miser *n* misert, nabal.
miserable-looking *adj* oorie.
miserable-looking person *n* soor-lik bodie.
miserly *adj* grippie, misert.
misfortune *n* mischief, mishanter.
misgivings *npl* doots.
mishandle *v* misguide.
mishap *n* skavie, mishanter.
misinform *v* mistell.
misinformed *adj* mislearit.
mislay *v* loss.
mismanage *v* misguide, blunk.
mismanaged *adj* ill-guidit.
mispronounce *v* misca.
miss *v* misgae, tyne; **miss something** miss yersel.
missel-thrush *n* storm-cock.
misshapen *adj* camshachelt, bachelt.
missing *adj* amissin.

mist *n* rouk, haar, reek.
mistake *n/v* mistak.
mistaken *adj* mistaen.
mistress *n* guidwife, hersel (head of house); limmer (abusive), bidie-in (lover).
mistrust *v* misdoubt.
misty *adj* roukie, haarie, reekie.
misunderstood *adj* mistaen.
misuse *v* disabuse.
mitigate *v* licht.
mitten *n* pawkie.
mix *v* mell; **mix up** *v* taigle.
mixture *n* mixter-maxter.
mix-up *n* snorl.
mixed up *adj* row-chow.
moan *n/v* complain.
moaning *adj* greetin-faced.
mob *n* canaillie.
mock *v* jamph, lant.
mockery *n* afftakin, jamph.
mocking *adj* afftakin.
mocking remark *n* afftak.
moderate *adj* middlin. • *v* lowden.
moderately *adv* middlins.
moderation *n* mense.
modern *n* modren.
modest *adj* blate.
moist *adj* sappie.
moisten *v* slock.
moisture *n* moister.
molar *n* aisle-tuith.
molasses *n* traicle.
mole *n* mowdieworp, rasp.
mole-catcher *n* mowdie.
molehill *n* mowdiehill.
moleskin *n* mowdieskin.
molest *v* sturt, steer.
mollycoddle *v* daut, fraik.
moment *n* blink.
momentum *n* virr.
Monday *n* Monanday.
money *n* siller, bawbies.
moneybox *n* pig, thrifite.
monied *adj* sillert.
mongrel *n* tike.
monkey *n* pug.
monotonous *adj* dreich.
monotonously *adv* dreichlie.
monster *n* cleisher.
monstrous *adj* wappin.

month *n* muin.
monument *n* moniment.
mood *n* muid, tune.
moody *adj* tunie.
moon *n* muin.
moor *n* muir, moss.
mooring post *n* pall.
mop *v* swaible.
mope *v* mump.
moral person *n* unco guid.
morass *n* slag, flow.
more *adj/adv* mair.
moreover *adv* mair.
morning *n* forenoon.
morose *adj* still.
morsel *n* bittock.
mortal illness *n* deid ill.
mortar *n* lime.
mortgage *n* hypothec. • *v* hypothecate.
mortuary *n* deid-hoose.
moss *n* fog, flow.
moss-covered *adj* fogged.
mossy *adj* foggie.
most *adj* maist.
mostly *adv* maistlie.
most of *adj* feck o.
moth *n* moch.
moth-eaten *adj* mochie.
mother *n* mither.
mother-in-law *n* guid-mither.
motion *n* mudge.
mottled *adj* marlie.
motley *adj* mixter-maxter.
mould *n* foost, mool.
moulder *v* moolder.
moulding *n* mooldin.
mouldy *adj* foostie.
mouldy smell *n* foost.
moult *n/v* moot.
mound *n* moond, tulloch.
mount[1] *n* munt. • *v* munt, lowp on.
mount[2] *n* muntain.
mountain *n* muntain, ben.
mountain ash *n* rowan.
mountain pass *n* bealach.
mounting-stone *n* lowpin-on stane.
mourn *v* murn, croon.
mourner *n* soulie.
mournful *adj* dowie.
mournfully *adv* dowielie.
mournful sound *n* mane.

mourning *n* murning.
mourning clothes *npl* blacks, murnings.
mouse *n* moose.
mousetrap *n* moose-fa.
moustache *n* mouser.
mouth *n* mou, mooth.
mouth-organ *n* moothie.
move *v* muve; **move along** hirsel yont; **move house** flit; **move to and fro** wampish.
movement *n* mudge.
movements *npl* mudgins.
mow *v* maw.
mower *n* mawer.
Mrs *n* Mistress.
much *adv* muckle, meikle.
much alike *adj* neibours, eeksy-peeksy.
much less *adv* forby.
muck *n* clart.
muck-rake *n* hack.
mucus *n* goor, glit.
mud *n* glaur, clart.
muddle *n* fankle.
muddle along *v* puddle.
muddled *adj* raivelt.
muddle-headed *adj* bumbazed.
muddle-headedness *n* throuitherness.
muddy *adj* clarty. • *v* glaur.
muddy place *n* plowter.
muff *n* wristie.
muffler *n* gravat.
mug *n* moog.
muggy *adj* mochie.
mugwort *n* muggart.

mullet *n* pelcher.
multicoloured *adj* lyart.
multitude *n* crood.
mum *n* mam, mammie, maw.
mumble *v* mump, mummle.
mummer *n* guiser.
mummy *n* mammie.
mumps *n* branks.
munch *v* hash.
murder *n*/*v* murther, malky.
murderer *n* murtherer.
murk *n* mirk.
murky *adj* mirksome.
murmur *n* curmurrin, murmuration. • *v* croon, hummer.
murmuring *adj* corrieneuchin.
mush *n* powsowdie. • *v* poach.
mushroom *n* puddock stuil.
musician *n* musicker.
mussel *n* clabbydhu.
mussel-bed *n* mussel scaup.
must *v* maun.
mustard *n* mustart.
musty *adj* foostie.
mute *n* dummie.
mutilate *v* mar, massacker.
mutilated *adj* mankit.
mutter *v* mump.
mutton *n* traik.
mutual assistance *n* giff-gaff.
muzzle *n*/*v* mizzle.
my *pron* ma, mi.
my own *pron* mine ain.
myself *pron* masel.
mysterious *adj* eldritch.

N

nag[1] *n* jaud, yaud.
nag[2] *v* natter; **nag at** threap.
nagging *adj* natter.
nail *n* caddle.
naive *adj* hielan.
naked *adj* scuddie, in the scud.
nakedness *n* bare scud.
name *n*/*v* nem.
nap *n* dover. • *v* dwam.
nape *n* cuff, howe.
napkin *n* naipkin.
nappy *n* cloot, hippin.

narcissus *n* lily.
nark *v* yap.
narrow *adj* sma.
narrowly *adv* near.
narrow-minded *adj* nippit.
narrow part *n* hause.
nasty *adj* naistie, nestie.
nasty-minded *adj* ill-thochit.
nasty person *n* skite.
native *adj* hameart, kin.
native district *n* cauf kintra.
natural *adj* kindly, naitral.

natural death *n* strae daith.
nature *n* naitur.
naught *n* nocht.
naughty *adj* coorse.
naughty child *n* wick.
nausea *n* scunner.
nauseate *v* scunner.
nauseating *adj* scunnersome.
nauseous *adj* stawsome.
navel *n* nyle.
navelwort *n* maid-in-the-mist.
navvy *n* cley davy.
near *adj* nar, nearhan. • *adv* nar, aside. •
  prep nar, nearaboot.
nearby *adj* narby.
nearer *adv/prep* narrer.
nearest *adv/prep* narrest.
nearly *adv* nar, near.
neat *adj* nate, dink.
neaten *v* snod, trig.
neatly *adv* ticht.
neatly-made *v* pretty.
necessaries *npl* necessars.
necessary *adj* necessar.
necessitate *v* necessitat.
neck *n* craig, hause.
necktie *n* owerlay.
needle *n* wire.
needlecase *n* hussie.
needlewoman *n* shewster.
needlework *n* shewin.
needy *adj* needful.
ne'er-do-well *n* dae-na-guid.
neglect *n* negleck. • *v* negleck, mislippen.
neglected *adj* brookit.
negligent *adj* thrieveless.
negligent action *n* quasi-delict.
negotiation *n* transack.
negro *n* bleck.
neice *n* brither-dochter
neigh *n/v* nicher.
neighbour *n* neibour.
neighbourhood *n* neibourheid.
neighbouring *adj* nearhan.
neighbourliness *n* neipert.
neighbourly *adj* neibourlik.
neither *conj* naither.
nephew *n* nevoy.
nervous *adj* nervish, timorsome.
nervousness *n* swither.
nest *n* est.

nestle *v* coorie in.
nestling *n* younker.
nets *n* fleet.
nettle *n* jennie-nettle.
neuter *v* lib, dress, sort.
never *adv* niver.
never mind *adv* nivver heed.
nevertheless *adv* still an on.
new *adj* split-new, spleet-new.
newcomer *n* ootrel.
newfangled *adj* new-farran.
newly *adv* newlins.
news *npl* newings, speirings, uncos.
newt *n* ask.
New Year gift *n* Ne'erday.
New Year's Day *n* Ne'erday.
New Year's Eve *n* Hogmanay.
New Year visitor *n* first fit.
next *adj* nixt, neist.
next but one *adj* next.
nib *n* neb.
nibble *v* mowp.
nice *adj* cliver.
nickname *n* teename.
nick of time *n* clippin time.
niggard *n* nipscart, niggar.
niggardly *adj* nippit.
night *n* nicht.
night before last *n* erethestreen.
nightcap *n* nicht mutch.
nightfall *n* mirkin, dayligaun.
nightgown *n* goonie.
nightingale *n* nichtingale.
nightjar *n* fern owl.
nimble *adj* nimmle, knackie.
nimbly *adv* soople.
nineteenth *adj* nineteent.
ninepins *npl* kyles.
ninth *adj* nint.
nip *n* nib. • *v* chack, sneck.
nipple *n* tit.
nippy *adj* nebbie.
nit *n* neet.
no *adj/adv* nae.
noble *n* thane.
nobody *pron* naebodie.
nodding *adj* nid-noddin.
node *n* knot.
nod off *v* dover.
noise *n* soon, roar.
noisy *adj* roarie.

nominate *v* leet.
nondescript *adj* orra.
none *pron* nane.
nonentity *n* vision, roun o.
nonplus *v* raivel.
nonsense *n* blethers.
nonsensical *adj* haiverin.
non-traveller *n* scaldie.
nook *n* neuk.
nooks and crannies *n* creeks an corners.
noon *n* nuin.
noose *n* mink, kinch.
normal *adj* kindly.
normally *adv* for ordinar.
north *n* nor.
northerly *adj* norlin.
northern *adj* norlan.
northerner *n* norlander.
northern lights *n* merry dancers, pretty dancers.
northernmost *adj* normost.
northwards *adv* northart.
nose *n* neb, snotterbox. • *v* snoke.
nosebag *n* mou-poke.
nostril *n* nosethirl.
nosy *adj* nebbie.
nosy person *n* neb.
not *adv* nae, no.
notable *adj* markit, namelie.
not any *pron* nae, nane.
notary *n* writer.
notch *n* nitch, natch. • *v* sneck, natch.
note *n* line, spatril. • *v* mark.

notebook *n* jotter.
noted *adj* namelie.
notepad *n* scroll.
noteworthy *adj* parteeclar.
nothing *n* naethin, nocht.
nothing at all *n* deil a haet.
notice *n* tent. • *v* tak tent.
notion *n* norie.
notorious *adj* notour.
notwithstanding *prep* neithers.
nought *n* naet.
nourish *v* nourice.
nourishment *n* fushion.
novel *adj* new-farran.
novelty *n* newin.
now *adv* noo, the noo.
nowadays *n* nooadays.
now and again *adv* ilka sae lang.
now and then *adv* whiles.
nowhere *adv* nae place.
noxious *adj* ill, hurtsome.
nude *adj* nakit.
nudge *n*/*v* nidge, nodge.
nuisance *n* fash.
nullification *n* irritancy.
nullify *v* irritate.
numb *adj* taibetless.
number *n*/*v* nummer.
numerous *adj* lairge, thrang.
nurse *n* nourice. • *v* cuiter, sort.
nurture *v* fess up.
nut *n* nit.
nuzzle *v* snoozle.

O

oaf *n* sumph.
oak *n* axik.
oar *n* air.
oatcake *n* bannock, aitcake.
oatcakes *npl* breid.
oaten *adj* aiten.
oat-grass *n* swine arnit.
oatmeal *n* meal, male.
oatmeal pudding *n* mealie pudding, brose.
oath *n* aith.
oats *n* aits, corn.
obedient *adj* bowsome.

obey *v* obtemper.
object *n*/*v* objeck.
objection *n* pleen.
objectionable *adj* scunnersome.
obligation *n* obleegement.
obliging *adj* bowsome, helplie.
oblique *adj* sklent, squint.
obliquely *adv* agley, asklent.
obliterate *v* disannul.
obnoxious *adj* ill-faured.
obscene *adj* ruch, groff.
obscenity *n* sclatrie.
obscure *adj* dern, mirk. • *v* smoor.

obsequious *adj* sleekit.
observant *adj* tentie.
observation *n* observe.
observe *v* leuk til.
obsessed *adj* thirled tae, unable tae see past.
obstacle *n* stick.
obstinate *adj* thrawn, unbowsome.
obstinately *adv* rizzon or nane.
obstreperous *adj* ramstam, radge.
obstruct *v* mar, stap.
obstruction *n* hinder.
obvious *adj* kenable.
occasion *n* tid, use.
occasional *adj* orra, antrin.
occasionally *adv* at a time, at the edge o a time.
occupied *adj* fest.
occur to *v* glance on.
ocean *n* tide.
odd *adj* orra, unco.
oddity *n* magink, queerie.
odd jobs *n* jots.
odd-jobs man *n* orraman, jotter.
odd-looking person *n* ticket.
odd person *n* queerie.
odds and ends *npl* orras.
odour *n* waff, guff.
of *prep* o.
off *adv/prep* aff; • *adj* foostie.
offal *n* emmledeug.
offence *n* gee.
offend *v* offen, miscomfit.
offended *adj* struntit.
offender *n* fauter.
offensive *adj* ill-faured.
offer *n/v* bode.
offhand *adj* affluif.
office *n* offish.
officer *n* offisher.
officious *adj* inbearing.
offset *n* intak.
offshore *adj* ooterlie.
offspring *n* bairn, wean.
often *adv* afen, aft.
ogle *v* blink.
ogre *n* etin.
oil *n/v* ile, uilie.
oilcan *n* poorie.
oilcloth *n* waxcloth.
oil jar *n* uilie pig.

oil lamp *n* eelie dolly, cruisie.
oily *adj* ilie, sleekit.
old *adj* auld, aul.
old age *n* eild.
oldest *adj* aul.
old-fashioned *adj* aul-farran.
old-fashioned girl *n* grannie mutch.
old-fashioned woman *n* Aunty Beeny.
old-maidish *adj* primsie.
old man *n* bodach.
old woman *n* cailleach, carline.
omen *n* warnin.
ominous *adj* uncanny.
omission *n* pass-ower.
omit *v* hip.
on *prep* in, o.
once *adv* aince, yince.
once or twice *adv* a time or twa.
one *adj/n* ane, yin.
one after another *adv* efter ither.
one and only *n* wha but he.
one kind *adj* ilk ither.
one another *pron* ilk ither.
one kind *adj* eeksie-peeksie.
oneself *pron* yerself.
onion *n* ingan.
only *adj* ainly, ae.
only child *n* bird-alane.
onset *n* onding.
onslaught *n* onding.
onward *adv* forrit.
ooze *n* seep, glaur. • *v* weeze.
oozings *npl* sypins.
open *adj/v* apen.
opening *n* open.
openly *adv* fair.
open-mouthed *adj* gyping.
opponent *n* unfreen.
opportune *adj* timeous.
opportunity *n* inlat, scowth.
oppose *v* conter, thorter, gainstand.
opposed *adj* contrair.
opposite *n* contrair, conter. • *prep* anent, forenent.
oppress *v* haud doon, owergang.
oppressed *adj* hauden-doon.
oppressive *adj* gurthie, sair.
oppressively hot *adj* muith.
opulent *adj* fouthie.
orange *n* oranger.
orchid *n* balderie.
ordain *v* ordeen.

ordeal n throu-come.
order n ranter. • v speak, ca.
orderliness n ranter.
orderly adj trig.
ordinary adj ordinar.
ordinary person n scone o the day's baking.
organ n kist o whustles.
organically sound adj hert-hale.
organs n harigals.
organise v guide.
origin n oreeginal.
original adj oreeginal.
original n principal.
ornament n affset. • v fineer.
ornamental adj wallie.
ornate adj fantoosh.
orphan n orphant.
ostentation n bladrie.
ostentatious adj palaverin.
ostentatious behaviour n palaver.
other pron ither.
other times adv itherwhiles.
otherwise adv itherwise.
ought n ocht.
ounce n unce.
our pron oor, wir.
ourselves pron oorsels, wirsels.
out adv oot.
out and out adj ringin.
outbuildings npl steading.
outburst n eruction, gowster.
outcast n ootlan, ootcuissen.
outcome n upcome, aftergait.
outcry n sang, scronach.
outdo v cowe, bang.
outdoor adj oot aboot.
outer adj ooter.
outer room n but, oot-room.
outfit n graithin.
outflow v stour.
outgoing adj gracious.
outing n veage.
outlandish adj haithen.
outlaw n ootlin.
outlay n ootgang.
outlet n ootlat.
outline n rinnin.
outlying adj oot, ootby.
outlying land n ootlan.
out of prep ooten.
out of doors adj ootby.

out of hand adj oot o theat.
out of place adj misbehadden.
out of sorts adj oorlich, peely-wally.
output n through-pit.
outrageous adj maroonjous, abstraklous.
outright adv ootricht.
outset n affset.
outside adv ootside, ootwith. • prep furth.
outsiders n the fremd.
outskirts n ootby.
outsmart v win ahin.
outspoken adj tongue-be-trusht.
outstanding adj by-ornar.
outstanding person n beezer, dancer.
outwards adv ootwan, ootby.
outwit v raivel.
ouzel n chack.
ovary n egg-bed.
oven n ovven.
over adv/prep ower.
overall n carsackie, ovies.
over and above prep forby.
over and done adj by wi.
over-anxious adj rackie.
overawe v coonger.
overbalance v coup.
overbearing adj ringin.
overburden v trachle.
overburdened adj trachelt.
overcast adj owercast, loorie.
overcharge v saut.
overcoat n muckle coat.
overcome adj owertaen. • v owercome.
overcooked adj sair duin.
overdressed adj fantoosh.
overdue adj ahin the haun.
overeating n gutsin.
overexcited adj raised.
overflow v skail.
overgrown adj grown-up.
overhang v owerhring.
overhead adj abuneheid.
overheads npl oncost.
overlook v owerleuk, mislippen.
over-particular adj fykie.
overpower v owerpooer.
over-precise adj perjink.
overrate v owerrate.
overreach v owerrax.
over-refined adj prick-ma-dentie.
overrun adj hoachin. • v ower-rin.

oversee v oversee.
overseer n grieve, owersman.
oversleep v sleep in.
overstep v owerstap.
overtake v owertak.
overtax v hash.
overthrow v owerthraw, ding doon.
overtime n by-oors.
overturn v coup.
overturning adj coup.
overweening adj heich.
overwhelmed adj trachelt.
overwork v hash.

overworked adj trachelt.
owe v awe.
owing adj owe.
owing to conj wi.
owl n ool, hoolet.
own adj ain. • v awn; **own up to** haud wi.
owner n awner.
ownership n aucht.
ox n owse.
oxen n owsen.
ox-eye daisy n horse gowan.
oyster n oo.
oyster-catcher n sea-pyot.

P

pace n pass, spang. • v pass, reenge.
pacify v peecifee.
pack n bunnle. • v stap.
packed adj stowed.
packed lunch n piece, denner-piece.
packed lunch box n piece box.
pack of cards n pair o cairds.
pack-saddle n sheemach, clibber.
pad n pluff.
paddle v paiddle.
paddock n parroch.
pail n cog, bowie.
pain n bide, fash.
painful adj sair.
painful injury n sair yin.
painfully adv sair.
painstaking adj fash.
paint n/v pent.
painted adj pentit.
paintwork n pent.
pair n twasome, perr.
palace n pailace.
palatable adj suppable.
palaver n carfuffle.
pale adj whitelie, peely-wallie, gash.
paling n pailin.
palisade n peel.
pall n mortclaith.
pallid adj palie, peely-wally.
palm n luif.
palpitate v flaff, dunt.
palpitation n dunt.
paltry adj fouterie.

pamper v cuiter, daut.
pamper oneself v socher.
pampered adj leepit, deltit.
pan n tillie-pan, pingle-pan.
panache n panash.
pancake n screever, English pancake.
pancreas n breeds.
pane n peen.
panelling n boxin.
pang n stang, stoun.
panic n swither.
pannier n packet.
pant n/v pech.
pantry n aumrie.
paper bag n poke.
parade n parawd.
paralyse v paraleese.
paralysed adj blastit.
paralysis n paraleesis.
parapet n ravel.
paraphernalia npl orders.
parasite n eat-mait.
parasitic adj sornie.
parboil v leep.
parcel n/v paircel.
parch v birsle.
parched adj drouchit.
pare v white.
parent n pawrent.
paring n scruiffin.
parish n pairish.
parish church n muckle kirk.
parishioner n pareeshioner.

park n pairk.
park-keeper n parkie.
parlour n chaumer, room.
paroxysm n rapture.
parrot n papingo.
parry v kep.
parsimonious adj ticht, grippie.
part n/v pairt.
particle n ressum.
particular adj parteeclar, perjink.
particularly adv parteeclar.
parting n (of hair) shed.
parting drink n deoch-an-dorus.
parting of the ways n shedding.
partition n parteetion.
partly adj pairtlie, halflins.
partner n pairtner, neibour.
partnership n partnerie.
partridge n paitrick.
party n pairtie, ploy, ceilidh.
pass n bealach, slap. • v weir in, see, pit
  by, win by; **pass away** win awa; **pass
  by** haud by; **pass over** win ower, hip.
passageway n gang, close, entry, vennel.
passing bell n deid bell.
passing by adj by-gaen.
passion n feem, patience.
passionate adj birsie, heidie.
passive adj fushionless.
past adv bygane. • prep by.
paste n/v batter.
pastime n play.
pastries npl snashters.
pasture n paster, gang. • v girse.
pasturage n girsin, lizour.
pasty-faced adj peely-wally.
pat n/v clap.
patch n/v eik, cloot.
patch up v souder.
patella n knap.
paternity n filiation.
path n pad, roadie.
pathetic adj sair.
patience n thole.
patient adj tholemoodie.
patronage n cheenge.
patter v whitter.
pattern n pattren.
paunch n painch.
pause n still. • v hover.
pave v causey.

pavement n causey, plettiestanes.
pavilion n paveelion.
paw n spag, luif. • v pawt.
pawn n/v pawnd.
pawnshop n pawn.
pay n/v pey; **pay attention** tent; **pay
  dearly** cauk; **pay for** pey.
pea n pey.
peace n pace, lown.
peaceable adj greeable.
peaceful adj lown.
peaceful place n lown.
peacefully adv lown.
peacock n paycock.
peahen n paysie.
peak n peen, kip, skip.
peaked adj skippit.
peaky adj peakit.
peal n jow, brattle. • v jow, dinnle.
peanut n puggie nut.
pea pod n cod, shaup.
pear n peer.
pearl n pairl.
pearlstring n pearlin.
peashooter n scooter.
pea soup n pey bree.
peat n pate, turf.
peat basket n creel, cassie.
peat bog n moss, hill.
peat-cutter n peat-caster, tusker.
peat-cutting v peat-castin.
peat dust n drush, coom, smoorach.
peat fire n peat lowe.
peat-stack n ruck, stack, bing.
peat working n peat-hag, moss-hag.
peaty water n peat bree.
pebble n chuckie, peeble.
pebbly adj rocklie.
peck n dorb. • v pick.
peckish adj hungert.
peculiar adj unco, parteeclar.
peculiarity n unconess.
pedantic adj lang-nebbit.
peddle v cadge.
pedestrian n ganger.
pedestrians npl fit-fowk.
pedlar n cadger, packman, troker.
pedlar's wares n troke.
peel v pilk.
peep n keek, glent. • v keek, pleep.
peephole n keekhole.

peeping Tom *n* keeker.
peer[1] *n* maik.
peer[2] *v* stime.
peevish *adj* fashious, girnie.
peewit, pewit *n* peesweep.
peg *n* nag, nab.
pellet *n* skirp.
pellets *npl* hail.
pelt *n* pellet. • *v* clod, dad.
pen *n* cruive, fank. • *v* pumphal, fank.
penance *n* mends.
pencil-point *n* nib.
pendulum *n* pendle.
penetrate *v* prog, thirl; **penetrate into** howk.
penis *n* pintle, whang, wan.
penmanship *n* hanwrite.
pen-nib *n* neb.
penniless *adj* plackless.
penny *n* stuir.
penny-farthing *n* speeder.
pensioner *n* foggie.
pensive *adj* pensefu.
pent up *adj* inhauden.
penurious *adj* scuddie.
penury *n* puirtith.
peony *n* speengie rose.
people *n* fowk.
pepper *n* spice.
pepper and salt *n* dab-at-the-stuil.
peppermint *n* sweet pan drop.
peppery *adj* spicy.
perceive *v* fin, feel.
perceptive *adj* nizwise.
perch *n* spaik.
percolate *v* seep, seek.
peremptory *adj* cuttit.
perfect *adj* perfit.
perfectly *adv* perfit.
perfidious *adj* slidderie.
perforate *v* thirl.
perhaps *adv* aiblins, mebbe.
pericardium *n* huil.
peril *n* wanchance.
period *n* stoun.
perish *v* tyne.
perjure *v* manswear.
perjured *adj* mansworn.
perk *n* chance. • *v* spunk.
perky *adj* birkie.
permit *v* lat, leeve.

perpendicular *adj* evendoon.
perpetually *adv* for aye.
perplex *v* kittle, fickle.
perplexed *adj* bumbazed.
perplexity *n* swither.
perquisite *n* chance.
persecute *v* pursue, murther.
persevere *v* stick in, hing in.
persevere in *v* haud at.
persevering *adj* through-gawn.
persist *v* haud at.
persistent *adj* dreich.
persistently *adv* even on.
person *n* bodie.
perspire *v* sweet.
persuade *v* wice.
pert *adj* forritsome.
pert child *n* nacket.
pert person *n* nyaff.
perturb *v* fash.
perverse *adj* thrawn, camstairie.
perverse streak *n* thrum.
perversity *n* thraw.
pervert *v* thraw.
pest *n* provoke, scunner.
pester *v* pest, steer.
pestle *n* champer.
pet *v* browden, daut.
petrify *v* fricht.
petted *adj* deltit.
petted child *n* sookie.
petticoat *n* coat.
petty *adj* pea-splittin.
petulant *adj* tiftie.
pew *n* dask.
pewit *see* **peewit** *n* peesweep.
pewter *n* pewther.
phantom *n* adhantare, bogle.
pharmacist *n* poticary.
pheasant *n* feesan.
phlegm *n* glit.
phosphorescence *n* fire-burn.
phrase *n* rame.
physics *n* natural philosophy.
pick *n* pike • *v* pike; **pick at** pewl at; **pick out** chap; **pick up** lift, cock.
pick and choose *v* lift an lay.
pickle *n* picher.
picnic *n* kettle.
picture *n* picter.
piddle *v* strone.

piddling *adj* drutlin.
piebald *adj* pyotie.
piece *n* dorle, nip, dad.
piece of work *n* hanlin.
pieceworker *n* tasker.
pie dish *n* ashet.
pied wagtail *n* willie-wagtail.
pier *n* shore.
pierce *v* prog, jab.
piercing *adj* snell.
pig *n* grice.
pigeon *n* doo.
pigeonhole *n* doocot.
pigeon-toed *adj* hen-taed.
piggyback *adj/n* coalie-back.
piggy-bank *n* pirlie pig.
pig-headed *adj* thrawn.
pig in a poke *n* blin bargain.
pignut *n* arnit.
pigsty *n* cruive.
pigswill *n* swine-mait.
pigtail *n* pleat.
pike *n* ged, pickstaff.
pile *n/v* bing, rickle.
pilfer *v* pauchle.
pilgrim *n* pilgrimer.
pill *n* peel.
pillage *v* reive, herrie.
pillar *n* pall, stoop.
pillow *n* pillae.
pillowcase *n* pillowbere.
pilot *n* lodesman. • *v* airt.
pimple *n* pluke, plouk.
pimply *adj* plukey.
pin *n/v* peen, preen.
pinafore *n* peenie.
pincers *n* pinchers.
pinch *n* nip. • *v* nirl, skech.
pinched *adj* scrimp, shilpit.
pincushion *n* preen-cod.
pine[1] *v* dwine, peenge.
pine[2] *n* bonnet fir.
pine cone *n* fir yowe.
pine needle *n* preenack.
pinhead *n* preen-heid.
pink *n* spink.
pinpoint *n* neb.
pins and needles *n* prinkle.
pious *adj* gracie.
pip *n* paip.
pipe *n* gun.

pipe band leader *n* pipe major, pipie.
pipeclay *n* camstane.
pipe cleaner *n* pipe riper.
pipit *n* lintie.
piquant *adj* sherp.
pique *n* heelie.
piqued *adj* struntit.
pirate *n* caper.
pirouette *v* wheel.
pit *n* heuch, winning, delf.
pitch[1] *n* pick (tar).
pitch[2] *v* keytch, pick (throw).
pitch-dark *adj* pit-mirk.
pitcher *n* pig, graybeard.
pitchfork *n* fowe.
pith *n* sense, fushion.
pithead *n* hill.
pit-heap *n* pit bing, coal bing.
pithless *adj* fushionless.
pitiable *adj* peetiful.
pitted *adj* coinyelled.
pity *n* shame. • *v* mane.
placate *v* dill.
place *n* bit, spat. • *v* stell, steid.
placenta *n* cleanin.
placid *adj* fine.
plagiarise *v* thig.
plague *n* pest. • *v* deave, pest.
plaice *n* plash.
plaid *n* plaidie.
plain *adj* hamelt. • *n* carse (land).
plaintiff *n* pursuer.
plait *n* plet, pleat. • *v* warp, plet.
plan *n* ploy, schame. • *v* ettle, mint.
plane *n* han-plane (for wood). • *v* scrunt.
plank *n* clift.
plant *v* lay, set doon, stell.
plantain *n* curl-doddie.
plantation *n* plantin.
plant out *v* set aff.
plaster *n* plaster, stookie. • *v* plaister, cleester.
plate-rack *n* bink.
platter *n* ashet.
plausible *adj* fair-farran, sleekit.
play *n* ploy. • *v* rampage.
play fair *v* play fair hornie.
playful *adj* geckin.
playing cards *n* cairts, deil's picter buiks.

plaything *n* playock.
play truant *v* troon, jouk.
plead *v* prig.
pleading *adj* priggin.
pleasant *adj* canty, couthy.
pleasantly *adv* mirkie.
please *v* pleesure.
pleased *adj* prood.
pleasure *n* pleesure.
pleat *n/v* plet.
pledge *n* wad. • *v* wad, hecht.
plentiful *adj* rife, rowth.
plentifully *adv* rife.
plenty *n* fouth, rowth.
pliable *adj* dwaible.
pliant *adj* dwaible.
pliers *n* pinchers.
plight *n* pliskie.
plimsolls *n* sannies.
plod *v* stodge.
plodder *n* stodger.
plop *n/v* plowp, plowt.
plopping noise *n* plump.
plot *n* dale, glebe. • *v* collogue.
plough *n/v* pleuch.
plough-handle *n* pleuch-stilt.
ploughman *n* pleuchie.
ploughshare *n* pleuch-sock.
plover *n* pliver.
pluck *n* gumption.
plucky *adj* stuffie.
plug *n* prop. • *v* stap.
plum *n* ploom.
plume *n* pen.
plump *adj* plumb, sonsie.
plump person *n* fodgel.
plunder *n* spulyie, creagh. • *v* spulyie, reive.
plunderer *n* reiver.
plunge *n/v* plowt, plype.
plunger *n* plumper.
pneumoconiosis *n* stourie lungs.
poach *v* spoach.
poacher *n* spoacher.
poacher's hook *n* geg.
pocket *n/v* pootch.
pocket money *n* Seturday penny.
pock-marked *adj* pockarred.
pod *n* huil, cod. • *v* shaup, huil.
podgy *adj* pudgie.
poem *n* pome.

poet *n* makar, bard.
point *n/v* pint.
poison *n/v* pooshion.
poisonous *adj* pooshionous.
poke *n/v* powk, prog.
poke about *v* ruit.
poker *n* proker.
pole *n* powl, pall.
polecat *n* foumart.
police *n* polis.
policeman *n* polis.
polish off *v* perish.
polite *adj* menseful.
pollack *n* lythe.
polled *adj* hummel.
pollute *v* fyle, smit.
polysyllabic *adj* lang-nebbit.
pompom *n* toorie.
pompous *adj* fou, pensie.
pond *n* pound, dub.
pony *n* pownie.
pooh-pooh *v* hoot.
pool *n* puil.
poor *adj* puir.
poor fellow *n* puir sowl.
poorly *adj* badly, tender.
pop *v* lowp.
pope *n* pape.
popery *n* paperie.
popgun *n* spoot-gun.
popish *adj* paipish.
popping noise *n* plunk.
poppy *n* puppie.
popular *adj* faur ben.
porcelain *n* wallie.
porch *n* rochel, entry.
pork *n* purk.
porpoise *n* pellock.
porridge *n* parritch.
porridge bowl *n* cap.
porridge stirrer *n* spurtle.
port *n* herbour.
portend *v* bod.
portent *adj* warnin.
portfolio *n* blad.
portion *n* lab, dale.
portrait-painter *n* limner.
possess *v* aucht.
possession *n* haddin.
possessions *npl* gear.
possibility *n* maybe.

possibly *adv* mebbe.
post *n* stoop, stob.
posterior *n* dowp.
postman *n* postie.
postpone *v* continue.
postponement *n* continuation.
posture *n* shape.
posy *n* bob.
pot *n* pat.
potato *n* tattie.
potato bag *n* tattie poke.
potato basket *n* tattie creel.
potato cake *n* tattie scone, tattie bannock.
potato clamp *n* tattie bing.
potato digger *n* tattie howker, tattie deevil.
potato field *n* tattie pairk.
potato harvest *n* tattie howkin.
potato leaves *n* tattie shaws.
potato masher *n* tattie champer.
potato peeler *n* tattie parer.
potato pit *n* tattie pit.
potato seedbox *n* tattie ploom.
potato skin *n* tattie peelin.
potato soup *n* tattie bree.
pot-bellied *adj* guttie.
potbelly *n* cog wame.
potent *n* stieve.
potential *n* scowth.
potful *adj* pottle.
pot handle *n* pat-bool.
pot-hanger *n* swee.
pothole *n* powe.
pot-leg *n* pat-fit.
pot lid *n* pabrod.
pot-scourer *n* scrub.
potted meat *n* plowt, potted heid/hoch.
potter *v* plowter, fouter.
pottering *n* kirn.
pottery *n* lame.
pouch *n* pootch, poke.
poultry *n* pootrie.
poultry woman *n* hen wifie.
pound[1] *n* pun.
pound[2] *v* champ, pun.
pour *v* poor; pour off shire; pour out tuim.
pout[1] *v* poot.
pout[2] *n* siller fish.
poverty *n* puirtith.
poverty-stricken *adj* ill-aff.
powder *n/v* poother.

powdery *adj* pootherie.
power *n* pooer.
powerful *adj* poorfae.
powerless *adj* mauchless.
practicable *adj* prestable.
practical joke *n* pliskie.
practice *n* haunt.
practise *v* practeese.
praise *n/v* ruise.
prance *v* brank.
prank *n* pliskie.
prattle *n/v* gash, gibble-gabble.
prawn *n* praan.
pray *v* engage.
prayers *n* guid words.
preacher *n* missionar.
precarious *adj* kittlie, tolter.
precious *adj* praicious.
precious stone *n* jowel.
precipice *n* heuch, scaur.
precipitous *adj* brent.
precocious *adj* aul-farran.
precocious child *n* nacket.
predicament *n* snorl.
predict *v* spae, weird.
prediction *n* spae, weird.
pre-eminence *n* gree.
pregnant *adj* boukit, on the road.
prejudiced *adj* nairra-nebbit.
premature *adj* afore the pint.
premonition *n* warnin, forego.
preoccupied *adj* taen up wi, jammed.
prepare *v* graith.
prepared *adj* boden, boon.
prepare for *v* mak for.
preposterous idea *n* megrim.
prescience *n* moyen.
prescription *n* line.
present *adj* forrit. • *n* praisent. • *v* gift.
presentable *adj* faisible, weel tae be seen.
presently *adv* the noo.
preserve *v* preser.
preside *v* moderate.
president *n* preses, convener.
press *n/v* preese, birze; press on *v* bode.
pressure *n* birze, thrangitie.
presume *v* jalouse.
presumption *n* hard neck.
pretence *n* pit on.
pretend *v* mak on; pretend to do mak a fashion o; pretend to be busy haiver.

pretended *adj* simulate.
pretentious *adj* fantoosh.
pretentious person *n* knab.
pretext *n* scug.
pretty *adj* bonny. • *adv* gey.
pretty well *adv* geylies.
prevail upon *v* weir roon.
prevaricate *v* hunker-slide, whittie-whattie.
prevarication *n* whittie-whattie.
prevent *v* kep, pit fae.
previous *adj* umquhile.
previously *adv* afore.
price *n* wanworth, dearth, ransom.
prick *n/v* prog, jag.
pricker *n* progger.
prickle *n* jag. • *v* prinkle.
prickly *adj* jaggie, prickie.
prickly feeling *n* prickle.
prig *n* primp.
priggish *adj* perjink, pensie.
prim *adj* mim, perjink.
prime *v* fang.
primly *adv* mim, perjink.
primrose *n* pink.
primula *n* dusty miller.
principal *adj* heid. • *n* rector.
print *n/v* prent.
printed book *n* prent buik.
printer *n* prenter.
prior to *adv/prep* afore.
prison *n* jile.
prisoner *n* panel.
private *adj* quate.
privet *n* privy.
privy *n* wee hoose, cludgie, watterie.
prize *n* gree, tak.
probable *adj* lik.
probe *n* speiring, prog. • *v* speir, prog.
problem *n* tickler, kinch.
proceed *v* ca awa; **proceed against** pit at; **proceed with** insist in.
procession *n* parawd.
proclaim *v* lat wit.
proclamation *n* scry.
procrastinate *v* latch.
procrastinating *adj* snifflin.
procrastination *n* weeshie-washie, aff-pit.
procrastinator *n* aff-pit.
prod *n/v* prog, pork.

prodigal *adj* wastrif.
produce *n* ootcome.
produce young *v* ferry.
production *n* ootcome, through-pit.
profane *adj* ill.
proficient *adj* profite.
profit *n* ootcome, fore.
profound *adj* lang-heidit.
profuse *adj* rowth.
profusion *n* rowth.
progeny *n* get.
progress *n* ongae, oncome. • *v* spin.
progressive *adj* fordel.
prohibit *v* interdict.
project *n/v* projeck.
projection *n* neb.
prolific *adj* breedie.
prominent *adj* kenspeckle.
promise *n/v* hecht.
promising youngster *n* lad o pairts, lass o pairts.
promontory *n* ness.
promote *v* forder.
prompt *adj* gleg, yare.
prone *adj* grooflins.
prong *n* prang, tae.
pronounce *v* pronoonce.
pronouncement *n* speak.
proof *n* pruif.
prop *n* prap, haud. • *v* prap, stuit.
propel *v* pile.
proper *adj* wicelik.
properly *adv* richt.
property *n* gear, pack.
prophecy *n* spae.
prophesy *v* spae.
prophetess *n* weird wife.
propitious *adj* seilful.
proportion *n* plenty.
proposal *n* speiring.
propose *v* propone, speir for.
proprietor *n* awner.
propriety *n* honesty.
prose *n* screed.
prosecute *v* pit at.
prosecutor *n* complainer, procurator fiscal.
prosper *v* luck, thram.
prosperity *n* seil.
prosperous *adj* fouthie, bien.
prostitute *n* limmer, hairy.

prostrate *adj* awald, felled. • *v* fooner.
protect *v* proteck.
protection *n* beild, hap.
protest *n* plaint. • *v* murmell.
protrude *v* boggle.
protuberance *n* knap.
proud *adj* prood.
proudly *adv* heich, voostie.
prove *v* pruive.
proverb *n* wice-sayin, say.
provide *v* fend.
provide for *v* sort.
provided *conj* boden.
provident *adj* forehandit.
provocation *n* provokshin.
provoke *v* chaw.
provoking *adj* angersome.
prow *n* horn.
prowler *n* scunger.
prowling *adj* skechin.
prudent *adj* canny, forethochtie.
prudish *adj* mim.
prune[1] *n* ploom damas.
prune[2] *v* sneck, sned.
pry *v* spy, neb.
prying *adj* lang-nebbit.
psalm *n* saum.
pub *n* howf.
publican *n* brewster.
publish *v* proclaim, cry.
pucker *n* bumfle.
pudding *n* puddin.
puddle *n* dub, hole.
puddles *n* gutters.
puerile *adj* bairnlie.
puff *n/v* pluff, fuff.
puffball *n* blin man's buff.
puff out *v* pluff.
puffed out *adj* bumfelt.
puffin *n* Tammie norrie.
puffy *adj* pluffie.
pugnacious *adj* fechtin.
pugnacity *n* fecht.
pull *n/v* pul, pou, click; **pull about** touse; **pull a leg** draw a leg; **pull apart** spelder; **pull oneself together** gaither; **pull through** thole throu; **pull to pieces** rive; **pull up** hale.
pullet *n* poullie.

pulley *n* block.
pullover *n* gansey.
pulp *n* potterlowe. • *v* pran.
pulpit *n* poopit.
pulsate *v* putt.
pulverise *v* murl.
pummel *v* nevel, knuse.
punch *n/v* nevel.
Punch-and-Judy show *n* puppie show.
punctilious *adj* pintit.
punctiliously *adv* pintitly.
punctual *adj* pintit.
punctually *adv* pintitly.
puncture *v* prog, jag.
pungent *adj* snell.
pungency *n* nip.
punish *v* pey, sort.
punishment *n* pey.
punt pole *n* sting.
puny *adj* drochlin, shilpit.
puny person *n* drochle.
pup *v* whalp.
pupil *n* scholar, sicht.
puppet show *n* puppie show.
purchase *n/v* coff.
purchases *npl* messages.
purge *v* wark, scoor.
purify *v* shire.
purl *v* pearl.
purple *n* purpie.
purpose *n/v* ettle, mint.
purposeless *adj* fushionless.
purr *n* murr. • *v* curmur.
purse *n* spung, spleuchan. • *v* thraw.
purulent *adj* attrie.
pus *n* etter, humour.
push *n/v* pouss; **push along** hurl.
pustule *n* plook.
put *v* pit; **put aside** pit by, set by; **put away** wa-pit; **put down** plunk; **put in order** redd; **put off** pit fae; **put out** set oot, smoor; **put together** rattle up; **put up with** thole, bide.
putrefy *v* muilder.
putrid *adj* humphed.
putty *n* pottie.
puzzle *n* tickler. • *v* fickle, tickle.
puzzling *adj* kittle, ticklie.

Q

quack *v* quaik.
quaff *v* coup.
quagmire *n* bobbin-quaw.
quail *v* jouk.
quaint *adj* orra, aul-farran.
quake *v* quak.
quaking grass *n* shaker.
qualify *v* qualifee.
qualm *n* doot.
quandary *n* swither.
quantity *n* amoont.
quarrel *n/v* thraw, threap.
quarrelling *adj* flytin.
quarrelsome *adj* carnaptious.
quarrelsome woman *n* randie.
quarry *n* quarrel. • *v* howk.
quarter *n* airt.
quarter day *n* term day.
quarter pound *n* quarter.
quarters *n* up-pittin.
quaver *v* tremmle.
quay *n* shore.
queer *adj* clem.
queer-looking person *n* magink.

quench *v* slock, smoor; **quench one's thirst** weet yer thrapple.
querulous *adj* girnie.
query *n/v* speir.
quest *n* fork.
question *n* speir. • *v* speir at, streek.
questioning *adj* speiring.
quibble *n* fittiefie.
quick *adj* gleg, cliver.
quickest *adj* suinest.
quickly *adv* swith.
quick-tempered *adj* snappous.
quick-witted *adj* gleg, sparkie, knackie.
quiet *adj* quate, quietlik. • *n* quate, saucht.
quieten *v* quaten.
quietly *adv* quate.
quill *n* pen.
quilt *n/v* twilt.
quirk *n* fittiefie.
quite *adv* hail, raither.
quits *adv* equals-aquals.
quiver *n* hotter. • *v* quither, queever.
quota *n* pairt.

R

rabbit *n* kinnen.
rabbit's burrow *n* clap.
rabbit's tail *n* bun, fud.
rabble *n* clamjamfrie.
rabid *adj* wuid.
race[1] *v* stour.
race[2] *n* ilk, etion.
rack *n* heck.
racket *n* ricket.
racquet *n* clackan.
radiance *n* lowe.
radish *n* reefort.
raffle *n* lucky-poke.
rafter *n* raft, bauk.
rag *npl* cloot.
ragamuffin *n* tattie-bogle.
rage *n* tirrivee. • *v* fizz.
ragged *adj* raggit.
ragman *n* ragger.

rags *n* duds, cloots.
ragwort *n* ragweed.
raid *n* creach, spreath.
raider *n* reiver.
rail[1] *n* ravel.
rail[2] *v* flyte.
railing *n* ravel.
railway points *n* snecks.
rain *n* weet, sowp. • *v* plump, pish doon.
raindrop *n* spark.
rainy *adj* saft, plowterie.
rainy day *n* sair fit.
raise *v* heeze.
rake *n* scartle, rap. • *v* quile; **rake together** *v* harl.
ram *n* tup.
ramble *v* rammle, rander.
ramshackle *adj* ricklie.
ramsons *n* ramps.

rancour *n* gum.
random *adj* beguess.
randy *adj* radgie.
range *n/v* reenge; **range over** raik.
rank *adj* ramsh, ruch.
ransack *v* ransackle.
rant *v* rane, natter.
rap *n/v* knap.
rapacious person *n* gled.
rape *n* rap.
rapid *adj* strick.
rare *adj* seendil.
rarities *n* uncos.
rascal *n* laidron.
rascally *adj* waffie, coorse.
rash[1] *adj* ramstam.
rash[2] *n* rush.
rashly *adv* ramstam.
rasp *n/v* risp.
raspberry *n* rasp.
raspberries *npl* thummles.
raspberry picking *n* berry-pickin, the berries.
rat *n* ratton.
rat-trap *n* stamp.
rate *n* raik.
rather *adv* raither.
ratify *v* chap.
ration *n/v* raition.
rational *adj* wicelik.
rattle *n/v* dirl, blatter.
raucous *adj* roupit.
ravage *v* herrie.
rave *n* raverie. • *v* rame.
ravel *v* fankle.
raven *n* corbie.
ravenous *adj* geenyoch.
ravine *n* heuch, gill.
raving *adj* gane, radge. • *n* raverie.
raw *adj* hard, oorie.
raw-boned *adj* runchie.
ray *n* leam.
razor *n* razzor, malky.
razorbill *n* scoot.
razor-fish *n* spootfish.
reach *n/v* reak; **reach out** *v* rax; **reach over** rax ower.
ready *adj* olite.
ready cash *n* lyin siller.
real *adj* rael.
really! *interj* fegs!

realm *n* kinrick.
reap *v* raep.
reaper *n* cutter.
rear[1] *adj/n* hint.
rear[2] *v* fess up, park.
reason *n* rizzon.
reasonable *adj* wicelik.
rebellious *adj* heidie.
rebound *v* skite, stot.
rebuff *n* turn. • *v* snuil.
rebuild *v* rebig.
rebuke *n/v* rebook.
recalcitrant *adj* reestie.
recall *v* mind.
receipt *n* quittance.
recent *adj* raicent.
recently *adv* newlins.
reception *n* innin.
recess *n* crannie, neuk.
recipe *n* receipt.
recitation *n* scrift.
recite *v* rame.
reckless *adj* rackless.
recklessly *adv* racklessly.
reckless person *n* ramstam.
reckon *v* rackon.
reckoning *n* rackonin.
reclaim *v* rive.
recline *v* lean.
recluse *n* mowdiewort.
recognise *v* ken.
recognition *n* kennin.
recoil *n* putt. • *v* resile.
recollect *v* mind.
recollection *n* mindin.
recommend *v* moyen.
recompense *n* rewaird.
reconcile *v* gree.
reconsider *v* forethink.
record *n* writ.
recount *v* screed aff.
recover *v* win ower, gaither.
recovery *n* betterness.
recrimination *n* back-come.
recruit *v* list.
rectify *v* richtify.
recuperate *v* sturken.
red *n* rid, reid.
redcurrant *n* rizzar.
redden *v* rid, reid.
redress *v* remeid.

redshank *n* pleep.
reduce *v* lowden.
reduction *n* inlaik.
reed *n* sprot.
reef *n* skellie.
reel *n* pirn, spring. • *v* slinger.
referee *n* thirdsman.
refined *adj* perjink.
reflect *v* refleck.
reform *v* mend.
refrain *n* owerword.
refresh *v* caller.
refreshing *adj* caller.
refuge *n* bield.
refund *v* repeat.
refurbish *v* replenish.
refurnish *v* replenish.
refuse[1] *v* deny.
refuse[2] *n* hinneren, redd.
refuse-collector *n* scaffie.
regale *v* treat.
region *n* kintra.
register *n* catalogue.
regret *v* rue.
regular *adj* raiglar.
reign *v* ring.
reimburse *v* repey.
reiterate *v* threap.
relapse *n/v* back-gang.
relate *v* effeir, screed aff.
related *adj* sib.
relation *n* kin, sib.
relationship *n* sibness.
relative *n* sib.
relax *v* lint.
release *v* lowse.
reliable *adj* sicker.
relief *n* easement.
relieve *v* exoner, souder.
relinquish *v* quate.
reluctance *n* sweirtie.
reluctant *adj* sweirt, thrawn.
rely *v* lippen.
remain *v* bide.
remainder *n* lave.
remains *npl* orrals.
remark *n* say, observe.
remarkable *adj* unco.
remedy *n/v* remede.
remember *v* mind.
remind *v* mind.

reminiscence *n* minding, recoll.
remnant *n* remainder.
remote *adj* ootlan, farawa.
removal *n* shift, flit.
remunerate *v* mak up, pey.
rend *v* rive.
render *v* rind.
rendezvous *n/v* tryst.
rennet *n* yirnin.
renovate *v* replenish.
rent *n* rive.
reopen *v* tak up.
repair *v* sort, fettle.
reparation *n* mends.
repartee *n* giff-gaff.
repay *v* repey.
repayment *n* repetition.
repeat *v* rane, say ower.
repent *v* mak a rue, remorse.
replete *adj* fou.
replica *n* limn.
reply *v* speak back.
report *n* din. • *v* clype.
repose *v* rist.
repress *v* haud in aboot.
repressed *adj* doon-hauden.
reprimand *v* scaud.
reproach *n* wyte. • *v* rag.
reprobate *n* laidron.
reproof *n* rub, waukening.
reprove *v* repree.
repudiate *v* rejeck.
repugnance *n* scunner.
repulsion *n* hert-scaud.
repulsive *adj* ugsome, ill-faured.
reputation *n* word.
request *v* speir, seek.
require *v* requare.
research *v* speir oot.
resemble *v* favour.
reserve *n* fordel. • *v* hain.
reserved *adj* ootward, still.
reservoir *n* pound.
reside *v* bide, stay.
resident *n* residenter.
residue *n* lave.
resin *n* roset.
resinous *adj* rosettie.
resist *v* gainstan.
resistance *n* fend.
resolute *adj* stieve.

resolve *v* redd up.
resort *n* howff.
resound *v* stoun.
resourceful *adj* fendie, quirkie.
respectable *adj* douce.
respectability *n* honesty.
respite *n* lissance.
responsible *adj* pensie.
rest[1] *n* rist, lave (remainder).
rest[2] *n/v* rist (repose).
restive *adj* skeer.
restless *adj* fykie, hotchin.
restlessness *n* fyke.
restitution *n* repetition.
restore *v* kep.
restrain *v* tether, haud in aboot.
restrained *adj* mim.
restraint *n* rander.
restricted *adj* scrimpit.
result *n* affcome, eftercast.
retailer *n* merchant.
retain *v* kep.
retch *n/v* boak.
retinue *n* trevaille.
retirement *n* retiral.
retort *n* back-chap. • *v* speak-back.
retract *v* resile.
retreat *n* place o haud. • *v* tak leg bail.
retribution *n* dirdum.
return *n* hame-comin.
reveal *v* kythe.
revel *n* splore. • *v* rant.
revelation *n* clearance.
revelry *n* gilravage.
reverberate *v* dunner, dirl.
reverberation *n* dunner.
reverie *n* dwam.
reverse *n* conter.
review *n/v* scance.
revile *v* misca, abuise.
revive *v* spunk up.
revolting *adj* scunnersome.
revolve *v* birl.
revolving *adj* row-chow.
revulsion *n* scunner, grue.
rheumatism *n* rheumatise.
rhythm *n* lilt.
ribald *adj* reebald.
ribbed *adj* rigged an furred.
ribbon *n* trappin.
rich *adj* fouthie, bien.

rick *n* steck.
rickety *adj* shooglie.
ricochet *n* skite.
rid *v* redd.
riddle *n* guess, ree. • *v* ree.
ride *n/v* hurl.
ridge *n* hirst, drum.
ridicule *v* mak a bauchle o.
riff-raff *n* scruff.
rifle *v* reive, ripe.
rift *n* rive, split.
rig *v* pauchle.
right *adj* richt.
rightly *adv* richtlie.
rigid *adj* stieve, stench.
rigmarole *n* lay-aff.
rigorous *adj* snell.
rim *n* fillie.
rime *n* cranreuch.
rind *n* huil.
ring *n* raing. • *v* tingle.
rinse *n/v* reenge, syne.
riot *n/v* gilravage.
riotous *adj* randie, dinsome.
rip *n/v* rive.
ripe *adj* maumie.
ripple *n/v* swaw.
rise *n* fluther, spate. • *v* heave, tak up.
risky *adj* unchancie.
river *n* watter.
rivet *n/v* ruive.
rivulet *n* strintle.
roach *n* braze.
road *n* rod, roadie.
roadway *n* causey.
roam *v* stravaig, reenge.
roaming *n* stravaig.
roan *adj* grim.
roar *n/v* rair.
roaring *adj* roarie.
roast *v* sneyster.
rob *v* reive.
robber *n* reiver, briganer.
robbery *n* rapt.
robin *n* reid Rab.
robust *adj* stoot, hail.
rock[1] *n* craig.
rock[2] *v* shoogle, coggle.
rocket *n* racket.
rocky *adj* stanie.
rod *n* wand.

roe *n* rae, rawn.
rogue *n* dyvour.
roguish *adj* pawky.
roisterous *adj* rantin.
roll *n* rowe; bap (bread). • *v* rowe, pirl.
rollicking *adj* tousie.
romp *n*/*v* rant.
romping *adj* hempie.
roof *n* reef, ruif.
rook *n* craw, corbie.
rookery *n* craw widdie.
room *n* en, chaumer.
roomy *adj* sonsie.
roost *n* reest.
root *n* ruit. • *v* howk.
rope *n*/*v* raip.
rose *n* breer.
rosehip *n* dog-hip.
rot *v* daise.
rotate *v* birl.
rotten *adj* daised.
rough *adj* roch, ruch.
roughen *v* faize, hack.
round *adj* roon.
rouse *v* roose, roust.
rout[1] *n* scatterment.
rout[2] *v* skail.
route *n* road.
routine *adj* ornar.
rove *v* raik.
rover *n* traik, land-louper.
roving *adj* rinaboot.
row[1] *n* raw (line).
row[2] *n* threap, stushie (quarrel). • *v* threap.
row[3] *v* rowe (a boat).
rowan *n* roden tree.
rowdy *adj* tousie.
royalty *n* lordship.
rub *n*/*v* dicht, screenge.
rubber *n* guttie.
rubbish *n* rubbage, clamjamphry, troke.
• *interj* blethers!
rubbish dump *n* coup.
ructions *n* stushie, rammie.

rude *adj* ill-mou'd, indiscreet.
rudely *adv* ramstam.
rue *v* forthink.
ruffian *n* rochian, keelie, ned.
ruffle *n* bord. • *v* runkle.
ruffled *adj* touslie, rouchled.
rug *n* hap.
rugged *adj* umbersorrow.
ruin *n* rummle, wrack. • *v* durk, wrack.
ruination *n* ruinage.
ruined *adj* shent, awa wi it.
rule *v* ring.
rumble *n*/*v* rummle, dunner.
rummage *v* ruit, howk; reesle throu.
rummaging *adj* kirn.
rumour *n* clatter. • *v* clash, clack.
rump *n* curpin.
rumple *n* lirk, bumfle. • *v* lirk, touse.
rumpled *adj* bumfelt.
rump-steak *n* Pope's eye, heuk-bone.
rumpus *n* splore.
run *n* rin (water), race. • *v* rin, leg; **run away** tak leg.
runabout *n* rinaboot.
runaway *n* fugie.
rung *n* spar.
runnel *n* trink.
runner *n* slipe.
runny *adj* snotterie.
runt *n* titlin, rag.
rupture *v* ripter, ripture.
ruptured *adj* rimbursin.
rural *adj* landward.
ruse *n* wimple.
rush *n* rash, scoor. • *v* stour; **rush about** widder.
rust *n*/*v* roost.
rustic *adj* landward. • *n* jock, teuchter.
rustle *n*/*v* reesle, souch.
rustling *adj* reishlin.
rusty *adj* roostie.
rut *n* rat, trink.
rutted *adj* trinket.
ruthless *adj* fell.

S

sack[1] *n* seck.
sack[2] *v* spulyie (plunder).

sackcloth *n* harn.
sacrament *n* the table.

sad *adj* sod, dowie.
saddle *n/v* saidle.
saddler *n* saidler.
sadly *adv* dowielie.
sadness *n* sair, sorra.
safe *adj* sauf.
safe-conduct *n* conduck.
safety *n* sauftie.
sag *v* swag.
sagacious *adj* wicelik.
sagacity *n* wit.
sagging *adj* dwamfle.
sailor *n* tarry-breaks.
saint *n* saunt.
saintly *adj* sauntlie.
salary *n* sellarie.
sale *n* roup.
saliva *n* slavers.
salivate *v* slerp.
sallow *adj* din.
salmon *n* saumon, fish.
salt *n* saut.
salt-cellar *n* saut dish.
salt water *n* saut bree.
salty *adj* sautie.
salve *n* saw.
salver *n* server.
same *adj* samen.
sample *n* preein. • *v* pruive.
sanctimonious person *n* Holy Willie.
sanctimonious people *n* the unco guid.
sanction *v* chap.
sanctuary *n* bield, haud.
sand *n* san.
sand-eel *n* sanle.
sandman *n* Willie Winkie.
sand-martin *n* sannie-swallow.
sandpiper *n* san laverock.
sandpit *n* bunker.
sandstone *n* brie-stane.
sandwich *n* piece.
sandy *adj* sannie.
sane *adj* wicelik.
sanity *n* judgement, wit.
sapwood *n* sap-spail.
sarcasm *n* afftakin.
sarcastic *adj* snell.
sardonic *adj* mockrif.
sash *n* chess.
Satan *n* Sawtan

sate *v* ser.
satiate *v* ser, sta.
satisfactory *adj* no bad.
satisfied *adj* fittit.
satisfy *v* pleesure.
satisfying *adj* hertsome.
saturate *v* drook.
Saturday *n* Seturday.
sauce *n* gravy.
saucer *n* flat.
saucy *adj* pauchtie.
saunter *v* dander.
sausages *npl* links.
savage *adj* gurlie.
save *v* sauf, gaither.
savings *n* hainins.
savour *v* saur.
savoury *adj* gustie.
saw *v* risp.
sawdust *n* sawins.
say *v* moot.
saying *n* say.
scab *n* scur.
scabbed *adj* scabbit.
scabby *adj* scawt.
scabious *n* curl-doddle.
scaffolding *n* sentrices.
scald *v* scaud.
scalding *adj* plot het. • *n* scaudin.
scale *n* shall, skelf.
scales *npl* wechts.
scallop *n* clam.
scallywag *n* loon, nickum.
scalp *n* scaup.
scalpel *n* lance.
scamp *n* skellum, loon..
scamper *v* skleter.
scan *v* scance.
scandal *n* souch.
scandalmonger *n* clatterer.
scandalmongering *n* speak.
scandalous *adj* michtie.
scant *adj* scrimp.
scantily *adv* jimp.
scantiness *n* scrimpness.
scanty *adj* scrimpit.
scapegoat *n* burry man.
scar *n/v* scaur.
scarred *adj* pockarrd.
scarce *adj* scrimp.
scarcely *adv* scarcelins.

scarcity *n* scant.
scare *v* scar, fleg, gliff.
scarecrow *n* bogle, tattie-bogle.
scared *adj* fleggit.
scarf *n* gravat, cosie.
scarlet fever *n* rush-fivver.
scatter *v* splatter, skail.
scatterbrain *n* scatterwit.
scatterbrained *adj* scatterwittit.
scattering *adj* skail.
scavenge *v* scunge.
scent *v* snoke.
scheme *n* ploy. • *v* schame.
scheming *adj* lang-drauchit.
scholarship *n* bursary.
school *n* scuil.
schoolchild *n* scuil bairn.
scissors *npl* chizors.
scoff *n* afftak. • *v* geck at.
scold *n/v* scaul.
scolding *adj* scauling.
scoop *n/v* scuip.
scope *n* scouth.
scorch *v* scowder, birsle.
score *n/v* rit.
scorn *n* laith. • *v* lichtlie.
scornful *adj* mockrif.
scot-free *adj* hailscart.
scoundrel *n* scoonrel.
scour *v* scoor.
scourer *n* scrub.
scouring *adj* scoor.
scourge *v* screenge.
scowl *n/v* scool, glunsh.
scowling *adj* gowlie.
scrabble *v* scraible.
scraggy *adj* mean, ill-thriven.
scramble *n/v* scrammle.
scrap *n* perlicket.
scrape *n/v* scrap, rit.
scraper *n* scartle.
scrapings *npl* scartlins.
scraps *npl* orrals.
scratch *n/v* scrat, scart.
scrawl *n* scrape o the pen.
scream *n/v* skirl, skelloch.
screaming *adj* yellyhooin.
scree *n* sclenters.
screech *n/v* skreek, scrauch.
screeching *adj* scrauchin.
screen *n* sconce. • *v* scug.

screw *n/v* feeze.
scribble *n/v* scart.
scribbler *n* scriever.
scrimp *v* jimp.
script *n* scrieve.
scripture *n* scripter.
scrofula *n* the cruels.
scrotum *n* courage-bag.
scrounge *v* scroonge.
scrounger *n* scunge.
scrounging *adj* scran, skech.
scrub *n* scrogs. • *v* screenge.
scrubbing brush *n* rubber.
scruff *n* cuff, tattie bogle.
scruffy *adj* scawt, scoorie, schemie.
scruple *v* stickle.
scrupulous *adj* perneurious.
scrutinise *v* sicht.
scrutiny *n* sicht.
scud *v* whid.
scuff *n/v* skliff.
scuffle *n* rammie. • *v* tullyie.
scullion *n* scodgie.
scum *n* quinkins, bratts.
scurf *n* scruif.
scurry *n* fudder. • *v* skelter.
scutter *v* skelter.
scuttle *v* skelter.
scythe *n* hey-sned. • *v* maw.
sea *n* sey, tide.
sea anemone *n* pap.
sea-eagle *n* earn.
sea fog *n* haar.
seagull *n* maw.
seal *n* signet, selkie, selch.
seam *n* saim.
seaman *n* killick.
sea-pink *n* sey-daisy.
seaport *n* seytoon.
search *n/v* fork; **search for** *v* seek.
seashore *n* ebb.
seaside *n* saut-watter.
season *n/v* saison.
seasoning *n* kitchen.
seat *n* sate. • *v* set.
sea-thrift *n* sey-daisy.
sea urchin *n* hairy hutcheon.
seaweed *n* tangle.
second *n* saicant.
second-hand *adj* second-handit.
secret *adj/n* saicret.

secrecy *n* hidin.
secretly *adv* hidlins.
sect *n* profession.
section *n* lith.
secure *adj/v* sicker.
securely *adv* sicker.
security *n* caution, wad.
sedate *adj* douce.
sedge *n* seg.
sedge-warbler *n* Scotch nightingale.
sedgy *adj* seggie.
sediment *n* gruns.
seduce *v* mistryst.
see *v* sei.
seed-potato *n* set.
seed-time *n* sawin time.
seedy *adj* bauch.
seek *v* sik.
seemly *adj* wicelik, menseful.
seep *v* sook.
seer *n* spaeman, spaewife.
seesaw *n* shoggie-shoo.
seethe *v* hotter.
seething *adj* hoatchin.
seething mass *n* hotter.
segment *n* leaf, lith.
seize *v* saize.
seizure *n* poinding, straik.
seldom *adv* seendil.
select *v* seleck, wale.
selection *n* walin.
self *n* sel, ainsel.
self-assured *adj* poochle.
self-confident *adj* poochle.
self-conscious *adj* strange.
self-important *adj* pauchtie, pensie.
self-important person *n* wha but he.
self-indulgent *adj* free-living.
selfish *adj* sellie.
selfishness *n* sellie.
self-righteous person *n* the unco guid.
selfsame *adj* self an same.
self-satisfied *adj* croose.
self-willed *adj* thrawn.
sell *v* roup.
semi-detached *adj* hauf.
send *v* sen, set; **send off** set aff; **send out** ootpit.
senile *adj* dottelt.
sensation *n* fushion, gliff.
sense *n* mense, sinse.

senseless *adj* glaikit.
sensible *adj* mensefu.
sensibly *adv* wicelik.
sensitive *adj* kittle.
sentence *n* doom.
sentiment *n* souch.
separate *adj/v* saiprit; **separate from** *v* spean fae.
separately *adv* sindry.
septic *adj* atterie.
serene *adj* at yersel.
sergeant *n* sairgint.
sermon *n* preachin.
servant *n* servan.
servants *npl* fowk.
serve *v* ser, lift.
service *n* onwaiting, preachin.
serviette *n* servit.
servile *adj* sleekit.
serving *adj* service.
serving spoon *n* divider.
set¹ *n* pair.
set² *v* mak, jeel; **set aside** pit by; **set down** plunk; **set off, set out** set awa, tak the road; **set to** yoke tae; **set up** stell; **set upon** set tae.
setback *n* thraw.
settle *v* sattle.
settlement *n* doonset.
set-to *n* fa-tae.
seven *adj/n* saiven, seeven.
seventeenth *adj* seeventeen.
seventh *adj* seevent.
seventy *adj/n* seeventie.
sever *v* saiprit, pairt.
several *adj* severals.
severe *adj* snell, fell, dour.
severely *adv* snell.
sew *v* shew.
sewing *n* shewin.
sewing kit *n* hussie.
sewer *n* jaw-hole.
sex *n* tail-toddle, houghmagandie. • *v* sicht.
sexually excited *adj* radgie.
sexton *n* beadle.
shabby *adj* scuffie, ill-faured.
shabby person *n* ticket.
shackle *n/v* sheckle.
shade *n* scug, mention. • *v* sky.
shadow *n/v* shedda.

shady *adj* leesome.
shaft *n* tram, shank.
shaggy *adj* tautit.
shake *n/v* shak; **shake hands** *v* chap hauns; **shake off** shachle aff; **shake up** cadge.
shaking *adj* hotter.
shaky *adj* shooglie.
shall *v* will.
shallow *adj/n* shalla.
sham *adj* leesome. • *n* pit-on. • *v* fraik.
shamble *v* shachle.
shambles *n* reel-rall, Paddy's mairket.
shamefaced *adj* hingin-luggit.
shameful *adj* michtie.
shameless *adj* braisant.
shape *n* set. • *v* coll.
shapeless *adj* shachlin.
share *n* dale. • *v* pairt; **share equally** gae halfers.
shark *n* sherk.
sharp *adj* shairp.
sharp-eared *adj* gleg-luggit.
sharpen *v* shairpen.
sharpening *n* shairp.
sharp-eyed *adj* gleg-eed.
sharp-featured *adj* peesie-weesie.
sharply *adv* shairplie.
sharpness *n* glegness.
sharp-nosed *adj* nairra-nebbit.
sharp-pointed *adj* gleg.
sharp-tongued *adj* snippie.
shatter *v* chatter.
shave *v* skive.
shavings *npl* spailins.
shawl *n* hap.
she *pron* shae.
sheaf *n* shaif.
shear *v* share.
shebeen *n* bothan.
shed[1] *n* puidge.
shed[2] *v* cast.
sheep *n* yowe, tup.
sheepdog *n* collie.
sheep-flock *n* hirsel.
sheepfold *n* fauld.
sheepish *adj* bauch.
sheepmark *n* kenmairk.
sheep-shearing *n* clippin.
sheep-shears *n* gangs, shears.
sheepskin *n* fell.

sheep-tick *n* taid.
sheep track *n* rodding.
sheer *adj* evendoon.
sheldrake *n* burrow duck.
shelf *n* skelf, bink.
shell *n/v* shall.
shelter *n* howf, shalter. • *v* scug, beild.
sheltered *adj* lown, hiddlie.
shelving *adj* shelvie.
shepherd *n* herd.
shepherd's crook *n* crummock, nibbie.
shepherd's purse *n* leddy's purse.
sheriff *n* shirrif.
shield *n* shiel.
shift *n* yokin. • *v* mudge.
shiftless *adj* haiveless.
shifty *adj* loopie.
shilling *n* shullin.
shilly-shally *v* waffle.
shimmer *n* oam. • *v* skimmer.
shin *v* sclim.
shine *n* gleet, glent. • *v* scance, sheen.
shingle *n* chingle.
shiny *adj* glancie.
ship *n* bait.
shipwreck *n* wrack.
shirk *v* slope.
shirker *n* sloper.
shirt *n* sark.
shiver *n* grue. • *v* chitter.
shivery *adj* oorie.
shoal *n* drave, scuil.
shock *n* gliff, conflummix, hassock. • *v* conflummix, stammygaster.
shocking *adj* awfu.
shoddy *adj* scuffie.
shoe *n/v* shae, shee.
shoelace *n* shae pint.
shoemaker *n* souter, cordiner.
shoemaking *n* souterin.
shoot *n* imp, hempe. • *v* shuit, pap; **shoot up** rapple.
shooting star *n* fire-flacht.
shop *n* shap.
shop assistant *n* coonter-lowper.
shopkeeper *n* merchant.
shopping *n* messages.
shore[1] *n* strand, stron.
shore[2] *v* stuit (support).
short *adj* jimpit.
shortage *n* shortcome.

shorten *v* dock.
shortbread *n* shortie.
short cut *n* near cut.
shortly *adv* shortlins.
short person *n* dottle.
short-tailed *adj* fuddie.
short-tempered *adj* fuffie, short i' the trot.
short-winded *adj* pechie.
shot *n* tooch.
shoulder *n* shouder, spaul.
shoulder bone *n* spaul.
shoulder joint *n* shouder heid.
shout *n* roust, goller. • *v* goller, cry.
shove *n* jundie. • *v* shuve.
shovel *n/v* shuil.
show *n/v* shaw; **show off** *v* pross.
showy *adj* fantoosh.
shower *n* shour, scoor.
showery *adj* plowterie.
shred *n* shreed.
shreds *npl* flitters.
shrew *n* screw, shirrow.
shrewd *adj* canny, pawky.
shrewdness *n* rumgumption.
shriek *n/v* skirl.
shrill *adj* snell.
shrimp *n* screw.
shrink *v* crine, skrunkle.
shrink back *v* scunner.
shrivel *v* crine, nither.
shrivelled *adj* skrunkit, wizzent.
shroud *n* shrood.
Shrove Tuesday *n* festern's een.
shrub *n* buss.
shrug *n* thring, fidge. • *v* hirsel.
shrunken *adj* picket.
shudder *n/v* shither, shidder.
shuffle *n/v* scush. • *v* shiffle.
shuffling walk *n* shachle.
shun *v* evite.
shut *v* steek, sneck.
shutters *npl* shuts.
shuttle *n* spuil.
shut up *v* parrock, haud yer wheesht.
shy *adj* freff, ergh. • *v* skeich, funk.
shy away *v* scar.
sickbed *n* carebed.
sicken *v* scunner.
sickle *n* Rob Sorby.
sickly *adj* unweel, peely-wallie.

sickly-looking *adj* fauchie.
sickness *n* unweelness.
side *n* cheek.
side by side *adj* fit for fit.
sidelock *n* haffet.
sidelong *adj* sidelins.
sidesaddle *n* side legs.
sideways *adj* sidieweys.
sidle *v* siddle.
sift *v* bout, search.
sigh *n/v* sich.
sight *n* sicht.
sightless *adj* sichtless.
signify *v* beir.
silence *n* lown. • *v* wheesht.
silicosis *n* stourie lungs.
sill *n* sole.
silly *adj* daft, sully.
silly person *n* gomerel, sodie-heid.
silly talk *n* jibber.
silt *n* sleek.
silver *adj/n/v* siller.
silver coins *n* white siller.
silvery *adj* lyart.
similar *adj* siclik.
similarly *adv* siclik.
simmer *v* hotter, sotter.
simper *v* smudge.
simple *adj* semple, blate, hamelt.
simple-minded *adj* wantin, nae richt.
simpleton *n* daftie, gowk.
simply *adv* een.
simulate *v* mak on.
simulated *adj* made on.
since *adv/conj* sin, syne.
sincere *adj* aefauld.
sinew *n* sinnen.
sing *v* tweetle.
singe *n/v* sing.
single *adj* aesome, free.
single-minded *adj* aefauld.
singsong *n* horoyally.
singular *adj* parteeclar.
sinister *adj* weirdlie.
sinister-looking person *n* huidie craw.
sink *n* jaw-box. • *v* lair.
sip *v* sirple.
siren *n* whustle.
sissy *n* Jessie.
sister *n* tittie.
sister-in-law *n* guid-sister.

sit *v* hunker, dowp doon.
sit-down *n* set-doon.
site *n* stance, larach, pairt.
sitting *n* doon-sittin.
sitting room *n* room.
situation *n* pouster.
six *adj/n* sax.
sixpence *n* saxpence.
sixteen *adj/n* saxteen.
sixteenth *adj* saxteent.
sixth *adj* saxt.
sixty *adj/n* saxtie.
size *n* bouk.
sizeable *adj* roon.
skate *n/v* skeet, sketch.
skater *n* skeetcher.
skein *n* hank.
skeleton *n* skelet, rickle o banes.
sketchy *adj* stake an rice.
skewer *n* speet.
skid *n/v* skite.
skilful *adj* skeelie, knackie.
skill *n* skeel.
skim *v* ream, scum.
skimmed milk *n* scum milk.
skin *n* huil. • *v* scruif.
skinflint *n* nipscart.
skinny *adj* skrank, shilpit.
skinny person *n* skinnymalink.
skip *n* link. • *v* skiff.
skip along *v* skelp.
skipper *n* mannie.
skipping rope *n* jumpin raip.
skirmish *n/v* skrimmish.
skirt *n* coat.
skirting board *n* skiftin.
skittish *adj* flisky.
skittles *npl* kyles.
skive *v* dog.
skua *n* allan, bonxie.
skulk *v* skook.
skulking person *n* skook.
skull *n* pan, powe.
sky *n* lift.
skylark *n* laverock.
slab *n* skelp, leck.
slack *adj* haingle. • *v* jauk.
slacker *n* fouter.
slackening *n* slack.
slag *n* danders.
slag-heap *n* bing.

slake *v* slocken.
slam *v* clash.
slander *n* ill-tongue. • *v* misca.
slandering *adj* ill-tonguit.
slanderous *adj* ill-speakin.
slant *n/v* sklent.
slanting *adj* skellie.
slap *n/v* skelp.
slapdash *adj* rummlin. • *adv* ramstam.
slash *n* screed. • *v* hash, chib.
slat *n* rin.
slate *n/v* sclate.
slattern *n* laidron.
slatternly *adj* slutterie.
slaughter *n/v* slauchter.
slaughterhouse *n* butch-hoose.
slave *n* sclave.
slaver *v* slabber.
slay *v* en.
sledge *n* sled.
sleek *adj* sleekit, slaip.
sleep *n* sowff. • *v* snoozle.
sleepless *adj* wakrif.
sleepy *adj* sleeperie.
sleight *n* slicht.
slender *adj* sclinner.
slender person *n* spirlie.
slice *n* sleesh, shave. • *v* shave; **slice open** speld.
slick *adj* gleg.
slide *n* sly. • *v* scurr, skite.
slight[1] *adj* slicht.
slight[2] *n* heelie. • *v* lichtlie.
slightly *adv* a wee.
slim *adj* slamp.
slime *n* goor, glaur.
slimy *adj* glittie.
sling *v* thraw.
slink *v* sleek.
slip *n* slidder. • *v* sklyte.
slip away *v* skice.
slip-knot *n* rin-knot.
slip past *v* glent.
slipperiness *n* slipper, glaur.
slippery *adj* slippie.
slipshod *adj* hashie.
slipper *n* baffie, rovie.
slit *n* fent, spare. • *v* slite.
slither *n/v* sclidder.
sliver *n* slive.
slobber *n/v* slubber, slabber.

slobberer *n* slabber.
slobbering *adj* blibberin.
sloe *n* slae.
slop *n* slutter. • *v* skiddle.
slope *n* sklent, brae. • *v* sklent.
sloping *adj* sidelins.
slops *n* slaister.
sloppy *adj* slitterie.
sloppy food *n* slubber.
slosh *v* skiddle.
sloth *n* sweirtie.
slothful *adj* sweirt.
slough *n/v* sloch.
slovenly *adj* sclafferin.
slovenly person *n* habble, guddle.
slow *adj* slaw, blate.
slow down *v* ca canny.
slowly *adv* huilie.
slow-witted *adj* donnert.
slow-witted person *n* mowdiewort.
slow-worm *n* slae.
sludge *n* slutch.
slug *n* snail.
sluggard *n* sclidder.
sluggish *adj* thowless.
sluice *n* sloosh.
slumber *n* sowff.
slum-dweller *n* keelie.
slump *v* fa.
slur *n* smitch.
slush *n* slash.
slushy *adj* slashie.
slut *n* besom, clatch.
sluttish *adj* slutterie.
sly *adj* slee.
slyly *adv* slee.
smack *n/v* skelp.
small *adj* wee, sma.
small amount *n* sma.
small change *n* smas.
smallholding *n* croft.
small piece *n* bittie, bittock.
small person *n* smowt.
smart *adj* smairt. • *v* nip.
smash *n* stramash. • *v* smatter.
smear *n* sclatch. • *v* slairy.
smell *n* waff, guff. • *v* snoke.
smelly *adj* minging.
smelt *n* spirling.
smile *n/v* smirk.
smirk *n/v* smirtle.

smith *n* bruntie, gow.
smithereens *npl* shivereens.
smithy *n* smiddy.
smock *n* carsackie, wrap.
smoke *n* reek, smeek. • *v* smeek, smuik.
smoke-covered *adj* reekit.
smoke-cured *adj* reekit.
smoke-filled *adj* reekie.
smoke-stained *adj* smeekit.
smoky *adj* smeekie.
smooth *adj* smuith. • **smooth down** *v* daik; **smooth out** stracht; **smooth over** glaze.
smoothly *adj/v* smuithlie.
smoothness *n* sneith.
smooth-tongued *adj* sleekit, slidderie.
smother *v* smoor, smudder.
smoulder *v* smooder.
smudge *n* smit. • *v* slair.
smug *adj* croose.
smuggling *n* free trade.
smuggling boat *n* bucker.
smut *n* smit.
smutty *adj* brookie, groff.
snack *n* piece, snap.
snag *v* thraw.
snail-shell *n* buckie.
snap *n/v* knack, snack.
snapdragon *n* grannie's mutch.
snare *n/v* girn.
snarl *n* girn. • *v* snag.
snatch *n* glamp. • *v* sneck; **snatch at** glaum at; **snatch away** wheech awa; **snatch up** clink up.
sneak *n* hinkum. • *v* snaik.
sneaking *adj* snoovin.
sneer *n* sneist. • *v* girn.
sneering *adj* sneistie.
sneeze *n* neeze. • *v* sneesh.
sniff *n* snift. • *v* snifter.
snigger *n/v* snicher.
snip *v* sneg, nick.
snipe *n* heather-bleater.
snob *n* cockapentie.
snobbish *adj* pridefu.
snooze *n/v* dover, gloss.
snore *n* snocher. • *v* snifter.
snort *n/v* snirt, snirk.
snot *n* snotter.
snotty *adj* snotterie.
snout *n* snoot.

snow *n/v* snaw.
snow bunting *n* snawfleck.
snow-covered *adj* snawsel.
snowdrift *n* wreath, blin smoor.
snowfall *n* onfa.
snowflake *n* flichan.
snowstorm *n* yowdendrift, stour.
snowy *adj* snawie.
snub *n* chaw. • *v* saut.
snuff[1] *n* sneesh.
snuff[2] *v* snite.
snuffbox *n* sneeshin-mill.
snuffle *v* snifter.
snug *adj* snod, cosh.
snuggle *v* coorie; **snuggle up** *v* coorie in.
so *adv* sic, sae.
soak *v* drook; **soak through** seek throu.
soaked *adj* drookit.
soaking *adj* plashin. • *n* dookin.
soap *n/v* saip.
soapsuds *npl* sapples.
soapy *adj* saipie.
soar *v* tove.
sob *n/v* sab.
sober *adj* fresh, douce.
sociable *adj* sonsie, couthy.
sock *n* fittock.
socket *n* hose.
sod *n* clod, divot.
soda *n* sodie.
sodden *adj* steepit.
soft *adj* saft, feel.
soften *v* saften.
softly *adv* saftly.
soggy *adj* sotterie.
soil[1] *n* sile, muild.
soil[2] *v* sile, suddle.
soiled *adj* brookit, dirten.
solder *v* sowder.
soldier *n* sodger, kiltie.
sole[1] *adj* ae.
sole[2] *n* howe o the fit, tobacco fleuk.
solely *adj* allenarly.
solicit *v* peuther.
solicitor *n* writer, agent.
solicitous *adj* helplie.
solid *adj* sonsie
solitary *adj* aesome, lane.
solve *v* redd.
sombre *adj* mirksome.

some *adj* fyow.
somehow *adv* someway.
somersault *n* simmerset.
something *pron* sumhin.
sometimes *adv* whiles.
somewhat *adv* some.
somewhere *adv* someplace.
somnolent *adj* sleeperie.
son *n* sin, lad.
son-in-law *n* guidson.
song *n* sang.
song festival *n* sangshaw.
song thrush *n* throstle, mavis.
soon *adv* suin.
sooner or later *adv* suin or syne.
soot *n* suit.
soothe *v* soother.
soothsayer *n* spaeman, spaewife.
sop *v* drook.
soppy *adj* sappie.
sops *npl* saps.
sorcerer *n* warlock.
sorceress *n* wutch.
sore *adj/n* sair.
sorely *adv* sairlie.
soreness *n* sairness.
sorrel *n* soorock.
sorrow *n* sair, sorra.
sorrowful *adj* sairie, sorraful.
sorry *adj* sairie, bauch.
sort *n* keind. • *v* redd.
soul *n* saul.
sound *adj* soon. • *n* soon, kyle.
soup *n* bree.
soup plate *n* deep plate.
sour *adj* shilpit, soor.
sour grapes *npl* soor plooms.
sour look *n* glumsh.
sour-looking *adj* soor-faced, glumsh.
souse *v* sloonge.
south *n* sooth.
southern *adj* soothlan.
southwards *adv* suddart.
souvenir *n* minding.
sow[1] *n* soo.
sow[2] *v* saw.
space *n* waygate, piece.
spade *n* spaad.
span *n/v* spang.
spank *v* skelp.
spanking *n* skelpin.

spar *n* strunt.
spare *adj* orra.
spare time *n* by-time.
sparing *adj* jimp.
sparingly *adv* jimp.
spark *n/v* sperk, gleid.
sparkle *n/v* glent.
sparrow *n* sparra, sprug.
spasm *n* drowe.
spatter *v* splatter.
spavin *n* spavie.
spawn *n/v* redd.
spawning ground *n* redd.
speak *v* spek; **speak of** mint at; **speak one's mind** say awa; **speak out** set up yer gab.
spear *n/v* leister.
special *adj* by-ornar.
specially *adv* aince-eeran.
species *n* speshie.
specify *v* condescend on.
specimen *n* sey.
specious *adj* fair-farran.
speck *n* smitch.
speckle *n/v* spreckle.
speckled *adj* spreckelt.
spectacles *npl* spentacles.
spectre *n* doolie.
speculate *v* ettle, jalouse.
speech *n* speak, say, leid.
speechless *adj* dumfoonert.
speed *n* raik. • *v* smack.
speedily *adv* swith.
speedwell *n* cat's een.
speedy *adj* gleg.
spell *n* speel, cantrip.
spellbind *v* daumer.
spend *v* ware.
spendthrift *n* spendrif.
spent *adj* matit.
sperm *n* melt.
spew *v* boak.
spice *v* kitchen.
spider *n* speeder, webster.
spider's web *n* moose wab.
spigot *n* spile.
spike *n* stug. • *v* pike.
spiked *adj* pikie.
spiky *adj* stobbie.
spill *v* skail.
spin *v* birl.

spindle *n* spinnle.
spindly *adj* spirlie.
spindrift *n* speendrif.
spine *n* backsprent, rig.
spinning wheel *n* spinnie.
spinster *n* maiden.
spirit *n* speerit, wicht, smeddum.
spirited *adj* speeritie, spankie.
spiritless *adj* fushionless.
spirits *n* aquavitae.
spit[1] *n* speet.
spit[2] *n* spittle • *v* slerp.
spite *v* maugre.
spiteful *adj* ill-willie.
spiteful person *n* ettercap.
spittle *n* spits.
splash *n* plash, jaup. • *v* splairge, plout; **splash about** plouter.
splashy *adj* jaupie.
splay *v* skew.
splay foot *n* splash fit.
splay footed *adj* skew-fittit.
splay-footed person *n* kep-a-gush.
spleen *n* melt.
splendid *adj* braw.
splendour *n* brawness.
splice *v* wap, skair.
splint *n/v* spelk.
splinter *n* splinder, skelf, spelk. • *v* spelk, sklinter.
split *adj* gelled. • *v* spleet.
split peas *npl* spilkins.
splodge *n* splatch.
splotch *n* splatch.
splutter *n/v* splairge.
spluttering *adj* splairgin.
spoil *n* spulyie. • *v* spile.
spoilt *adj* daised.
spoilt child *n* sookie.
spoke *n* spaik.
spoked *adj* spaikit.
spokesman *n* preses.
sponge *n* spoonge. • *v* cadge.
sponger *n* skech.
spongy *adj* fozie.
spook *n* ghaist.
spool *n* spuile.
spoon *n* spuin.
spoonful *adj* spuinful.
sport *n* play. • *v* ramp, daff.
sportsman's assistant *n* ghillie.

spot *n* spat, plook.
spotted *adj* spreckelt.
spouse *n* marrow.
spout *n/v* spoot.
sprain *n/v* staive, rax.
sprat *n* garvie.
sprawl *v* sprachle.
spray *n* stour. • *v* spairge.
spread *n/v* spreed; **spread about** skail; **spread gossip** clish; **spread out** speld.
spreadeagle *v* spelder.
spree *n* splore, rammle.
sprig *n* rice.
sprightly *adj* spree.
spring *n* spoot, voar. • *v* lowp, sten; **spring forward** breist; **spring up** breist.
spring onion *n* sybie.
sprinkle *v* splatter.
sprinkler *n* skoosher.
sprinkling *adj* splatter.
sprint *v* sprunt.
sprite *n* brownie.
sprout *n/v* sproot.
spruce[1] *adj/v* sproosh.
spruce[2] *n* sprush.
spry *adj* spree.
spume *n* seagust.
spur *n* brod.
spurious *adj* fause.
spurn *v* cast oot.
spurt *n* scoot, skoosh. • *v* jaw, jilp.
sputter *v* sotter.
spyglass *n* prospect.
squabble *n* stushie. • *v* scash.
squabbling *n* nip-lug.
squalid *adj* fousome.
squall[1] *n* skelp (blast of wind).
squall[2] *v* squaik.
squally *adj* scourie.
squander *v* squatter.
square *adj* squerr. • *v* quader.
squash *v* grush, brizz.
squat *adj* setterel. • *v* hunker, coorie hunker.
squawk *n/v* squaik.
squeak *n/v* squaik.
squeal *n/v* squile.
squeamish *adj* waumish.
squeeze *n* chirt. • *v* knuse.
squelch *v* chork, plodge.
squelching *adj* plashin.

squib *n* squeeb.
squid *n* ink-fish.
squint *n* gley, skelly. • *v* skew, sklent.
squint-eyed *adj* skelly-eed.
squirm *v* wimple.
squirt *n/v* scoot.
stab *n/v* stug.
stable[1] *n* travise.
stable[2] *adj* sicker.
stably *adv* stieve.
stack *n/v* steck.
stack up *v* ruck.
stackyard *n* cornyaird.
staff *n* steek.
stagger *n/v* stoit.
stagnant *adj* staignant.
stagnant pool *n* stank.
staid *adj* douce.
stain *n/v* tash, smad.
staircase *n* stair.
stairs *n* stair.
stake *n* stob, stunk.
stale *adj* haskie.
stalk[1] *n* shank, pen.
stalk[2] *v* steg, dilp.
stalks *npl* shaws.
stall *n* sta, stan.
stallion *n* staig.
stalwart *adj* buirdly.
stamina *n* strenth.
stammer *n/v* stut, stot.
stammerer *n* manter.
stamp *n/v* stramp, tramp.
stampede *v* prick.
stanch *v* stainch,
stanchion *n* staincheon.
stand *n/v* stan, staun; **stand up** win up.
standard *n* stannert.
standard-bearer *n* cornet.
staple *n* stapple.
star *n* starn, blinker.
starboard *adj* farran.
starch *n* stairch. • *v* stiffen.
stare *n* gowp. • *v* glower.
starfish *n* scoskie.
starlight *n* starnlicht.
starry *adj* starnie.
stark *adj* sterk.
starling *n* stirlin.
start *n/v* stert.
startle *v* start.

starve *v* sterve.
starved *adj* hungert.
starved-looking *adj* shilpit.
state *n* tift, set.
statement *n* speak.
station *n/v* stance.
station master *n* station agent.
stature *n* lenth.
staunch *adj* stench.
staunchly *adv* stieve.
stave *n* stap. • *v* brak.
stay *n/v* bide.
steadfast *adj* sicker.
steady *adj* sicker, canny.
steak *n* collop.
steal *v* nip, sneck.
stealthily *adv* stowlins.
stealthy *adj* sneck-drawing.
steam *n* stame. • *v* stove.
steel *n* fleerish.
steelyard *n* steel.
steep[1] *adj* brent, stey.
steep[2] *v* drook, sapple.
steer[1] *v* airt.
steer[2] *n* stirk.
steersman *n* lodesman.
stem *n* pen, shank.
stench *n* guff, stew.
step *n/v* stap, staup.
step-child *n* stap-bairn.
step-father *n* stap-faither.
step-mother *n* stap-mither.
stepping-stone *n* stappin-stane.
stern[1] *adj* raucle, dour.
stern[2] *n* starn.
sternly *adv* fell.
stew *n/v* stove.
steward *n* factor.
stewed *adj* sitten.
stick *n/v* steek; **stick up** *v* stert.
stickleback *n* banstickle.
sticky *adj* claggy.
stiff *adj* stieve, stechie.
stiffly *adv* stieve.
stifle *v* smoor.
stifling *adj* smochie.
stigma *n* tash.
still[1] *adj* lown, quate. • *adv* aye, yet (continue to).
still[2] *n* stell.
stilletto heel *n* peerie heel.

stillness *n* lithe.
stilt *n* stult.
stimulation *n* upsteerin.
stimulus *n* kittle.
sting *n/v* stang.
stingy *adj* nippit, ticht.
stink *n/v* stew.
stinking *adj* minging.
stint[1] *n* yokin.
stint[2] *v* stent.
stir *n/v* steer; **stir up** *v* taisle, set up; **stir round** to whummle.
stirrup *n* strip.
stirrup-cup *n* deoch-an-dorrus.
stitch *n/v* steek, stick.
stoat *n* whitrat.
stock *n* etion, bree, stockin. • *v* hain, fordel.
stockade *n* peel.
stocking *n* moggan.
stocky *adj* short-set.
stomach *n* waim.
stomach ache *n* bellythraw.
stomach-rumble *n* curmurrin.
stone *n* stane, chucky, paip. • *v* stane.
stonebreaker *n* stane-knapper.
stonechat *n* chack.
stonemason *n* dorbie.
stone's throw *n* stane-clod.
stony *adj* stanie.
stool *n* stuil.
stoop *n* lootch. • *v* coorie.
stop *n/v* stap; **stop for a moment** *v* haud a wee; **stop in the middle** stick; **stop short** reest; **stop up** clag.
stoppage *n* stick.
stopper *n* prop.
store *n* fordel. • *v* kist.
storekeeper *n* Jenny a' thing, Johnny a' thing.
storey *n* flat.
storm *n* weather. • *v* heckle.
storm about *v* rammish.
stormy *adj* weatherful.
story *n* say, crack.
storyteller *n* upmakar, seannachie.
stout *adj* stoot.
stout-hearted *adj* stoot-hertit.
stow *v* stowe.
straddle *v* striddle.
straggle *v* traik.

straight *adj/adv/n* stracht.
straight ahead *adv* enweys.
straight away *adv* stracht.
straight down *adv* evendoon.
straighten *v* stracht.
straightforward *adj* stracht-forrit.
straight on *adv* enlang.
strain *n/v* streen, leed.
strait *n* kyle.
strait-laced *adj* perjink.
strand *n* ply.
strange *adj* unco, fremmit.
strangeness *n* unconess.
strange person *n* wedgie.
stranger *n* ootrel.
strangers *n* unco fowk.
strange sight *n* ferlie.
strangle *v* thrapple.
strap *n* tawse.
straw *n* strae.
stray *adj* waff. • *v* gae will.
streak *n/v* straik.
streaked *adj* brookit, randit.
stream *n* strin, burn. • *v* teem.
stream out *v* tove.
street *n* causey, gate.
street-sweeper *n* scaffie.
strength *n* strenth, macht.
strengthen *v* souder.
strenuous *adj* sair.
stress *n* sweet, flocht.
stretch *n/v* streetch; **stretch out** to streek, rax oot; **stretch over** to rax ower.
stretched *adj* streekit.
strew *v* strinkle.
stricken *adj* strucken.
strict *adj* strick.
strictly *adv* stricklie.
stride *n/v* striddle.
strident *adj* groff.
striding *adj* stilpin.
strife *n* stour.
strike *v* strick, chap, paik; **strike at** lay at; **strike down** fooner; **strike off** skite; **strike out** loonder; **strike up** yerk aff.
string *n* skainie.
string together *v* strap.
strip *n* ran. • *v* tirr.
stripe *n/v* straik.
striped *adj* strippit.
stripling *n* lad, loon, callant.

strip off *v* tirl.
strive *v* kemp; **strive for** seek tae.
stroke *n/v* straik.
stroll *n/v* dander, dauner.
strong *adj* strang, hard.
strongly *adv* stranglie.
strong-tasting *adj* wild.
struggle *n/v* fecht, chaave; **struggle on** *v* warsle on; **struggle through** warple.
struggling *adj* warslin.
strut *n* dwang (wooden). • *v* bairge.
stubble *n* stibble.
stubbly *adj* stibblie.
stubborn *adj* thrawn.
stubbornness *n* thraw.
stucco *n* stookie.
stuck-up *adj* big.
stud *n* mud.
student *n* collegianer.
study *v* bore at.
stuff *n* graith. • *v* stap.
stuffed *adj* stappit.
stuffing *n* stappin.
stuffy *adj* smochie.
stumble *n/v* stummle.
stumbling-block *n* bumlack.
stump *n* stug. • *v* stodge; **stump along** stramp.
stumpy *adj* stumpit.
stun *v* daze, daumer.
stunned *adj* donnert.
stunned state *n* stoun.
stunted *adj* scruntit.
stunted-looking person *n* shargar.
stupefied *adj* donnert.
stupefy *v* daver.
stupid *adj* daft, stupit.
stupid person *n* fuil, daftie.
stupor *n* stoun, dwam.
sturdy *adj* stieve.
stutter *n/v* stitter.
sty *n* cruive.
stye *n* styan.
style *n* souch.
stylish *adj* tippie.
suave *adj* fair-faced.
subdue *v* lowden.
subdued *adj* lown.
subject *n* speak.
subjugate *v* warsle.
sub-lease *n/v* subset.

sublet *n/v* subset.
submissive *adj* patientfu.
submit *v* knuckle, snuil.
subside *v* seg.
subsistence *n* leevin.
subsoil *n* sole.
substantial *adj* sonsie, sufficient.
substitute *n* by-pit. • *v* speel.
subterfuge *n* scug.
subtle *adj* gleg.
succeed *v* mak weel, luck.
succeeding *adj* incoming.
success *n* seil, thrive.
successful *adj* seilful.
successfully *adv* enweys.
succinct *adj* cuttit.
succour *v* fend.
succulent *adj* sappie.
such *adj* sic.
suchlike *adj* siclik.
suck *v* sook.
sucker *n* sooker.
suckle *v* sook.
suckling *adj* sookie, suckler.
suck up to *v* sook in wi.
suction *n* fang.
sudden *adj* suddent.
suddenly *adv* suddentlie.
suddenness *n* suddenty.
suds *npl* sapples.
sue *v* law.
suet *n* shuet.
suffer *v* thole.
suffering *n* dool, pine.
suffocate *v* smeek, smoor.
sugar *n* succar.
sugar-candy *n* candibrod.
suggest *v* propone.
suit *n/v* shuit.
suitable *adj* sitable.
suit of clothes *n* cleedin.
sulk *v* fung, hing the pettit lip.
sulks *npl* dorts.
sulky *adj* glumsh.
sulky-looking *adj* glumsh.
sullen *adj* derf, dour.
sullenly *adv* dourlie.
sully *v* fyle.
sultry *adj* smochie.
sum *n* soum.
summarily *adv* short an lang.

summer *n* simmer.
summit *n* heid, heicht.
summon *v* cry.
summons *n* cry.
sums *n* coonts.
sun *n* sin.
sunbeam *n* sunblink, leam.
sunrise *n* keek o day.
sunset *n* sundoon.
Sunday *n* Sawbath.
sunder *v* sinder.
sundry *adj* sindry.
sunken *adj* howe, clappit.
sup *v* sowp.
superb *adj* ferlie.
supercilious *adj* dortie, pauchtie.
superimpose *v* onlay.
superior *adj* a king tae.
supernatural *adj* eldritch.
superstition *n* freit.
superstitious *adj* freitie.
supervise *v* owersee.
supervision *n* owerance.
supper *n* sipper.
supplant *v* pit oo ane's ee.
supple *adj* soople.
supplement *n* eik.
supplement *v* eik tae.
supply *v* plenish.
support *n* haud, prap. • *v* stuit, tend; **support oneself** fend.
supporter *n* stoop.
suppose *v* jalouse.
suppress *v* smoor.
suppurate *v* etter.
supremacy *n* gree.
sure *adj* shair, shuir.
surely *adv* shuilie.
surety *n* caution.
surf *n* jaup.
surface *n* sruif.
surfeit *n* stap. • *v* scunner.
surfeited *adj* sairt.
surge *n* hurl. • *v* jaw.
surgical instruments *n* irons.
surly *adj* gurlie.
surmise *v* jalouse.
surmount *v* win over.
surpass *v* cowe, bang; **surpass everything** cowe the cuddie.
surplice *n* sark.

surplus *adj* owerplus.
surprised *adj* taen.
surrender *v* renounce.
surreptitious *adj* hidlins.
surreptitiously *adv* hidlins.
surround *v* humfish.
survey *n/v* leuk, scance.
survive *v* pit ower.
surviving *adj* tae the fore.
suspense *n* tig-tire.
sustain *v* keep, pit ower.
sustenance *n* mait.
swab *n/v* swaible.
swagger *n* swash. • *v* strunt.
swaggerer *n* gowster.
swamp *n* flow, moss, gullion.
swampy *adj* mossie.
swampy place *n* stank.
sward *n* swaird.
swarming *adj* hoatchin.
swarthy *adj* black-avised.
swathe *in* sway. • *v* sweel.
sway *n/v* swey, shog.
swear *v* sweer.
swear word *n* sweer, sweerie.
swear words *n* sweerie-words, ill-tongue.
sweat *n/v* sweet.
sweaty *adj* sweetin.
swede *n* neep, swad.
sweep *n/v* soop.
sweet *adj* douce, hinny. • *n* sweetie.
sweetbreads *n* breids.
sweetheart *n* jo, sweetie, quine.
sweet-jar *n* sweetie bottle.

sweets *n* snashters.
sweetshop *n* sweetie-shop.
sweet-stall *n* sweetie stan.
swell *n* lift, jow. • *v* swall.
swelling *adj* swallin.
swelter *n/v* swither, plot.
sweltering *adj* sweltrie.
swerve *n* swey, jee. • *v* jee, sklent.
swift *adj* swith, cliver. • *n* cran.
swiftly *adv* swith.
swig *n* wacht. • *v* scaff.
swill *n/v* sweel.
swilling *n* sweel.
swim *v* sweem.
swindle *n/v* swick, pauchle.
swindler *n* swick.
swindling *adj* swickerie.
swingboat *n* shoogieboat.
swingle *n* scutcher.
swingle-tree *n* threap.
swipe *n/v* wheech.
swirl *n/v* swurl.
switch off *v* sneck aff.
swollen *adj* swallen.
swollen-headed *adj* gigsie.
swoon *n* dwam, soon. • *v* swelt, dwam.
sword *n* swurd.
sycamore *n* plane tree.
sycophant *n* sook, lick-ma-dowp.
syllable *n* syllab.
symbol *n* whirligig.
sympathetic *adj* couthy, innerlie.
symposium *n* collogue.
syrup *n* trykle.

T

table *n* buird, brod.
table leg *n* standart.
table mat *n* bass mat.
table napkin *n* daidle.
tablet *n* taiblet.
taciturn *adj* dour, derf.
tack *n* airt, road, taik (direction). • *v* taik.
tackle *n/v* taickle.
tact *n* mense.
tactful *adj* canny.
tadpole *n* taddy.

tag *n* shod.
tail *n* rumple.
tailor *n* tylor.
taint *n* humph. • *v* smit.
tainted *adj* humphie.
take *v* tak, hae; **take in** *v* intak.
takeaway *n* cairry-oot.
tale *n* spell, spin.
talent *n* ingine.
talk *n/v* crack, blether say.
talkative *adj* bletherie.

tall *adj* lang, heich.

tally *n* nickstick.

talon *n* clowe.

tame *adj* caif. • *v* cuddom.

tamper *v* prat wi.

tan *v* barken.

tangle *n* fankle, raivel, snorl. • *v* fankle, taut, taigle.

tangled *adj* fankelt, raivelt.

tangy *adj* snell.

tankard *n* stoup.

tanner *n* barker.

tansy *n* stinkin Tam.

tantrum *n* fung.

tap[1] *n* cran, well.

tap[2] *n* chap *v* chap, tip.

tape *n* trappin.

taper *n* spail.

tapioca *n* birdie's een.

tap-root *n* taupin.

tar *n/v* taur.

tardy *adj* dreich, hint-haun.

tare *n* fitch.

target *n* prap.

tarnish *v* ternish, scuff.

tarnished *adj* scuffie.

tarry *adj* taurie. • *v* dwadle.

tart[1] *adj* saur, snar.

tart[2] *n* tairt, tert.

tartan *adj* chackit. • *n* plaidin.

task *n* troke.

tassel *n* toorie.

taste *n* saur, gust. • *v* lip, gust.

tasteless *adj* wersh, gustless.

tasting *adj* preein.

tasty *adj* gustie.

tattered *adj* duddie.

tatters *npl* flitters.

taunt *n/v* upcast.

taunting *adj* sneistie.

taut *adj* tacht.

tauten *v* stent.

tavern *n* howf.

tawdry *adj* hudderie.

tax *n/v* stent.

tea *n* tae.

tea-break *n* piece-break.

teach *v* learn.

teacher *n* dominie, schoolie.

tea-drinker *n* tea-haun, tea-Jenny.

tea-leaf *n* blade.

team *n* pass, rink.

tea party *n* tea skiddle.

teapot *n* snippy.

tear *n/v* sklent; **tear apart** *v* rive; **tear at** rive; **tear off** screeve.

tearaway *n* ned, clip.

tearful *adj* bubblie.

tear-stained *adj* begrutten.

tease *v* kittle, touse.

teasing *adj* rub, taisle.

teat *n* tit.

tedious *adj* taiglesome, dreich.

tedium *n* hing-on.

teeming *adj* hoatchin.

teeth *n* gams.

teetotal *adj* total.

tell *v* mou, clype.

telltale *adj/n* clype, clasher.

temper *n* tune, cut, birse. • *v* licht.

temperate *adj* lown.

tempest *n* bowder, blatter.

tempestuous *adj* ramballiach, gowstie.

temple *n* haffet.

tempt *v* temp.

temptation *n* provokshin.

ten *adj/n* dek, dick.

tenement *n* backland.

tenant *n* tacksman.

tend *v* keep, tent.

tender *adj* frush.

tendon *n* tenon.

tenon *n* tenor.

tense *adj* strait.

tenterhooks *n* heckle-pins.

tenth *adj/n* tent.

tepid *adj* teepid.

term *n* tairm.

termagant *n* shirrow.

terminate *v* en.

termination *n* hinneren.

tern *n* pirr.

terrible *adj* terrel.

terrier *n* terrie.

terrified *adj* fair fleggit.

terrify *v* fricht.

terrifying *adj* frichtsome.

terror *n* terrification.

terse *adj* nippit.

test *v* pruive.

testament *n* settlement.

testicle *n* cull, stane.

testy *adj* crabbit, cranky.
tetchy *adj* carnaptious, crabbit.
tether *n/v* tedder.
tethering post *n* baikie.
text *n* grun.
than *adv* nor, as.
thank *v* thenk.
that *pron* at, it.
thatch *n/v* thack.
thatched cottage *n* thackit biggin.
thatcher *n* thacker.
thaw *n/v* thowe, fresh.
the *adj/adv* e, de, da.
theft *n* stootherie.
them *pron* thaim, dem.
theme *n* leid, owercome.
themselves *pron* thaimsels.
then *adv/conj* than, an.
thence *adv* syne.
thereabouts *adv* thereaway.
thereafter *adv* syne.
therefore *adv* syne.
thereupon *adv* syne.
these *pron* thae, thir.
thick *adj* guttie, stieve.
thicken *v* lithe, mak.
thickening *n* lithin.
thicket *n* buss, shaw.
thick-headed *adj* mappit.
thickness *adj* ply.
thickset *adj* thick.
thief *n* briganer.
thievery *n* rapt.
thigh *n* thee.
thigh-bone *n* hunker-bane.
thighs *npl* fillets.
thimble *n* thummle.
thin *adj* slink, skleff, shilpit. • *v* sinder.
thin person *n* skelf.
third *adj* trid.
thirst *n/v* thrist, drouth.
thirst-quencher *n* slockener.
thirsty *adj* drouthie.
thirteen *adj/n* therteen.
thirteenth *adj* therteen.
thirty *adj/n* threttie.
this *adj/pron* is.
thistle *n* thrustle.
thither *adv* theretill.
thong *n* whang.
thorax *n* kist.

thorn *n* jag.
thorny *adj* jaggie.
thorough *adj* thorow.
thoroughfare *n* througang.
thoroughly *adv* evendoon.
those *adj/pron* thae.
though *adv* but.
thought *n* thocht.
thoughtful *adj* pensefu.
thoughtless *adj* glaikit.
thousand *adj/n* thoosan.
thraldom *n* thirlage.
thrash *v* bate, ding, bash; **thrash about** spelder.
thrashing *n* skelping, loonderin.
thread *n* threid.
threadbare *adj* pookit.
threat *n* thrait.
threaten *v* thrait.
threatening *adj* unchancie.
three *adj/n* chree.
three-pronged *adj* three-taed.
thresh *v* thrash.
thresher *n* barnman.
threshold *n* thrashel.
thrift *n* trift.
thriftless *adj* thrieveless.
thriftlessness *n* wanthrift.
thrifty *adj* fendie.
thrill *n* dirl. • *v* thirl.
thrive *v* trive, dae guid.
thriving *adj* growthie.
throat *n* thrapple.
throb *n/v* stoun, thrab.
throe *n* thraw.
throng *n/v* thrang.
throttle *v* thrapple.
through *prep* throu.
throw *n* thraw, jass. • *v* thraw, clod; **throw away** ort; **throw down** doosht; **throw off** cast. **throw on** hudder on; **throw up** boak.
thrust *n* thrist, punce. • *v* thrist, dird.
thrust into *v* stap in.
thud *n/v* dunt, dad.
thug *n* rochian.
thumb *n* thoum.
thump *n* belt, dunt. • *v* dunch, cloor.
thunder *n* thunner, brattle.
thunder shower *n* thunner-plump.
thwart *v* conter. • *n* thaft.

thwarted *adj* lummed.
tick *v* skelp.
ticking *n* tike.
tickle *n/v* kittle.
ticklish *adj* kittle.
tiddly *adj* cornt.
tide *n* rug.
tidings *npl* speirings.
tidied *adj* red up.
tidily *adv* ticht.
tidiness *n* purpose.
tidy *adj* trig. • *v* redd.
tie *v* tether; **tie together** leash; **tie up** hankle.
tiger *n* teeger.
tight *adj* ticht.
tighten *v* tichten.
tight-fitting *adj* nippit.
tightly *adv* ticht.
tile *n* wallie tile.
tiled *adj* wallie.
till *v* teel.
tillage *n* laborin.
tiller *n* tillie.
tilt *n* thraw. • *v* coup.
timber *n* timmer.
timbre *n* souch.
time *n* tid.
time-consuming *adj* taiglesome.
time-wasting *adj* fouterie.
timid *adj* blate, timorsome.
timidity *n* erghness.
timorous *adj* timorsome.
tinsmith *n* tinnie.
tinder *n* tindle.
tine *n* tae.
tinge *n/v* teenge.
tingle *v* dingle, thirl.
tingling *adj* dinnle.
tinker *n* tink, mink.
tinkle *v* tingle.
tinkling *adj* plinkin.
tint *n/v* spraing.
tiny *adj* wee, peedie, peerie.
tip *n* tap, neb. • *v* coup.
tipple *v* taste, dribble.
tippler *n* drouth, toot.
tipsy *adj* hauf-cock, cornt.
tiptoe *v* tipper.
tiptoes *npl* taptaes.
tire *v* fornyaw.

tired *adj* fornyawed, forfochen.
tired-looking *adj* disjaskit.
tiredness *n* tire.
tiresome *adj* stawsome.
tiring *adj* taiglesome.
tissue *n* tishie.
titbit *n* hire.
titbits *n* snysters.
tithe *n* teind.
titillate *v* kittle.
titivate *v* prink.
titter *n/v* snicher.
tittle-tattle *n* clavers, clishmeclaiver.
to *prep* tae, till.
toad *n* taid, puddock.
toadstool *n* puddock stuil.
toady *n* sook.
toast *v* birsle.
toasted *adj* roastit.
tobacco ash *n* dirrie.
tobacco pouch *n* spleuchan.
today *n* the day.
toddle *v* tottle, hotter.
toddler *n* tottie.
toe *n* tae.
toe-cap *n* freuchan.
toffee *n* taffie.
together *adv* thegither.
toil *n* trachle, chaave. • *v* trachle, swink.
toilet *n* watterie, cludgie, wee hoose.
toilsome *adj* pinglin.
token *n* taiken.
tolerable *adj* tholeable, middlin.
tolerably *adv* middlin.
tolerance *n* thole.
tolerate *v* thole, bide.
toll *n/v* towl.
toll-keeper *n* tollie.
tomboy *n* gilpie.
tomboyish *adj* hallockit.
tombstone *n* lairstane.
tomcat *n* gibcat.
tomfoolery *n* flumgummerie.
tomorrow *n* the morn.
tomorrow morning *n* the morn's morn.
tomorrow night *n* the morn's nicht.
tone *n* souch.
tongs *npl* tangs.
tongue *n* melt, gab.
tongue-tied *adj* tongue-tackit.
tonight *n* the nicht.

too *adv* tae.
tool *n* tuil.
tools *npl* graith.
too many *adj* ower monie.
too much *adj* ower muckle.
tooth *n* tuith.
toothache *n* teethache, worm-i-the-cheek.
top *n* tap, heid.
toper *n* drouth.
topknot *n* toorie.
topmost *adj* heidmaist.
top up *v* eik up.
topic *n* speak.
topple *v* coup.
topsy-turvy *adj* tapsalterie.
torch *n* ruffie.
torment *v* deave.
tornado *n* skailwin.
torrent *n* spate.
tortoise *n* tortie.
torture *n/v* torter.
toss *n/v* fung; **toss about** *v* towin; **toss down** doss doon.
tot *n* tottie, dram.
total *n* hail.
totter *n* stotter, stoiter. • *v* stacher, stoiter.
tottery *adj* shooglie.
touch *n/v* tig, scuff.
touchy *adj* tiftie, pernickitie.
tough *adj* teuch. • *n* rochian.
tour *n* gate.
tourist *n* towerist.
tournament *n* rink.
towel *n* tool.
tower *n* toor.
town *n* toon.
town hall *n* toon hoose, tolbooth.
townspeople *npl* toonsers.
toy *n* playock, wheerum.
trace *n* tress. • *v* speir oot.
trachea *n* wizzen.
track *n* pad, steid. • *v* steid; **track down** speir oot.
tract *n* track.
trade *n* tred, traffeck. • *v* dale, niffer.
tradition *n* threap.
traffic *n/v* traffeck.
trail *n* steid. • *v* trachle.
trailing *adj* sloggerin.
train *v* cuddum.
training *n* upbring.

trait *n* track.
traitor *n* tratour.
tramcar *n* skoosh-car.
tramp *n* gangin body, caird, gaberlunzie. • *v* traik, stramp.
trample *v* patter, paidle; **trample down** paddit; **trample on** stramp.
trampling *adj* stramp.
trance *n* dwam.
tranquil *adj* lown, lithe.
tranquillity *n* lown.
transact *v* transack.
transaction *n* transack.
transactions *n* traffeck.
transfer *v* translate.
transferable *adj* prestable.
transfix *v* skiver.
transform *v* cheenge.
transgress *v* mistak.
translate *v* owerset.
translation *n* owersettin.
transport *v* convoy.
transverse *adj* thort.
transversely *adv* thort.
trap *n* girn, stamp. • *v* girn, fankle.
trappings *n* graithin.
trash *n* troke.
trashy *adj* peltrie.
travel fast *v* spank.
travelling bag *n* pockmantie.
travelling salesman *n* fleeing merchan.
traverse *v* reenge.
tray *n* server.
treacherous *adj* traicherous.
treachery *n* traison.
treacle *n* traicle.
tread *n/v* stramp; **tread down** *v* paidle; **tread on** stramp.
treadle *n* fit brod.
treason *n* traison.
treasure *n* traisure.
treasurer *n* thesaurer.
treatise *n* libel.
treatment *n* guideship.
treble *adj/v* threeple.
tree-creeper *n* tree-speeler.
tree stump *n* stog.
tree trunk *n* caber.
trefoil *n* triffle.
trellis *n* tirless.
tremble *v* tremmle.

trembling *adj* grue, chitterin.
tremendous *adj* unco.
tremor *n* grue.
trench *n* sheuch, track.
trencher *n* truncher.
trend *n* fasson.
trendy *adj* fantoosh.
trepidation *n* feerich.
tress *n* flacht.
trestle *n* tress.
tribulation *n* tribble.
tributary *n* leader.
trick *n* cantrip, swick. • *v* jouk, jink.
trickery *n* swickerie.
trickle *n* dribble. • *v* seep.
tricky *adj* fickle, ill-trickit.
trifle *n* triffle. • *v* fouter; **trifle with** glaik wi.
trifling *adj* skitterie.
trigger *n* tricker.
trim *adj* trig, nate. • *v* sned, shaw.
trimmed *adj* snibbit.
trimly *adv* dinklie.
trimming *n* squirl.
trimmings *npl* trappin.
trinket *n* whigmaleerie.
trinkets *npl* trokes.
trip *n* gate. • *v* stammer.
tripe *n* painches.
triple *adj/v* threeple.
triplet *n* threeplet.
trivet *n* cran.
trivial *adj* fouterie.
troll *v* harl.
trolley *n* barra.
trollop *n* cookie, hairy-tail.
trot *n* jundie. • *v* troddle.
trot along *v* pad.
trouble *n* tribble. • *v* fash.
troubled *adj* trachelt.
troublemaker *n* rochian.
troublesome *adj* tribblesome, fashious.
trough *n* troch.
trounce *v* lamp, bang.
trouncing *adj* lamping.
trousers *n* troosers, breeks.
trouser braces *npl* galluses.
trousseau *n* muntin, waddin-braws.
trout *n* troot.
trowel *n* truan.
truant *n* troon.

truce *n* barley.
truck *n/v* troke.
truculent *adj* turk.
trudge *n* traik. • *v* trodge.
trudge on *v* dodge awa.
true *adj* suithfast.
truly *adv* truelins.
truth *n* trowth.
truthful *adj* truthfae.
trump card *n* trumph.
trumpery *adj* trumpherie.
trumpet *n* tooter. • *v* toot.
truncate *v* sned.
truncheon *n* rung.
trundle *v* trunnle.
trunk *n* kist, caber.
truss *n/v* turse.
trust *n* truist. • *v* lippen.
trustworthy *adj* suithfast.
trusty *adj* stieve, trest.
try *v* ettle, pruive.
tub *n* bine, boyne.
tuck *n/v* touk.
tuck up *v* kilt.
Tuesday *n* Tyseday.
tuft *n* toosht.
tufted *adj* tappit.
tug *n/v* teug, chug.
tumble *n/v* tummle; **tumble about** *v* row-chow; **tumble over** play wallop.
tummy *n* stamack.
tumour *n* clyre.
tumult *n* stushie.
tumultuous *adj* camstarrie, arrachin.
tumulus *n* law.
tune *v* kittle.
tuneless *adj* timmer.
tunic *n* slop, jupe.
tunnel *n* cundie.
turbid *adj* drumlie.
turbot *n* rodden fluke.
turbulence *n* stushie.
turd *n* tuird, jobbie.
turf *n* turr.
turf-cutter *n* flauchter-spade
turf seat *n* sunk.
turf wall *n* truff dyke.
turkey *n* pullie.
turkey cock *n* bubbly-jock.
turmeric *n* tarmanick.
turmoil *n* dirdum.

turn *n/v* birl; **turn aside** *v* skewl; **turn
  back** kep again; **turn out** oot; **turn
  round** birl; **turn up** lay in.
turned up *adj* kippit.
turnip *n* neep.
turnip lantern *n* neep lantern.
turnip slicer *n* neep-cutter.
turnip top *n* neep shaw.
turnpike *n* toll.
turnpike-keeper *n* tollie.
turnstile *n* tirless.
turnover *n* owerturn.
turn-up *n* flype.
turret *n* tappietoorie.
tussle *n/v* tissle.
tussock *n* boss.
tutelage *n* tutory.
tutorship *n* tutory.
twang *n* tune.
tweed mill *n* oo-mill.
tweezers *n* pinchers.
twelfth *n* twalt.
twelve *adj/n* twal, qual.
twelvemonth *n* twalmond.
twelve o'clock *n* twaloors.

twenty *adj/n* twintie.
twice *adj* twicet.
twiddle *v* tweedle.
twig *n* boucht.
twilight *n* gloamin.
twill *n/v* tweed.
twin-bedded *adj* twa-beddit.
twine *n* skaenie. • *v* whip.
twinge *n* rug, twang.
twinkle *n/v* glent.
twirl *n* swirl. • *v* pirl.
twist *n* skew. • *v* thraw, chowl.
twisted *adj* thrawn, snorlie.
twister *n* dyvour.
twit *v* geck.
twitch *n/v* fidge.
twite *n* heather lintie.
twitter *v* tweeter.
two *adj/n* twa.
two-faced *adj* sleekit.
two-faced person *n* sneck-drawer.
two-fold *adj* twa-fauld.
type *n* teep.
typhus *n* purpie-fever.
tyrant *n* tirran.

U

udder *n* aidder, ether.
ugly *adj* ill-faured, ooglie.
ulcer *n* bealin.
ultimate *adj* hinmaist.
ultimately *adv* at the hinneren.
ululation *n* hwll.
umbrage *n* umrage.
umpire *n* owersman.
unabashed *adj* furthie.
unable *adj* useless.
unaffected *adj* hameower.
unaired *adj* mothie.
unappetising *adj* wersh.
unappreciative *adj* perskeet.
unassuming *adj* canny.
unattractive *adj* ill-faured.
unawares *adv* unawaurs.
unbalanced *adj* cat-wittit.
unbending *adj* stieve.
uncanny *adj* oorie, eldritch.
uncertain *adj* slidderie, dootsome.

uncivil *adj* sneistie.
uncomfortable *adj* unoorament.
uncommon *adj* orra.
uncompromising *adj* stench.
unconditionally *adv* simpliciter.
unconventional *adj* owerlie.
uncouth *adj* raucle.
unctuous *adj* sappie.
uncultured *adj* coorse.
undaunted *adj* undauntit.
undecided *adj* dootsome.
undemonstrative *adj* lown.
under *adj* nether.
under *prep* alow.
under-age *adj* within eild.
underclothing *n* linens.
undercut *v* boss.
undergo *v* dree.
undergrowth *n* scrogs.
underhand *adj* sleekit.
underhand person *n* mowdiewort.

underneath adv aneath.
undernourished adj ill-thriven.
underrate v lichtlie.
undersized adj scrimpit.
understanding n uptak.
undertake v tak on haun.
undertaking n prottick, ploy.
undervalue v lichtlie.
undiluted adj hard.
undisciplined adj ill-deedie.
undistinguished adj raploch.
undo v lowse.
undress v tirl, tirr.
undulate v kelter, wammle.
unearth v howk.
unearthly adj eldritch.
unease n thocht.
uneasiness n wanrest.
uneasy adj on nettles.
unemployed adj orra.
unemployment n idleset.
unemployment benefit n broo.
unequalled adj marrowless.
unexpectedly adv in a hurry.
unfair adj nae fair.
unfamiliar adj unkent.
unfastened adj lowse.
unfinished adj stickit.
unfit adj no able.
unfortunate adj mischancie.
unfriendly adj thin.
ungainly adj ill-shakken.
ungrateful adj pick-thank.
unhappy adj dowie.
unharmed adj hail-heidit.
unhurt adj hail-heidit.
uninspired adj fushionless.
uninteresting adj smeerless.
unite v knit, souder.
university n college.
university student n collegener.
unjust adj unricht.
unkempt adj tashie, ill-farran.
unkind adj ill.
unknown adj unkent.
unlatch v unsneck.
unless conj onless.
unlike adj unalik.
unload v disloaden.
unlucky adj unchancie.
unmanageable adj royat.

unmannerly adj unfarran.
unmarried adj marrowless, free.
unmatched adj orra.
unmethodical adj throwder.
unmusical adj timmer.
unnatural adj nae canny.
unobserved adj unkent.
unoccupied adj tuim.
unpalatable adj humphy.
unpleasant adj unoorament, pooshiona-
  ble.
unploughed adj white.
unpolished adj raucle, unfarran.
unpopular adj ill-likit.
unpredictable adj kittle.
unpunctual adj mistimeous.
unravel v unraivel.
unrefined adj unfarran, raucle.
unrelated adj fremmit.
unreliable adj slidderie.
unrest n wanrest.
unrestrained adj camstairie.
unruly adj ill-deedie.
unsafe adj uncanny.
unsatisfactory adj ill.
unscathed adj hailscart.
unscrew v feeze aff.
unsettled adj lowse, wanrestful.
unsheathed adj bare.
unshorn adj ruch.
unskilful adj kweerichin.
unskilled adj ill, hielan.
unsociable adj stickin.
unsophisticated adj unfarran.
unspeakable adj past a.
unstable adj skeer, shooglie, cogglie.
unsteady adj shooglie, cogglie.
unsubstantial adj silly.
untidy adj tashie.
untidy person n ticket.
untidy place n Paddy's mairket.
untie v lowsen.
until conj/prep gin, while.
untrustworthy adj sleekit.
unusual adj by ornar, unco.
unusually adv nae ornar.
unwashed adj unwashen.
unwell adj nae weel, bad.
unwholesome adj ill.
unwieldy adj untowtherlie.
unwilling adj sweirt.

unworthy *adj* wanwordie.
unwrinkled *adj* brent.
unyielding *adj* unbowsome, dour.
up *adv/prep* oop.
upbraid *v* scaul.
upbringing *n* upfessin.
uphold *v* uphaud.
upkeep *n* keep-up.
upland *adj* upthrou. • *n* brae.
upper *adj* iver.
upper hand *n* owerhaun.
uppermost *adj* umost.
uppish *adj* heich.
upright *adj* upricht.
uproar *n* stushie, stramash.
uproarious *adj* rantin.
uproot *v* howk.
upset *adj* uggit. • *n/v* coup, whummle.
upshot *n* upcome.
upside down *adv* tapsalteerie.

upstairs *adv* upby.
upward *adj* upwart.
upwards *adv* upwith.
urchin *n* gorlin.
urge *v* threap at.
urge on *v* ca.
urgent *adj* clamant.
urgently *adv* sair.
urine *n* pish, peeins.
urinate *v* pish, strone.
us *pron* uz, wiz.
use *n/v* eese.
useful *adj* eesefae.
useless *adj* eeseless, daeless.
usual *adj* eeswal.
usually *adv* for ordnar.
utensil *n* tuil.
utmost *adj* utmaist.
utter[1] *adj/adv* fair.
utter[2] *v* mint.

V

vacant *adj* tuim.
vacate *v* redd.
vacillate *v* switherg.
vacillating *adj* switherin.
vagabond *n* scurryvaig.
vagina *n* fud.
vagrant *adj* waffie, vaigin. • *n* gaun-a-boot, gangrel, hallanshaker.
vagrants *npl* waunnerin fowk.
vague *adj* dootsome.
vain *adj* pridefu, tuim.
valance *n* pan.
valet *n* wally.
valiant *adj* wicht, croose.
valley *n* glen, howe, strath.
valour *n* saul.
value *n/v* vailye.
valueless *adj* wanworth.
valve *n* toby.
vanishing *adj* eelyin.
vanquish *v* defait.
vapid *adj* smerghless.
vapour *n* reek.
varied *adj* sindry.
variegated *adj* spreckelt.
variety *n* kin.

various *adj* sindry.
vary *v* cheenge.
vast *adj* gowstie, muckle big.
vat *n* fat.
vault *n/v* vowt.
vaulted *adj* coomed.
vaulted passageway *n* pend.
vaunt *v* bla.
vegetation *n* growthe.
vehement *adj* swith wi virr.
vehemently *adv* sair.
vehicle *n* machine.
velvety *adj* feel.
veneer *v* fineer.
venereal disease *n* Canongate breeks.
venom *n* pooshion.
venture *n* ploy. • *v* ettle.
verge *n* leemit.
verger *n* beadle.
verily *adv* verilies.
veritable *adj* jonick.
verity *n* troth.
vermin *n* baists.
vernacular *adj* hameower.
verruca *n* werrock.
verse *n* screed.

vertebra *n* link.
very *adv* verra, awfie, gey.
vest *n* semmit.
vestibule *n* rochel.
vestige *n* glint, stime.
vetch *n* fitch.
veteran *n* foggie.
veterinary surgeon *n* ferrier.
veto *n/v* na-say.
vex *v* fash.
vexation *n* fasherie.
vibrate *v* dirl.
vibration *n* dirlin.
victory *n* owerhaun.
victuals *npl* scran.
vie *v* kemp.
view *n* vizzy. • *v* leuk.
vigilant *adj* waukrif.
vigorous *adj* hail, caller.
vigorously *adv* fell.
vigour *n* birr, smeddum.
vile *adj* wile.
vilify *v* splairge.
village *n* clachan, toon.
villain *n* limmer.
villainous *adj* gallus, hangit-faced.
vindictive *adj* ill-willie.

violate *v* abuise.
violence *n* strouth.
violent *adj* bang, snell.
violently *adv* fiercelins.
violin *n* fiddle.
virago *n* shirrow.
virile *adj* pretty.
virtuous *adj* gracie.
virulent *adj* strang, fell.
vision *n* sicht.
vitality *n* smergh.
vivacious *adj* speeritie.
vivacity *n* lifieness.
vivid *adj* gleg, vieve.
voice *n/v* vice.
void *n* tuim, boss.
volatile *adj* wafflie, allevolie.
vole *n* lan-moose.
voluble *adj* gleg-tonguit, glib.
vomit *n/v* boak.
voracious *adj* gutsie.
vouch for *v* uphaud.
vow *v* voo.
voyage *n* veage.
vulgar *adj* groff, coorse.
vulva *n* fud.

W

wadding *n* colfin.
waddle *n* hoddle, plowd. • *v* widdle, rowe.
wade *v* wad, plowter.
waders *n* wyders.
wading *adj* wad.
wag *n* tear. •*v* to wingle.
wage *n* wauge.
wager *n/v* wauger.
waggle *n/v* waiggle.
wagon *n* wain.
wagtail *n* seed-bird.
waif *n* waff.
wail *n/v* yowl.
wainscoting *n* boxin.
waistband *n* heidban.
waistcoat *n* weskit.
wait *n/v* wyte.
wait a while *v* bide a wee.

wait for *v* wyte on.
wake *v* wauk.
wakeful *adj* waukrif.
walking *n* shanks' naig.
walking stick *n* staff, crummock.
wall *n* wa, dyke.
wall-clock *n* wag-at-the-wa.
wallet *n* walgan.
wall-eye *n* ringle ee.
wall-eyed *adj* ringit.
wallop *n/v* loonder.
wallow *n/v* wammle, wallae.
wan *adj* wabbit, peely-wally.
wand *n* wan.
wander *v* wauner, stravaig, rove, reenge.
wanderer *n* traik.
wandering *adj* waunert.
wangle *v* pauchle, scraible.
waning *n* dwine.

want *n* wint. • *v* seek.
war *n* weir.
warble *n* chirm. • *v* chirl.
war-cry *n* slogan.
ward *v* weir.
warehouse *n* warehoose.
wares *n* plweirs.
warlike *adj* weirlik.
warm *adj* het. • *n* glaise. • *v* birsle.
warn *v* wairn.
warning *n* telling.
warp *n/v* worp.
warrant *n/v* warran.
warren *n* cuningar.
warrior *n* kemp.
wart *n* wrat.
wary *adj* sicker.
wash *n/v* wesh.
wash down *v* sweel.
washer *n* shangie.
washerwoman *n* washerwife.
wash out *v* syne oot.
wasp *n* waasp.
wasp's nest *n* byke.
waste *n* redd. • *v* connach; **waste away** dwine.
wasted *adj* gowstie, ill-wared.
wasteful *adj* wastrif.
wastepaper basket *n* bucket.
waster *n* prod.
waste time *v* pit aff, daidle.
watch *n* gaird. • *v* tak tent o, leuk ower.
watchful *adj* waukrif.
watchmaker *n* watchie.
water *n/v* watter.
water-bucket *n* stan.
water-closet *n* watterie, cludgie, wee hoose.
watercress *n* wa girse.
waterfall *n* linn.
water-hen *n* stankie.
watering can *n* rooser.
water pistol *n* scoot.
water rat *n* watter dog.
water sprite *n* kelpie.
water tap *n* stroop.
watertight *adj* thight.
watery *adj* wabblie.
wave *n* swaw, waff. • *v* waff, wampish.
waver *v* waffle.
wavering *adj* weegletie-waggletie.

way *n* wey, airt.
wayward *adj* waywart.
we *pron* oo.
weak *adj* waik, wabbit, traikie.
weaken *v* tak doon.
weakling *n* schachle.
weakly *adv* tender.
weak-minded *adj* glaikit.
weak-willed *adj* sapsie.
weal *n* score.
wealth *n* walth, graith.
wean *v* spean.
weapon *n* wappen.
wear *v* weir.
wear and tear *n* docher.
weariness *n* tire.
wearisome *adj* stawsome.
weary *adj* wabbit, forjeskit. • *v* deave.
weary-looking *adj* disjaskit.
weasel *n* wheasel.
weather *n* wather.
weave *v* warp, wyve.
weaver *n* webster.
web *n* wab.
wed *v* wad.
wedding *n* waddin.
wedding cake *n* bridecake.
wedding clothes *n* waddin braws.
wedge *n/v* wadge.
Wednesday *n* Wodensday.
weed-infested *adj* growthie.
weeds *n* growthe.
week *n* ook.
weekday *n* ilkaday.
weekly *adj* ooklie.
weep *v* greet.
weepy *adj* greetie.
weft *n* waft.
weigh *v* wey, wecht.
weight *n* wecht.
weighty *adj* wechtie.
weir *n* caul.
weird *adj* unco, eldritch.
welcome *n/v* walcome.
weld *v* well.
well[1] *adj/adv/interj* weel.
well[2] *n* wall.
well-behaved *adj* gracie.
well-bred *adj* gentie.
well-built *adj* buird.
well-deserved *adj* weel-wared.

well-dressed *adj* braw.
well-earned *adj* weel-wared.
well-endowed *adj* weel-tochert.
well-fed *adj* mait-lik.
well-grown *adj* growthie.
well-informed *adj* wice.
well-known *adj* kenspeckle.
well-made *adj* slee, trig.
well-mannered *adj* menseful.
well-meaning *adj* weel-willie.
well-off *adj* weel-daein.
well-preserved *adj* weel-hained.
well-protected *adj* weel-happit.
well-read *adj* far I the buik.
well-spent *adj* weel-wared.
well-stocked *adj* weel-plenisht.
well-to-do *adj* weel-daein.
well-trodden *adj* paddit.
welt *n* walt.
welter *n* walter.
west *n* wast.
western *adj* waster.
westernmost *adj* wastmost.
westwards *adv* wastle.
wet *adj/v* weet, wat.
wet-nurse *n* nourice.
wether *n* wedder.
whack *n/v* whauk, loonder.
whale *n* whaul.
wharf *n* shore.
what *pron* whit, wha, fit.
whatever *pron* whatsomever.
wheat *n* white.
wheatear *n* stane chack.
wheedle *v* wheetle.
wheedler *n* whillywha.
wheedling *adj* licklip.
wheedling *n* whillywha.
wheel *n* trinnle, whurl. • *v* hurl, rowe.
wheelbarrow *n* hurl-barra.
wheeze *n/v* wheezle.
wheezing *adj* purfelt. • *n* sowff.
wheezy *adj* pechie.
whelk *n* wulk.
whelp *n/v* whalp.
when *adv/conj* whan, fan.
whence *adv* whaur fae.
where *adv* whaur, far.
wherever *adv* whaurivver.
whet *v* what.
whetstone *n* set-stane.

whether *conj* whither, whuther, gif.
which *adj/pron* whilk, filk.
whiff *n* whuff.
while *conj* whill, file. • *n* stoun.
whim *n* wheem.
whimbrel *n* Mey bird.
whimper *n/v* fumper.
whimsical *adj* maggotie.
whin *n* whun.
whinchat *n* whun-chacker.
whine *n/v* girn, draunt.
whining *adj* girnie. • *n* girn.
whinny *v* nicher.
whip *n/v* whup.
whiplash *n* whang.
whipping *n* skelping.
whip-round *n* lift.
whirl *n/v* whurl.
whirligig *n* turlie.
whirlpool *n* swelch, belth.
whirlwind *n* whidder.
whirr *n/v* whurr.
whish *n/v* whush.
whisk *n* wheech. • *v* wisk.
whisker *n* fusker.
whisky *n* whuskie, barley bree, the craitur, usquebae.
whisky and beer *n* hauf an hauf.
whisky jar *n* kirstie.
whisky measure *n* dram, hauf.
whisper *n/v* whusper.
whispering *adj* hudgemudgin.
whistle *n/v* whustle, fussle.
white *adj* fite.
whitebeam *n* mulberry.
white-faced *adj* hawkit.
whither *adv* whaur till.
whiting *n* whitie.
whitish *adj* whitelie.
whitlow *n* whittle-bealin.
whittle *v* white, futtle.
whizz *n* swiff. • *v* wheech.
who *pron* wha, whae.
whoever *pron* whasomever.
whole *adj* hail.
wholesome *adj* haisome.
wholly *adv* haillie.
whom *pron* wham.
whoop *v* hooch.
whooping cough *n* kink-hoast.
whopper *n* whulter.

whopping *adj* wappin.
whore *n* howre, limmer.
whorl *n* whurl.
whose *pron* whase.
why *adv* hoo, foo.
wicked *adj* wickit, ill-deedie.
wickedly *adv* ill.
wicker *n* wan.
wickerwork *n* wickers.
wide *adj* braid.
widely *adv* abreid.
widely known *adj* weel-kent.
width *n* boon.
wield *v* wage, wald.
wife *n* wifie, wumman.
wild *adj* wull, will.
wild cat *n* wullcat.
wild garlic *n* ramps.
wile *n* wimple.
wilful *adj* willsome, heidie.
will *n/v* wull.
willing *adj* wullint.
will-o'-the-wisp *n* spunkie, daith-cannle.
willow *n* willie, sauch.
willow warbler *n* willie-muff.
wilt *v* wult.
wily *adj* pawky.
win *v* wun; **win over** weir roon.
wince *v* jouk.
winch *n* iron man.
wind[1] *n* win, wun.
wind[2] *v* rowe, wimple; **wind up** rowe.
windbag *n* blether.
windbreak *n* sconce.
windfall *n* peeled egg.
winding *n* loop. • *v* wuppit.
winding sheet *n* shrood.
windless *adj* lown, quate.
windmill *n* win-mull.
window *n* winda, windae, winnock.
window-frame *n* chess.
window-sill *n* windae-sole.
windpipe *n* thrapple.
wing *n* weeng, jamb.
wink *v* glimmer.
winnow *v* win.
winter *n* wunter.
wipe *n/v* dicht.
wire *n* weer.
wisdom *n* wit.
wise *adj* wice, slee.

wish *n/v* wiss, wush.
wishbone *n* thochtbane.
wishy-washy *adj* fushionless.
wisp *n* wusp.
wistful *adj* pensefu.
wit *n* wut.
witch *n* wutch, carline.
witchcraft *n* glamourie.
with *prep* wi, in.
withdraw *v* hen, resile.
wither *v* wuther.
withered *adj* fushionless, wallan.
within *adv* wi'in. • *prep* intae.
without *prep* wi'oot, wantin.
withstand *v* gainstan.
witless *adj* doitert.
witness *n* wutness.
wits *n* judgement.
witty *adj* knackie, auld-farran.
wizard *n* warlock.
wizzened *adj* wuzzent.
wobble *n* wachle. • *v* wabble.
wobbly *adj* shooglie.
woe *n* wae.
woebegone *adj* waebegane.
woeful *adj* waeful.
wolf *n* oof.
woman *n* wumman, wifie.
womb *n* wame.
wonder *v* wunner.
wonderful *adj* wunnerfae.
wonderfully *adv* ferlie, wunnersome.
wont *n* hant.
woo *v* oo.
wood *n* wuid, wud, timmer, plantin.
wooden *adj* wudden.
wooden leg *n* pin leg.
woodland *n* plantin, shaw.
woodlouse *n* slater.
wood-pigeon *n* cushie-doo.
woody *adj* wuddie.
wool *n* woo, oo.
woollen *adj* ooen.
woolly *adj* ooie.
word *n* wird.
work *n* wark, thrift, seam.
worker *n* warker.
workhouse *n* puirhoose.
workings *npl* intimmers.
workshy *adj* hanigle, sweirt.
world *n* warld.

worldly *adj* wardlie.
worm *n* wirm.
worn-out *adj* forfochen.
worry *n/v* wirry, fash.
worse *adj* warse, waur.
worst *adj/adv/v* warst.
worsted *n* worset.
worth *n* wirth.
worthless *adj* weirdless.
worthy *adj* wordie, braw.
wound *n* stang, dunt, scrat. • *v* brain, mairtyr.
wraith *n* ghaist.
wrangle *n/v* raggle.
wrap *n* hap. • *v* wap, hap; **wrap up** rowe up.
wrath *n* wreth.
wreck *n/v* wrack, wreak.
wreckage *n* stramash, spreath.
wren *n* wrannie.

wrench *n/v* runch.
wrestle *v* warsle.
wretch *n* wratch, dring.
wretched *adj* donsie.
wriggle *v* wammle.
wring *v* thraw.
wrinkle *n/v* runkle.
wrinkled *adj* runklie.
wrinkly *adj* wirlie.
wrist *n* shackle.
writ *n* summons, letter.
write *v* wreat, scribe, scrieve.
writer *n* scriever.
writing *n* write, writ, scrieve.
writhe *v* warsle, twine.
wrong *adj* wrang, ill-deein. • *n* ill.
wrongdoing *n* ill-daein.
wrongful *adj* wrangous.
wrongfully *adv* wrangouslie.
wry *adj* thrawn.

YZ

yacht *n* yatt.
yap *v* yowl.
yard *n* yaird.
yardstick *n* ellwan.
yarn *n* yairn.
yawn *n/v* gant.
yawning *adj* ganting.
yearling *n* yearaul.
yearn *v* green for.
yell *n/v* yowl, gowl.
yellow *adj* yella, yellae.
yellowhammer *n* yella lintie, yorlin.
yellowish *adj* fauchie.
yelp *n/v* yowl.
yes *adv* ay, yea.
yesterday *adv* yestreen.
yet *adv* still an on. • *conj* yit.
yield *n* profit. • *v* loot.

yob *n* ned, clip.
yoghurt *n* soor dook.
yoke *n* yock.
yokel *n* yochel, geordie, teuchter.
yolk *n* yowk.
yon *adv/pron* thon.
yonder *adj/adv* yonner, thonder.
you *pron* ye, yiz.
young *adj* green. • *n* follower.
youngster *n* younker.
your *pron* eer, yer.
yourself *pron* yersel.
youth *n* youtheid, lad, loon, callant.
youthful *adj* green, youthie.
Yule *n* Yeel.
zealous *adj* guid-willed.
zigzag *v* jink.